THE
ETHICAL VISION
OF THE BIBLE

LEARNING GOOD FROM KNOWING GOD

PETER W. GOSNELL

IVP Academic
An imprint of InterVarsity Press
Downers Grove, Illinois

InterVarsity Press
P.O. Box 1400, Downers Grove, IL 60515-1426
World Wide Web: www.ivpress.com
E-mail: email@ivpress.com

*InterVarsity Press® is the book-publishing division of InterVarsity Christian Fellowship/USA®, a movement of
students and faculty active on campus at hundreds of universities, colleges and schools of nursing in the United
States of America, and a member movement of the International Fellowship of Evangelical Students. For
information about local and regional activities, write Public Relations Dept., InterVarsity Christian Fellowship/
USA, 6400 Schroeder Rd., P.O. Box 7895, Madison, WI 53707-7895, or visit the IVCF website at <www.
intervarsity.org>.*

Scripture quotations, unless otherwise noted, are from the New Revised Standard Version of the Bible, *copyright
1989 by the Division of Christian Education of the National Council of the Churches of Christ in the USA. Used by
permission. All rights reserved.*

*While all stories in this book are true, some names and identifying information in this book have been changed to
protect the privacy of the individuals involved.*

Cover design: Cindy Kiple
Interior design: Beth Hagenberg
Images: book pages: © Maica/iStockphoto
        book icons: © Alex Belomlinsky/iStockphoto

ISBN 978-0-8308-4028-1 (print)
ISBN 978-0-8308-6479-9 (digital)

Printed in the United States of America ∞

Library of Congress Cataloging-in-Publication Data
A catalog record for this book is available from the Library of Congress.

P 26 25 24 23 22 21 20 19 18 17 16 15 14 13 12 11 10 9 8 7 6 5 4 3 2 1

Y 36 35 34 33 32 31 30 29 28 27 26 25 24 23 22 21 20 19 18 17 16 15 14

To Bee

wife, companion,

partner in life and ministry

CONTENTS

PREFACE

This book is written for students—for undergraduates, seminarians, those in theological college, even those in ministry who want a gentler orientation to biblical issues. The world of biblical ethics often appears uninviting to the nonexpert. I have tried to take many of the core ideas from that scholarly world and present them in a way that makes them more accessible and less intimidating. I frequently take the time to explain basic introductory issues relevant to biblical writings before beginning to trace their developing ideas. I never refer to a scholar by name in the main body of the writing, even though occasionally I may place competing scholarly conclusions side by side. Instead, I have tried to lead readers through the basic train of thought of biblical writings, with sustained readings of those texts in their final form.

The book should work best when read alongside of the Bible, not in place of it. It does offer lots of explanations of biblical matters. It is also designed to make readers think. Reflection questions at the end of each chapter are meant to encourage readers to contemplate more concretely and practically on some of that chapter's more theoretical issues.

I hope professional scholars will engage with this material also, even if they are not my primary audience. The endnotes are mostly for them, to assure them that I am in touch with important aspects of the wider scholarly dialogue, while taking certain points made in the main body a bit further. Students, of course, may read the notes and obtain both a sense of where others support the ideas of this book and of where they can begin to go, with discernment, to probe the ideas further. Several of the notes are actually more fitting for students; the suggestions for further reading at the end of each chapter are entirely for them.

I am a biblical studies person, not a theologian. Biblical studies people are about clarifying biblical texts. Theologians, among other things, are about establishing theological positions. As a biblical studies person, I aim to explain the biblical text, rather than to conform to a theological position. Declaring this up front, I hope, will explain why I am focusing on ethical patterns as they develop from the flow of thought of individual texts considered in their more extended context, rather from ideas rooted in individual statements excerpted from those texts. This book grows out of a high regard for the Bible. I want to go where its words take me, even if that means sidestepping valid theological ideas often associated with certain statements. I want to listen to the voices of its texts. I want to see where they, in their flow of thought, are pointing.

This book has also been years in the making—more than twenty, in fact. It began as a sprout in the desert, in Tucson, Arizona, where we as a family had moved after I had completed my doctoral studies at the University of Sheffield. We had to relocate somewhere in the United States, and Tucson offered us certain advantages. There we also ran into both the kindness of the church and the callousness of American universities and colleges that all too often fill teaching needs by hiring part-time faculty at unlivable wages, with no benefits. I worked under that adjunct system for nearly ten years, eventually teaching ten to sixteen classes per year, spread between several institutions.

We could not have survived as a family without the microethical encouragement, and sometimes financial support, of members of our church there. I could also not have ended up where I did without the microethical treatment of singular individuals at various institutions in Arizona where I worked, people who gave me opportunities not only to teach but to expand my horizons into the worlds of ethics and ancient philosophical texts.

Muskingum University, then Muskingum College, hired me in 2002, so we moved from Tucson to New Concord, Ohio. One of my privileges has been to develop a course on biblical ethics. After getting it wrong the first time I taught it, I totally redesigned the course. This book has emerged out of that redesigned course. My doctoral work had focused on the New Testament. Being the only biblical studies specialist in the department of religion and philosophy, and being determined not to be a Marcionite, I chose to spend a significant portion of that course in the Old Testament. That accounts for the broader scope of this work.

Muskingum University granted me a full year sabbatical to help me finish this project, for which I am grateful. So I set out in September 2011 with my wife and my youngest daughter to Cambridge, England, to avail myself of the library at Tyndale House. That meant not only access to relevant books. It also led to significant interaction with scholars from all over the world, many of whom listened to my ideas and offered constructive input. Just as significant, though, was the microethical ministry of Eden Baptist Church in Cambridge, whose extraordinary outreach to the foreigner in their midst extended to me, my wife and daughter. People opened their hearts and homes to us, even knowing how brief our stay would be.

At the end of that sabbatical, to my delight, IVP accepted my proposal for this book. My thanks to Brannon Ellis and the team—external readers, editors, marketers, designers, indexers and everyone else—who have all helped to make this a much better book than what I had first submitted.

To say none of this is possible without family is cliché. I could not have survived the exploitative adjunct system without the ongoing microethical support of my wife, Bee, and our five children. They were models of patience, gladly accepting humbling circumstances—dining out usually meant the occasional $1 special at fast food restaurants, with water. I have also watched with delight as each of our children has consistently sought and maintained inclusive friendships. Four of our children are married now, to outstanding people who all share the full range of their morality and connection to God, especially as pro-marriage people.

My wife continues to be astounding, full of affirmation. She has spent years interacting with me about ideas in this book. An outstanding wife and mother, she not only held us together in the desert, she became a model for others, both in Arizona and now Ohio, who sought, and continue to seek, her input on marriage and family issues. An exceptional thinker and encourager, the effect of her input into my life and work is incalculable.

What Is Biblical Ethics?

Defining Ethics

What makes for good behavior? What makes for bad? How can people decide what is good and what is bad? And why should anyone care in the first place? People from an assortment of cultures spanning a variety of eras have asked these kinds of questions. Thinking people pursue answers to such questions to help them make sense of the world they live in. These happen to be the questions of ethics.

What is *ethics*? That word refers to the basic ways that people use to distinguish right from wrong behavior. The discipline of ethics aims to assess the rightness and wrongness of people's activities. It also offers motivations and reasons for why a person should choose to do what is right and avoid what is wrong.

Consider a basic interaction between a child and parent:

> *"Mom, why do I have to brush my teeth?"*
>
> *"Because I told you to."*

There is a system in place here. It is a command-like system. A person should perform an activity not because of any rightness or wrongness of that activity, but simply because an authority has ordered it. According to that system, one should never question authority. It is a system that usually works based on the control of one person over another. Parents can often get away with that kind of interaction until their children come under influences outside of the home. As children grow up in many of the world's societies today, they begin to learn that authorities can be blocked. Parental appeals to their own authority become dissatisfying and ineffective.

So, consider the following upgrade:

"Mom, why do I have to brush my teeth?"

*"To keep your teeth healthy. If you don't, they'll rot
and fall out."*

Now a new element has been added—consequences. If people perform well, they benefit; if they perform badly, they can be harmed. The interaction now appears to be fairly reasonable. But compare the explanation from the preceding parent with those following:

*"Because if you do, I'll take you to the zoo
tomorrow."*

Or

"Because if you don't, I will spank you."

These also are consequences, but something is a bit off. The consequences do not seem to be tied to the behavior. There is no genuine connection between tooth brushing and the zoo, or tooth brushing and spanking. Rather, the interaction appears disturbingly manipulative, perhaps symptomatic of a flawed relationship. The parents here appear to be on subtly weak ground. In one case, the parent is bribing the child. In the other, the parent is threatening the child.

Ethics provides the rationale for performing certain behaviors. If the reasons for performing a behavior make sense, the system makes sense. If they do not, the system begins to falter.

Ethics involves another important element. The two scenarios may be instructive in the area of parenting, but are they really dealing with ethics? Brushing teeth may be polite. It may be healthy. But is it right in the same way that one would consider helping a person in need would be, or is failing to do it wrong in the same way that murdering someone would be? Brushing teeth reflects social upbringing, to be sure. It has health consequences, certainly. Refusing to do so when asked to may indicate troublesome attitudes that themselves do come into the sphere of ethics—rebelliousness, stubbornness, selfishness. But people would hardly call someone who fails to brush teeth an unethical person merely because he or she happened not to perform an act of personal hygiene.

So what else does ethics involve? We are talking, ultimately, about how someone is guided to become a good person who performs good deeds. That would involve matters such as how people treat others or how they treat themselves. It would more fully involve how one treats the world around oneself.

The following scenario swerves more fully into the world of ethics:

> *"Alicia, please share your toy with Junie."*
>
> *"Why?"*
>
> *"Because you want to be a good friend to her. She ought to enjoy coming to visit you."*

Here we are dealing with behavior that affects people's expression of their humanness. We are observing Alicia's parent instructing her about right and wrong behavior that affects another person.

That kind of interaction, even between parent and child, shows a regard for behavior that goes beyond the bounds of mere politeness. It reflects a concern for others. It ultimately reflects a concern for what kind of person the child should aim to become and the kinds of things she should be doing as that sort of person. In this scenario Alicia is being urged to advance good, or well-being, on her world. She is also being urged not to advance harm in her world. That basic pattern will serve as the working definition of what ethics involves for this book. In other words, *ethics involves championing behavior that advances good or hinders harm in one's world.*

People who aim to be ethical people are good people. We like good people. Good people do what is right. They refrain from what is evil. We like associating with people who are kind to us, who give to us, who care for us. Conversely, we don't like people who are nasty to us, who take from us, who harm us. So, what does it mean to be good? Why should we do good? Answers to those questions will reveal the kind of ethics we are applying.

BIBLICAL ETHICS

In this book we are considering what the collection of writings known as the Bible contributes to the world of ethics. What is considered right and wrong behavior according to biblical writings? What thought patterns do writings in the Bible encourage in helping their readers distinguish right from wrong? What reasons and motivations do biblical writings offer for why their readers should perform what is good and refrain from what is bad?

In addressing such questions, let's first note an important difference between what some would call "Christian ethics" or "religious ethics" and what we are exploring here in this book. Christian or religious ethics might address the question, What do the tenets of the religious faith contribute to distinguishing right from wrong on life's issues? Or, more personally, Since I call myself a Christian, how should I behave as a Christian over this issue? These are great questions. They launch the inquirer on a prescriptive task that looks to the religion, including the Bible as Christian Scripture, to advise about or make behavioral demands for the present moment.

Biblical ethics should also inform those kinds of questions. But before we can determine how, we must first try to discern what the biblical texts appear to be communicating.[1] Note, biblical *texts,* not simply biblical statements. We're aiming to learn to observe the sustained lines of reasoning offered by individual biblical writings or clusters of related writings. Instead of imposing our interests on them—What does the Bible say about X?—we want to discern the issues that the words of individual writings appear to be designed to address. The biblical ethics we are pursuing here is largely a descriptive task. We will aim to understand what the Bible's writings themselves promote ethically, exploring them with a regard for their literary, cultural and historical contexts. What we discover through this kind of biblical ethics should then be the basis of conversation between Bible readers, who can help each other understand more deeply what to do with the kinds of ideas disclosed by this sort of investigation. Our primary pursuit in this book is to observe the ways of distinguishing right from wrong that are encouraged within biblical writings, and what rationale and motivations those writings offer for performing right activities and avoiding wrong ones. Based on those, people can begin to discuss the prescriptive role these texts can have in their lives now, no matter the culture.[2]

Since much of Christian ethics is interested in using the Bible, how is what we are doing here different? Our task will not be to *use* the Bible as a source of moral statements, but to *describe* the Bible's ethical vision, how its writings themselves shape the readers' views of moral right and wrong. For example, some Christian thinkers are interested in exploring the implications of humans being made in God's image, a point made twice in the early chapters of Genesis, as we'll soon see. "If humans are said to be in God's image," the reasoning goes, "then I should always treat other humans as fellow image bearers." That's not a bad line of reasoning. But it is not strictly biblical in the way we are considering here. How so? Because that line of reasoning is never explicitly found or encouraged by any words in biblical writings. In fact, the last use of the expression "image of God" in the large first part of the Bible, the Old Testament, is in Genesis 9. Biblical writings appeal to the concept differently. Those writings instead follow other identifiable, sustained lines of reasoning that offer consistent and persistent ways of thinking about right and wrong. Learning to trace those lines is the point of this book.

In some religious contexts people are told, prescriptively, to do one certain kind of activity or refrain from others "because the Bible says so." Such people could then go so far as to say that such a reason makes their ethics biblical. Though that religious approach may appeal to the Bible, it also tends not to reflect consistently what the writings themselves communicate and should also not be confused with the biblical ethics we are pursuing here. It rather tends to assume that the Bible is a collection of moral injunctions and stories that declare and demonstrate what is right and wrong for the faithful. According to that view, those who want to be considered faithful should do what the Bible says, without hesitation. Though, as we'll see, biblical writings expect their words to be taken seriously, the words of those writings present a much richer set of ideas than the rationale of rote obedience allows for.

Further, the Bible's words shouldn't be pressed into service to communicate ideas foreign to them. If we impose assumptions from our culture onto what the Bible's words communicate in their original settings, we introduce distortions. For example, we may want a biblical ruling on when human life begins definitively, but if we assume that biblical writers know exactly what we may know about human conception, we would be introducing ideas foreign to the biblical texts. The female ovum was not discovered until the early nineteenth century. Appeals to the Bible for such uses tend to reflect what religious authorities claim about biblical texts more than what those texts themselves may actually be advancing. They do not reflect biblical ethics but rather a form of religious ethics that appeals to biblical texts, sometimes validly, other times not.

As we explore biblical texts here, we will discover that those texts together do not really speak with one voice. The expression "the Bible says" reflects a religious attitude, but it does not always reflect accurately what we find biblical texts advancing. There are varieties of thought within the Bible because the Bible itself is a collection of writings produced over a wide time span and addressing varieties of cultures, even as many of those writings also show a high degree of consistency in disclosing an unfolding divine program.

Though that will lead us to consider a variety of ethical approaches in the Bible, we should also recognize one constant to all biblical texts: people's ethics flow from their relationship with God. To begin to explore that point, let's briefly return to the illustrations in the opening section of this chapter. Some people assume that God in the Bible is like an obnoxiously strict parent. Right is defined purely in terms of what God says. One should do what is right because God said so. Period. No questions asked.

Such rationale would be legitimate to consider if biblical writings actually communicated those thoughts in that way. And, if that were the case, they could be severely criticized for encouraging nothing better than "Do this or else!" Biblical writings would not be worthy of deep ethical examination, disclosing instead a harsh, authoritarian religion.

Now, suppose instead other assumptions that, for example, God manipulates people into behaving a certain way by threatening them with tough consequences, such as punishment or hell, or bribes them with good consequences, such as heaven or at least good things in life—the Santa Claus god who "knows when you've been bad or good, so be good, for goodness' sake!" And in return, if people bribe or manipulate that god enough by promising to behave a certain way, maybe god will be fooled into thinking they are better than they know they really are, deep down, hoping to avoid bad outcomes and attain good ones. Again, such a system would not be worth examining ethically, whatever unbiblical, personal religion it might disclose.

Many writings in the Bible do talk about God's undeniable authority and about rewards, punishments and heaven and hell. But biblical writings do so in ways that defy uninformed, popular-level assumptions. When examining the Bible's words in their actual contexts, readers will make surprising observations that may defy their assumptions about the sense of religion advocated by the Bible's varied writings. For example, eternal rewards and punishments, concerns with life after death, even hell avoidance and heaven attainment are generally side issues in the Bible. (When we explore the Gospel of Matthew, though, we will see aspects of those issues emphasized.) And in those few places in the Bible where hell is referred to, it is portrayed not as a scare or bribery tactic, but as a serious outcome for the end of the age. What happens to a person upon dying is scarcely a topic in the Bible, even if it becomes so for some expressions of Christianity so closely connected to those writings. Let Bible readers beware: when observed carefully, the words of the Bible will reveal, criticize and correct their sloppy religious assumptions.

Now, if biblical writings advocate various approaches to ethics that flow out of people's relationship with God, and if that God is neither a brute, authoritarian parent demanding rote obedience, nor a weak, manipulative parent threatening with punishment and bribing with rewards, what do we actually see? Let's look briefly at the first writing, Genesis.

Our original introduction to God in that writing displays the Creator, whose acts resemble more those of a beneficent monarch or king than of a parent.[3] That king commands, and it is so. Even more revealing, that king evaluates to see that all is good. That kingly activity results in an ordered creation that humans are asked collectively to manage. When we see God instructing the first human, a man known eventually as Adam, he issues a specific charge: "You may freely eat of every tree of the garden; but of the tree of the knowledge of good and evil you shall not eat, for in the day that you eat of it you shall die" (Gen 2:16-17).

Notice, first of all, that this is not an ethical scenario. Rather, this shows a boundary-setting restriction. That is important to observe. Why? Not everything in the Bible is about ethics. Think about it. What is inherently wrong in eating fruit? Of course, this is a particular kind of fruit—a unique kind, in fact, that is said to give "knowledge of good and evil," important categories for ethics. But eating it is said to have severe consequences—death. Certainly the rationale eventually offered for disobeying God's command has implications for ethics: "When the woman saw that the tree was good for food, and that it was a delight to the eyes, and that the tree was to be desired to make one wise . . ." (Gen 3:6). How, after all, can a person overcome strong desires and refrain from doing what she or he ought not do? But the scenario itself does not address the topic of how to distinguish right from wrong behavior, or why one should choose to perform right behavior, the concerns of ethics. If we expect everything in the Bible to be about morally good and bad behavior, we might want to reexamine our assumptions.

But notice further that in his initial injunction God provides the rationale for why one certain fruit should not be eaten: "for in the day that you eat of it you shall die" (Gen 2:17). Though another character questions that reason in a subsequent scene, it remains a reason that does not show any weakness or arbitrariness. Rather, it displays a concern for the well-being of the man, implying some sort of built-in consequence for the particular kind of disobedience. It also implies the expectation that the man can process, understand and adhere to the injunction for his own good.

Though that initial interaction is not ethical, it is instructive about the kinds of interactions that we can expect between God and people in the world of the Bible. It helps set the tone for what follows.[4] Who God is, what God wants and what God does with people become important issues to bear in mind when evaluating the approach to proper behavior. So also are the ways people are encouraged to think and act in response to God, his activities and his expectations. Some of what God wants from people does fall under the category of behavior often considered moral or ethical—learning to advance good on others, on oneself, on one's world or hindering behavior that advances harm in one's world. Examples of that kind of behavior include concerns for refraining from murder, refraining from wickedness, not treating others roughly, and pursuing love instead of vengeance. Some of what God wants from people does not involve what we normally consider under the category of ethics. Examples of that include abstaining from certain kinds of foods, keeping certain days special, offering proper sacrifices to God, responding to God when he says to move to a particular land, or even obeying God when he instructs a person not to eat the fruit from a specific tree.

That gives way to an important additional category for ethics—the morally neutral. Some behaviors may be important for some people in specific situations but are not inherently morally right or wrong. Those behaviors may fall into the areas of cultural customs and manners, or even situation-specific instructions, but not ethics. When considering morally neutral behaviors, we will have to consider the ethics of pursuing those behaviors, knowing that someone might be bothered, or the ethics of forcing people to conform to neutral standards, however important those standards may be culturally or religiously to those enforcing them.

It will also require people recognizing that some of their own culturally or religiously conditioned behaviors may actually be neutral, not genuinely moral. People should not expect biblical writings to affirm their own culture's manners and expectations. For example, being prompt or timely, an important cultural value for some people in the West today, is not really an issue that falls into the category of ethics, even though it may be wise to be prompt in many circumstances familiar to us. It's really only a culture-bound value near and dear to many people. Certainly biblical writings don't count promptness among the issues that God cares about. Being impatient with others for being late, however, would be. So also is a refusal to honor another's known sense of timeliness by insisting on having one's own way.

What we will see throughout the Bible is the notion that how a person chooses to respond to God affects the kind of person he or she becomes. Thus, those who aim to do what God wants are ethical people, because much of what God is said to want is also what most people would consider to be good, ethical behavior, and because throughout the span of biblical writings, God is portrayed as being in the business of restoring rightness to his creation. In the world of the Bible those who choose to defy God do not know how to act consistently as ethical people, because they have chosen to cut themselves off from the ways and plans of God, and thus are incomplete in their sense of what right and wrong behavior actually include.

Obeying God, trusting God, having faith in God and responding to God are all central issues to the Bible, issues that affect the ethics that its varied writings promote. How one responds to God is reflected in a person's ethics. In fact, expect to see repeatedly how those who respond to God are often shown as good responders by doing ethical acts. Those who disregard God are often shown as bad responders with the unethical acts they perform.

Ultimately, what we see throughout the Bible are sets of ethics rooted in people's relationship with God—an ethic of relationship.[5] Doing good flows out of a person coming to know God and growing in that relationship with God. Doing wrong shows how out of touch a person is with God. Biblical writings are full of the language of devotion and commitment. It is not a mindless devotion but one that is highly attractive, showing people interacting with a God who gives, cares and accepts, even if that God also has high standards for those who are connected to him. Those standards are often shown to lead to personal well-being for those who interact with God.

Significantly, because people's relating to God is the one constant advocated by the varieties of biblical writings, how God relates to people also merits consideration. Biblical writings offer hope and restoration for those who mess up. An important element of that is a concept known as *repentance*: people turning away from their evil and embracing God's good. Along with that are *grace*: receiving good from God when one deserves the opposite, and *mercy*: receiving good from God when one is in a decidedly weak position. A sense of hope also emerges as a central feature of biblical ethics. People are allowed to be works in progress. Expect to discover imperfect people in biblical writings, people who, as they draw close to God, also become better people in the process, even if many of them have rough edges. In the world of the Bible God never rejects people who call on him.

MORALITY VERSUS ETHICS

People often use the concepts of morality and ethics interchangeably. Morals generally refer to a person's awareness of right and wrong. A moral person does the right kind of behavior in the sense we have been probing here, advancing good on the world while refraining from what inflicts harm. For that reason some people would say that a moral person is also ethical.

A moral person may be doing what is right, but may not know clearly what makes the activity right or why she or he should do that right. By contrast, ethics as we discuss it here deals with how to distinguish right from wrong, and why someone should do the right and hinder the wrong. In exploring the Bible we will see many statements weighing in on the moral rightness or wrongness of various behaviors. But we won't stop there. We will look for the ethics that will indicate what makes the activity right or wrong and that offer rationale and motivation for engaging in the right activity or refraining from the wrong. Moral people do what is right. So do people who have ethics, but they also know why.[6]

The distinction between morality and ethics is an important one. Two people can share the same moral convictions, but they could easily have very different ethics. How? Because the ethics will explain the answer to the question, Why is that wrong? For example, in the world that produced the New Testament section of the Bible, Greek and Roman philosophers commonly discussed the moral wrongness of being guided by our passions. Thoughtless passions lead people to do the wrong things. One writer, Paul, whose ethics we will explore in chapters nine and ten, would basically agree that people acting out their passions leads to misbehavior. But if you asked both sets of people why being guided by passion is wrong, you would get two entirely different sets of answers. Paul's answer connects directly to his awareness of the crucifixion and resurrection of Jesus. The philosophers know nothing of Jesus. Their answers are linked to their view of the psychology of the soul. Though we might think we see moral agreement between Paul and philosophers, we see totally different ethics. We will see the same thing in the Bible itself. The various places we will explore will frequently show common moral standards but different ethics. Ethics and morality are not the same.

The Bible's writings do communicate a strong set of morals. But they do much more than that. They portray genuine ethics. They show ways of life stemming from people living in attractive relationship with the true and living God. Reasons for living morally appear regularly, either stated or implied, because relationship with God is portrayed as wonderfully good and genuinely healthy. Relationship with God ultimately involves participating in God's process of remaking the world, a world filled with brokenness exhibited in and stemming from human misbehavior. As we probe biblical texts, we will discover ethical systems that are intriguing, inviting, enlightening and uplifting. People who read the Bible well will not only have a stronger sense of what is right and wrong, they will realize why, according to those writings, they also should do right, and why living that right is so fulfilling.

SUMMING IT UP

What is ethics?

- o Ethics refers to how a person distinguishes right from wrong behavior.

- o Ethics is also concerned with the reasons for why a person should choose what is good and abstain from what is not.

- o The kind of behavior that ethics is concerned with generally is behavior that advances good or hinders harm in one's world.

What do we mean by biblical ethics?

- o With biblical ethics, one is concerned with discerning the kinds of behavior biblical writings indicate are right and wrong.

- o One is also concerned with both how, according to biblical writings, to distinguish right from wrong and why its readers should do right and refrain from wrong.

- o Biblical ethics begins with describing what biblical writings communicate ethically. Only then can people see how those ethics might apply to their lives prescriptively.

- o Ethics is not the central concern of biblical writings.

- o Other behaviors besides ethical behaviors are dealt with in the Bible.

- o How people connect meaningfully with God is a central concern of biblical writings.

- o Ethics in the Bible flows primarily out of people's healthy relationship with God.

- o Ethics in the Bible offers hope for those who recognize their error and turn to God.

How is morality different from ethics?

o Morality is simply knowing what is right and what is wrong.

o Ethics involves both the reasoning for distinguishing right from wrong and the motivations for doing what is right and hindering what is wrong.

o Biblical writings regularly portray genuine ethics, not mere morality.

ALTERNATIVE ETHICAL SYSTEMS

Ethical questions and dilemmas appear consistently and prominently within human history. Some of the ethical systems Western civilizations developed to address those concerns are worth noting, briefly, as a way of comparing how biblical writings offer both similarities to and dissimilarities from them.[7] Some of these systems actually influenced aspects of ethics as found in parts of the Bible. Others of these have themselves been influenced by the sense of right and wrong found in biblical writings.

Virtue ethics. Also closely related to what is called "character ethics," virtue ethics focus on what kind of person one should become in order to attain a higher goal, such as happiness or well-being, emphasizing various virtues (e.g., courage, wisdom, justice, self-control, kindness, forbearance, friendliness, modesty).[8] Conversely, there are vices that one should avoid (e.g., cowardice, folly, wrongness, self-indulgence, meanness, short-temperedness, diffidence, extravagance). Many of those good character qualities are learned from observing people who are considered to be good, or by repeated practice of virtuous activities. Discussions of virtues and vices were especially important to the ancient Greeks and Romans. Some writings in the New Testament reflect awareness of the fruit of such discussions, but also offer their own unique perspectives on virtues and vices.

Ethical egoism. Also coming from ancient Greece, ethical egoism advocates pursuing behaviors with outcomes that maximize personal pleasure while minimizing personal pain. Rather than resorting to out-and-out hedonism (i.e., selfish pleasure seeking), the point here is to evaluate long-term outcomes or consequences. Some immediate pleasures may result in such horrible pain in the end that they should be avoided altogether. But some pain may be necessary to endure in order to attain the benefit of a long-term pleasure.

Utilitarianism. Utilitarianism is similar to ethical egoism with its concern for maximizing pleasure and minimizing pain, but does so with societies in view, not merely the individual. Whatever advances pleasure for the greatest number of people is to be preferred. Further, it recognizes that there are higher-order pleasures in life beyond mere physical gratification. People's failure to exercise their minds or their pursuit of personal selfishness are two major obstacles to good being advanced. In current popular, everyday practice, both ethical egoistic and utilitarian ways of thinking can lead people to line up physical, psychological and sociological conclusions in order to prove that a genuine pleasure is being advanced or pain is being avoided. But sometimes those conclusions prove more tentative than their communicators may indicate at the time, especially when they are really interested in justifying their own misbehavior.

Duty. With duty, one should do what is right and refrain from what is wrong because that is the most reasonable form of activity to pursue as a thinking human being. One has a duty to live consistently with one's being. Right and wrong are independent of human existence. Right corresponds with what is true; to pursue what is false is self-contradictory and internally inconsistent. Practically speaking, living by duty means functioning in a world of beings. As a human being, one has a duty to recognize people as people. Whenever one treats another, or even oneself, solely as an object, one is violating one's duty to a fellow creature. This way of thinking partly resembles a well-known maxim attributed to Jesus, often called the Golden Rule—"Do to others as you would have them do to you." But it has little regard for people thinking empathetically about others with a desired ideal good for them the way Jesus' words do.

Divine command theory. Divine command theory assumes that rightness comes directly from divinity, and whatever any divinity commands, the religious person must obey. When applied to the Bible, this approach assumes that the Bible is full of commands meant to be obeyed. So as a reader, one should look diligently for those commands. Whatever is commanded must be followed because it comes from God. To obey God is to do what is right. To disobey God is to do what is wrong. While to many this would seem to be biblical ethics in a nutshell, it falls short by not seeing how biblical ethics involves much more than obeying commands. Often associated with this approach at the popular level is an attitude that treats the Bible as a sort of guiding constitution to scan for moral rulings; discovering "what the Bible says" about a topic then becomes the primary pursuit.

Teleology. Many of these approaches to ethics also try to organize life around a focused goal, a teleological approach. For example, for some virtue ethicists and ethical egoists, achieving a form of happiness or well-being is the goal for which virtues are exercised or pain is minimized. By contrast, the approach emphasizing duty regards the duty to be right all by itself, independent of any ultimate human goal or ideal.

ETHICAL SYSTEMS AND THE BIBLE

The Bible and teleology. In the Bible we will see varieties of teleological thought, stronger in some places than in others. Concerns, for example, with conformity to the created order or to God's merciful acts in a moment known as the exodus are common in the first writings we will probe.[9] Even stronger will be the awareness that life is advancing toward a future, ultimate moment of reordering, a major component to the later writings being studied here.

The Bible and virtue ethics. There are many places where biblical writings champion conformity to a good character model.[10] But good character is advanced neither as a means to some sort of end nor merely as an end in itself the way it is in traditional virtue ethics. Obtaining good life outcomes or avoiding bad ones is not the main goal of being good. Rather, good character in biblical writings is often seen as a reflection of the God who is being served. It is both an outcome of associating with God and a measuring stick of how in touch one is with God. Further, in addition to character issues, biblical texts also champion specific behaviors such as taking care of the poor, standing up for the weak or loving the unlovely. Those behaviors may reflect good character, but they are to be done regardless of one's overall character. Many in Christianity have traditionally thought of love as a virtue. But biblical writings often focus on love as an activity, even a responsibility.

Attention to character formation is a major topic of discussion for scholars examining the use of the Bible in ethics.[11] That would be close to virtue ethics, but not identical. It focuses on how encouragement in the practice of certain biblical instructions shapes the lives of those who do them, influencing what kind of people they become. Like virtue ethics, this recognizes that a person must be trained in the right way of living to be able to become good. It does receive major support from the Bible's writings themselves, which encourage a lifestyle that is always growing in its awareness of God and God's desires for humans. Still, the ethics of the parts of the Bible we will explore here will also provide more than material for character formation. They will also provide guidelines that help people make reasoned decisions about the rightness and wrongness of certain activities as they ponder them.

The Bible, ethical egoism and utilitarianism. Some biblical writings promote appraising harmful or beneficial outcomes of behaviors in ways that may seem to resemble the ethical egoist or the utilitarian. They tend to do so to show the wisdom or folly of certain activities, or to speak approvingly of advancing the goodness or well-being of one's neighbor. They do not make the avoidance of personal pain or the acquisition of personal pleasure the ultimate goal. Rather, they measure consequences observed from the activities of others and offer advice based on what is observed to have worked and what genuinely does not, founded on how one studies the world as God created it. Other writings talk about growing in character from enduring hardships such as persecution. Again, the point is not to focus on the personal gain from such growth but on the ultimate goal, the remade, hardship-free creation one is destined to.

The Bible and duty. Various biblical writings urge their readers to treat others as people, rather than objects, but they do so in a manner that takes into consideration the frailties of the environment people live in and the realities of human existence and weakness, encouraging readers to be aware of their own. Though obedience itself, in some contexts, may be perceived as a duty, further probing of those contexts often discloses that obedience flows more out of a sincere relationship with God and a high regard for others than from a sense of resolute, duty-bound obligation.

The Bible and divine command theory. The Bible is also full of commands. But many of those commands come in specifically defined contexts that are not meant to apply directly to people in most contemporaneous settings. And outside of those contexts, much of what is often regarded as command is really instructional advice, which is quite a different form of expression—ordering someone to "Slow down!" is not the same as advising someone to "Take your time," yet both communicate what grammarians call imperatives. Further, much of the Bible's advice appears in contexts that point to clear supporting reasons behind it. Focusing on the advice without dealing with its supporting rationale misses the actual ethics being advanced. Finally, there are many ethical topics about which the Bible does not issue any direct command or instruction, leaving readers with no guidance or worse, as we have already seen, leading people to twist the Bible's words into making points not really there. Discovering God's will emerges as a major concern in some of the writings we will explore for their ethics. But we will see how doing that leads a person beyond a search for direct statements or interpretive moral rulings.

When people probe the Bible to learn what it might say about a certain moral topic, they are really acting under a basic assumption of divine command theory: an act is right or wrong because God says so.[12] And yet, without ever having read the Bible, people all over the world have views similar to biblical writings' views about the morality of certain acts. A sense of right and wrong can exist independent of the Bible. In this book we will proceed under the assumption that *an act is not right or wrong just because the Bible says so. The Bible says so often because the act is right or wrong.* Why is an act right or wrong? Answering that from the Bible's writings will put readers in touch with the ethics those writings advance.

The observations from the previous paragraphs should not lessen any respect that a reader gives to biblical texts. They should, in fact, increase it. The writings of the Bible encourage more than they often receive credit for. Throughout the variety of ethical approaches we will examine in this book, we will see attitudes expressed by biblical texts that expect their words to be taken seriously, precisely because they are connected to God, who is trustworthy, who has made the world with purpose and who is in the process of moving its events to an ultimate, restorative climax. Doing something because one is prompted by a saying in a biblical text is an attitude encouraged directly by the words of the Bible's writings. But studying biblical ethics means much more than searching for and then obeying divinely established commands or discovering what the Bible says about a topic. That may sometimes be a good starting point, but the Bible's words often lead its readers to think about how to do even more than they say directly. People who care about the Bible should let their ethical vision be shaped by that.

A VARIETY OF ETHICS AND A CONSISTENT MORALITY

The Bible is not a book written by a single author with a collection of chapters reflecting a beginning, a middle and an end. It is a collection of writings, emerging over a large time span and produced by a wide variety of authors, nearly one third of whom are not identified. It falls into two unequal portions: (1) the much larger Hebrew Bible (or to Christians, the Old Testament), the product of hundreds of years of activity, focusing on the people of Israel and their covenant with God, and (2) the New Testament, produced within the second half of the first century C.E. or A.D., the writings of which all reflect issues and events related to the person named Jesus, the Christ. Many of the writings of both Testaments disclose threads of an unfolding story to which they persistently connect, divulging an emerging divine plan. Some writings connect to that plan with more detail than others. And not all of the writings try to advance that unfolding story.

In this book we are probing only four broad sections of biblical ethics: (1) The Torah (minus Numbers) and (2) proverbial wisdom from the Old Testament; (3) two of the Gospels (Luke and Matthew) and (4) two of Paul's letters (1 Corinthians and Romans) from the New Testament.[13] Prophetic thought from Isaiah in the Old Testament will be addressed briefly as well, not for separate ethical inquiry as much as to bridge the ethical worlds of Torah and the Gospels. Immediately, some may fault this listing as incomplete and too limiting.[14] Yes, it is. But these four basic sections each have broad, unique, identifiable features that disclose significant depth of ethical thought. What Torah communicates, ethically, is quite distinct from what Proverbs conveys. And though the Gospels of Luke and Matthew each display their own special ethical approaches, their similarities offer a significantly different slant from what Paul advances. We will be looking at four distinct emphases: covenant, consequences, kingdom and transformation. The Bible does not portray a single, unitary ethical vision. We see multiple visions, each connecting people with God, who has made the world and will remake it.

Evidence within the biblical writings suggests that all four of the approaches we are exploring can interact not only with each other but with those biblical approaches that we are not exploring in this book.[15] We are looking at a useful, basic starting point. Those wanting to pursue a fuller range of approaches and thought forms can then build from here.

Recognizing that there are different, complementary ways of thinking advocated by biblical texts should give Bible readers a greater appreciation for the richness of thought the writings encourage. It should also caution them about the shallowness of approaches that disregard that variety in favor of coming up with a "biblical" position about a moral topic. Though one might be able to discern common moral perspectives on some issues, one would be missing out on the ethical reasoning individual sets of writings advance.

SOME LIMITATIONS OF THIS APPROACH

Many biblical writings invite their readers to distinguish right from wrong. Though the Bible does not speak univocally (i.e., with one voice), its writings display a remarkably consistent concern for distinguishing right from wrong, even within the diversity of their expressions. Consider the following statements from a wide range of biblical books, all but one of which we will eventually survey.

Moses, the leader of God's people in the Torah, instructs them concerning God's commands:

> *You must observe them diligently, for this will show your wisdom and discernment to the peoples, who, when they hear all these statutes, will say, "Surely this great nation is a wise and discerning people!" For what other great nation has a god so near to it as the LORD our God is whenever we call to him? And what other great nation has statutes and ordinances as just as this entire law that I am setting before you today?* **Deut 4:6-8**

In Proverbs, a father instructs his son:

> *Do not enter the path of the wicked,*
> *   and do not walk in the way of evildoers.*
> *Avoid it; do not go on it;*
> *   turn away from it and pass on.*
> *For they cannot sleep unless they have done wrong;*
> *   they are robbed of sleep unless they have made someone stumble.*
> *For they eat the bread of wickedness*
> *   and drink the wine of violence.*
> *But the path of the righteous is like the light of dawn,*
> *   which shines brighter and brighter until full day.*
> *The way of the wicked is like deep darkness;*
> *   they do not know what they stumble over.* **Prov 4:14-19**

When accusing Israelite people of a series of wrongdoings, the prophet Isaiah writes,

> Ah, you who call evil good
>   and good evil,
> who put darkness for light
>   and light for darkness,
> who put bitter for sweet
>   and sweet for bitter! **Is 5:20**

In one Gospel, Jesus invites hearers to accept a set of his teachings, many of which address moral behavior:

> Enter through the narrow gate; for the gate is wide and the road is easy that leads to destruction, and there are many who take it. For the gate is narrow and the road is hard that leads to life, and there are few who find it. **Mt 7:13-14**

When disturbed that believers in Corinth are not distinguishing right from wrong, that church's founder, Paul, says,

> Can it be that there is no one among you wise enough to decide between one believer and another, but a believer goes to court against a believer—and before unbelievers at that? **1 Cor 6:5-6**

In a totally independent writing, when disturbed at the immaturity displayed by his readers' willingness to wander away from the faith, the writer of the epistle to the Hebrews identifies spiritually mature as

> those whose faculties have been trained by practice to distinguish good from evil. **Heb 5:14**

Biblical writings clearly advocate that people distinguish moral right from moral wrong.

That said, let's note once more how focusing on ethics to the exclusion of other issues is potentially misleading. We will see that immediately in exploring the first part of the Bible, the Torah. In Deuteronomy, for example, we will find activities identified as evil that our working definition of ethics would call immoral: false witness, adultery, kidnapping (Deut 19:19; 22:22; 24:7). But that same writing identifies false prophets and idolaters with the same label— evil (Deut 13:5; 17:7). Are idolaters and false prophets immoral or something else? Elsewhere in the Bible we will see ethical activity such as loving enemies (Mt 5:44-46) placed on the same reward level as facilitating the work of those who spread the message of the kingdom (Mt 10:40-42). Is supporting the spread of the kingdom's message moral or something else? Biblical writings often portray a more integrated view about life than our strict definitions allow. We might like to put certain decisions into an ethics box. Living in relationship with the Bible's God is all encompassing, not easily separable into box-like categories—a worship box, a sacrifice box, a religion box, an ethics box.

So why are we doing this? Because the list of statements we have just looked at is one piece of evidence among many we will see that encourages us to think ethically as a natural way of living in relationship with God. Failure to live in ways that emerge out of our definition of ethics is regularly condemned in biblical writings (e.g., Is 1:10-17; Mt 23:23-24). But living in relationship with God involves much more than ethics. Our study of ethics should not keep us from realizing that.

BIBLICAL ETHICS TENDS TO BE MICROETHICAL

Ethicists generally do not use the expression *microethical* or its noun, *microethics*. Those terms are unique to our discussions here. They appeal to concepts from the world of economics. Economists speak of microeconomics and macroeconomics. The former refers to how people interact in day-to-day business transactions. Whenever people buy or sell items from a store, they are engaging in microeconomics. The latter refers to larger, national and global issues that determine economic policies set by governments. Whenever people announce state or national employment figures, or whenever people are concerned about the prime rate being set by the Federal Reserve Bank, they are dealing with macroeconomics.

Similar concepts are being applied here. Microethics refers to what people do when they interact directly with someone else. "Should I be kind or rude to that woman who won't give me the time of day?" "Should I get angry at that man who just cut me off in traffic, or should I simply smile pleasantly?" "Should I join in the conversation about our friend, who is not present, or should I change the topic?" "Should I step in and help protect someone whom I see being mistreated, or should I just walk away?"[16] By contrast, macroethics appeals to larger matters concerning policy and programs. "Should I be in favor of policies that penalize the rich and champion the poor?" "Are programs that advocate abortion correct?" "Should I join a protest against a government policy that I think is a bad idea for society?" "Should I support the war?"

When we observe popular media, especially television and movies, we tend to see a macroethical emphasis. We see more concern for policies and programs than for individuals themselves being good people doing good things. Thus, a person who advocates the "right" causes, champions the "right" policies or supports the "right" programs is considered by many to be more ethical than someone who may see differently about such policies, but who is always ready to lend a helping hand whenever the opportunity arises, who regularly gives away money to individuals in need and who, as a nonmarried person, remains sexually celibate. In the meantime the activist who champions the "right" causes but who is not the nicest person to be around, or who may even be loose sexually, can be celebrated in the media for being good, in spite of the fact that people are being harmed in their interpersonal interactions. What people do in private is said to be their own business. Hence, one can be heralded for speaking well in front of the camera while being a person who does not get along well with others when the cameras are off. The world is filled with such people. They would not be considered moral within the worlds reflected in biblical writings.

Describing the *macroethical* and the *microethical* in this way tends toward a simplistic generalization. But the purpose of introducing these two categories is to point out that the various approaches to biblical ethics that we will examine tend to emphasize microethical responses. No matter where a person is reading in the Bible, one will see texts that frown on people who refuse to get personally involved in doing what is right to the people immediately in front of them. It is useless to be a public advocate for the poor while never actually giving anything to the poor nearby, or worse, never talking to or befriending people who are poor. The rich politician who advocates taxing the rich but who maintains an affluent lifestyle while donating minimal amounts of money to poor people would not be treated well in the world of biblical ethics. Neither would the sexually loose-living activist who shouts angry words at political opponents for the sake of the cause, no matter how worthy the cause. Biblical texts favor interpersonally enacted concern for people as the starting point for policies and programs. The individuals one interacts with are always more important than the causes one advocates, no matter how valid those causes may be.

The terminology of micro- and macroethics should not undermine an important subcategory for many discussing the Bible and ethics, namely that of social ethics. Social ethics emphasizes how various groups of weak people in societies are easily marginalized and mistreated, rather than helped. Such social concerns will appear in all four approaches to ethics we will explore here. For example, early on we will discover texts that talk about caring for poor people, for widows, for fatherless (or unprotected) children and for foreigners or aliens.[17] Though neglect of such weak people can and does become part of wider social issues needing to be addressed by biblical texts, the words we first see about such issues will be aimed at people in local, interpersonal situations. The care for the weak neighbor is portrayed as the responsibility of the person who crosses that neighbor's path, not some impersonal, outside source. The person ignoring the weaker neighbor whom he or she could help would be acting immorally. A concern for living properly within one's own community is first and foremost a microethical concern.

SUMMING IT UP: WHAT WE SHOULD (AND SHOULDN'T) EXPECT FROM BIBLICAL ETHICS

- Biblical writings have points in common with other ethical systems outside of the Bible, but they display their own unique approaches to ethics.

- The attempt to discover what "the Bible says" about a topic does not reflect *biblical* ethics. It reflects some other system of ethics being imposed on the Bible.

- The Bible contains a variety of approaches to ethics, not a single, unitary ethical vision.

- The pursuit of biblical ethics should not hinder our attention to other biblical concerns.

- Biblical ethics favors people over policies and programs—it is more microethical than macroethical.

Since biblical texts focus on interpersonal interactions rather than broad policies, expect to feel pinched. The various approaches to biblical ethics that we will observe do not let people get away with bad interpersonal behavior.

Reflection Questions

1. What is the relationship between morals and ethics?

2. How does biblical morality differ from biblical ethics?

3. Consider the list of ethical approaches under this chapter's subhead "Alternative Ethical Systems": virtue ethics, ethical egoism, utilitarianism, duty, divine command theory. What aspects of any of these have you ever observed at least partially in practice?

4. What are the problems of assuming that divine command theory is all that the Bible advocates?

5. How is microethical activity different from macroethical activity? Toward which do you find yourself most often tending in your own thinking?

FOR FURTHER READING

Wilkens, Stephen. *Beyond Bumper Sticker Ethics.* Downers Grove, IL: InterVarsity Press, 1995.

FROM DISORDER TO ORDER

Ethics in Torah 1

We begin, appropriately, with the opening section in the Bible known as the Torah. We will test some of our basic principles right from the start, principles such as people's sense of ethics flowing from their relating to God, and that not everything in the Bible centers on trying to get people to behave morally. To help us do that, let's explore some basic issues.

WHAT IS THE TORAH?

The first large segment of the Bible was written in Hebrew. *Torah* (plural *tôrôt*) is a Hebrew word meaning "law" or "instruction." The Torah consists of the first five writings of the Bible: Genesis, Exodus, Leviticus, Numbers and Deuteronomy. Scattered throughout those writings, in various concentrations, are individual laws (*tôrôt*) that instruct. Genesis and the first half of Exodus contain stories in which God establishes his ways, initially in the creation of "the heavens and the earth" and then in his creation of a nation known as Israel. Those stories do not emphasize ethical human behavior, even if aspects of them have strong implications for ethics, in places wrestling with the messiness of life and the moral inconsistencies of people whom one would expect to know better.[1]

The rest of Exodus presents instructive laws for God's people and directions for building a special structure (the tabernacle) that enables God to dwell in the midst of his people, the Israelites.[2] Leviticus continues with more instructive laws. Numbers contains two censuses (hence the title of the writing), a series of stories regularly highlighting God's punishment of, but also faithfulness to, his people. It also has further sets of laws. Deuteronomy offers a re-presentation of instructive laws, spoken in the form of a farewell speech delivered by Moses. Much of the content of those writings presents actual laws that exist as part of the covenant between God and his people, the Israelites. The Israelites are to enact the laws in the land that God is giving them. Many of the laws and instructions in the Torah have implications for ethics, but certainly not all of them. We must begin to recognize that legality and morality are separate ideas, even if the two can be related. We'll explore that point more in chapter three.

As we examine the Torah, we will focus on two major features: foundation stories and legal instruction. The foundation stories will tell us about God, his activities, his motivations for acting and his plans for people. In them we will find some bases for ethical reasoning. We will also find some motivational points that provide reasons for why good ethics should be pursued. Our approach to legal instruction will have to recognize the difference between legality and morality. No matter the society, laws exist for a variety of reasons, one of which includes the need to curb abuse. Just because a law exists to regulate an activity does not mean that that activity in and of itself is good. Furthermore, just because an activity is not regulated by law does not mean that the unregulated activity is ethical. Again, we will explore these legal points more in chapter three.

GENESIS AND FOUNDATIONS

Genesis is a Greek word. It is also an English one. The English definition refers to "beginnings" or "origins." Though those meanings are also possible for the Greek term, another more appropriate definition would be "genealogical descent." Genesis was originally written in Hebrew. The Hebrew title of the writing, *běrē'šît*, translates into English as "In the beginning," a restatement of the first words of the writing. All of the books of Torah acquire their titles the same way. Thus, Exodus is originally "These are the names"; Leviticus, "And he said"; Numbers, "In the wilderness"; and Deuteronomy, "These are the words." Where did Torah's book titles in our English Bibles come from? When Greek became the major language of the Eastern Mediterranean world, the Hebrew Bible was translated into Greek in a version known as the Septuagint. The Septuagint gave the writings its own set of titles. Those titles appear to summarize, in one word, the major thrust of the beginning information of each writing. One need not read that far in Genesis to be able to see that the writing is filled with lists of genealogies.

So why the notion of beginnings? Because Genesis begins with the beginning, as its opening words declare: "In the beginning . . ." It offers a rendering of the beginning of all sorts of entities: for example, "the heavens" (the Bible's term—our term *space* reflects the materialistic way that we think of things), earth, animals, sea creatures, humankind. This is an origins story. The notion of beginnings is often distorted, however. Many of Genesis's early stories—the creation, the Garden of Eden, the flood, the tower of Babel— also appear to many readers to have a mythic feel to them. Thus, modern and postmodern Westerners often jump to the conclusion that Genesis is portraying an undeveloped, primitive way of thinking in an attempt to explain origins. Are they correct in so doing? Not necessarily. Why?

We should first begin to understand what the stories are communicating to their broader target culture before criticizing them for not directly addressing ours. Not to do so could lead to a subtle form of prejudice. Some people, especially modern (and postmodern) Westerners could assume that "We are certainly more advanced than those silly primitives. What they say about things that we know more about needs to be taken with a grain of salt." Now, without denying that Genesis's explanation of origins deviates significantly from the materialistic origins story of Western cultures, we, as Westerners, have no right to any smug superiority. Technologically we may be more advanced. But that does not mean that all of our ideas and behaviors stemming from our basic thought world are. If the practice of ethics is any indication of human advancement, the widespread prevalence of evil in our societies should give us pause. Perhaps before dismissing Genesis's origins stories out of hand, we should exercise some humility and slow down to explore more carefully what their words are communicating.

In discerning the ethical vision taking shape in a writing such as Genesis, we will have to pay attention to the origins stories. What they say about certain foundational issues will establish a basis for the sense of right and wrong that emerges from these texts. In talking about these foundational stories, however, we will need to keep in mind that their context is not merely one attempting to explain the mysteries of the origins of life. Rather, they are introducing the uniqueness of God over against assumptions about deity found among the nations surrounding God's people, the Israelites. As foundational to the covenant that God eventually makes with his people, the Israelites, they also disclose a sense of God's purposes in the world in response to human wickedness, with implications for the roles that the Israelites play in addressing that.[3]

FOUNDATIONAL ISSUES

Order from disorder. Genesis begins with a chaotic setting: the earth is a formless void, darkness is over the deep, and wind is blowing over the waters. With one set of words, God begins to tame that disorder, creating in sequence: light (day 1); a separation of the waters into an "above" and "below" arrangement, with a "dome" or an expanse called "sky" or the "heavens" in between (day 2); a further separation of the waters below, with dry land appearing, and with vegetation emerging on the dry land (day 3). Those all appear as elements that define structure. In the next three days of creation elements that fill or contain the structure are formed: sun, moon and stars (day 4, corresponding with day 1); birds for the expanse above and fish for the waters below (day 5, corresponding with day 2); animals and, the pinnacle of creation, humankind in God's image to fill the dry land and vegetation (day 6, corresponding with day 3). God then proclaims all that he has done to be "*very* good" and rests on the seventh day.[4]

This may sound strangely primitive to the ears of modern and postmodern readers. Within its original cultural setting, however, the story offers something quite profound. This is a story for God's people, the people of Israel. The nations surrounding the people of Israel think differently. In their view, their gods and goddesses are actually portrayed as powerful parts of the world, such as the sun or the sea. Further, the nations' gods and goddesses are also subject to the uncertainties of chaos. In their stories, their gods and goddesses have moments when they are overcome by elements beyond themselves. So one set of gods and goddesses needs to ally itself against another.[5] The people of Israel declare that what the surrounding nations worship, their God actually made. Genesis offers a creation story that communicates loudly to its culture of origin that non-Israelites worship the wrong gods. Israel's God is God alone, existing apart from the creation as the only being who has overcome chaos, establishing order from disorder. He presides over an ordered creation that he made through his own spoken word. God alone is king.[6]

As king, God delegates his reign to humans, made in his image, made like him. He designs humans to create order within the creation, just as God does initially. God is the supreme ruler and appoints all humans, not just an elite few, to reign over his creation in a manner that reflects his order.[7] Thus, people fashioned in God's image become a symbol of God's own creative supremacy. God alone can tame the chaos. God brings order from disorder. People in his image are on the earth to fill it by procreation, and subsequently subdue it, perhaps organize it, as a reflection of God's own royal activity in making the world. When people bring order from disorder, they reflect God's own reign over the heavens and the earth.

Further, it's a beneficent reign. When God made the first living creatures, birds and water creatures, he blessed them (Gen 1:22). He likewise blessed humankind (Gen 1:28). Here Genesis introduces a term that becomes an important part of its basic vocabulary. God is for his creation, desiring it to flourish. Eventually we will see Genesis demonstrating the role to be played by one group of humans as agents of blessing for the entire earth (Gen 12:1-3).[8] Here an emerging pattern also useful for ethics begins to take shape. God is advancing well-being on the earth. Humans are to be doing the same.

Genesis 2:4 begins a new moment for Genesis. Though certainly connected to Genesis 2:3 and the preceding creation story, it does not claim to pick up exactly where verse 3 leaves off. Rather, it begins with a fresh telling of the creation of humankind, as though elaborating more on the climactic moment from the previous account.[9] A man is formed out of the ground, followed by the planting of vegetation and a special garden. The man is placed in the garden, commissioned to till the ground and instructed to eat from any tree except a special one, the tree of the knowledge of good and evil. Should he eat of that tree, he would die. God then declares that the man should not be alone, promising to make him "a helper as his partner" (2:18). As part of that process God forms animals out of the ground, bringing them before the man to name. Genesis concludes that from those animals there was no "helper as his [i.e., the man's] partner" (2:20). Only then does God form such a partner, from the man's rib. That partner is not a different creature but from the same composition as the man, coordinating with the thought from the previous creation story of *both* male *and* female being created by God in his image (Gen 1:27). When the man sees the woman, he declares her to be the one suited for special relationship with him. Genesis then remarks, "Therefore a man leaves his father and his mother and clings to his wife, and they become one flesh. And the man and his wife were both naked, and were not ashamed" (Gen 2:24-25).

We still have a basic, created order here that resembles aspects of the order established in Genesis 1, though also with its own special emphases. Note what is part of that order in Genesis 2. Humans are given dominion over God's creation. Humans are distinct from animals, being in charge of them. Human males are not females, but also are not of a makeup different from females (making any sense of superiority-inferiority between the sexes impossible to sustain).[10] Animals are unsuitable helpers as partners for humans, a point with implications not only for companionship but also for sexual activity. Marriage is a divinely established relationship, with a husband and wife forming a unique conjugal bond meant to endure through life's ups and downs;[11] being "one flesh" not only includes appropriate sexual activity for a husband and wife, but implies other interactions that also fall within the category of "helper as partner."[12] A husband and his wife are naked before each other and not ashamed. All of this is part of God's created order.

Each of those points of the original created order has ethical implications, even if ethics is not their main topic. For example, when humans exercise dominion over the creation, they cannot be simultaneously dominated by it. Land erosion from chopping down trees, extermination of species through overhunting, infestations of killer bees and pumpkin bugs, and invasions of kudzu vines smothering the landscape—all products of human mismanagement—show improper dominion, perhaps even dictatorial or tyrannical dominion.[13] If the creation can act back with negative consequences, then improper dominion has been exercised. Coupled with the notion of humans in God's image from Genesis 1, proper management of the created order would reflect God's beneficent rule. When people manage improperly, they reflect that they are out of touch with how God, the master designer, brings order to the world. They are, in some sense, out of touch with God.

Consider the implications for sexual ethics:

- Humans are made for sex with each other, a man and a woman.

- A man has no grounds for treating his wife either as an inferior or as an object.

- Sex with animals offers no valid partnership, but rather cruel violation of the dominion mandate.

- A man and a woman as a married couple form a special, lasting unit separate from their parents.

- Being naked and unashamed is good—for married couples.

- Sex between a husband and a wife is bonding activity—the two become one flesh.

- Sex between a husband and a wife is a good aspect of the divinely created order.

- When coupled with the mandate from Genesis 1, sexual activity has both a procreative *and* a bonding function, but does not exist as a mere personal pleasure. To enter into sexual activity with any other awareness would be to distort divinely established order.

Torah draws on aspects of this picture in its establishment of sexual and familial laws, especially in Leviticus 18 and 20.[14] Those chapters strongly imply, with their language, a reflection of the created order in proscribing incest and other illicit sexual activities.[15]

Disorder from order. Genesis 2 ends with a declaration of unashamed nakedness between a man and a wife as part of God's created order. Genesis 3 introduces a new event that changes the direction of the story for the rest of the writing. Tricked by the serpent, the man and woman eat from the tree from which God had forbidden them to eat, the tree of the knowledge of good and evil. As a result, with their eyes opened, they recognize their nakedness and hide, not only from each other but from God. The hiding is Genesis's way of signaling that God's order has been disrupted, a disruption resulting from human disobedience. In response God initiates a series of consequences on the perpetrators of this disorder—the man, his wife and the beguiling serpent. Pain in childbirth, marital strife, work by sweat, a cursed ground, and ultimately death itself are all imposed on people and their world as part of an emerging disorder that makes the fulfillment of God's original purposes for humanity in Genesis 1:28 more difficult.[16]

That God's order has been permanently overturned becomes clear from the story of Genesis 4, when one brother murders another, in spite of God's warning that "if you do not do well, sin is lurking at the door; its desire is for you, but you must master it" (Gen 4:7).[17] Here we see a new wrinkle: sin as some kind of lurking power, needing to be mastered, but overcoming the angry brother Cain in the end, who murders his brother Abel. The first time the word *sin* is used in the Bible, it is talking about a destructively powerful force or entity, not a violation of a behavioral norm.

Notice another important element emerging in the text, mercy. God confronts Cain with the heinousness of his act of murdering Abel:

> *What have you done? Listen; your brother's blood is crying out to me from the ground! And now you are cursed from the ground, which has opened its mouth to receive your brother's blood from your hand. When you till the ground, it will no longer yield to you its strength; you will be a fugitive and a wanderer on the earth.*
> **Gen 4:10-12**

God certainly inflicts a punishment on Cain. He will be unable to settle anywhere with any success. Cain's complaint in response is instructive: "My punishment is greater than I can bear! Today you have driven me away from the soil, and I shall be hidden from your face; I shall be a fugitive and a wanderer on the earth, and anyone who meets me may kill me" (Gen 4:13-14). Cain may be reading more into God's words than is warranted, but note how God responds: "'Not so! Whoever kills Cain will suffer a sevenfold vengeance.' And the LORD put a mark on Cain, so that no one who came upon him would kill him" (Gen 4:15).

Rather than dispute Cain's claim that he will be hidden from God's face, God instead places a mark on Cain to identify him as a protected being. Consider the implications. Instead of condemning him forever, God offers him protection. That is an act of mercy, and an instructive one for developing a sense of the ethics related to the God of the Bible. God is not encouraging people to behave in such a way that they try to manipulate him with what they do. Earning favor from God based on behavior is not sanctioned activity. Performing in order to gain a reward or avoid a punishment is not an approved motivation. Instead, we see a merciful God who addresses the weaknesses of those who call on him. He most certainly is not hiding his face from Cain.

Again, little of this is directly about ethics. But ethical implications are shouting out from the stories. People are responsible for introducing disorder into God's ordered creation. The result is people being unable to function consistently in God's image, unable to foster God's sovereign reign over his creation. With that comes a powerlessness of people to overcome themselves. Here, from the beginning, we see one of the major principles of the varieties of biblical ethics. At the heart of the various approaches to ethics in the Bible is an ethic of relationship with God. People who are in touch with God show it by their good behavior. People who are out of touch with God show it by their bad behavior. The downward slide of humanity is portrayed vividly in the story of Cain's descendant Lamech at the end of Genesis 4. He tells his wives, Adah and Zillah,

> I have killed a man for wounding me,
>   a young man for striking me.
> If Cain is avenged sevenfold,
>   truly Lamech seventy-sevenfold. **Gen 4:23-24**

Now, we have escalating violence. We have threatening language. We have the seeds of abusive domination. We have people out of touch with God.

Further disordering. Genesis shifts to a new set of stories, but continues to show the same descending spiral of human misbehavior. Human disorder appears to be the order of the day, as illustrated by the flood account of Genesis 6–9. In the process we get to see Genesis begin to wade into what is often called "the problem of evil"—if God is good and wants to advance his goodness on the world, then why is there evil?[18] Trying to solve that now would take us way beyond the scope of this exploration. The question is relevant here only because the existence of evil requires the existence of ethics. Further, how God begins to deal with the evil has implications for ethics.

Genesis has already shown creation becoming more disordered at the fault of humankind. Genesis then introduces the story of Noah and the flood with the following assessment: "The LORD saw that the wickedness of humankind was great in the earth, and that every inclination of the thoughts of their hearts was only evil continually. And the LORD was sorry that he had made humankind on the earth, and it grieved him to his heart" (Gen 6:5-6). Humans were evil. God was grieved. To deal with the wickedness, God proposed to destroy the earth with a flood, carrying out his plan through the righteous Noah. Though some people were preserved through Noah's ark, the rest of humanity was destroyed as an act of sorrowful judgment from God. Genesis says that they were wicked, evil and filled with violence.

At the end of the story, God again recognizes the permanence of human wickedness, after acknowledging the sincere devotion of the righteous Noah:

> I will never again curse the ground because of humankind, for the inclination of the human heart is evil from youth; nor will I ever again destroy every living creature as I have done.
>
> As long as the earth endures,
>   seedtime and harvest, cold and heat,
> summer and winter, day and night,
>   shall not cease. **Gen 8:21-22**

In spite of his grief toward human evil, God promises never again to destroy the earth in that way. Humans may be evil, but they may also connect well with God, as Noah does.

Note how this touches on the problem of evil. The alternative to allowing the existence of evil humans is to destroy on a cyclical basis the source of evil, human beings, whenever their cumulative evil gets to be too much to endure. Instead, God commits himself to showing compassionate mercy by allowing evil people to persist, since the human makeup is inclined toward evil. God makes a covenant never to destroy the entire earth that way again. As a result, more evil people now have the opportunity to become like Noah, choosing righteousness in relationship with God. We can expect God to do something else to address evil, as we will see.

In describing that covenant, furthermore, Genesis shows God making a declaration about the importance of human life. A death penalty is enacted:

> Whoever sheds the blood of a human,
>   by a human shall that person's blood be shed;
> for in his own image
>   God made humankind. **Gen 9:6**

The wanton taking of another human's life is portrayed as a direct affront to God's reign over the earth. Since people are made in God's image, the symbol of God being in charge, then the taking of another's life flies in the face of God. In effect, we have the establishment of the first law in the Bible, a law presented to Noah and his family. It is their law (Gen 9:6), but it is one that instructs all readers. The taking of a human life is the ultimate act of rebellion against God.

Notice the punishment—the taking of the life-taker's life. Is Torah being inconsistent? No. Torah is making an important distinction often made in societies. There is illegal killing and there is legal killing. Since the death penalty is enacted by those who are in charge in accordance with a law they are conforming to, it is not in itself illegal. How it could be moral is a discussion for other settings outside of this passage. The point here is to recognize that Torah shows thoughtful sophistication in distinguishing killing as an enactment of justice from killing as unbridled human activity. The wanton taking of another's life is so reprehensible that it merits the ultimate penalty—the death of the perpetrator. The death sentence here is not merely a punishment; it is a statement. The reckless killing of another human is intolerable activity. It is a direct affront to God himself, to his image and to his right to reign over the people of the earth. No one in touch with God would ever offend his character in that way.

That human disordering persists is shown in the account of people wishing to avoid being scattered (Gen 11). They unite to make a name for themselves by building a great tower to reach to the heavens. Though the incident does not in itself deal directly with ethical material, it does help set the stage for what follows in Genesis. For the time being, we must be content with the basic observations that human beings, when left to themselves, choose to defy God and his ways.[19] That defiance, according to Genesis, leads ultimately to improper activity, some of which is also unethical. No amount of divine intervention aimed at evil can stop human evil without destroying humans. Unethical activity is the byproduct of the basic human condition, and the symptom of humans being out of touch with God. The chapters that follow in Genesis portray a shift in God's activities, a shift that shows God forming a people for himself. Those people, as they engage in sincere relationship with God, demonstrate changes in their lives. Some of those changes are displayed through ethical activity.

SUMMING IT UP:
WHAT HAVE WE LEARNED SO FAR?

o Order and disorder are related to ethical and unethical activity, although not equivalent to them.

o God's order in creation offers a foundation for establishing ethical and unethical behavior.

o Human beings are made in God's image, reflecting that God is ultimately in charge in the world.

o Environmental ethics and sexual ethics are rooted in God's sense of order.

o Human violence reflects unethical disorder.

o Evil in the world is a human problem that a merciful God chooses to put up with rather than continually destroy.

o When people are out of touch with God, they show it with their unethical behavior.

o When people are in touch with God, they show it with their good behavior.

A NEW PROGRAM: PROMISE AND COVENANT (GEN 12–22)

Genesis 12 begins a new segment of the Genesis account. Where Genesis 1–11 have presented us with brief stories—creation, flood, confusion of languages—each separated by lists of names of genealogical descent, implying the passing of considerable time, Genesis 12–25 offers us tidbits from the life of one man, Abram, whom God renames Abraham.[20] When we meet Abram, he is seventy-five years old. Most of the significant activity concerning him takes place between his seventy-fifth and one-hundredth (plus) years (Gen 12–22). Even then, we only learn selected details, singled out to convey a special set of points. Though we are told that he is 175 when he dies (Gen 25), we are told very little about what happens between his 100th and his 175th year, apart from three significant stories and a final summary. Most of the points relevant to our discussion of biblical ethics are found in Genesis

12–22, even if relevant ethical material appears elsewhere in Genesis.[21] For that reason, our exploration here will probe those chapters only, leaving to the reader the opportunity to explore the rest of the writing.

Consider the contrast. In the first eleven chapters we learn about three distinct events, separated by "generations." In the next eleven chapters, we learn about one man, illustrated by selected events. Something new is taking place. Genesis is slowing down the pace of its presentation. That slowing down itself indicates a new direction. That direction, we are about to see, indicates a new way of God dealing with the world in view of what has been happening previously.[22] That new way, in turn, will have a profound influence on the shape of the ethical vision projected by the Torah and other parts of the Bible.

A set of promises. Abram is first introduced to us in the genealogy of Genesis 11. There we learn that he is originally from the city of Ur (200 miles southeast of present-day Baghdad). His father moves him and his family to the town of Haran (in modern Turkey, on the Syrian border, about 150 miles east of the Mediterranean). He has a nephew named Lot, and a wife named Sarai, who, we are told, is "barren" (i.e., infertile). At the beginning of Genesis 12, God appears to Abram in Haran and tells him,

> Go from your country and your kindred and your father's house to the land that I will show you. I will make of you a great nation, and I will bless you, and make your name great, so that you will be a blessing. I will bless those who bless you, and the one who curses you I will curse; and in you all the families of the earth shall be blessed. **Gen 12:1-3**

Note what God promises Abram, as signified by the words *I will*: He will show Abram a land where Abram will live; he will make Abram a great nation; he will bless Abram; he will make Abram's name great; he will make a blessing of Abram to others; he will bless those who bless Abram; he will curse those who curse Abram; he will bless all families of the earth in Abram. Those can be neatly summarized with three objects of promise—land, descendants and blessing—objects that correspond well with what has already been introduced to us since Genesis 1, an earth to be filled with humans, blessed by God.[23] Though the focus here is initially on one person, Abram, the final outcome leads to blessing or well-being for the entire earth as coming through Abram. He is not a lone object of God's lavishing. God's acts on behalf of Abram are for the ultimate benefit of the entire earth. We have here the declaration of promises that appear to signal a new program of establishing order to the disordered world.[24] That program is enacted through God's initiative.

What must Abram do besides accept God's offer? Nothing. God's promises are presented here unconditionally, with no strings other than the obvious one to accept the deal in the first place. That is an important point to recognize, because it reaffirms a major principle we have already seen in the Cain story, a principle that applies positively to ethics. God's acts are not necessarily conditioned by human behavior. Said differently, humans are not encouraged to behave a certain way in order to gain a special outcome from God. The implications of that for Torah's ethics, and ultimately for all of biblical ethics, are enormous. People are not to perform morally in order to convince God to do something special for them. What should motivate Abram to respond here? His expectation that God will be reliable to do what he said he would. Genesis shows Abram both growing and failing in his ability to trust God. But Genesis shows an eventual, overall improvement in that trust.

Note that we have nothing here that directly concerns ethics. What we do have is the declaration of promises that will eventually affect the entire earth. Those promises point to a program that is certainly different from what Genesis has been portraying to this point. Instead of special divine acts that curb human disordering activities, we see God cultivating a relationship with an individual through a big picture set of interventions, promising unmerited benefits. In the tower of Babel incident, God faulted people for wanting to make a name for themselves (Gen 11:4). By contrast in Genesis 12, God promises to one individual, Abram, that he, God, will make Abram's name great. God will do the intervening to make that possible. Abram is to respond to God based on his hope that God will keep his promises. As we watch that program begin to be enacted in the life of Abram, we also see that he grows in his relationship with God. Genesis's language purposefully reflects growth and development in Abram's life, indicating those aspects to be the significant points of the account. God offers and Abram responds. Genesis lets us know whether he responds well or badly. One of the ways that Genesis portrays the quality of Abram's response is through his moral activity.

Up and down in the life of Abram. Let's briefly survey the episodes in Genesis 12–22.[25] We have just seen God call Abram from Haran (Gen 12:1-3). Remarkably, he accepts the deal from God and heads out with his family. He ends up south, in the land of Canaan, his Promised Land, and travels through it, building altars at places called Shechem and Bethel, where he worships God (Gen 12:4-9). Those acts of worship signal that he is in right relationship with God. When a famine strikes the territory, however, he heads further south, to Egypt, where he instructs his wife Sarai to tell the ruler there, the Pharaoh, that she is Abram's sister (Gen 12:10-20). Genesis tells us that Abram fears for his life; Pharaoh might kill him to take his beautiful wife, but would negotiate with Abram to marry his sister. When Abram's duplicity is discovered, Pharaoh banishes him from the territory. Abram returns to Canaan and worships God at Bethel (Gen 13:1-4).

That gives way to two stories that feature Abram interacting with his nephew, Lot. In the first, in response to quarrels breaking out between Abram's herders and Lot's, Abram generously offers Lot first pick of where to settle. Lot chooses the greenest territory, though we're told it's in the vicinity of a notoriously wicked city, Sodom (Gen 13:5-18). In the second, Lot is caught in the middle of a battle between rulers, with the king of Sodom being overtaken and his subjects, including Lot, being carried away as captives. When word of this reaches Abram, he musters his servants and defeats the rulers, reclaiming his nephew and all the captives (Gen 14:1-24). When returning from his victory, Abram accepts a blessing from a "priest of God Most High," named Melchizedek, but refuses a monetary reward offered him by the king of Sodom.

In the aftermath of those incidents, God appears to Abram and promises him a great reward (Gen 15:1-21). Abram questions God about how that will happen while he is childless, and when God reaffirms that he will indeed have a son, we learn that Abram believes God, prompting God to regard Abram as righteous (v. 6). When Abram then continues to question God about land, he receives an amazing response. God (remarkably!) binds himself to his promises by creating a covenant with him, without requiring anything from him in return (vv. 9-21).[26] God's promises are now legally binding in some sense, indicating his purposeful, relational commitment to Abram. In the next scene, however, Abram accepts Sarai's offer to have children with her slave girl Hagar (Gen 16:1-16), an offer that leads to discord, disorder and a son named Ishmael. We learn from the next scene that Abram will have a son through Sarai (Gen 17:1-27). Both then receive new names, Abraham and Sarah, indicating God's assurance to them of that son. Additionally, Abraham accepts the act of circumcision as a sign of the covenant that God has made with him, and willingly circumcises not only Ishmael and all the male servants in his household, but himself as well, at the age of ninety-nine.[27]

That leads to a lengthy segment where Abraham extends hospitality to three angelic visitors, one of whom not only affirms that Abraham will have a son through Sarah but also barters with Abraham over the fate of the cities of Sodom and Gomorrah, where Lot lives (Gen 18:1–19:38). Two of those angels then visit Sodom, where they are rudely received. They rescue Lot and his two daughters from the city's destruction; we leave them after an ugly scene involving conniving and incest. The story that follows this one offers drama in the household of King Abimelech, where Abraham tells him that Sarah is his sister, endangering the possibility that he be the true father of Sarah's promised son (Gen 20:1-8). God intervenes to resolve the problems and tensions this creates, and then some time later, Isaac is born, Ishmael is banished from the household and further interaction takes place with Abimelech (Gen 21:1-34).

In our final, climactic episode of the sequence, Abraham is tested by God, who asks him to offer his son Isaac to him as a burnt offering (Gen 22:1-19).[28] Abraham willingly complies, even hinting that he expects a different outcome when he tells others that he and Isaac will return after they depart (v. 5). The angel of the Lord spares him from having to follow through with the sacrifice and then commends him: "now I know that you fear God, since you have not withheld your son, your only son, from me" (v. 12). Fear God? That indicates that he is in proper relationship with him. God is to be fully respected, not trifled with. In the language of biblical texts, people who know God fear him (whereas people who are afraid of God generally do not know him).[29] In this case Abraham is trusting God to fulfill his promise, even though God has asked Abraham to destroy the very one whom God has promised. God responds by reaffirming his promises, not only to give him land, descendants and blessing, but to bless all nations through him (vv. 17-18). We end where we began, with a promised program. In between we have seen stories that have portrayed the ups and downs of Abraham's faith and unfaith.[30]

If Abraham is a model of anything, he is a model for coming to believe with certainty that God will do all that he has promised, leading to the blessing of the whole world through him and his descendants. Abraham must buy into the program that God initiates here. So also must the readers of Genesis. As Abraham buys into it, he changes. How do we know that he is buying into it? Sometimes through his moral behavior. When we see Abraham enacting good, moral behavior, we see him close to God, full of faith. When we see bad morality, we see him distant from God, faithless.

Faith and morality. Ethics has not been the main point of the section we have just surveyed. God beginning to establish a new order to the world has. Out of that new program, however, trusting relationship with God has emerged as a healthy focus. Morality appears closely connected to a thriving relationship with God. Consider those moments when we see both obvious moral and immoral behavior:

- Obvious bad, immoral behavior
  - Abraham and Sarah lying to Pharaoh and to Abimelech (Gen 12; 20)
  - Pregnant Hagar's scorn for Sarai, and Sarai's harshness toward Hagar (Gen 16)
  - The hideousness of the people of Sodom, Lot and his daughters (Gen 19)
- Obvious good, moral behavior
  - Abram giving Lot the first pick of the land (Gen 13)
  - Abram refusing to accept dirty money (from the king of Sodom; Gen 14)
  - Abraham showing hospitality to angelic visitors (Gen 18)
  - Abraham setting up a covenant with Abimelech (Gen 20)

Let's revisit these in a bit more detail. First the bad behavior. In each case words in Genesis point to something lacking in how Abram/Abraham should be relating to God. Consider the first of the two cases of deception. Genesis tells us the story to contrast Abram's faithlessness with God's faithfulness.[31] Though it is tempting to moralize the story to show that lying is bad, Genesis's words offer no such emphasis. In fact, Abram gets rich from his deception! God continues to bless him regardless of his performance. We know that the story is about Abram's failure to respond well to God from its context. God has promised to make him a great nation and to bless those who bless him, while cursing those who curse him (Gen 12:1-3). That would be undone if the people of Egypt were to kill or even harm him. The language of the story shows us that Abram is not counting on God to rescue him. Genesis's language of God's interventions with Pharaoh shows us that God has not forgotten his promises.

. The second deception shows the same features. God will keep his promises regardless of the poor performance of his chosen agents. In the aftermath of the events surrounding Sodom and Gomorrah, Abraham journeys into the territory of King Abimelech. Here, in fear of his life, he repeats the falsehood he and Sarah had perpetrated on the king of Egypt. Abimelech takes Sarah as his wife. Abraham's act is rash because it potentially obstructs God's promise that Abraham will be the father of Sarah's son.

God intervenes directly by appearing to Abimelech in a dream. Abimelech affirms his own righteousness in the situation, a point also acknowledged by God.[32] Abimelech has not yet had sex with a married woman. God points Abimelech to Abraham as a prophet with the power to pray effectively for him. When Abimelech questions Abraham about his deception, Abraham says that he was afraid because none of the people in that household feared God (i.e., they worshiped other gods). Abraham expects bad morals from those who do not know God. And yet he has been amazingly faithless, regardless of the technical excuse he gives about Sarah being a half-sister.[33]

Rather than punishing Abraham and Sarah for their act, however, God continues to fulfill his promises. We learn that he had "closed fast all the wombs of the house of Abimelech because of Sarah, Abraham's wife" (Gen 20:18). Abimelech cannot become the true father of Sarah's son and thus overturn God's promise. God not only continues to bless Abraham, he also blesses Abimelech, who in the end treats Abraham well. God has made an unconditional deal with Abraham. Abraham is to respond to God because of that. When he responds well, he shows it with his behavior, which can sometimes be directly moral. When he responds badly, a diminished morality emerges. But God has remained faithful.

Sarai's giving of Hagar for Abram to impregnate leads to another significant moment of immorality, but not the kind some might initially conclude. What Abram does is never directly addressed by anyone in the passage. Further, the language of Genesis is not focused on the morality or immorality of surrogate parenthood. Taking the slave of one's wife as a surrogate mother is a common enough practice for that culture.[34] Ethics, or a lack of ethics, of that kind of activity is not the focal point of the passage. Abram and Sarai needing to trust in God to fulfill his promises is.[35] We learn eventually that the son born to Abram is not the son whom God had in mind (Gen 17:16).

More immediate in the story in Genesis 16 is the point that the pregnancy of Hagar and the birth of Ishmael resulting from the surrogacy lead to discord and disorder. Hagar shows contempt to her mistress. Sarai responds by treating Hagar harshly, so that Hagar runs away with her baby son. Contempt and harsh treatment are both harmful activities. Abram's act of impregnating Hagar is not being portrayed as immoral (or moral). He and Sarai are showing a degree of faithlessness in their resorting to surrogate parenthood, which is what led to the rift between Sarai and Hagar. Though people taking matters into their own hands need not be bad in itself, their diminished trust in God and in his reliability to do what he has promised emerges as a problem here.[36] Once more, it has led to a measure of immorality.

The final moment of obvious immorality is closely connected to a moment of good behavior that we will soon explore. The people of Sodom hideously want to commit homosexual rape against two angels, the height of an affront to God, and outrageously symptomatic of their being out of touch with him.[37] It stands in strong contrast with Abraham's offer of blind hospitality to those same visitors, even before he knew who they were. Though his nephew Lot also welcomes two of those visitors, it quickly turns into hospitality gone amiss. Lot tries to protect his guests from gang rape by offering his daughters instead—a twisted offer, indeed. The angels rescue Lot and his two daughters, but the story of incest that follows (Gen 19:30-38) shows how far away from God his clan has drifted, again, in contrast with Abraham, whose children are to become those who do "righteousness and justice" (Gen 18:19). In the end Lot is rescued, not because he is terribly special himself but because of Abraham's pleading with God for mercy (Gen 19:29). The whole story affirms the point that ethics flows out of people's relationship with God. People act immorally because they are out of touch with God.

We have seen some moments of immorality. The cumulative effect of all those moments may prompt readers to question the morality of the strategies of the faithless.[38] But the focus of these stories has been faithlessness, with immoral acts as the symptom. Damaged connections to God can lead to damaged behavior.

So, let's consider the moments of moral behavior listed earlier. The first two involve Abram and Lot and can be addressed together. Faced with the situation of arguments between his herders and Lot's, Abram proposes that Lot take his flocks elsewhere (Gen 13:2-13). Abram gives him the first pick of the land that God had promised Abram, an extraordinary act of generosity.[39] Lot chooses the best territory, lush and well-watered. Abram's openhandedness receives direct approval from God, who expands his original promise to give Abram the land (Gen 13:14-17). It's a faith-affirming moment, not a moral one. The next scene in Genesis 14 shows that Lot's decision to settle near wicked Sodom (Gen 13:10-13) leads to his being captured, along with the entire city, by marauding kings from the north. Abram is able to rescue them with a meager force—God did promise to bless Abram. He accepts a prayer of blessing from Melchizedek, the king of Salem and a "priest of God Most High" (Gen 14:18-20), when the king comes out to greet him after the battle. By contrast he turns down a physical reward when the king of Sodom urges him to keep the spoils of battle. Abram declines, saying, "I have sworn to the LORD, God Most High, maker of heaven and earth, that I would not take a thread or a sandal-thong or anything that is yours, so that you might not say, 'I have made Abram rich'" (Gen 14:22-23). Abram shows his connection to God by refusing to receive tainted wealth. *God* will bless him, not some wicked king.

A third episode of moral behavior also reflects Abraham's solid relationship with God. He sees three travelers in front of his desert tent in the heat of the day and offers them immediate, lavish hospitality (Gen 18:1-15). Only later does he learn that these are not ordinary guests. When one of them speaks, we are told that it is God who speaks. What began as a kindness to strangers has turned out to have been an extension of hospitality to God himself. The words of Genesis show his hospitality merging with his relationship with God. Genesis depicts his overflowing kindness to strangers as sincere, a reflection of his genuine character. Out of that kindness comes an amazing interaction with God, which we will soon explore in more detail.

In our final moment with clear moral implications, we see Abraham once more interacting with Abimelech (Gen 21:22-34), promising to deal honestly with him and making a covenant with him. Abimelech sees that God is with Abraham. In the upshot of all of that, Abraham settles there, calling on God. He is relating well with God, as his now honest interaction reflects.

With each of these episodes of limited immorality or morality we have seen a close connection between people's trust in God and the quality of their behavior. But moral instruction has not been the point of this section of Genesis. Rather, all the episodes demonstrate that God can be relied on to fulfill his set of promises, which will also ultimately enhance the well-being of the entire earth. To underscore the seriousness of his intent, God even binds those promises into a covenant. These are relational and programmatic issues. Covenantal promises imply commitment. Here God is committing himself to Abraham and his descendants over the long term. As Abraham responds in commitment to God and to his promises, he changes. Aspects of that change sometimes appear in the moral acts he performs.

So let's observe again statements relevant to the core issue, God's promises to Abram/Abraham reflecting the establishment of a new program to restore order to the world. Note the moments when God states and restates his promises:

- God initially promises land, descendants and blessing, with the ultimate blessing of all nations in view (Gen 12:1-3).

- God reaffirms that Abram will receive a land, full of his descendants, in response to his giving his nephew Lot the first pick of grazing area (Gen 13:14-17).

- God reaffirms that Abram will have numerous descendants along with the land where he dwells. When Abram questions God about how he will know whether he will get the land, God turns his promises into a covenant (Gen 15:1-21).

- God renews his covenant with Abraham, specifying that he will have a multitude of descendants, along with the land. Moreover, his son will come through Sarah. In response, he is to accept circumcision for himself and all males in his household (Gen 17:1-27).

- God repeats his promise of giving Abraham a son through Sarah (Gen 18:10).

- God repeats his promise of making Abraham a mighty nation (Gen 18:17-19).

- Sarah gives birth to Isaac, as God had promised (Gen 21:1).

- As Abraham passes God's test for him, God repeats the terms of his covenant, promising abundant blessing, numerous descendants, a land and through his offspring, ultimate blessing for all the earth (Gen 22:16-18).

Can God be trusted to reorder the world through Abraham and his descendants? The ways that God affirms and begins to fulfill his promises to Abraham would indicate yes. So also would God's dealings with Abraham's descendants Isaac, Jacob and Joseph in the rest of Genesis. Significant to our exploration in ethics, however, two of those moments of affirmation begin to connect trusting God and relating to God with ethics, not just morality: Genesis 15:6 and Genesis 18:18-19. Trusting God to reorder the world can be expected to have a positive effect on the moral quality of the lives of those who respond to him. Let's consider these two passages more fully.

- Abraham is deemed righteous by believing God (Gen 15:6).

- Because Abraham is to be the father of a nation through whom the whole earth is to be blessed, he needs a high regard for righteousness, a regard that he is to pass on to his children and their children (Gen 18:18-19).

The first of these flows out of Abram's faithful responses to God shown in how he dealt with his nephew Lot. God appears to Abram in a vision assuring him that he will receive a great reward (Gen 15:1). Abram responds by questioning how God will fulfill his promises if he has no son. When God graphically declares the certainty not only of a son but of innumerable descendants, Abram "believe[s] the LORD; and the LORD reckon[s] it to him as righteousness" (Gen 15:6). That is both a startling response from Abram, and a startling result from God. Abram and God here exhibit a tight relationship. Abram believes God. God considers that as righteousness.

What is righteousness? While an expansive term, it certainly communicates strong, positive, moral overtones.[40] That would include correct, proper behavior. While proper behavior can incorporate more than morality, morality is a significant aspect of that. The first time in Genesis we are led to consider someone as righteous, we meet Noah. He is described as righteous and blameless (Gen 6:9), in contrast to other inhabitants of the earth who are described as having hearts continually inclined toward evil (v. 5), wicked (v. 5), corrupt (v. 11) and violent (v. 11). In Genesis 7:1, God tells Noah that he alone is righteous in all that generation.

The very next time Genesis refers to righteousness is in Genesis 15, with Abram. Merely by believing God, Abram is deemed by God to be righteous, as someone who does what is right. His relationship gives him favorable moral standing of some sort from God's perspective. His personal performance of righteous acts is not what is said to give him that standing. It cannot be overstated what that means for the ethical foundation established here for the rest of the Bible. Remember, ethics includes reasons for why one does what is right. Gaining right standing with God by moral performance would lead to a manipulative ethic. Righteousness based on trust in God working out his programmatic promises is, by contrast, a positive relational ethic.

So where does righteous performance come in? The second passage is even more profound, showing an interplay between what God does morally and what God expects from those connected to him. It reflects the same sense of moral expectation in its use of the terms *righteous* and *righteousness* that we have been talking about. It grows out of Abraham's hospitality to the angelic visitors. As they get up to leave, one of the visitors, the one speaking such that it is the Lord who speaks, says,

> *Shall I hide from Abraham what I am about to do, seeing that Abraham shall become a great and mighty nation, and all the nations of the earth shall be blessed in him? No, for I have chosen him, that he may charge his children and his household after him to keep the way of the LORD by doing righteousness and justice; so that the LORD may bring about for Abraham what he has promised him.* **Gen 18:17-19**

God certainly has high regard for Abraham. God is about to disclose to Abraham his intentions to destroy the wicked cities of Sodom and Gomorrah. His words have strong ethical implications: "that he may charge his children and his household after him to keep the way of the LORD by doing righteousness and justice" (Gen 18:19). God is declaring himself to be a righteous God, one who does not tolerate unrelenting unrighteousness. Since Abraham's descendants are also to be connected to God, they too must live righteously, morally. In that way, God will work out his promises to Abraham, promises that extend to the entire world.[41] We see further particulars of those words in the subsequent books of the Torah. But here, we must observe how good ethics are expected to flow out of a good relationship with God, who has a reputation for *justice*, another good word with moral implications.

Abraham responds in this scene by appealing to God's mercy and justice: "Will you indeed sweep away the righteous with the wicked?" (Gen 18:23). God

is being asked to be ethical![42] That begins a bartering sequence between God
and Abraham. With terminology reminiscent of the flood story and its aftermath,[43] Genesis portrays God's judgment as neither thoughtless nor irre-
sponsible; God is willing to flex with even the smallest righteous exception.[44]
Significant to our inquiry here, Abraham has engaged in a marvelously bold
interaction with God, who is encouraging people to relate to him. What began
with moral hospitality has led to a moment reflecting remarkable closeness
between God and Abraham, also disclosing more about God, his righteous
character and his expectations of righteousness from those who belong to him.

From these two scenes we learn of direct connections between God's restoration promises and his desire for human righteousness. The first indicates
that trust in God to enact his promised program can give someone righteous
standing. It is a relationship-based righteousness, founded in trust. The second
shows that part of the program that God is establishing will lead to righteous
behavior on the part of Abraham's descendants. Connection with God through
Abraham and his descendants will bring about blessing for the entire earth,
and a major aspect of that blessing is righteous, moral behavior.

SUMMING IT UP:
ETHICAL INSIGHTS FROM THE ABRAHAM STORY

In the Abraham stories we have indeed encountered evidence to support some of the basic principles mentioned at
the beginning of this chapter. We have seen that

o People's morality, or lack of morality, has tended to flow
   out of their relationship, or lack of relationship, with God.

o Genesis has not centered on God, or anyone else, trying
   to get people to behave morally. Rather, it has been about
   people needing to respond to God and his programmatic activities aimed at restoring order to the world.

As we continue with Torah and other parts of the Bible, we will see the program
begun with Abraham shaping the Bible's ethical vision more concretely.

Reflection Questions

1. How can Genesis's origins stories influence the way people think about such issues as marriage, family or the environment?

2. How do the origins stories of your own wider culture actually affect the moral views of that culture?

3. What are the relationships between order, disorder and morality?

4. How does the promise to bless the world through Abraham and his descendants lead to good, moral performance? What role does growing trust in God play in that?

FOR FURTHER READING

Bartholomew, Craig G., and Michael W. Goheen. *The Drama of Scripture: Finding Our Place in the Biblical Story*, pp. 29-59. Grand Rapids: Baker Academic, 2004.

Wenham, Gordon J. *Story as Torah*. Edinburgh: T & T Clark, 2000.

MERCY, COVENANT AND INSTRUCTING LAW

Ethics in Torah 2

INTRODUCTORY POINTS

Before launching into a fuller investigation of the world of Exodus, let's revisit some core issues. Recall the following:

- Ethics refers to the methods people use to distinguish right from wrong behavior.

- Ethics is concerned with behavior that advances good and hinders harm in one's world.

- Ethics also provides reasons and motives for why one should advance good and restrain harm in one's world. Answering the question, Why should I do what I think is right? will lead one to embark on a track that discloses one's own personal ethics.

We are moving into a world dominated by two central concepts: covenant and law. When understood rightly, law in Torah should be viewed as an element of the covenant we will be exploring. Without that understanding, we would be left observing a system that would look ominously like a set of obnoxious rules imposed by the powerful on the powerless. If that were the case, when answering the question, Why should I do what is right? we would have to resort to very weak answers: Because it says so, or variations such as Because the Bible says . . . or Because God commands. . . . Why are those weak? To do something just because a law or a person says to do so may reflect a strong, legitimate sense of trust for the authority behind the words, but it does not show any understanding of why the words exist in the first place. What happens if the laws are broken? What is the purpose of the laws in the first place? Doing something merely because it says so is not enough.

Imagine a man coming home after work, saying to his wife, "Honey, I really wanted to have sex with one of the girls at work today, but then I remembered that there was a commandment in the Bible about not committing adultery, so that was the only reason I didn't do it. Aren't you pleased with me?"

Well, at least he didn't do it! But if a moral rule was all that hindered him, we would have to fault the weakness of his thinking. His wife certainly wouldn't be pleased. What about her feelings? What about their relationship? What about the woman at work? What kind of man is he anyway? A whole host of other questions should emerge from such a scenario. And would any of this really change if he added, "And don't you think God is also pleased?"

The "learn the rules and keep them" kind of system observed in this (ridiculous) scenario reflects conditioned conformity more than thoughtful deliberation. It can also appear somewhat impersonal, with rules keeping almost an end in itself. The fact is that Exodus and the rest of Torah offer a covenant, of which laws, not rules, are an essential part. (And laws are quite different from rules, even if the concepts overlap. For one, rules are more trivial; laws more grand. Games have rules. Nations have laws.) For the Torah, the keeping of those laws is not an end in itself. Rather, keeping both the laws and the lifestyle they inform, uphold and protect stems from a kindly, merciful relationship initiated by God with his people, the Israelites. That relationship is sealed with a covenant. Any separation of Torah's laws from its covenant would distort the ethical vision projected by Exodus and subsequent writings.

THE EXODUS STORY

Foundational issues. Exodus clearly and specifically connects its story world with the book of Genesis that precedes it. One must have an awareness of the basic Genesis plot in order to begin to understand what Exodus is doing initially. Exodus expects its readers to be aware of God's covenant with Abraham. Exodus also expects its readers to know that the covenant promises are reissued to Abraham's son and grandson, Isaac and Jacob, whose name God changes to Israel. Exodus begins where Genesis leaves off, with the situation of Jacob, or Israel, having moved eleven of his twelve sons into Egypt along with their families. Another son, Joseph, had been forced into Egypt previously by ten of his brothers and then had jumped from the rank of imprisoned slave to the position of Pharaoh's viceroy.

In spite of those basic continuities, Exodus offers its own self-contained story. It is an account of how God blesses the descendants of Abraham, delivering them from the misery of slavery in a foreign land, bringing them to his sacred mountain on their way to receive the land he had promised to their ancestors Abraham, Isaac and Jacob/Israel. It is also an account about how the numerous descendants of Abraham move from the nonblessed state of not knowing God to being blessed with their own covenant with God, having God's presence actually dwell with them in the tabernacle, the portable temple they build at his request, while they move toward a permanent residence in the Promised Land. Further, that covenant is meant to bring ultimate benefit to the entire world, not simply to a select group of people.

The writing abounds with moments that show people coming to know God.[1] Sometimes that reflects a remarkable deepening relationship. Moses, God's designated leader of his people, initially shows mistrustful hesitation when God calls him from a burning bush (Ex 3:1–4:17). But toward the end of Exodus, he knows God so well that he even dares to ask God to be able to see his glory (Ex 33:18). Though that is not possible, God is said to pass before him, declaring who he is and what he stands for—an amazing revelation (Ex 34:6-7).

Sometimes people are resistant to God as they learn about him. When Moses tells Egypt's Pharaoh to set God's people free, Pharaoh responds that he does not know God (Ex 5:2). By the time God is finished inflicting the land of Egypt with plagues, however, he and the Egyptians certainly do know him (Ex 7:5, 17; 8:10, 22; 9:14, 29; 10:2; 11:7; 14:4, 18). In spite of that, Pharaoh remains hardened to God and his desires (Ex 7:3, 13-14, 22; 8:15, 19, 32; 9:7, 12, 34-35; 10:1, 20, 27; 11:10; 14:4, 8, 17).

The most significant, burgeoning relationship in the writing is between God and the Israelites. Exodus implies that the Israelites initially do not know God in their slavery (Ex 2:23). Moses anticipates that they might doubt that God is actually sending them help (Ex 3:13-17), and so learns God's sacred name YHWH (translated as "the LORD") by which they are to know God. But after experiencing God intervening on their behalf (Ex 6:7), they learn deeply that God is for them and they can wholeheartedly rely on him. They eagerly enter into a covenant with him when he offers one (Ex 19:3-8). Even God's recognition of the state of his people at the outset of the story is a factor in fostering this relationship. As the Israelites groan and cry out in their slavery, Exodus declares that those groans rise up to God, who hears them. He "took notice of them" (Ex 2:25): the Hebrew expression there indicates more clearly that God *knew*, not in the sense of recovering from ignorance, but in a renewed concern for Abraham's descendants.[2] God moves to liberate, care for and offer his people their own covenant with him. At the end of the story, God's presence dwells with his people, a remarkable reversal from the opening misery.

The ethics that begins to emerge in this setting flows from the laws associated with the covenant that God makes with his people. It also flows from the fact of the covenant itself, a covenant between God and those whom he calls "my people." There is a relationship between God and the Israelites. It is to be a deepening relationship. God extends himself to them. They are to extend themselves to him, growing in their trust in him. One chief way they are to do that is to keep the laws of the covenant. They don't keep them to get something from God. They do so because they have already received and have every prospect of continuing to receive.

The story line. Many popular approaches to Exodus focus on the story line of deliverance, sometimes excluding other elements found in the writing. When considering the writing as a whole, one must see that the elements of the deliverance story are merely foundational to the central concerns of Exodus,[3] God's establishing of a covenant with the Israelites as a means of continuing to work out his earlier covenant with Abraham, Isaac and Jacob.[4]

The basic story line is simple and dramatic. We'll have to be careful not to rob the Exodus account of its own unique emphases by embellishing that story. We see from the outset the Abrahamic promises of large numbers of descendants (Gen 15:5) merging with the creation mandate to be fruitful, multiply and fill the earth (comp. Gen 1:28 with Ex 1:7). We learn in quick fashion how those Israelites come to be enslaved, eventually being perceived as threats. Though the king of Egypt tries to exterminate them, others defend them.[5] In the process we learn of the birth of Moses and of his being rescued from destruction. We learn that he is raised in Pharaoh's household, but we are told nothing of that upbringing. Suddenly Moses is a grownup who senses his responsibility to help his fellow Israelites, but he must flee for his life after he kills an Egyptian who is mistreating one of the Israelite slaves. Escaping across the desert, he ends up in the company of a Midianite priest when he kindly helps the priest's daughters water their flocks. The story informs us that the Israelites continue to groan under the burden of slavery, that those groans rise up to God and that upon hearing them God remembers his covenant with Abraham, Isaac and Jacob (Ex 2:24).

At that point the story moves into high gear. God speaks to Moses through a bush that burns without being consumed, commissioning him to declare to Egypt's Pharaoh that he must set God's people free. After a series of objections, Moses heads out to begin his task. The Pharaoh rebuffs him, placing more burdens on the Israelites. They in turn reject Moses. After a series of ten plagues, however, the Israelites begin to know that God is indeed rescuing them. Pharaoh must let them go, and does so after losing his own son. In the tenth plague, all the firstborn sons in that land are killed, except in those households—the Israelite households—where the blood of an unblemished year-old male lamb is painted on the doorposts and lintel. The Israelites ask for and receive riches from the Egyptian inhabitants and depart from the land, though not on the most efficient travel route. Pharaoh is incited once more to subdue the Israelites, pursuing them with his army and entrapping them with their backs against the sea. The Israelites complain, the first of several complaints in the writing, but are protected in dramatic fashion, not only by a cloud that separates them from the pursuing army, but with a wind from God that blows all night after Moses strikes the sea with his rod. The result is that they can cross over to the other side on dry land. When the Egyptians try to pursue them, they are drowned. The Israelites praise God as the Warrior who fights for them, setting out on their way to their Promised Land.

The desert wilderness proves to be a major obstacle. Exodus records three more major scenes where the Israelites complain. In the first they find bitter water where they expected sweet. God shows Moses a stick to place in the water to make it potable. Then the Israelites complain they have no food. God provides them with quail for meat and a daily ration of a bread-like substance they call "manna," Hebrew for "What is it?" Then the Israelites complain that they have no water. God shows Moses a rock to strike, out of which water gushes. The Israelites must endure a battle with the Amalekite people, and they are also visited by Moses' father-in-law, who both marvels at what God has done for them and offers advice as to how Moses can more effectively adjudicate issues brought before him by the Israelites.

After that, God makes a remarkable offer:

> *You have seen what I did to the Egyptians, and how I bore you on eagles' wings and brought you to myself. Now therefore, if you obey my voice and keep my covenant, you shall be my treasured possession out of all the peoples. Indeed, the whole earth is mine, but you shall be for me a priestly kingdom and a holy nation.* **Ex 19:4-6**

In summary fashion, we see previous activities encapsulated by two expressions: what God has done to the Egyptians, and how he has borne the Israelites on "eagles' wings."[6] What has happened in Exodus to this point is apparently a setup for God's offer. The Israelites are given the opportunity officially to become God's covenant people, his "treasured possession out of all the peoples." Though God is concerned for all, Israel uniquely is to become his people in a way that implies ultimate benefit for all.[7] In return for that, they are to keep his covenant, which God is about to unfold. That covenant, as it turns out, consists of laws. In acting on their behalf God has shown how he is for them. They can expect, therefore, that the laws God offers them will be good laws, for their ultimate benefit. The people readily accept the proposition: "Everything that the LORD has spoken we will do" (Ex 19:8).

The rest of Exodus emphasizes the giving of laws, and the following through with instructions to build a special structure, the tabernacle, a portable temple that enables God's presence to dwell with his people as they travel from Mount Sinai, their present location, to the land that he has promised to give them, "a land flowing with milk and honey" (Ex 3:8). Within those two broad segments appear two dramatic stories. The first concludes the giving of the covenant with a striking covenant ratification ceremony involving both sacrifice and a meal eaten in the presence of God (Ex 24:1-11). The second separates the plans for the tabernacle from its actual building with a story of God displaying his forgiving mercy after the Israelites violate their covenant in a serious way by building and then worshiping a golden calf as an idol (Ex 32–34). Exodus ends with God's presence inhabiting the newly built tabernacle. God has made a covenant with his people, the Israelites. God abides with them in a unique relationship that fosters their coming to know him more.

The basic deliverance story itself has been punctuated, sometimes even interrupted at key points, with moments that anticipate the offering of the covenant:

- In response to Moses' first objection to being the one to approach Pharaoh, God tells him that he will bring the Israelites back to that very same mountain to worship him as a sign that God has sent him (Ex 3:12). It is at that mountain where the Israelites, in Exodus 19, eventually receive their covenant offer from God.[8]

- After receiving an initial rebuff from Pharaoh, Moses is instructed that when God delivers the Israelites, they will formally become God's people as they set out on their way to their Promised Land (Ex 6:6-8), a promise that is eventually realized in the actual covenant offering (Ex 19:5).[9]

- The people of Israel are first referred to as God's people in Exodus 3:7, even though they are not formally his people until Exodus 19.

- Moses tells the Pharaoh God's words, "Let my people go" (Ex 5:1), and in an intensifying way, the people of Israel are distinguished from other non-Israelite people with the succeeding plagues in Exodus 6–10. That underscores the sincerity of God's covenant offer to the Israelites in Exodus 19.

- In the final plague, the killing of the firstborn sons of the Egyptians, the story is interrupted with the very first specific regulations for the Israelites. In anticipation of their covenant, the instructions mark out the celebration of the Passover festival, along with the Feast of Unleavened Bread.[10] Those festivals are meant as perpetual rehearsals of God's merciful interventions on their behalf.[11] God's merciful acts are to be an ongoing aspect of their covenantal awareness.

Even the stories recounting moments of the Israelites complaining to God are told with an instructive purpose. The incident involving the bitter water at Mara (Ex 15:22-27) concludes with these words:

> There the LORD made for them a statute and an ordinance and there he put them to the test. He said, "If you will listen carefully to the voice of the LORD your God, and do what is right in his sight, and give heed to his commandments and keep all his statutes, I will not bring upon you any of the diseases that I brought upon the Egyptians; for I am the LORD who heals you." **Ex 15:25b-26**

The words of the story give us the distinct impression that the Israelites are to anticipate receiving something special, from which they are meant to benefit dramatically.[12] That same mode continues with the provision of the manna in Exodus 16. The words God speaks to Moses indicate that bodily sustenance is not its sole purpose:

> Then the Lᴏʀᴅ said to Moses, "I am going to rain bread from heaven for you, and each day the people shall go out and gather enough for that day. In that way I will test them, whether they will follow my instruction or not. On the sixth day, when they prepare what they bring in, it will be twice as much as they gather on other days." **Ex 16:4-5**

The people are being prepared to accept the laws, more specifically the sabbath law. That law emerges eventually as a sign of the covenant between God and the Israelites (Ex 31:13-17).

All of this reinforces Exodus as a covenant-making story, not a mere deliverance story. Deliverance forms the basis of that covenant and appears as a motivation for the Israelites to accept the covenant from God. When they accept it, they do so with awareness that God is for them. The covenant is special. The covenant also provides the chief motivation for obedience to the laws it comprises. The Israelites are God's covenant people. They obey because they are in covenant relationship with God, whose desire is to bless them in the land he is leading them to. God has shown them mercy in their setting of weakness. He has shown himself to be reliable, powerful, trustworthy and caring. His offer of laws to them is a gracious offering. Their obedience is to be a response to their awareness of God's ongoing concern for their well-being. When considering Torah's ethics, therefore, one must see covenantal issues offering the primary motivations for ethical reasoning. We have a strong ethic of relationship.

Implications for Torah's ethics. Ethics involves distinguishing right from wrong behavior. But just as important, it includes the rationale, the reasons for choosing what is right and avoiding, even opposing, what is wrong. As we begin to explore individual laws, many of which do have implications for appropriate, moral behavior, we must see that the circumstances surrounding the granting of the covenant do in fact supply the motivation for keeping the laws, many of which have ethical bearing. Implied in the Exodus story is one answer to the question, Why do you do that? That answer, as inferred from the story, would look something like the following: "We are God's covenant people. We are in covenant relationship with the true and living God. We know God. God has given us these laws for our well-being. We keep them to express our relationship with him. We were desperate in our condition as slaves. God rescued us from slavery and provided for us in our departure. Because we belong to him, we do what he wants. And what he wants is for our good."[13]

What we have here, therefore, is a foundation for Torah's ethic of relationship. The Israelites do good things, not in order to receive but because they have received. Their obedience is to be a response to their covenant relationship with God, who is continually for them. Not all of Torah's laws intersect with moral issues as we are defining morality here.[14] But from Torah's perspective, people who obey God's laws will also be moral people.

LAWS IN EXODUS

Torah's laws should feel strange to most readers. They address a culture that is radically different from many in the world today, though much nearer to cultures found in the Middle East. They address concerns relevant to a time and place foreign to most modern readers. That does not make them irrelevant.[15] People can learn from them without distorting them, even if people do not belong to the laws' culture of origin. Many of the laws contain points of instruction that communicate beyond their initial cultural boundaries.[16] We can get that sense from reading them in the settings in which we find them, gathered in books such as Exodus, Leviticus and Deuteronomy.[17]

If we try to slot these laws directly into our own circumstances, we can expect to run into difficulties. We will have to think about each one, especially when there are conditions expressed for the situations they apply to. For example, we will see a law in Exodus 22:26-27 about returning a person's cloak if taken in "pawn." Most of us would wonder what is being addressed here. We would need to know that in the agrarian society where the law exists, people put up personal property as collateral for loans. The poorest would only have their clothes. The law states that the cloak a person uses as a garment by day and a blanket by night must be returned. Entering into the cultural circumstances being addressed by a law is a necessary first step. We will have to work at seeing what many of the laws address before we can start to discern any morality that they appear to uphold.

Topics in Exodus's laws. As we explored in chapter one, ethics covers activities that advance good or hinder harm in people's worlds. Exodus's laws appear in two major groupings: the Ten Commandments in Exodus 20:1-17, and the Book of the Covenant or Covenant Code, spanning Exodus 20:22–23:33. They cover a variety of topics, many with moral implications.

Let's consider the Ten Commandments. The first several address connecting to God, as opposed to connecting with other people. They shape the core of how God's people live in relationship with him, knowing God as the one who has rescued them from Egypt. God has exclusive relational rights. His people must never serve other gods or make images of God or any other deity to worship. They must honor the sacredness of his name, YHWH, never misusing it. And they must revere God's postcreation rest in view of the order God established on the earth in six days. The story in Exodus 32–34 about the Israelites worshiping a golden calf illustrates both the shortcomings of their relational knowledge of God and the sense of God's perfection and forgiving patience that the Israelites must come to know in their covenantal relationship with him. That moment grows out of their impatience with God, leading them to ask Aaron to make them an idol. They need to relate to God with a fuller awareness of God as one who is

> The LORD, The LORD,
> a God merciful and gracious,
> slow to anger,
> and abounding in steadfast love and faithfulness,
> keeping steadfast love for the thousandth generation,
> forgiving iniquity and transgression and sin,
> yet by no means clearing the guilty,
> but visiting the iniquity of the parents
> upon the children
> and the children's children,
> to the third and fourth generation. **Ex 34:6-7**

Those words directly echo the words of the commandment forbidding the making and worshiping of images (Ex 20:5-6). God's people have lots to learn in knowing God better.

More germane to our exploration here are those laws that deal with tangible, concrete interactions, not just spiritual ones. The Ten Commandments have at least six basic laws with such import: (1) parents must be honored, and (2) murder, (3) adultery, (4) theft, (5) false witness against a neighbor, and (6) the coveting of anything belonging to a neighbor are all to be avoided.

It is important to recognize that morality is only one offshoot from looking at such laws. For example, each of these laws also upholds a basic sense of social or civil order, which is something quite different from morality.[18] The same can be said about other laws beyond these. Exodus 21–23 appear to embellish on some of the basic categories found in the Ten Commandments, offering their own special nuances on some while adding entirely new categories not covered by the Ten:

- Slaves must not be mistreated (Ex 21:1-11, 26-27).

- Purposeful harming of others must be avoided (Ex 21:12-14).

- Vengeance is to be replaced by a measured penalty meted out by a neutral third party (Ex 21:13, 23-25).

- Accidental harm must be put right, even when it involves several innocent victims, including the prematurely born (Ex 21:22-25).

- Parents are to be neither cursed nor hit by their children (Ex 21:15, 17).

- People are held liable for hurt caused by their livestock and even by their own carelessness (Ex 21:28-36).

- Differing cases of theft require various forms of restitution (Ex 22:1-4).

- Property damage caused by negligence requires reparations (Ex 22:5-15).

- Neither sex between an unmarried man and a virgin nor sex between people and animals is permitted (Ex 22:16-17, 19).

- The poor, widows and orphans must receive special care and protection (Ex 22:21-27).

- Cursing a leader is placed on the same level as addressing God with abusive language (Ex 22:28).

- Slander is proscribed (Ex 23:1).

- Joining in with deceiving majorities is forbidden (Ex 23:1-2).

- Neither partiality to the poor nor denying them justice is to be countenanced (Ex 23:3, 6).

- People are responsible for looking after the property of others, even of their enemies (Ex 23:4-5).

- Uprightness is to be upheld, the innocent are to be protected and bribery is to be avoided (Ex 23:7-8).

- Foreigners living in their land need to be treated well (Ex 23:9).

- Farmlands, vineyards and olive orchards should be given rest every six years, out of regard for the poor and the wild animals (Ex 23:10-11).

- All laborers, whether animal, slave or foreign born, must receive a day of rest and refreshment on the sabbath (Ex 23:12).

We have a wide-ranging list of topics, yet scarcely an exhaustive list. What sort of sense are we to make of this?

Torah's laws instruct. The upholding of Torah's laws is to flow out of Israel's relationship with God. Remember, the word *tôrâ* means more than "law." God's relationship with Israel is rooted in his merciful acts on their behalf, not in brute, authoritarian claims. Torah does contain laws. But those laws instruct and guide, not merely regulate. God wants them to learn. Exodus indicates that when God calls Moses to receive the stone tablets containing the Ten Commandments: "The LORD said to Moses, 'Come up to me on the mountain, and wait there; and I will give you the tablets of stone, with the law and the commandment, *which I have written for their instruction*'" (Ex 24:12, italics added).

God's laws are meant to instruct. When God's covenant people, the Israelites, do what God instructs in his laws, they learn an overall lifestyle that reflects their covenant relationship with him. Moral living becomes one aspect of what emerges from the lifestyle being instructed. Upholding regulations would never be the sole purpose. Laws are only a starting point.

Laws exist in societies for a variety of reasons. They "protect interests . . . restrict power . . . try to balance the rights of different and possibly competing groups in society . . . promote social objectives according to the legislators' vision of what kind of ideal society they would like to see."[19] They offer guidelines and boundaries that provide principles that enable people to conduct their lives in an ordered fashion. They can help resolve conflicts. Often they curb abuse. They offer protection for people who otherwise might be harmed. They primarily exist not for good people but for the bad who, when left alone, would ultimately advance harm on others. Consider, for example, what many view as the Tenth Commandment: "You shall not covet your neighbor's house; you shall not covet your neighbor's wife, or male or female slave, or ox, or donkey, or anything that belongs to your neighbor" (Ex 20:17).[20]

To whom is such a law addressed?[21] At the very least, it speaks to a person desiring to overstep the bounds of another's property to long for what rightfully belongs to another. It can equally reflect the mental activity of both the weak and the powerful. The language indicates that it is aimed principally at a male, not surprising given that it is a law emerging from a patriarchal society, a society where men were in charge. Does a man who is content with his wife and all that God has blessed him with need such a law? Not really. But there are unprincipled men out there who treat others as objects for their own consumption. That kind of man needs to know that his neighbor's house is not his house, his neighbor's wife is not his wife, his neighbor's slaves are not his slaves, his neighbor's animals are not his animals. Everything that is his neighbor's belongs to his neighbor.

Such laws offer more than protection. They can underscore what the society deems important. In this case, in a law described as coming from God, it would also underscore what God would think is important.[22] People are to be content with what they have. They are to respect what belongs to others. In fact, they may even rejoice in how God has blessed others. Laws do protect. In the Torah they also instruct.

Of course, some might be offended by this particular law. Are wives no better than donkeys and slaves? And why would anyone have slaves anyway?

In this case it is helpful to recognize that the law appears to restrain those who would overstep the bounds of what is rightfully theirs. This is a law designed to curb various forms of harm or abuse. There is a basic problem being addressed, coveting, even if some examples of coveting might give us pause because of our particular culture's sensitivities. The Tenth Commandment is not aimed at upholding slavery or advancing patriarchy. Rather, it is aimed in part at immoral men who reach for what is not rightly theirs. Women are not being relegated to the animal level. Wives are being protected from unscrupulous men. Slavery is not being promoted as a proper institution. Slaves are being protected from being caught up as objects in an ongoing tussle between unfriendly landowners. Other laws in Exodus (see, for example, Ex 21:2-6), in fact, indicate that slaves are not only to be treated properly but to be set free every seven years. (Slavery in that society, it turns out, offered one way for people who got into debt trouble to pay back what they owed.)[23] Those who learn from a law such as the Tenth Commandment—whether men, women, children, slave, free—all learn to respect what does not belong to them.

In considering how all laws in the Torah instruct, one must move beyond their mere legality. The law against coveting can lead a person positively to respect what others have. It also potentially advocates contentment. Those who learn from such a law, whether male or female, develop a regard for others that is to transcend their own ambitions. Others are ultimately as important as oneself—perhaps even more so.

We will find the task of moving beyond legality easier for some laws than for others. For example, consider the following: "You shall not follow a majority in wrongdoing" (Ex 23:2). Officially that is a law further specifying how people should not join with those who are perpetrating grand falsehoods, even though initially it may sound to us like a piece of good advice. No one can legitimately appeal to the majority to justify participating in a conspiracy to alter the truth. As a mere law, it has limitations. Practically it can only be enforced against those members of that majority who are caught. When one considers these words not merely as law but as instruction, then an additional perspective emerges. Those who belong to God's covenant have a responsibility to deviate from the crowd when the crowd is promoting falsehood. One could even begin to see that such a standard could apply to any piece of morally wrong behavior. Any departure from the wrongdoing crowd pleases God.

Torah offers instructive laws, not mere morals. In recognizing that one must move beyond a law's mere legality, a reader must also be careful not to ignore the legality entirely, assuming that the laws are the standards of a moral code. Torah principally portrays a legal code that instructs, not a moral code that instructs.

For example, the commandment preceding coveting declares: "You shall not bear false witness against your neighbor" (Ex 20:16). Note, it does not say "You shall not lie."[24] We have an instructive law, not a moral rule. The legal situation addresses someone being called on to give account about what another has done or said. That account must be truthful. It is not restricted to something as formal as testifying in court; hence, it is not the same as perjury. It is much more expansive than that. Whenever someone tells a falsehood about another, one is bearing false witness. It is against the law. A person can learn from that, morally, that truth telling is a good practice and falsehood evil, but the law itself is not a moral rule against lying.

Distinguishing legality from morality needs further consideration. We have just been exploring the Tenth Commandment, one that proscribes coveting. But how does that prohibition work? How can coveting be detected? Is this commandment a sudden insertion of an unprosecutable moral edict into an otherwise enforceable law code?[25] Presumably God knows what people are thinking, but how would humans?[26] Detailed studies on the terms used for *covet* in this law and its counterpart in Deuteronomy 5:21 (where the Ten Commandments are repeated) indicate that it involves deep, internal desires that are not initially plainly visible.[27] That would not make it equivalent to greed, lust or any other immoral vice, which instead would seem to be the source of coveting. Yet we do have a law that appears to regulate the thought life in a way that is difficult to prosecute independently. Coveting would perhaps be a first step leading to a visible illegal act such as, for example, stealing (see esp. Deut 7:25 and Josh 7:21). It would not be the same thing as stealing.[28] But the legal instruction against coveting would point to mental activity that may not be that far removed from activity forbidden by laws that we may know of in Western societies that outlaw conspiring to commit a crime, a different illegal act from the crime itself. This law seems to instruct in a fashion similar to the advice "Don't even think about it" when a person is exposed to someone to whom or something to which that one has no legitimate belonging.[29] To begin to learn from a law, it helps first to try to envision how a prosecutable violation of that law could take place.[30] From there one can begin to derive any potential moral implications from it.

Ultimately, we must make an important distinction. Legality and morality are not the same. We can see that to be true in contemporary social contexts. In most countries with laws regulating alcohol use, for example, a man or woman would be operating totally within the bounds of the law if that person were over the legal age for drinking and were, on a daily basis, to get drunk in the privacy of his or her own locked bedroom, staying put until the effects wear off. But we could question that person's morality. What is legal need not always be moral.

Likewise, what is moral need not always be considered legal. A man or woman may consider it a moral duty to pay city government for the amount of time parked at an expired parking meter, even if no parking ticket were to have been issued. Some might consider that to be excessive action, but it is an example of someone who is seeing beyond mere legality to attempt to live by higher principles. Additionally, we should note that a significant number of current laws have absolutely nothing to do with moral issues. Declarations of national holidays, laws governing what constitutes a valid corporation, or laws regulating procedural transactions, whether governmental, business or real estate, all reflect elements of an ordered society, but are not necessarily directly concerned with ethical issues.

Let's all now consider what a Torah observant Jew would already have concluded by this point. In trying to observe how a law might work in an ancient Near Eastern setting, which is foreign to us, we are introducing thought patterns foreign to those who, over millennia, have learned to adapt those laws to their new cultural settings. Our approach to morality and laws sounds decidedly like the perspective of the peoples surrounding the nation of Israel, referred to in Deuteronomy 4:6.

Just as in many contemporary societies, so it is in the kind of society being addressed by Torah's laws. Not every law has moral implications. We will have to distinguish between legality and morality. The command regarding the sabbath in Exodus 20:8-11 could certainly illustrate that. Based on the definition of morality being applied here, there is nothing immoral about laboring on Saturday, the seventh day of the week.[31] But for Israelites to do so would be a significant violation of their covenant with God, especially since further explanations in Exodus 31:13-17 portray the sabbath as the sign that the Israelites are in covenant relationship with God. There could be moral implications dancing around that law. An Israelite who labors on Saturday would be showing disrespect to God and his covenant, which itself is a source of ethics. The person would also be disloyal. What kind of person binds him- or herself to another but disregards the mandated sign of being in relationship with that other? Nevertheless, the mere act of working on Saturday is not itself immoral as, for example, the act of having sex with another's spouse would be. Viewed that way, working on Saturday is not inflicting harm in one's world.

Some activities that may be regulated in the Torah appear to have very little, if anything, to do with morality: dietary restrictions, purity rites, sacrificial practices, celebrations of festivals. Other activities that Torah does regulate may not themselves be moral—one could even make a case that they are immoral. For example, Torah in one instance regulates an unjust situation growing out of a man having more than one wife, polygamy (Deut 21:15-17), but that does not mean that Torah, with that law, promotes polygamy as a moral practice.[32] The same could also be said about regulations in Deuteronomy affecting divorce (see Deut 22:13-19; 22:28-29; 24:1-4). Torah may regulate slavery, as we have seen, but Torah does not instruct that slavery is a good social option. The import of the words about slavery is to offer protection to those in a weak situation, not to create an ideally ethical social order that is said to include slaves.[33] Torah is ultimately concerned with informing the Israelites, God's covenant people whom he has freed from slavery, about activities that keep them distinct as God's people, eventually reflecting, as we will see in Leviticus and Deuteronomy, two very important characteristics about God himself: his holiness and his loyal love. Torah's regulations are certainly tied into their cultural setting. But they have strong implications for developing a sense of moral understanding that goes beyond that setting.

We have to be discerning as readers. Let's not forget our operating definition of ethics as addressing issues of the rightness or wrongness of activities that advance good or hinder harm in one's world. If the main thrust of a law has direct implications for advancing good or hindering harm against others (including God), it has implications for the core ethical picture that Torah presents. If not, then it is of less value for acquiring ethical sensitivity.

Having to make such a distinction for Torah is certainly an artificial imposition. Ethics is not a focal point of discussion within the Torah. However, when we consider what ethics is, we can see that Torah's laws do advance a strong sense of rightness and wrongness about activities that deal with good or harm against others. Remember our initial observation. Not everything in the Bible is about good, moral behavior. Torah certainly demonstrates that.

So the basic rule of thumb is this: a law is not the same as a moral standard. A law may express or uphold a sense of morals. Beginning with a statement's overt legality can be a useful starting point. That involves discerning the basic harm that the law appears to restrict and the basic good it appears to advance. From there, we can learn to distinguish between moral implications a law may have and implications for other kinds of behavior that have no bearing on ethics. Here is where our working definition of what comprises ethics must govern our explorations. Not every law has implications for ethics. We must read carefully.

From legal penalty to moral point. Though Torah's laws are designed to instruct, an essential purpose of them as laws is to regulate. That means that we, as readers, come to recognize that in their social and literary contexts the laws often provide a neutral platform to help sort out issues between two parties at odds with each other, sometimes calling on outside help.[34] In many contemporary social contexts that platform involves the work of judges and the courts. Those judges are to apply the principles established by laws, also arbitrating between presentations offered by experts in laws, lawyers. Though displaying a different sort of legal system, some laws in Torah clearly indicate that others are involved in applying them, not exclusively the immediate parties involved.

Take the following words as an example:

> When people who are fighting injure a pregnant woman so that there is a miscarriage [or perhaps more properly, a premature birth], and yet no further harm follows, the one responsible shall be fined what the woman's husband demands, paying as much as the judges determine. *If any harm follows, then you shall give life for life, eye for eye, tooth for tooth, hand for hand, foot for foot, burn for burn, wound for wound, stripe for stripe.*[35] **Ex 21:22-25, emphasis added**

People can easily focus on the words *eye for eye, tooth for tooth* as comments justifying revenge.[36] Understood in context, however, they communicate the opposite. The expression "paying as much as the judges determine" indicates a layer that stands between the wrongdoer and the potentially vengeful wronged person. The statement actually conveys a legal principle similar to one employed in many contemporary law-based societies: The punishment must fit the crime. A man is not allowed to kill another for knocking out the man's tooth. Another milder, proportionately appropriate penalty is to be handed down by others who are in charge.

In that regard, then, the statement appears here as more of a guiding principle than a pronouncement of exact penalties.[37] The statement demarcates the nature of the punishment that a guilty perpetrator must endure. It is not primarily for the victim. The victim is not being instructed "He took your eye. Get his!" Rather, the judge or arbiter, not the victim, is the one for whom this offers the most immediate guidance. The victim learns from this that vengeance is not his or her right. The perpetrator learns that his harmful activity has damaged another, and at the very least experiences a similar type of damage to that inflicted. Among the set of ethical messages one could derive from the penalty for violating such a law would be the necessity for people to consider the potential harm their rash actions may actually cause others. People cannot live as independent, self-seeking individuals. Whenever they cause harm, they must do what they can to compensate for it. That lesson is for the perpetrator of the action, not the victim.

Other laws have automatic penalties built into them. They are presumably meted out by the existing judicial system. The death penalty exists for premeditated killing (Ex 21:12-14), for owners of oxen with reputations for goring others when another human has died (Ex 21:28-32) and possibly, as cited earlier, for the death of a pregnant woman or her prematurely born child when that is the fallout of her being a bystander in a fight between two men (Ex 21:22-25).[38] But other activities merit the death penalty, even when another human does not die. Kidnapping (Ex 21:16), children hitting or cursing parents (Ex 21:15, 17) and people having sex with animals (Ex 22:19) also warrant death. The extreme penalty would appear to accent the contemptibility that the illicit behavior is thought to express. With such penalties, Torah appears to place a high value on human life, family structures and proper sexual expression, issues also reflected in both the initial creation order and its recommissioned state (see Gen 1–2; 9).

Lesser penalties exist for other offenses, including the requirement for restitution for various kinds of property loss, whether through theft or negligence (Ex 22:1, 4-13). Thieves who sell stolen livestock pay back four or five times the value of the animals stolen, probably heightening what the loss means to the farmer being stolen from.[39] They may in no way profit from inflicting such harm. Thieves caught with the goods not only restore what they stole; they also experience the exact same loss themselves, having to pay back double the amount. Such laws, when considered for their instructive value, indicate that people are to have a sense of responsibility for what belongs to their neighbor instead of merely getting on with their own lives. In fact, they need to do what they can to uphold what belongs to their neighbor, so that their neighbor's well-being is upheld. They are to have a deep sense of responsibility in relating to their neighbors.[40]

A man who seduces an unengaged virgin and then is caught must be subject to the decision of the girl's father (Ex 22:16-17). Though the law reflects a patriarchal, male-dominated culture that may be foreign, even objectionable, to many Western readers, it has overarching principles that do transcend some of the culture-bound particulars of the law.[41] Note that the seduction makes the activity more consensual than forced.[42] The fact that the virgin is unengaged would indicate that another's wife is not being interfered with. Such delineations and protections are important for the patriarchal society that the law addresses, curbing the whims of those who would overstep the bounds of their control. The young man must pay the girl's father the bride price for the girl he had sex with as the first step to marrying her—unless the father rejects him![43] Such a law supports keeping sexual activity within the bounds of marriage, a value equally significant for men and women.[44] It simultaneously curbs the selfishness of an unmarried person manipulating another's emotions for sexual gratification. Though the law itself protects vulnerable women from certain kinds of men, its restrictions against seeking sexual pleasure outside of marriage are equally instructive to men and women alike. In the end, the integrity of marriage as the sole God-pleasing sphere of sexual activity is the core ethical issue upheld by such a law, again reflecting creation order.

Only in one set of laws is divine intervention threatened as a consequence: "You shall not abuse any widow or orphan. If you do abuse them, when they cry out to me, I will surely heed their cry; my wrath will burn, and I will kill you with the sword, and your wives shall become widows and your children orphans" (Ex 22:22-24).

Though appearing less severe, the following also implies a form of divine activity: "If you take your neighbor's cloak in pawn, you shall restore it before the sun goes down; for it may be your neighbor's only clothing to use as cover; in what else shall that person sleep? And if your neighbor cries out to me, I will listen, for I am compassionate" (Ex 22:26-27).

That is amazing. No other issues in Exodus's laws carry the direct threat of divine intervention. That threat underscores the seriousness of mistreating poor people, widows and orphans. It also trumpets the importance of caring for the disadvantaged in anyone's circle of personal interaction. Such a responsibility belongs to each individual Israelite. It is activity that is near to the heart of God, reflecting God's own merciful interventions on their behalf.

That point becomes even clearer when considering how foreigners are to be treated. Exodus 23:9 states, "You shall not oppress a resident alien; you know the heart of an alien, for you were aliens in the land of Egypt." In this case, their regard for that category of socially disadvantaged is to be rooted in their own national history. They knew how they were mistreated. They themselves should not mistreat others they know in similar circumstances. Note the concrete rationale for its adherence also in line with the activity being talked about. It, like the law of Exodus 22:26-27, offers a motivation statement that supports why the law should be kept.[45] This statement provides a basis for individuals to address any setting where they see others being harmed—"You know what it's like to be mistreated. Sympathize with others in their weakness and do what you would have wanted to have happened to you when you were in similar straits." In this law we have the basis for some profound ethical reasoning. A person who takes advantage of the weakness of others is evil. The Israelites know of such evil firsthand. Instead, they should do for the weak what the weak need, lest they inflict the same sort of harm that they themselves experienced.[46]

With these laws one can begin to see how people can move beyond dependence on regulatory words. The basic principle of the importance of looking out for all people is reflected in laws that themselves reflect the history of God's intervention on behalf of his people in their moment of supreme weakness. Whenever God's people, who are in covenant relationship with him, look out for others in weak situations instead of taking advantage of them, they are being as God was when he looked out for them.[47] Growing in their covenantal knowledge of God, who is for them, should inform their moral behavior.

In learning ethics from laws one must learn how to move from legality to general life principle. The legal dimensions exist to protect against potential harm rooted in actual possibilities. But more than protect, they also steer God's covenant people to uphold what is good for others, what advances the well-being of others. These laws flow out of the covenant between God and Israel, where God has acted mercifully and mightily on their behalf. God has brought initial order to the world, with a desire to bless the whole world. The laws point to an environment where God's people should show similar concern to others they encounter in their midst, whether or not those others do not belong to their own group. In so doing, not only can they expect to be blessed (Ex 23:25-26). They fulfill their role as a bridge between God and the rest of the nations (Ex 19:5-6).

The laws' ethics affect a community, not simply individuals. One more important point flows from all of this, one that has already been hinted at throughout. We tend to think of ethics as a personal choice. Torah's laws additionally reflect social conditioning.[48] One person's lack of ethics encourages another to be unethical. Majorities can be followed in their wrongdoing. But also one person's ethical choices affect the positive ethical stance of others. Consider the following law as a demonstration: "When you come upon your enemy's ox or donkey going astray, you shall bring it back. When you see the donkey of one who hates you lying under its burden and you would hold back from setting it free, you must help to set it free" (Ex 23:4-5).

It's against the law to say, "That was my enemy's donkey. That's why I let it die." Why protect an enemy's property? Notice the responsibility to look after others in weakness extends even to those with whom one would wish to have no involvement. What does such a law do for the one who enacts it? What also does it do for those who receive the action? Over time, the sense of someone being an enemy is greatly reduced. And what is the affect on others who see known enemies enacting kindness to one another? If one exercises such responsibility for an enemy's property, what does that say about the importance of caring for others?

SUMMING IT UP:
WHAT HAVE WE LEARNED FROM EXODUS?

o The laws flow out of Israel's covenant with God, who has acted mercifully on their behalf to rescue them from misery in Egypt.

o The laws are to be kept as Israel's responsibilities in their covenant with God.

o The Israelites are to keep the laws because they are God's people.

o Such motivations are relational motivations. Obedience is to flow out of their covenant knowledge of God, whose desire is to show them mercy, patience, love and faithfulness.

- The laws cover a variety of topics with moral relevance, but they do not attempt to exhaust the possibilities of topics.
- The laws are designed to instruct, not merely legislate.
- Legality is not the same as morality or ethics.
- Laws that regulate practices that some could regard as unethical do not necessarily ask us to consider those practices to be ethical (e.g., slavery).
- Not all laws have relevance for ethics, only those that advocate the advancing of good or the hindering of harm against others.
- Legal penalties and rationale provide a basis for further moral and ethical reasoning.
- The ethics flowing out of the laws affect a community. Individuals learn morals from living with people who are behaving morally to each other.

Since legality and morality are not the same, readers must think carefully to discern the moral or ethical significance of a law. A simple approach to that would

- Begin by recognizing that you are reading a law, not a moral rule.
- Identify the central point of a law, not getting entangled in side issues.
- Begin to envision a situation of how a law could be broken in a prosecutable way.
- Move beyond the mere legality.
- Identify the basic harm being restricted and the basic good being advanced by such a law; if you can't see how the law hinders or advances the well-being of others and their world, move on—it would not be immediately morally instructive.

> o Consider what any legal penalties may reinforce about the harm being inflicted or the good being advanced.
>
> o Consider how any motivation statements in a law may point to ethical principles affecting other related moral issues not addressed by the specifics of the law.[49]

Of course, Torah's ethical vision is bigger than this. We are just getting started.

Reflection Questions

1. What do God's acts on behalf of his people communicate about God's regard for them, and how does that affect the way they know God, in covenant relationship with him?

2. How does the covenant relationship between God and his people provide a significant motivation for behaving ethically?

3. How does the covenant between God and Israel represent movement toward a world that more reflects the created order?

4. How can a person learn ethics from a law?

5. How do the laws, as part of this particular covenant, affect how God's people are to think about life? Families? Others' property? Society's weak?

FOR FURTHER READING

Wijk-Bos, Johanna W. H. van. *Making Wise the Simple: The Torah in Christian Faith and Practice*. Grand Rapids: Eerdmans, 2005.

Wright, Christopher J. H. *Old Testament Ethics for the People of God*. Downers Grove, IL: InterVarsity Press, 2004.

4

HOLINESS AND LOVE
IN THE COVENANT

Ethics in Torah 3

INTRODUCTORY ISSUES

The story line. The world of Exodus introduced the covenant between God and the Israelites. The story lines of Leviticus and Deuteronomy progressively develop from that world. Leviticus is set at Mount Sinai (aka Mount Horeb), the same site where the Israelites were dwelling at the end of Exodus. It begins as though a continuation of the Exodus story, but quickly becomes a self-contained unit with its own special concerns and emphases, the most key being that of the holiness of God and his people. In the basic story line God continues to speak to Moses, issuing further laws that Moses records. The main initial event in Leviticus is the installation of Aaron and his sons as priests of God in the newly constructed tabernacle, with those sons suffering extreme consequences for imprecise attention to their priestly duties. Deuteronomy, by contrast, is set in another time and location. The principal speaker is Moses, not God. The entire writing is in the form of a farewell speech from Moses to a new generation of Israelites who finally are on the verge of entering their Promised Land.

In between those two story lines are two military censuses taken in the world of Numbers. Those censuses themselves are the focal points of two movements of the Israelites, the first from Mount Sinai (Horeb) to the southern border of the Promised Land, and the second from some undisclosed southern wilderness territory to the eastern border of the Promised Land, just northeast of the Dead Sea. The turning point in that story is the refusal of the Israelites to enter their land after the first census. The members of that generation are sentenced to wander forty years in the wilderness, dying off without entering their land, which their children, instead, will inherit. Those children, as grownups with their own families, are the ones counted in the second census. Numbers, and indeed all of Torah, is uninterested in what happened during those forty years, conveying instead the buildup to the rejection of the land by the first generation of Israelites and then the immediate run-up to the second generation's imminent entry to the land. Sprinkled around those plot elements are various laws relevant especially to sacrificial offerings and officiants, and to land settlement. Deuteronomy begins with Moses' rehearsing the movements of the next generation of Israelites from the wilderness to the edge of the land as an introduction to his restatement of the covenant for that new generation.

Numbers is certainly relevant to an understanding of Torah's covenant and of God as a covenant-keeping God in spite of the covenant unfaithfulness of his people. But in terms of helping to shape Torah's ethical vision, its contribution is not as transparent. That is why we will examine it no further.

Basic principles learned from Exodus. The points established from Exodus carry over when reading laws both in Leviticus and in Deuteronomy. The following principles are worth keeping in mind from chapter three:

- The laws cover a variety of topics with moral relevance, but they do not attempt to exhaust the possibilities of topics.

- The laws are designed to instruct, not merely legislate.

- Legality is not the same as morality or ethics.

- Laws that regulate practices that some could regard as unethical do not necessarily ask us to consider those practices to be ethical (e.g., slavery).

- Not all laws have relevance for ethics, only those that advocate the advancing of good or the hindering of harm against others.

- Legal penalties and rationale provide a basis for further moral and ethical reasoning.

- The ethics flowing out of the laws affect a community. Individuals learn morals from living with people who are behaving morally to each other.

LEVITICUS AND HOLINESS

Some introductory points for Leviticus. With the exception of two story segments, Leviticus consists of laws and instructions that mostly regulate sacrificial offerings and the clean fitness of people and priests to participate through the tabernacle in sacrificial and ritual expressions to God. That activity is firmly centered on the covenant between God and his people. Everything that Leviticus presents facilitates proper connection between God and his people.

Ethics would not appear initially to be a major concern for Leviticus.[1] That thought is thoroughly challenged by a series of statements found in the middle of a section of the writing, a section often referred to as the Holiness Code. That code is generally considered to span Leviticus 17–26; many of the laws found in Leviticus 18–20 deal with behaviors that directly involve God's people advancing good and hindering harm on others in their world. Additional laws in Leviticus 25 introduce a fascinating concept of property ownership, also instructing how to care for poverty stricken kin among the Israelites. The laws of chapters 18–20 and 25 will receive the primary attention here. At the very least they will show that piety and ethics must go together because they both reflect people in relationship with God. Leviticus does not permit any thinking that separates good religious behavior from good moral behavior.[2]

Before discussing those chapters, let's explore the overall context of their laws. They appear in a writing that is deeply concerned with the concept of holiness. This concept needs to be described and defined because it affects not only the ethics reflected in Leviticus's laws but the covenant expressing those ethics. The entire writing of Leviticus emphasizes how the Israelites, God's people, are in covenant relationship with a holy God. Since God is holy, they too must be holy to maintain that relationship: "Be holy, for I . . . am holy."[3] Holy people have a clearer understanding of who God is, and so, how to relate to him. To understand holiness in this context is to understand more of God. People can know God well only if they know his holiness.

Being ethical is not the same as being holy. But in the world of Leviticus, ethics clearly and significantly flows out of a regard for holiness. Performing a moral deed does not make one holy. Rather, because one aims for holiness, one performs moral deeds among a host of other behaviors. People who are holy in Leviticus's ways will be ethical people, with a clearer sense of the kind of activity that is right or wrong. They will also have a clearer, God-focused motivation for doing the right and refraining from the wrong, since they will understand how that activity reflects God's holiness. Though much of that stems from activities such as eating appropriate foods and offering proper sacrifices, a significant portion of holiness maintenance directly advances good and hinders harm in the world, working for the betterment of others.

What is holiness? The word *holy* and its related terms *sacred, holiness, consecrate, sanctuary* and *sanctify* appear 153 times throughout the writing.[4] We see them directly in twenty of Leviticus's twenty-seven chapters, though the concept they convey is present everywhere. It is not foreign to other parts of Torah. Exodus uses those same terms 109 times throughout its forty chapters. The vast majority of Exodus's usages (ninety-five of them), though, appear in Exodus 25–40 in their discussion of the tabernacle, the portable temple built by the Israelites for God to dwell in their midst while they proceeded to their Promised Land. Clearly holiness affects the connection between God and his people. Leviticus expands on the concept, indicating that holiness involves much more than performing pious duties for the tabernacle. As part of their covenant relationship with God, they must perform ritual activities such as sacrifice. But with those, they must be holy and that relates to a host of activities, including morality.

Throughout the book of Leviticus, *holy* and its related terms are applied directly to the following issues: the special place where sacrifices are to be offered, the proper mode and conduct of various sacrifices, portions of sacrifices designated for priests, and proper priestly conduct in offering sacrifices. It also is the standard for these kinds of activities: determining the proper kind of food to eat; cleansing from impurities resulting from childbirth and from various bodily emissions; cleansing from various skin diseases and other forms of leprosy that even affect objects; maintaining laws that resemble the Ten Commandments; showing a righteous regard for all people, even including poor, blind, deaf, foreigners and elderly; judging with proper, consistent standards; keeping animals, fabrics and fields as "one kind"; prohibiting certain practices belonging to other religions; maintaining honesty; and refraining from a variety of illicit sexual interactions. The priests and their sacrificial activities receive significant attention, but clearly holiness affects everyday life as well.

Holiness plainly has wide-ranging import. We must avoid distorting the concept by focusing on a single cluster of items on the list. Still, we have to try to get a handle on what is going on here. Leviticus reflects an expansive view of what the concept incorporates. The primary dimension, especially emphasized in priestly and sacrificial settings, would appear to be a sense of hallowedness and, combined with that, set-apartness.[5] Objects, or even people, considered holy for unique functions are to be reserved in a special category and handled with respectful care. Priests, who must offer the holy sacrifices in a holy manner and place, must themselves follow a stricter set of limits on items that have nothing to do with the behavioral issues we explore in ethics, items such as what they can touch, whom they can marry and what physical defects disqualify them from service.

In addition to this sense of reverential set-apartness, holiness reflects a strong sense of purity or cleanliness. Objects and practitioners, both officiants and participants, are maintained in holiness by being kept pure, separate from contact with nonholy objects or people. The sense of purity carries over to the Israelite understanding themselves to be uniquely set apart from the nations of the world, not defiling themselves in the same ways that they do.

Purity can also be a slippery concept to define. Social anthropologists are fond of characterizing the opposite of purity, dirt, as "matter out of place."[6] Consider, for example, saliva. For many cultures it always belongs in the mouth, then to be swallowed. That is where it is in place. But once someone spits, it is out of place, dirty or unclean. Fill a glass with spit, drink from it, and stomachs will turn.

Purity labels often provide clues to how different cultures perceive order. Leviticus's brand of purity appeals to concepts of order that would make sense within its culture of origin, concepts that could appear foreign to many of us. Consider, for example, the language of purity within the dietary instructions of Leviticus 11. Meat coming only from cud-chewing, cloven hoofed animals can be eaten. If our general culture happens to have no problems with eating pigs, which do have cloven hoofs but do not chew the cud, we might think this odd. But Leviticus presents a system that is ordered and easily applied within the understanding of its culture's worldview.

Other cultures' sense of unclean food may not be as easily determined. The thought of eating rat stew would not be appealing to some of us—in fact, it would probably gross us out (note the language of purity). Why? Many might consider how rats inhabit horrible, unhygienic places. Rats feel dirty. However, pigsties are not always the cleanest places in the world, yet those same people do not apply the logic about rats when eating pigs. Whatever it was that made pigs, rabbits and other animals not conform to the pattern established in Leviticus, it made cultural sense to those among whom it was initially shaped. They could be just as grossed out about eating pigs as someone from another culture would be about eating rats.

When appealing to purity assumptions about food commonly held within its culture of origin, Leviticus helps us understand holiness. The same can be said for the sense of purity reflected in some bodily discharges (Lev 15) or skin diseases (Lev 13), all of which offer God's people regular, daily reminders of the need to maintain holiness.[7] By applying purity concepts that make cultural sense, Leviticus shows that holiness also makes cultural sense.[8] Leviticus eventually addresses inappropriate sexual activities that are said to defile. They are dirty, out of place in some manner.[9] Refraining from sexually immoral activity maintains holiness.

Holiness can also apply to a sense of order without appealing directly to purity language. In its approach to holiness Leviticus sometimes depicts strong boundaries of the sort established in the created order of Genesis 1, which portrays plants and animals each made after its kind.[10] That sense of order can help explain why some activities promote unholiness, such as, for example, a human having sex with an animal (Lev 18:23-24), which is also said to be dirty (Lev 18:24-25), and a farmer mating an animal of one species with that of another, or sowing two different kinds of seed in the same field, or someone combining two different kinds of materials in a garment (Lev 19:19), none of which has any purity language attached to it. The sexual boundary between humans and animals may make sense to people in various cultures now. But the sense of order applied to animals, crops and clothing probably does not. Just as with purity, it would make total sense to Leviticus's culture of origin, offering visible reminders of holiness.

Related to the sense of order upholding holiness in the words of Leviticus is a sense of wholeness or completeness.[11] Certain patterns that show incompleteness may point to what cannot be holy. For example, animals being offered to God in sacrifice must have no blemish or defect (Lev 1:3, 10; 3:1, 6; 4:3, 23, 28, 32; 5:15, 18; 6:6; 9:2, 3; 14:10). That sense of wholeness and its lack, when connected to the sense of order reflected in creation, offers potential insight to how Leviticus encourages ethical reasoning in its holiness laws that have clear moral bearing. Activities that advance good on others and also reflect a sense of creation wholeness are holy. Activities that destroy creation wholeness while advancing harm are unholy. Holy people will be moral.

So, holiness refers to what is reverentially set apart from the common. In Leviticus the sense of holiness can be closely connected to senses of purity, order and wholeness. When applied to moral activity, it would indicate that some activities are impure, disordering or diminishing, while others are pure, ordering and completing. Why does holiness matter? The Israelites, God's people, are in covenant relationship with a holy God. That God dwells in their midst through the tabernacle. For them to come to his presence there, they must be holy or else perform purifying rituals that make them holy. To dwell with them the holy God must have a holy people. They must be holy because God is holy. That is a key ethical motive for the Torah. "Why should I do that behavior and avoid the other?" Leviticus's answer is: "To do the wrong behavior defies the holiness of God, who dwells with us. We are in covenant relationship with a holy God. We must be holy and thus do right, because our God is holy." People who know God in his holiness have a clearer understanding of God's sense of right and wrong when it comes to acts that advance good or hinder harm against others and against the world they live in.

Ethics in the Holiness Code: Leviticus 18–20. While ethics flows out of holiness, holiness in Torah is not principally about ethics. Holy people will be moral people. Good morals emerge from a regard for holiness. But because holiness in Torah is not principally about ethics, we can expect many laws in the Holiness Code to address behaviors outside of the sphere of ethics. Here is where, again, we apply our operating definition of ethics as pertaining to behaviors that advance good or restrain harm in one's world, especially when a person's well-being is concerned. If the law, or instruction, addresses the direct advancement of good or harm on the well-being of another, it offers potential moral insight.[12] If it does not directly address such activity, it will not be as useful for ethics.

Consider the restrictions on sexual behavior found in Leviticus 18. Sexual activity certainly deals with the direct inflicting of good or harm on another. Though the vocabulary of holiness is absent there, the senses of purity and distinctiveness connected to holiness remain. The term *holy* does in fact appear in Leviticus 20 when tough penalties are mandated for much of the same activity. Leviticus 18 begins with the following warning:

> *Speak to the people of Israel and say to them: I am the LORD your God. You shall not do as they do in the land of Egypt, where you lived, and you shall not do as they do in the land of Canaan, to which I am bringing you. You shall not follow their statutes. My ordinances you shall observe and my statutes you shall keep, following them: I am the LORD your God. You shall keep my statutes and my ordinances; by doing so one shall live: I am the LORD.* **Lev 18:2-5**

Distinctiveness rings out from these words. But so also does God's character: "I am the LORD." That reminder occurs twenty-three more times in Leviticus 18–20.[13] It calls on the Israelites to consider their covenant relationship with God. After those words appears a list of various forms of incestuous sexual relationships the Israelites are to refrain from (Lev 18:6-18), beginning with the words: "None of you shall approach anyone near of kin to uncover nakedness: I am the LORD" (18:6—"uncover nakedness" is a euphemism for "have sexual intercourse").[14]

As detailed as the list may appear to be, it is not thoroughly exhaustive.[15] For example, sex between a man and his daughter is not explicitly on the list.[16] The rationale offered for each appeals to the violation of a familial relationship; the one to whom "nakedness" is said to belong is the one who is dishonored.[17] That same kind of rationale is also applied to the similar activities listed in Leviticus 20. The words support the basic marital scene envisioned by the creation accounts, where people were to populate the earth (Gen 1:28) and where a man was to leave his mother and father and cling to his wife, with the two of them becoming one flesh in unashamed nakedness (Gen 2:24).[18] The prohibitions of sexual behaviors mentioned in both Leviticus 18 and Leviticus 20 make sense against that background. The illicit sexual acts damage core familial relationships and violate the unique one-fleshness of a husband and wife. The holiness advanced by these laws hinders harm against another. Incest appears to be immoral because its relational damage defies God's created order.

Not everything on the list in this chapter is about immoral sexual activity. Leviticus 18:19 forbids a man having sex with his wife "while she is in her menstrual uncleanness." It offers no motivational statements that point to any rationale, unlike other prohibitions in this section.[19] It does coordinate with purity

laws found in Leviticus 15:19-24, where women during menstruation are officially unclean, and thus are the men who have sex with them at that moment.
That same thought appears in Leviticus 20:18, which speaks against uncovering
a woman's flow of blood as a sacred violation. The prohibition also appears in a
context about God's people living uniquely from the nations. The words do not
point to issues that deal with hindering harm against another's well-being, even
if they reflect damage to covenantal holiness. In another example in Leviticus
18:21, child sacrifices to the god Molech are outlawed. They are not forbidden,
however, because explicit harm would be inflicted on the child. Leviticus
bundles the child sacrifice with Molech worship; the two work together to
profane God's name, not the act of child sacrifice alone (see also Lev 20:2-5).[20]

By contrast, three laws in Leviticus 18:19-23 do have language with moral
implications. "Sexual relations with [a] kinsman's wife" is called an act of
defilement (v. 20). Male same-sex intercourse and sex with animals are respectively referred to as an abomination (Lev 18:22; 20:13) and a perversion
(Lev 18:23; 20:15-16). They damage holiness as clear distortions of creation
boundaries, and thus are harmful to others and their world.

The list about illicit sexual activity shows that any sex going outside of the
creation boundaries is defiling, unholy sex. That kind of sex also advances
harm in one's world because it defies the order established in God's creation,
undermining the dignity of maleness and femaleness, the dignity of the
separate marital unit of a husband and his wife, along with the dignity of
humankind in God's image. It is to be avoided. The final words of Leviticus
18 provide further rationale:

> Do not defile yourselves in any of these ways, for by all these practices the nations
> I am casting out before you have defiled themselves. Thus the land became defiled;
> and I punished it for its iniquity, and the land vomited out its inhabitants. But you
> shall keep my statutes and my ordinances and commit none of these abominations,
> either the citizen or the alien who resides among you (for the inhabitants of the land,
> who were before you, committed all of these abominations, and the land became
> defiled); otherwise the land will vomit you out for defiling it, as it vomited out the
> nation that was before you. For whoever commits any of these abominations shall
> be cut off from their people. So keep my charge not to commit any of these abomi-
> nations that were done before you, and not to defile yourselves by them: I am the
> LORD your God. **Lev 18:24-30**

Similar language also appears in Leviticus 20:22-26, directly connecting inappropriate sexual activity to a violation of God's holiness. Only marital sex is holy sex. God's people are in covenant relationship with a holy God. Maintaining sexual purity is one aspect of honoring that covenant.

Leviticus 19 begins with some important words that govern the contents of all that follows in verses 1-37: "The LORD spoke to Moses, saying: Speak to all the congregation of the people of Israel and say to them: You shall be holy, for I the LORD your God am holy" (19:1-2). Fifteen times the statements are punctuated with the declaration "I am the LORD." That statement points to why God's people should obey by highlighting the importance of these laws for the covenantal relationship between the people of Israel and their holy God. The subsequent laws cover an amazingly wide range of activities, some dealing with morality, some not. At the heart of the chapter is perhaps Leviticus's best known saying, "love your neighbor as yourself" (19:18). Obedience to that is also an expression of holiness.

Topics with moral implications include:

- honoring parents (v. 3)
- taking care of the poor and the alien (vv. 9-10, 33-34)
- refraining from stealing (vv. 11, 13) and falsehood (vv. 11-12, 35-36)
- not mistreating the deaf and blind (v. 14)
- forbidding economic standing to influence the rendering of judgment (v. 15)
- refraining from slander (v. 16)
- refraining from hatred and vengeance (vv. 17-18)
- acting to reprove wrongdoers (v. 17)
- prohibiting sex with another's slave (v. 20)
- forbidding forcing one's daughter into prostitution (v. 29)
- acting to respect the elderly (v. 32)[21]

Attention to all those issues is portrayed as just as much a part of holiness as attention to other nonmoral issues, such as not obtaining tattoos (v. 28) or keeping the sabbath (v. 3). They are all sacred deeds.

Those issues overlap significantly with issues already observed in Exodus. The most obvious ones echo some of the Ten Commandments: the honoring of parents, the prohibition against stealing, and perhaps even the concern with falsehood.[22] There are also similar concerns with Exodus's Book of the Covenant. We can observe a common regard for the poor and the foreigner (Lev 19:9-10; Ex 22:21-24, 25-27; 23:9), with the same motivational reminder of the Israelites' status as aliens in Egypt (Lev 19:33-34). There is a concern for just judgment (Lev 19:15; Ex 23:6-7) and truthful reporting (Lev 19:11-12, 16; Ex 23:1-3).These laws also uphold the integrity of families, not only in terms of parent-child relationships (Lev 19:3; Ex 21:15, 17) but also in terms that support the marital unit as the only sphere for proper sexual activity (Lev 19:20, 29; Ex 22:16-17, 19). They also add to the picture of morality by instructing how the poor and the alien may be helped by leaving parts of fields unharvested so that they can collect food (Lev 19:9-10). They extend the sense of having a regard for the weak with two unique statements about the deaf and blind (Lev 19:14). They advocate an evenhandedness in judgment by forbidding any deference to economic standing, whether rich or poor (Lev 19:15), and they extend the sense of honesty into the commercial world by outlawing dishonest weights that are heavier when selling and lighter when buying merchandise (Lev 19:35-36). The echoes with Exodus invite the reader to extend Leviticus's sense of holiness back to Exodus, while considering how to expand the sense of rightness advocated by Exodus's laws.

As we saw in Exodus, so we see here. These laws are designed to instruct, not to regulate every aspect of a person's life. That appears quite clearly with two completely unique sets of laws in Leviticus 19:17-18, "You shall not hate in your heart anyone of your kin. . . . [Y]ou shall love your neighbor as yourself." How could those ever be enforced? In its context the first statement is the first part of a law that counters harboring inner hatred against someone with, instead, publicly rebuking one's neighbor. Likewise, the second statement is the second half of a longer sentence: "You shall not take vengeance or bear a grudge against any of your people, but you shall love your neighbor as yourself: I am the LORD." Open,[23] public reproof, or correction, is the alternative to internal hating, implying recourse to the guidance of outside judges;[24] love of neighbor is put forward as the alternative to vengeance-taking and grudge-bearing.[25] But how does someone enforce laws against internal hatred and for love of neighbor? One can see outward demonstrations both of hatred and of love, but against what standards does someone determine that a person is hating another, or a person has not shown enough love to another?

On the one hand, the instructions extend the sense of communal responsibility for others advocated by the law in Exodus 23:4-5, which requires mercy to be directed even to an enemy's beast of burden, or by the laws that governed accidental damage to another's property (Ex 22:5-6, 10-15). But they do more than that. They suggest that people must perform positive activity directed toward those around them that both protects others and actively seeks their well-being. Hatred, vengeance and grudge bearing are against the law. Direct correction and love are for the law.

Alternative to refraining from hidden hatred is a positive act: open, mediated reproof. Alternative to restrictions against committing vengeful acts or enacting grudges is a positive obligation: love of neighbor. Reproof points to taking responsibility for the improper acts of one's neighbor. Love acts for someone's well-being, not for that person's harm. Here, embedded in the midst of laws, is a core ethical principle. God's people are not only to look out for their own affairs; they are to engage positively and helpfully with the affairs of others. That principle is taken further in Leviticus 19:34, which advocates loving foreigners both with language identical to love of neighbor and with the motivation of recalling the experience of being aliens in Egypt: "The alien who resides with you shall be to you as the citizen among you; you shall love the alien as yourself, for you were aliens in the land of Egypt: I am the LORD your God."

That law includes the foreigner as a neighbor and supports the love of neighbor with reasoning that urges Israelites to consider their own moments in life when they have been mistreated. They would have wanted to receive love and care then. They ought to extend the same, not only to aliens but, by implication, to all in weak situations. This kind of connection between love and mercy, which extends help to people in weakness, forms the foundation of the golden rule statements that we will observe both in the Gospel of Luke and the Gospel of Matthew, in chapters seven and eight. Here in Leviticus, the connection furthers the life of holiness.

When God's covenant people love their neighbors, including the alien, rather than harm them, and set their neighbors on the right path rather than hate them, they are being holy. Active regard for a neighbor's well-being is hallowed activity directed to God. As part of the covenant it expresses relationship with God. God's people are to be holy because God is holy. A failure of God's covenant people to care for their neighbors is a failure to be holy. Success in holiness makes them ethical. Holiness is a necessary aspect of Torah's ethic of relationship.

People who understand holiness as Leviticus advances it will be people who love others. They will also be people who hold familial relationships in high esteem, who know the proper place of sexual activity, who take care of those in need, who place a high value on consistent, honest dealings with others. The ethics of holiness reflects God's sense of order, wholeness and propriety expressed in creation. Holiness distinctly shapes Torah's ethical vision.

Ethics in the Holiness Code: Leviticus 25. Leviticus 25 portrays two issues worthy of discussion: the Jubilee and poor relatives.[26] The first issue offers a general policy of land ownership. Unlike other issues we have explored in Leviticus, it has macroethical implications. It stems from two main thoughts. First, God declares that he owns the Israelites' Promised Land (Lev 25:23). The Israelites live as aliens themselves in God's territory. Israelite families receive control over specific parcels of property because God allows it. Only God has the ultimate right to give and take away land. Second, the land is apportioned according to families. Land control must always revert to the original family to whom the land was assigned in the first place (Lev 25:10). That is to happen every fifty years, effectively preventing the consolidation of large amounts of land in the hands of a few. The fiftieth year is to be a year of "liberty throughout the land" (v. 10). The reversion of property is supposed to be factored into the value of the land in all deals (Lev 25:15), discouraging any cheating that may stem from overvalued property going back too quickly to the original family and thus harming the one who had purchased it temporarily from the original family. Proper pursuit of the Jubilee policy reflects holiness (Lev 25:12).[27] It must be conducted honestly, with a regard for God (Lev 25:17). It flows out of Israel's covenant relationship with God.

The second issue addresses how the Israelites are to treat their own kin who fall on hard times financially, becoming dependent on them. The financially stronger relatives are to support their weaker relatives, lending without remuneration (Lev 25:35). They should be careful not to take advantage of the poverty of their relatives by causing them to become financially indebted to them. Any loans of that sort should be interest free (Lev 25:36), and anything sold to them should be solely at cost, with no profiting from their poverty (Lev 25:37). Should people need to sell themselves to get out of debt, they should not be treated as slaves but as laborers worthy of payment, until the year of Jubilee when all debts are to be forgiven (Lev 25:40). The grounding for all of this is God himself:

> I am the LORD your God, who brought you out of the land of Egypt, to give you the land of Canaan, to be your God. . . .
>
> For they are my servants, whom I brought out of the land of Egypt; they shall not be sold as slaves are sold. You shall not rule over them with harshness, but shall fear your God. **Lev 25:38, 42-43**

Both of these extraordinary sets of policies stem from God's covenant relationship with his people. They underscore how people who know God in his holiness will care well for others. God's people should not treat another improperly by taking advantage of that person's weakness. Neither should they become too possessive of land that they have only by virtue of God's granting it to them. Here, as elsewhere, we will have to distinguish legality from morality. What we learn is the value of the covenantal solidarity between God and his people, and between God's people and one another. People should not take advantage of the hard times of others. Instead, they should look out for the weak, offering dignified help with respect for their humanity. That would further uphold the principle of the weak being looked after by the strong in the same way that God has looked after them.[28] That also is holiness.

DEUTERONOMY AND LOVE

Some introductory points for Deuteronomy. There is a forty-year gap in time between the ending of the story line of Leviticus and the beginning of the story line of Deuteronomy. We have already seen the bridge that the book of Numbers offers between those two. Deuteronomy represents Moses' farewell speech to the people of Israel, his final charge to that new generation of Israelites.[29] In that charge he re-presents their covenant with God, urging them to obey. The reasons he offers them will be most instructive to us. They will provide further rationale for why God's covenant people should do what they are to do, supporting a strong sense of ethics. Though, as we'll see, some might be inclined to obey a god out of a sense of dread or out of a need to manipulate him into granting a desired outcome, Deuteronomy offers the language of healthy relationship between God and his people. Deuteronomy portrays God not as one people should be afraid of but whom they should respect. Deuteronomy also portrays God as one who cannot be manipulated or bribed. People cannot do something to get God to favor them.

Deuteronomy significantly balances the world of Leviticus. In theological terms Leviticus has emphasized God as transcendent, one who is above the moral messiness of the world. God's people approach him on his terms; they must not update their religious ideals to match cultural trends and expectations. The nations surrounding the Israelites are used to stories about gods and goddesses engaging in sexual and murderous encounters with humans.[30] Israel's God does not stoop to such unseemly activities. God's holiness keeps him separate from the world, even though it also drives moments of divine judgment directed against infractions of the covenant. Deuteronomy balances out the view of God emphasized by his separateness by also underscoring God's desire to advance the well-being of his covenant people. It is full of words such as *love, heart, bless* and *give*, which are distributed throughout the writing.[31] Deuteronomy presents God intervening for his people's well-being, without compromising his holiness. In theological terms God is said to be immanent, in some way present with them, intervening on their behalf. Leviticus and Deuteronomy together show Israel to be in covenant relationship with a transcendent-immanent God.[32]

Structurally, Deuteronomy appears highly organized. The first three chapters offer a historical retrospective from the events at Mount Horeb (Sinai) to the activities at the Israelites' current location on the east side of the Jordan River, opposite the city of Jericho. Deuteronomy 4–11 give a broad overview of the Israelites' covenantal obligations, repeating the Ten Commandments in chapter 5 while underscoring the people's need to be loyal to God, especially in refraining from idolatry. Deuteronomy 12–26 contain more detailed laws. It is the largest running section of laws in Torah. Deuteronomy 27–30 outline covenantal blessings and curses—promises of divine intervention for their well-being when the nation maintains covenant faithfulness; promises of divine intervention for their detriment when the nation violates their covenant, with their being sent into exile to another nation as the ultimate curse. That section ends with a final plea from Moses to the Israelites, urging them to choose the life that God offers them. The last segment, Deuteronomy 31–34, recounts the transfer of power from Moses to his successor, Joshua, ending with two hymns from Moses and a description of the manner of his death.

The language of healthy relationship. Israel, God's people, is in covenant relationship with God. The language of Deuteronomy depicts a healthy, sincere relationship. Consider one of the best known sayings from Deuteronomy, a saying known as the *Shema,* Hebrew for opening word *Hear*:

> *Hear, O Israel: the Lord is our God, the Lord alone. You shall love the Lord your God with all your heart, and with all your soul, and with all your might. Keep these words that I am commanding you today in your heart.* **Deut 6:4-6**

The command urges the Israelites, as God's people, to love God with their entire being.[33] That love cannot be faked. It must be sincere. Performing an act in order to acquire something does not count. The Israelites are not to attempt to manipulate God, as though he could be influenced. The Israelites are called to obey from their heart. Mere outward performance is unacceptable. When the behavior concerns moral activity, the ethics supporting those morals would stem directly from eager love for God expressed through obedience.[34] This is an essential, positive aspect of Torah's overall ethical vision.

Consider another, similar statement:

> *So now, O Israel, what does the Lord your God require of you? Only to fear the Lord your God, to walk in all his ways, to love him, to serve the Lord your God with all your heart and with all your soul, and to keep the commandments of the Lord your God and his decrees that I am commanding you today, for your well-being.* **Deut 10:12-13**

The Israelites are to obey God's laws sincerely, from their hearts. Some of those laws have moral bearing. When God's people live out the ethical motivations those words advocate, they are doing so because they are serving God. They are to love God with their entire being.

Deuteronomy 10 goes on to say:

> *Although heaven and the heaven of heavens belong to the LORD your God, the earth with all that is in it, yet the LORD set his heart in love on your ancestors alone and chose you, their descendants after them, out of all the peoples, as it is today. Circumcise, then, the foreskin of your heart, and do not be stubborn any longer. For the LORD your God is God of gods and Lord of lords, the great God, mighty and awesome, who is not partial and takes no bribe, who executes justice for the orphan and the widow, and who loves the strangers, providing them food and clothing.* **Deut 10:14-18**

Again, we have the language of healthy relationships. Here, God is portrayed as the one who has first loved his people, who has "set his heart in love" on their ancestors, and as a result has chosen the Israelites, their descendants, to be his people. This expresses God's willing choice, coming from his very core, his heart. In response to that, God's people are being urged to remove from their own core whatever hinders their sincere interaction with God. They are to circumcise their hearts, a metaphor rooted in the sign of the Abrahamic covenant.

The statement underscores the absolute supremacy of Israel's covenant God.[35] It also declares God's royal impartiality and his mercy for the weak. In reinforcing God's impartiality, Deuteronomy states that God takes no bribe. Bribery and manipulation belong to unhealthy relational systems. Here, Israel is being told that performing manipulative activity to try to get God to act on their behalf is an affront to the impartiality of the kingly character of God, whom they should know.[36] In that one statement Deuteronomy takes out of consideration one major, unhealthy motive for performing moral deeds. According to that language God does not countenance people doing good acts to obtain a desirable outcome, whether that behavior be moral or cultic/religious (e.g., saying a ritual prayer without meaning it or offering an animal sacrifice). God is a good God who helps those in need. He does that without partiality, without playing favorites. They should behave in the same way, which the words of Deuteronomy 10:19 declare: "You shall also love the stranger, for you were strangers in the land of Egypt." They should know God as the one who has cared deeply for them and acted for their well-being. They should do the same for others out of sincere regard for the well-being of those others in response to their needs.[37]

Israel is meant to take seriously its relationship with God. Deuteronomy 7–9 are filled with warnings for the Israelites to learn from the sins of their forbears in the wilderness. But those chapters also herald God's concern for them. Consider the following:

> It was not because you were more numerous than any other people that the LORD set his heart on you and chose you—for you were the fewest of all peoples. It was because the LORD loved you and kept the oath that he swore to your ancestors, that the LORD has brought you out with a mighty hand, and redeemed you from the house of slavery, from the hand of Pharaoh king of Egypt. Know therefore that the LORD your God is God, the faithful God who maintains covenant loyalty with those who love him and keep his commandments, to a thousand generations, and who repays in their own person those who reject him. He does not delay but repays in their own person those who reject him. Therefore, observe diligently the commandment—the statutes, and the ordinances—that I am commanding you today. **Deut 7:7-11**

Moses' speech here emphasizes that God loves his people, even as he also longs for their obedience. At the same time, God does not excuse disobedience. God's people are to obey willingly, out of their covenant relationship with him. Though there are divine consequences for disobedience, Deuteronomy is not advocating obedience so as to avoid punishment. Punishment will happen as a consequence of covenantal faithlessness. But in maintaining their covenant with God, they need not worry. Those in right relationship with God do what he wants as an outgrowth of that relationship.[38]

Deuteronomy 8 proceeds to urge the Israelites to maintain their covenant loyalty to God based both on how he has cared for them in the past (Deut 8:1-5, 14-16), and how he will bring them to a good land (Deut 8:6-10) and empower them to prosper there in the future (Deut 8:11-13, 18). Deuteronomy 9 reminds them that they are not righteous people who deserve what God is giving them. They deserve judgment. God is doing something different for them, while simultaneously judging the wicked inhabitants of the land the Israelites are about to acquire. God is righteous and moral, prosecuting those who need to be judged; he also desires to pursue a strong covenant relationship with his people. They are to come to know him well. He loves them. He wants them to love him. Mutual love also informs this ethic of relationship.

Laws that are meant to instruct. Let's revisit some words already quoted in the first chapter of this book:

> See, just as the LORD my God has charged me, I now teach you statutes and ordinances for you to observe in the land that you are about to enter and occupy. You must observe them diligently, for this will show your wisdom and discernment to the peoples, who, when they hear all these statutes, will say, "Surely this great nation is a wise and discerning people!" For what other great nation has a god so near to it as the LORD our God is whenever we call to him? And what other great nation has statutes and ordinances as just as this entire law that I am setting before you today? **Deut 4:5-8**

Notice that Moses' aim is to teach the laws. These words in Deuteronomy 4 are part of the beginning of a hortatory section, a set of words designed to urge its hearers/readers to accept and enact what it says. They suggest a form of teaching much more profound than rote memorization.[39] Though eventually the writing produces a listing of laws, that listing is full of language going beyond the merely legal, offering descriptions and explanations that differ in tone from the kinds of lists we observed in Exodus 21–23.

Notice, for example, the rationale behind the law requiring capital punishment for disobeying the legal ruling of a priest or judge: "So you shall purge the evil from Israel. All the people will hear and be afraid, and will not act presumptuously again" (Deut 17:12-13). The people are meant to learn not merely from what is written but from what is enacted.[40] Other rationale in laws with moral implications varies, from showing God's desire to bless them[41] to the need to protect the reputation of those who have been misused,[42] or even to avoiding what God abhors.[43] The specific stipulations listed in Deuteronomy 12–26 are full of such language.

Significantly Deuteronomy 4 declares that the writing's laws are instructive not only for the Israelites but for "the peoples," nations other than God's people. They can learn about God's covenantal nearness to his own people. That can lead them to observe the wisdom of God's people for having such laws. Those laws can teach them something too.[44]

The microethical orientation of Deuteronomy's laws. Though all of the laws we are exploring in Exodus, Leviticus and Deuteronomy are given to the entire nation, the laws tend to focus on local, interpersonal interactions within communities. We will note some significant exceptions to that, but observe that Deuteronomy urges its laws to be taught and enacted at the basic level of society, the home. We have already seen the initial words from the *Shema*. Those words continue:

> *Keep these words that I am commanding you today in your heart. Recite them to your children and talk about them when you are at home and when you are away, when you lie down and when you rise. Bind them as a sign on your hand, fix them as an emblem on your forehead, and write them on the doorposts of your house and on your gates.* **Deut 6:6-9**

The laws[45] are to become a way of life for families.[46] They are to form the core subject matter of instruction from parents to children at all times of the day, no matter where they may be. They are to be connected with what they see day in and day out. The laws are meant to be internalized, not imposed. They are to govern how people live among and interact with each other.

There are, however, some macroethical exceptions. Individual villages are to have storage facilities where people bring one-tenth of their produce every three years, collected for Levites, resident aliens, widows or orphans, all in need because of their landlessness (Deut 14:28-29). That sounds more like a policy one layer removed from the practice of individuals or families themselves giving directly to aliens, widows and orphans the way other laws instruct (Deut 24:19-22). Likewise, establishing cities of refuge to protect people from revenge when they have accidentally killed someone (Deut 19:1-10) is a national provision, not an individual's responsibility. It is especially concerned with establishing legitimate blame and curbing inhumane vengeance.[47] It is also microethically valuable. It upholds the importance of human life while discouraging dishonesty from someone trying to cast a murder as an accident.

These exceptions reinforce the communal aspect of laws, aspects that we saw reflected in Exodus and Leviticus. The laws are aimed at people or a nation who are God's people. They are not aimed simply at a collection of independent individuals.

Covenantal orientation of Deuteronomy's laws. As in Exodus and Leviticus, so in Deuteronomy: its laws are part of the covenant between God and his people, Israel. That covenant becomes the means by which God works out his covenant promises to bless Abraham and all nations. Even more than Exodus and Leviticus, Deuteronomy shows how obedience to the laws leads to God's people, the descendants of Abraham, being blessed in the land that God is giving them. Most of Deuteronomy's references to God as giver reflect God's covenantal faithfulness in upholding his promises to Abraham.[48] That faithfulness both displays what God is doing for Israel, the descendants of Abraham, and provides a major motive for why they should obey in the good land that God is giving them. God is for them. They must be for God.

Deuteronomy is full of language disclosing consequences both for obeying and disobeying the covenant.

> If you heed these ordinances, by diligently observing them, the LORD your God will maintain with you the covenant loyalty that he swore to your ancestors; he will love you, bless you, and multiply you; he will bless the fruit of your womb and the fruit of your ground, your grain and your wine and your oil, the increase of your cattle and the issue of your flock, in the land that he swore to your ancestors to give you. You shall be the most blessed of peoples, with neither sterility nor barrenness among you or your livestock. The LORD will turn away from you every illness; all the dread diseases of Egypt that you experienced, he will not inflict on you, but he will lay them on all who hate you. **Deut 7:12-15**

Does that mean that God's people should obey to get a reward and avoid a punishment? The consequences are part of the covenant between God and Israel. That covenant does not establish a merit system that advocates earning rewards and avoiding punishments. Pagan expectations may work that way, but the covenant between God and Israel does not.[49] Pagan expectations point to a manipulative relationship in which people, sometimes out of extreme fear, perform deeds to convince a deity to enact a good consequence or remove a bad. Deuteronomy displays something quite different. God overwhelmingly desires to lavish goodness on his people. Israel is in covenant relationship with God. That covenant involves an agreement. God promises to keep Israel as his people. Israel's responsibility is to obey, maintaining loyalty to God. As part of that agreement, God promises to intervene in the affairs of his people, for their good when they obey and for their correction when they disobey. But Israel always remains God's people, never abandoned, regardless of performance.[50]

Deuteronomy addresses a nation, not individuals. It emphasizes Israel's obedience as a people. It does not emphasize what God will do to individual Israelites for their own personal obedience or disobedience. When the nation, as God's people, upholds God's laws, God's people can expect his intervention for their national benefit, not as a crude reward for performance but as God's expressed covenantal desire for their well-being. When his people maintain their relationship with God through heart-centered, sincere obedience, God will give them sincere, heart-motivated blessing. The covenantal terms show God's desire focused on blessing his people out of his covenant loyalty to them.

But the flipside is also true. When God's people turn their heart away from God, neglecting their covenant, forsaking their loyalty to him and consequently disobeying his laws, God promises to intervene for their short-term detriment, not as flippant, angry punishment, but as strong correction to lead his people back to their senses. It also is part of the covenantal arrangement that God has offered them. God's intervention is not arbitrary but fixed, spelled out as part of the agreement. They should expect it when they fail to uphold their part of the bargain. They should not be surprised.

What we see in Deuteronomy vaguely resembles contractual features that people might know from their own cultures.[51] For example, consider the person who signs an agreement to rent or lease an apartment. That person promises to pay the exact amount of rent on time at the beginning of each month for the duration of the lease. If the renter fails to pay on time, the renter must also pay a late fee, not because the landlord is meanly punishing the renter for bad behavior, but because that fee is part of the rental agreement. If the renter skips out before the lease expires, the landlord can come after the renter for the amount owed, not because the landlord is punishing the renter but because the lease contract allows that to happen. Likewise, if something in the apartment wears out, for example a pipe bursts, the landlord is obliged to fix it, not as a reward to the renter for being a good resident but because that also is part of the lease agreement.

Those dynamics are important to recognize when considering laws in Deuteronomy. The Israelites are not being encouraged to obey to earn reward points from God, nor are they being warned against disobedience simply to avoid punishment. They are to consider their covenant relationship with God. They are being offered lists of benefits they can expect for covenantal faithfulness and detriments for disloyalty as part of their covenant with God.

Those lists certainly encourage obedience and discourage disobedience. But they are not primary motivators. The Israelites are to perform out of love for God, to whom they are connected by covenant. God desires to bless them as their God always. When they obey laws, they are to do so because they are God's people, not to get a positive or avoid a negative consequence.[52]

Deuteronomy 27–29 offers detailed lists of blessings for obedience and curses for disobedience. Those lists have been anticipated by the comments from Deuteronomy 7, quoted earlier, as well as from Deuteronomy 11. They point to the lengths that God will go to enforce their covenantal faithfulness while expressing his own. The words of the covenant expect all people to learn, including children and foreigners:[53]

> *The next generation, your children who rise up after you, as well as the foreigner who comes from a distant country, will see the devastation of that land and the afflictions with which the Lord has afflicted it . . . they and indeed all the nations will wonder, "Why has the Lord done thus to this land? What caused this great display of anger?" They will conclude, "It is because they abandoned the covenant of the Lord, the God of their ancestors, which he made with them when he brought them out of the land of Egypt. They turned and served other gods."* **Deut 29:22, 24-26**

Everyone will know from the Israelites' exile that they have broken their covenant with God, disloyally worshiping other gods. Their punishment provides visible evidence that God does what he says he will do.

Israel's covenant relationship with God is central to Torah's ethical vision. Israel must connect with God, stay connected with God and reconnect with God as part of its covenant with God. It is always important that Israel maintains steadfast loyalty to God and rekindles that loyalty whenever it diminishes. Moses' closing words in Deuteronomy 30 indicate that:

> *When all these things have happened to you, the blessings and the curses that I have set before you, if you call them to mind among all the nations where the Lord your God has driven you, and return to the Lord your God, and you and your children obey him with all your heart and with all your soul, just as I am commanding you today, then the Lord your God will restore your fortunes and have compassion on you, gathering you again from all the peoples among whom the Lord your God has scattered you.* **Deut 30:1-3**

Those are words that have been anticipated earlier in Deuteronomy 4:

> *When you have . . . become complacent in the land, if you act corruptly by making an idol in the form of anything . . . I call heaven and earth to witness against you today that you will soon utterly perish from the land that you are crossing the Jordan to occupy. . . . The LORD will scatter you among the peoples. . . . From there you will seek the LORD your God, and you will find him if you search after him with all your heart and soul. In your distress, when all these things have happened to you in time to come, you will return to the LORD your God and heed him. Because the LORD your God is a merciful God, he will neither abandon you nor destroy you; he will not forget the covenant with your ancestors that he swore to them.* **Deut 4:25-27, 29-31**

Deuteronomy makes relationship with God primary. The biggest affront to God is to go after other gods, who are not really gods at all. God's people should expect God to delight in their loyalty to him; they should also not expect God to tolerate disloyalty on their part. Deuteronomy advocates covenant loyalty to God. Good morals will flow out of that loyal relationship, which encourages God's people to know him more and more.

The range of Deuteronomy's laws. Let's recall our working definition of ethics: *ethics involves enacting behavior that advances good or hinders harm in one's world.* We are now probing how specific laws in Deuteronomy 12–26 advocate advancing good and hindering harm in the world. Many of those laws have clear moral bearing, even if many do not.

We have already considered the first most obvious of such laws in Deuteronomy 14:28-29, where Israelites are told to store produce within their towns as food for the landless and unprotected. Doing that results in God's direct blessing of their land, underscoring the value of people helping others in need. The same concern overflows into the next chapter of Deuteronomy where people are instructed to let off the hook, on a periodic basis, those who have borrowed money from them without paying back in full, activity similar to what we saw in Leviticus 25. The idea stems from the statement that they are to have no needy among them, since God will bless them (Deut 15:4). They are to be openhanded toward the needy in their midst (Deut 15:7-11), microethically to their neighbors, whom they know.[54] Though openhandedness initially is promoted in the context of relieving their debtors, it certainly applies beyond that.[55] Even those who have sold themselves as slaves to relieve their indebtedness need to be released on a periodic basis (Deut 15:12-18). And they are to be done so in an extraordinary manner, sent away with ample supply of produce from the land and flocks they have been tending (Deut 15:14). Why? God had intervened to release them from slavery in their past (Deut 15:15). All of this activity is rooted in God's benevolence. God's people should know him as a giving God; his covenant people should thus be giving people.

Activity reflecting a sense of morality does not appear again until Deuteronomy 16:18-20, where judges are urged to offer impartial judgment. They are told to pursue "justice, and only justice," referring to an evenhanded, impartial application of right and wrong. The words directly echo what has already been said in Deuteronomy 10:17-18 about their covenant God, "who is not partial and takes no bribe, who executes justice for the orphan and the widow, and who loves the strangers, providing them food and clothing." Even kings, when the people choose to have them, must be equally subject to the laws of the covenant (Deut 10:17-18; 17:14-20), rather than sidestepping them as words only for common folk. Though judges and kings are governing officials, they must perform their duties in the fear of God with covenantal faithfulness that offers among other things, a moral foundation.[56]

Remember again that we are exploring laws. They are not moral instructions, even if some are instructive morally. We should continue to distinguish between legality and morality. What kinds of harm do these laws aim to hinder? What kinds of good do they attempt to advance? By probing those questions we can begin to acquire a clearer sense of the ethics that Deuteronomy advances.

Let's now probe the morality of other relevant laws. They are listed in the order in which they appear, headed by a summary of the gist of their topics.

Protection against land theft (Deut 19:14). Though this underscores the sacredness of ancestral land, it also shows how what is given to another belongs to another.[57]

The necessity of truthful, multiple witnesses to establish public guilt (Deut 19:15-21). The law makes reliable, truthful information essential to fair court dealings. Punishing a malicious witness with the same harm intended for the victim shows how damaging falsehood can be. This carries further what we first saw in Exodus 23:1-3.

Instructions governing warfare (Deut 20:1-20), including releasing from military service both those who are in new life circumstances and those who are fearful, offering terms of peace to enemy towns and protecting fruit-bearing trees in the vicinity of besieged towns. The section is filled with covenantal language depicting God fighting for his people, complete with the realities of death in war. It, like Deuteronomy 7:1-6, offers a sober divine sanctioning of killing Canaanite inhabitants, a unique, specialized circumstance. Also reflected are attitudes about war to which some might object. Yet in discussing war Torah shows the same distinction made in many societies about the difference between killing in battle and in homicide, which has just been dealt with in part in Deuteronomy 19:1-13. Further, embedded in these laws is a merciful concern that restricts violence. In view of the possibility of death, those in new circumstances, along with the fearful, are excused from war.[58] Peace may be made with distant opponents. Senseless destruction of plants and vegetation is forbidden.

Protections for women taken captive in battle (Deut 21:10-14). Again, though the legal circumstances stem from war, activity that many could find morally objectionable, the laws here advocate treating captive women as humans, not as objects to be used and discarded. Against the background of men mistreating women in a patriarchal society, the law curbs harm against women found in an especially weak situation. The law fosters both familial and sexual respect.[59]

Protections for women in polygamous marriages (Deut 21:15-17). Without remarking on the morality of polygamy, this law deals with the messiness of that practice, hindering harm against the son of an unloved wife. Emotional attachment is not what governs familial responsibility. Rather, the existence of the familial relationship itself is paramount. Though polygamy may be messy, marriage itself upholds an order to life that must be maintained.

Consequences for disobedient sons (Deut 21:18-21). This takes further what we've already seen in Exodus 21:15, 21:17 and Leviticus 20:9, which dealt with children who strike or curse their parents. The language here in Deuteronomy implies an older child who has acquired a reputation for over-indulging in both food and alcohol, symptomatic of one who does not heed his parents. The death penalty for persistent, defiance may appear extreme, but the law underscores the importance of parent-child respect, protecting family integrity.

Responsibilities toward a neighbor's livestock and moveable property (Deut

22:1-4). Previously we had seen laws in Exodus portraying the responsibility to care for an enemy's donkey. The laws here hinder the harm stemming from people looking the other way when anyone's moveable property is out of place, whether stray animals or dropped garments. It upholds the value of people looking after those around them, instead of looking away or taking it for themselves—finders are not to be keepers.

Prohibition of cross-dressing (Deut 22:5). Probably prohibiting more than the mere wearing of unfit clothing, the law upholds the distinction between the sexes, important to the created order.[60]

Responsibilities toward nesting birds (Deut 22:6-7). Like the prohibition against destroying fruit trees when in siege against a city, this also supports the creation mandate of good land and animal care beyond the bounds of one's own home.

How to deal with false and true claims that a new bride is not a virgin (Deut 22:13-21). The legal circumstances may appear unusual to some readers. Why should evidence of a bride's virginity matter?[61] But the law supports marriage as the only sphere of proper sexual activity. More pointedly it protects a woman who might otherwise be discarded, left helpless and unwanted with an untruthfully sullied reputation.

How to deal with adultery (Deut 22:22) and other forms of inappropriate unmarried sex (Deut 22:23-30). As with similar laws in Exodus and Leviticus, these uphold the uniqueness of the marital bond as the only sphere for sexual activity, in accordance with the created order. A man having sex with another's wife or fiancée is subject to the death penalty. The married woman and the betrothed woman who appears to be complicit in the act are also to be killed. The man who forces himself sexually on an unbetrothed virgin must pay a fine and marry the girl. Sexual activity belongs in one place only—a marriage.[62]

How to treat escaped slaves (Deut 23:15-16). The laws in Torah do allow slavery to exist. But this law protects escaped slaves; they are to be harbored, not oppressed. When combined with the release of slaves mandated by the laws in Deuteronomy 15, these laws significantly soften the institution.[63]

Prohibitions against cult prostitutes and prostitutes' fees (Deut 23:17-18). See also Leviticus 19:29. The law here principally proscribes the religious practice of prostitutes serving at the temple (which will not be built until the reign of King Solomon, but which is anticipated in Deut 12:5-7). It labels that practice as abhorrent, along with the money any prostitute would earn.[64] By underscoring the damage to God's reputation from that kind of activity, the law again upholds the proper, God-pleasing sphere of sexual activity in marriage.

Prohibitions against charging interest to Israelites (Deut 23:19-20). Similar to Exodus 22:25 and Leviticus 25:36-37, the law forbids Israelites from charging interest to one another in commercial transactions; it may be charged to foreigners. The law upholds the exclusivity of the covenant between God and his people. Supporting that regulation, though, is the importance of not taking advantage of the weakness of others. People borrow money because they are in need. Interest would aggravate that need.[65] The law supports the broader importance of caring for people in one's immediate contact.

What one may and may not eat of a neighbor's produce (Deut 23:24-25). The law protects a landowner from freeloaders. Laws in Leviticus 19:9-10 require landowners to allow poor and alien to harvest certain sections of their fields. A similar regard appears in Deuteronomy 24:18-22. The laws here keep the beneficiaries of that practice from taking advantage of others' acts of kindness. Even the poor can be greedy. Though they have no property, they must still value the property of others. Combined, these laws foster mutual respect between the haves and the have-nots.[66]

Protections for divorced women (Deut 24:1-4). In regulating a practice that itself has questionable morality, Deuteronomy's laws once more curb immoral abuse stemming from legally permitted practices. In this case the law helps a woman who is in danger of being tossed about between two men who claim to find her objectionable.[67] Legally, the divorced woman cannot remarry her first husband after being divorced by her second. Morally, people cannot be reckless in terminating marriages, whose integrity is part of the created order.[68]

What to do with kidnappers (Deut 24:7). Similar to Exodus 21:16, the law here forbids stealing Israelites and selling them into slavery.[69] The death penalty for the perpetrators underscores the travesty of the activity as a direct affront to the sacredness of God's covenant people. In legally forbidding such dealings with Israelites, the law is not tacitly approving that activity for non-Israelites. The law points to all enslaving activity as an affront to others' humanness.[70]

Protections for poor people (Deut 24:10-15), for indebted people (Deut 24:6, 17) and for aliens and orphans, including allowing them access to personal fields to pick food (Deut 24:17-22). A series of laws protect various weak members, mandating justice to the poor, widow and fatherless; forbidding holding as collateral a mill, millstone (required for making bread, and hence for being able to eat) or a widow's only piece of property, her garment; leaving dropped crops for the alien, the fatherless and the widow. We have seen a similar set of laws in both Exodus and Leviticus. All those are supported by the reminder that they too had been oppressed in Egypt. Regard for the weak will bring God's blessing to them. By appealing for support to God's merciful acts on their behalf in rescuing them from Egypt, they elevate the moral correctness of helping out any people in weak situations.

Kindness to working animals (Deut 25:4). The law advocates humane treatment of animals that help the farmer obtain food; the ox treading out the grain for people's benefit should also be allowed to eat from it while doing the work. It is one more law (with Deut 20:19-20; 22:6) instructing people to treat the nonhuman creation well.

An improper way for wives to fight for their husbands (Deut 25:11-12). The law protects a man from potential genital mutilation at the hand (literally) of the wife of a man whom he is fighting. The harshness of the penalty, the loss of a hand (the only place we see that penalty), underscores the seriousness of an act that threatens the man's ability to reproduce.[71] Though the law addresses a family situation, it does uphold the importance of procreation, which again, is part of the created order.

Using honest weights and measures in commerce (Deut 25:13-16). The law enforces basic honesty in business dealings, similar to Leviticus 19:35-37. A person cannot use a lesser measure to sell produce (and thus sell less for more) and then use a greater measure to buy (and thus buy more for less). But the legal sense of honesty here points to the importance of honesty as a lifestyle. The references to God giving them land and to God being repulsed by dishonesty reinforce that importance.

The laws themselves end with a prayer to be recited at the giving of the tithe for the landless and unprotected (Deut 26:12-15). That prayer asks God to do what he had promised in his covenant with them—to bless both them and the ground of their land. Clearly, care for the disadvantaged must have a privileged place in the thinking of God's people.

As we observed with laws in Exodus and Leviticus, the wide-ranging list of legal issues is hardly exhaustive. It does not instruct about people's every act. When considering their relevance for morality, they can only provide a basic starting point. But that beginning is useful. Those who, as Deuteronomy 6:6 instructs, put the laws on their heart have a valuable moral compass.

According to the sense of ethics advanced within these laws in Deuteronomy, God's people are to be those who are kind, generous, merciful, honest and helpful. They should aim to uplift and protect those in their midst who are poor, weak or disadvantaged. They should know that sexual activity remains within the bounds of marriage. They should live to uphold the integrity of the family unit. They should also look after the belongings and concerns of others, not merely their own. Becoming people who do such things is to flow out of their relationship with God, whom they are to love and obey sincerely, from their heart. God has a high regard for them as his people. They too should have a high regard for others.

The ethics behind the morality being upheld is not always directly transparent. The most obvious rationale appears in support of caring for the weak, with appeals to the Israelite history of having been delivered from weakness in the land of Egypt. But Deuteronomy also communicates that the Israelites can expect to receive blessing from their covenant-keeping God. That encourages them to offer blessing and kindness to others. Because God is giving them a good land, they should pass that goodness to those in need. When applied to commercial transactions, dishonesty appears to be an affront to God's blessing to them. Less obviously implied is the sense of upholding the created order, though that certainly stands behind both the regard for marriage and family issues, and the regard for plants and animals. Deuteronomy, when combined with perspectives from Exodus and Leviticus, supports a way of thinking that draws a God perspective into all aspects of life. How God has formed them, treated them and wants to help them drives the way his people should think about treating others. They must come to know God more and more in awareness of his merciful, holy blessing of them in the good land he has given them, maintaining relationship with God by keeping their covenant, from their heart.

SUMMING IT UP: WHAT HAVE WE LEARNED FROM LEVITICUS AND DEUTERONOMY?

o The laws flow out of Israel's covenant with God.

o The laws are to be kept as Israel's responsibility for covenant maintenance.

o Israel is to keep the laws because Israel is God's people.

o These are relational motivations. Obedience is to flow out of the people's covenantal relationship with God.

o The laws are meant to instruct, not merely regulate. Legality and morality are not equivalents.

o Readers must consider the good being advanced and the harm being hindered by individual laws.

o The laws cover a variety of topics with moral relevance, but they do not attempt to exhaust the possibilities of topics.

o The ethics flowing out of the laws affect a community. Individuals learn ethics from living with ethical people.

o The ethics flowing out of many laws are connected to God's own activities and character.

With regard to Leviticus in particular, we have seen:

o God is holy.

o Because Israel is in covenant relationship with a holy God, Israel must also be holy.

o Righteously pure living is an essential aspect of that holiness.

o When God's people aim at God's holiness, being moral will be one outcome.

o The sense of morality will reflect purity, order and wholeness in relating to others while avoiding impurity, disorder and diminishment.

o That sense of morality will affect activities widely ranging from sexual behavior to a regard for the poor and the weak in their midst, to love of neighbor as an alternative to vengeance and grudge-bearing.

With regard to Deuteronomy in particular, we have seen:

o Deuteronomy emphasizes God's loving covenantal commitment to his people.

o Their covenantal responsibility is to return that love to God with all their being.

o Sincere obedience to God's laws is to be an expression of their love for God.

o The laws with moral import tend to point to God's people being kind, generous, merciful, honest, helpful and sexually upright.

o God's people must actively and concretely help the poor and disadvantaged they are in contact with.

o God's acts to rescue them and God's desire to bless them contribute to the sense of moral rightness they are to uphold.

o When God's people love God sincerely, they will learn from his laws to become people who bless others.

PULLING IT ALL TOGETHER

Our exploration of Torah's ethical vision began in Genesis with an introduction to the divine order established in creation. As part of that order God made people in his image, leaving them as his viceroys to procreate and to subdue his creation. The pattern of a husband and a wife in partnership setting up a distinct family unit was an explicit part of that order, as was the exclusive sexual unashamedness between them. The failure of humans to obey God's initial command in the Garden of Eden led to a violent, self-aggrandizing human population that God committed by covenant to allow to exist rather than repeatedly and justly to destroy. Genesis's ultimate solution to the restoration of world order was portrayed through God's special interactions with a man named Abram/Abraham, through whom he would eventually bless the entire world.

Exodus, Leviticus, Numbers and Deuteronomy offer details about the covenant that God makes with his people, the Israelites, the direct descendants of Abraham. That covenant appears as the means by which God begins to work out his promises to Abraham. The covenant formally makes Israel God's people, his treasured possession out of all the nations of the earth. In return for becoming his people, they agree to keep his laws, knowing God's mercy in having rescued them from oppression in accordance with his covenant with Abraham. God is a holy God. In entering into a covenant with God, the Israelites commit themselves to a life of holiness. When they follow his laws, they will be a holy people. God also loves them and desires to act for their well-being. He wants the Israelites to love him in return, sincerely, from their heart. They will show their love to him by obeying his laws from their hearts. Out of that obedience will flow blessing to others, which itself stems from God blessing them as he promises in his covenant.

God's mercy, holiness and love combine as the foundation for the strong sense of right and wrong emerging from the laws that God's people are to keep. In maintaining their covenant with God, God's people perform many behaviors that advance good and hinder harm in their world. Superficially this resembles a divine command system. Torah teaches God's people to put its words on their hearts. Those words provide an essential foundation to developing a basic moral sense of direction. A person whose moral compass is set to the words of the Torah can readily say "That is not good" when confronted with situations having potential for evil.

What Torah says is important precisely because it is perceived to come from the God of the covenant. God has shown himself to be trustworthy. He has rescued his people from bondage. He has extended his love to them (Deut 10:15). His laws are for their "lasting good" (Deut 6:24). What those laws say is important, and doing what they say because they say so has validity, precisely because God has shown himself to be consistently righteous, kind and merciful toward them. There is no arbitrariness about the Bible's God.

But Torah does more than advocate submission to the commands of a beneficent ruler. A closer examination reveals that Torah advocates something more than mere adherence to God's commands. Torah advances a covenant between God and Israel. Embedded in that covenant is a relationship between God and his people, a relationship begun in mercy, encased in holiness and sealed with loyal covenantal love. God's people are to know God more and more in his mercy, holiness and love, especially as those qualities are expressed through God's laws.

Some of the laws provide rationale for obedience, advocating more than rote compliance. Consider the laws governing treatment of the weak and disadvantaged. They instruct the Israelites to recall their own history of mistreatment to avoid damaging others. They themselves should uphold the weak and disadvantaged because they themselves were wronged; their own experiences of being hurt must help them to avoid hurting others. Since their covenant God rescues the weak, they must embrace the same concern, beginning at the very least with the poor, the widow, the fatherless and the alien. But these laws also encourage God's people to assist anyone in weak circumstances. In answer to, Why are you doing that? one might respond, "I belong to a people who know what it is like to be mistreated in weakness. Why would I leave anyone else to endure misery? God saved us. He wants us to help others as he helped us." A similar, more positive line of reasoning may be inferred from God's commitment to bless his people in the good land he is giving them. As recipients of that beneficence, they are encouraged to help others: "My hands are open to you, because God's hand has been open to me. All I have, I have from him. God's desire to bless us as his people leads me to bless others."

Other rationale flows from Torah's creation order. Israel is in covenant relationship with the Creator God, who brings order from disorder and wholeness from brokenness. Israel itself is brought from disorder to order in becoming God's people, coming into covenant relationship with the Creator God. That relationship itself is supposed to foster God's establishment of order in a disordered world that is out of touch with him. The covenant with Israel is established as a means by which God blesses all the nations of the world. Moral rightness upholds the good order created by God, as many of the laws do. But the world is now disordered and incomplete, with disordered people out of touch with God. Interpersonal actions that address the weaknesses and incompleteness of that disorder are also right. Torah-obedient people would reflect the basic created order in their actions. The laws encourage them to

- Preserve the order of the family unit, which includes a strong sense of the husband and wife sexual bond, a sense of children as a blessing, and respect for parents, even when leaving them to form a new family unit.

- Aim to manage their immediately surrounding environment well, including both land and animals.

- Be aware that the world is full of imperfect people, the most extreme of whom express themselves violently. They would do what they could to stem violence in their own lives, resisting whatever practices lead to harmful chaos in the lives of others. That would make them champions of life, even for the weakest in their society.

- Be honest, even-handed people who uphold the fullness of others' property, even the property of an enemy.

- Be responsible community members who shun destructive thoughts and actions in favor of correction and love.

- Have a sense of God's propriety, as expressed in his holiness, which they are to reflect in all they do and say.

- Be mindful of how God desires to bless them, encouraging them to extend that blessing to their interactions with others.

This is not a fully detailed system of distinguishing right from wrong.[72] But it encourages people to reflect the nature of the God they are connected to, the order of the world he initially designed, and the blessing he wishes to bring to it.[73] We have an ethic of relationship here. Ethics emerges from a sincere, growing love for the holy God, who has first loved his people, and whose desire is to bless them. The instructive words of Torah's laws promote that merciful, holy love.

The concerns here are largely microethical. People are being prodded to consider their day-to-day interactions with others. When people do what is right, they have a positive effect on their communities at large as others observe and are encouraged to do likewise. Torah advocates God's people eagerly living up to the standards of their covenant with him. When they do that sincerely, from their hearts, broader social issues get taken care of in the process.

Torah's ethic of relationship is exclusive. Torah depicts a covenant between God and his people, Israel. Unless people belong to Israel, they do not belong to that covenant. Torah presents hundreds of laws, many of which have no obvious bearing on ethics at all, but which God's covenant people Israel must obey. While many of those laws underscore the uniqueness of that relationship, they can also alienate outsiders, who may even find some of them objectionable.[74]

Still, the sense of good advanced by many of the laws is supposed to resonate with those outside of the covenant: "You must observe [the laws] diligently, for this will show your wisdom and discernment to the peoples, who, when they hear all these statutes, will say, 'Surely this great nation is a wise and discerning people!'" (Deut 4:6). The ethical vision is shaped by God's people knowing God in unique covenantal relationship with him, a relationship that is meant to be both distinct from the nations and to point the way for the nations (see Ex 19:5-6). Thus, outsiders can learn from the standards and from God's people enacting them; outsiders can learn about the God who establishes those standards; and outsiders can also note the sensible rationale upholding many of those standards. They can be drawn to the God who is intensely, lovingly loyal in fulfilling his covenants. But unless one belongs specifically to the covenant being portrayed in the Torah, a person has neither the same, specific obligation nor the same, specific motivation to perform Torah's instructions. This will contrast with what we will see in other approaches to ethics found in the Bible, starting with chapter five.

Reflection Questions

1. How does God's holiness inform the sense of moral right and wrong conveyed by Leviticus?

2. What is healthy about the covenantal relationship between God and his people projected by Deuteronomy?

3. How does that healthy covenantal relationship affect both the sense of moral right and wrong and the attitudes about doing right and hindering wrong?

4. Pick an issue from the list in chapter three's reflection questions: life, families, others' property, society's weak. How do Leviticus's and Deuteronomy's perspectives add to ethical ways of thinking about them?

FOR FURTHER READING

Clements, Ronald E. "The Book of Deuteronomy." In *The New Interpreter's Bible.* Vol. 2. Nashville: Abingdon Press, 1998.

Wenham, Gordon J. *The Book of Leviticus.* New International Commentary on the Old Testament 3. Grand Rapids: Eerdmans, 1979.

Wright, Christopher J. H. *Old Testament Ethics for the People of God.* Downers Grove, IL: InterVarsity Press, 2004.

5

WISDOM AND CONSEQUENCES

The Book of Proverbs

INTRODUCTORY ISSUES

Let's go back to some basic principles from the introductory chapter.

- Ethics refers to how a person distinguishes right from wrong behavior.
- Ethics is also concerned with the reasons for why a person should choose what is good and abstain from what is not.

When we come to the world of proverbial wisdom, we come to an entirely new way of thinking, different from what we have seen in Torah. Torah's was a world of covenant. God was portrayed as having made a binding agreement with Abraham, Isaac and Jacob, and then committing himself to working that out by making a major covenant with the nation of Israel. That Mosaic or Israelite covenant became the means by which the Abrahamic covenantal promises were to be implemented. Within the framework of that Israelite covenant, laws were given to instruct God's people in God's ways. Some of those ways included activities that fall within the sphere of ethics.

When we enter into Proverbs' ethical vision, we discover a parallel world. There is no mention of the covenant between God and Abraham. Though later in this chapter we will explore Abrahamic implications, the name Abraham never appears in Proverbs. Likewise, there is no mention of the covenant between God and Israel. In fact apart from the opening line of Proverbs 1:1, where "Solomon . . . king of Israel" is named, the word *Israel* never appears either. There is thus no direct appeal to specific laws or commandments found in Torah. The Ten Commandments, which clearly

formed a foundational base for much of the behavior of God's people in
Torah, are never referred to in the world of Proverbs, even if sometimes law
in general is mentioned (see Prov 28:4, 7, 9; 29:18). Though God spoke and
intervened all throughout the Torah, with some of those activities being
summarized by Moses in Deuteronomy, God never speaks any words in
Proverbs. We certainly find similar moral standards in both the Torah and
Proverbs.[1] But morality and ethics are not the same. The ways of discerning
and the reasons for enacting the morality are different in both environments.

That said, Proverbs appeals in exclusive fashion to the LORD (YHWH),
Israel's covenant God, using language also appearing in the covenantal environment of Torah, especially of Deuteronomy.[2] In doing this Proverbs
does not base its points on the Torah or any other part of the Bible. It offers
a separate ethical vision, even though that vision can fit side by side with
Torah's, not only reinforcing similar moral concerns, but filling in the gaps
that Torah leaves.[3] Consider the following words:

> My child, do not forget my teaching,
> 　　but let your heart keep my commandments,
> for length of days and years of life
> 　　and abundant welfare they will give you.
> Do not let loyalty and faithfulness forsake you;
> 　　bind them around your neck,
> 　　write them on the tablet of your heart.
> So you will find favor and good repute
> 　　in the sight of God and of people. **Prov 3:1-4**

The speaker here is not God but an ideally wise father.[4] The language
appears to echo the kind of language we observed in Deuteronomy.
"Teaching" (Hebrew: *tôrâ*) is to be remembered, "commandments" are to be
kept in the "heart," with the result being lifelong "blessing." Covenantal
loyal love and faithfulness are to be written "on the tablet of [the] heart."
This sounds like Torah. But it is not Torah. The wise teacher is talking about
his own instruction, not any law. It is his wise teaching that is referred to
as commandment, not anything resembling the Ten Commandments or
other laws.[5]

Earlier, words worth comparing with a similar speech in Deuteronomy are found in Proverbs 1:24-28, where the principal speaker is not the wise teacher but Wisdom, personified as a woman:

> *Because I have called and you refused,*
> *   have stretched out my hand and no one heeded,*
> *and because you have ignored all my counsel*
> *   and would have none of my reproof,*
> *I also will laugh at your calamity;*
> *   I will mock when panic strikes you,*
> *when panic strikes you like a storm,*
> *   and your calamity comes like a whirlwind,*
> *   when distress and anguish come upon you.*
> *Then they will call upon me, but I will not answer;*
> *   they will seek me diligently, but will not find me.*
> **Prov 1:24-28**

Contrast those words with words we have seen in Deuteronomy:

> *When you have had children and children's children, and become complacent in the land, if you act corruptly by making an idol in the form of anything, thus doing what is evil in the sight of the LORD your God, and provoking him to anger, I call heaven and earth to witness against you today that you will soon utterly perish from the land that you are crossing the Jordan to occupy; you will not live long on it, but will be utterly destroyed. The LORD will scatter you among the peoples; only a few of you will be left among the nations where the LORD will lead you. There you will serve other gods made by human hands, objects of wood and stone that neither see, nor hear, nor eat, nor smell. From there you will seek the LORD your God, and you will find him if you search after him with all your heart and soul.* **Deut 4:25-29**

Proverbs 1:28 says, "Then they will call upon me, but I will not answer; they will seek me diligently, but will not find me."

Deuteronomy 4:29 says, "From there you will seek the LORD your God, and you will find him if you search after him with all your heart and soul." Why the difference?[6]

The main answer to that question discloses a key variance between the world of Torah and the world of wisdom. Torah's is a world of covenant and divine intervention. The world of proverbial wisdom is largely a world of consequences.[7] And though Proverbs is certainly aware of God's interventions,[8] it does not accent them in quite the same way.[9] In Torah, God's people are to do as God directs. In Proverbs, all who want to be wise must do what the wise instruct. Though, as we'll see, they are in touch with the Lord, Israel's covenant God, the wise are not God. Neither is Wisdom, even though through wisdom God made the world (Prov 3:19-20). God is a being who intervenes in time and changes the course of events, even sometimes reversing the effects of consequences. Wisdom is not God. Wisdom cannot do that.

Remember, ethics refers to how one distinguishes right from wrong. It also refers to the motives or reasons for why one should do what is right and refrain from what is wrong. Answering the question, Why should I do that? discloses one's ethics. The Torah answer to that question might sound something like this: "I belong to the covenant people of the God who rescued us from slavery in Egypt. God's laws instruct us in the patterns of appropriate behavior. They reflect God's mercy, holiness and love, and help us be an ordered people. I do this out of my love for a holy God who loves his covenant people and whose laws exist for their well-being."

The Proverbs answer, by contrast, might sound something like this: "I aim to be wise. To be wise, I must be in touch with the One who made the world, God, highly respecting him. I must also actively seek wisdom by learning from those who are wise, who themselves are in touch both with God, the Creator of the universe, and the design with which he has made all things. When I learn from the wise and from God's wise design, I learn the best ways for life to work out. Life works out for wise people because they are living according to how God designed life to be lived. Fools, by contrast, defy God's design. Those who defy God's design are asking for disaster."

WISDOM AND CONSEQUENCES

Imagine a daughter whose mother tells her, "Don't touch that stove. It's hot." What happens to the daughter who ignores her mother's instruction and touches the stove anyway? She gets burned, and no amount of words of comfort, no amount of bandaging or medicating will take away the effects of the daughter's disobedience. If the burn is a bad one, the girl may carry her scars her entire life.

That is the world of Proverbs' Wisdom. Wisdom offers her valuable insight. Those who refuse her insight must pay the penalty because that penalty is the basic, natural, God-designed consequence of disregarding the pattern of the way things are supposed to be. That's what Proverbs 1:24-28 communicates. Those who would be wise listen to Wisdom. They listen to and heed the instructions of the wise, who know and respect Israel's covenant God, and who themselves discern how life is supposed to be lived in accordance with how it has been designed. They themselves eventually learn how to make wise observations of God's created order, knowing that when the order is defied, generally speaking, they can expect a bad outcome, and when the order is upheld, all things being equal, they can expect a good outcome.[10] Wisdom is powerless to take away the scars of folly. Only God could begin to do something like that.

Let's return to the words of Deuteronomy 4:25-29. With those, Moses informs God's people that they can expect God to intervene and send them off to exile in another country if they break their covenantal loyalty to the one true God and go after other deities, who are not really gods in the first place. God will give them the bad consequence of exile, not as a natural consequence but as a corrective act, since they are defying God and his covenant in the Promised Land, which he has given to them. When God's people come to their senses in captivity outside of their land, Moses claims, God will then intervene positively on their behalf, restoring them from exile in accordance with the covenant he has made with their ancestors.

In the world of proverbial wisdom, we are dealing with a very different way of thinking. If we drag into that world the same expectations and patterns of the world of Torah, we will probably misunderstand and, worse, misappropriate the instruction.

WHAT IS WISDOM?

Wisdom and smarts, or intelligence, are not the same. There are some very intelligent people all over the world today who commit foolish acts. Consider the following:

- A straight-A high school senior gets in a car accident because she drank (illegally) to excess at a party and then tried to drive home;

- A man who receives top marks studying economics at his university regularly overdraws his bank account because he never keeps track of his expenditures.

In these true scenarios both people are intelligent. But neither one is behaving wisely. Both suffer damaging consequences as a result.

Wisdom, as Proverbs portrays it, is in touch with life itself. It may involve what we sometimes call common sense. But it's much more than that. Wisdom is a way of life that someone should actively seek in order to live life fully, as God designed it to be. Wisdom aims to be in touch with the way things are and the way things should be. Those who are wise learn how everyday life works so that they can get the most out of it. Those who try to defy reality should expect to get into trouble. If they ignore reality, insisting that they will not be hurt, get caught or suffer normal, bad consequences, they should expect elements of their world to cave in.

Wisdom is in touch with life and with the way life is supposed to be lived in order that life may be lived well. Wisdom, as Proverbs declares in elegant poetry, was with God when he made the world (Prov 8:22-31; see also Prov 3:19-20). Wisdom is in touch with God, the Designer of life. When one knows the Designer, and commits to learning the design, then one is in the best shape to live. Wisdom therefore involves observations of God's created order rooted in the fear of God and thus filtered through a mind that is oriented toward God.[11] When people purposefully live within the bounds of God's created design, they are wise. When people attempt to defy the way things are supposed to be, they are fools.

God designed gravity. People who ignore that die when they jump from high places, unless they have learned how to create a counterforce to gravity, in which case they are still operating within the bounds of God's design. The same principles work in the world of morality. People who perform acts that are designed to hurt, but who ignore that they are hurting others, inflict harm in their world and must deal with the bad consequences. Speaking angry words would be an example of just that sort of act, and, no surprise, Proverbs has lots to say about it. Consider Proverbs 29:22 as one example among many:

> One given to anger stirs up strife,
>   and the hothead causes much transgression.[12]

Of course there are situations in the world where there appear to be exceptions to the design. People living foolish lives sometimes get away with it. We often hear people make claims such as: "I heard of a man who never ate vegetables and he lived to be 105. I don't need to worry about my diet." But people who act foolishly (like a man never eating vegetables) and get away with it generally are exceptions. Only fools base their lives on the exceptions.

Sometimes a bad activity may actually feel good. One popular saying goes, "If it feels good, do it." Technically that's a proverb. It strongly contrasts with Proverbs 14:12, which states:

> *There is a way that seems right to a person,*
> *but its end is the way to death.*

One may initially feel right about an activity because it may give a momentary emotional lift. But if that activity is actually morally bad, one can normally expect a bad outcome, regardless of the initially good feelings. Here we have two proverbs, one from popular culture outside the Bible, the other from the Bible's Proverbs. What makes Proverbs right?

How One Becomes Wise

Proverbs 1:7 states,

> *The fear of the Lord is the beginning of knowledge;*
> *fools despise wisdom and instruction.*

Proverbs 9:10 declares,

> *The fear of the Lord is the beginning of wisdom,*
> *and the knowledge of the Holy One is insight.*

In between those two statements exists a host of words in Proverbs that establish both what wisdom is and how one obtains it, urging the readers to embrace the life of wisdom.[13]

Consider the initial premise. Proverbs declares that people can only be truly wise if they know God and stay in touch with him, growing in deep respect. One must fear him. The same points we observed in Torah with regard to the fear of God do apply here. Those who know God fear him. They know that God is not to be trifled with. But those who do not know God, or are ignoring him, do not fear him. They may even laugh at the notion of God. Others who don't really know God as Proverbs expects its readers to know him may confuse fear of God with being afraid of God, as though God were like pagan gods who, according to the stories that exist about them, are sometimes known to do mean things to people for arbitrary or petty reasons.[14] There is a difference between fearing God and being afraid of God. The former involves respect and trust. The latter shows that one does not have awareness of who God is and what he does. People who fear God know him. Proverbs too advocates a strong ethic of relationship.

People who want to become wise must fear God, not just once but as an ongoing attitude. Those who refuse to fear God, or lose sight of the fear of God, are setting themselves up to become fools. Folly, according to Proverbs, stems from people being out of touch with God, the Creator and master Designer of the world. Fools cut themselves off from the source of wisdom in this world and blunt their capacity to make consistently reliable, moral decisions.

More specifically, Proverbs advocates the fear of the Lord, YHWH, Israel's covenant God, as the beginning of wisdom.[15] That's provocative. Wisdom was a common pursuit within the world of the ancient Near East, including both ancient Egypt and ancient Mesopotamia.[16] While aligning itself with that pursuit, Proverbs indicates that what it offers stands in strong contrast to those other approaches. By portraying wisdom as stemming from Israel's God, Proverbs points to a sense of order and morality counter to the views prevailing in the nations around Israel. Proverbs offers a correction and a standard to measure the legitimacy of others' wisdom. Sometimes the nations may have it right. But other times they have it wrong. The fear of Israel's God allows a person to discern both the rightness and wrongness of the wisdom of the nations. How so? By beginning with the point that God, as Creator, has established an ordered world. As someone studies that world, that person can expect to discern an order that reflects its creative design. Rather than seeing wisdom as a means of maintaining balance in an already existing harmony (as in Egypt) or as the means of triumphing over an ongoing struggle with chaos (as in Mesopotamia), Proverbs sees a basic created order to the world because God has established that order through wisdom

(Prov 3:19-20). Proverbs encourages people to study that order and then align themselves with its good consequences.

That is equally instructive to worldviews in today's cultures. Proverbs challenges all other thought systems that set themselves in opposition to the view of an ordered creation established by Israel's God. Proverbial wisdom would support pursuing the kinds of observations that can be made within the social sciences, for example. But the fear of the Lord would require someone to question conclusions from those observations that go counter to the basic order of God's creation. Proverbs would likewise allow the observations of conventional wisdom. But the fear of the Lord requires one to question that wisdom when it defies God's order.

Consider the statement quoted earlier in this chapter: "If it feels good, do it." That statement reflects a view that says, The world exists for me. I must grab what I can from it to achieve the most pleasure I can. It reflects the individual as his or her own god or goddess, needing to find happiness in a world of competing power gods and goddesses who are all trying to make sense of a random world that exists courtesy of an accidental collision of atoms.[17] Proverbs' perspective immediately falsifies that by starting with the view that God has established a basic order to the universe. Proverbs' perspective communicates that though some acts may feel good or seem right, those may ultimately be deadly.

"If it feels good, do it" is often associated with attitudes about seeking sexual pleasure—"How could something that feels so good be so bad?" Wisdom, as Proverbs presents it, would indicate that done improperly, that is, outside of marriage, sex harms. Sex outside of marriage may feel good, but it never really advances good, while it does produce all sorts of hurt: STDs, unwanted pregnancy, psychological distress. Sex within marriage is the created design from the good Creator. It is good, designed as a procreative bonding act that enhances the tie established between a wife and husband when they marry. Even an unplanned pregnancy is good in a committed marriage because there is an existing support structure to welcome a new life.

The fear of God is only the beginning, however. A mere declaration that one respects or fears God does not make a person wise, according to Proverbs. One must want to become wise.[18] One must have a hunger for or desire for wisdom. One must, in Proverbs' own language, respond to the invitation of Lady Wisdom herself. Proverbs 1–9 are filled with a heavy concentration of invitational language, where the reader is being urged to accept Wisdom and all that she offers, or to accept the teachings of the wise and all that they provide.

Note the following collection of statements, picked from a host of others, designed to encourage a positive response to Proverbs' instructions:

> My child, if you accept my words
>   and treasure up my commandments within you,
> making your ear attentive to wisdom
>   and inclining your heart to understanding;
> if you indeed cry out for insight,
>   and raise your voice for understanding;
> if you seek it like silver,
>   and search for it as for hidden treasures—
> then you will understand the fear of the LORD
>   and find the knowledge of God. . . .
> Then you will understand righteousness and justice
>   and equity, every good path;
> for wisdom will come into your heart,
>   and knowledge will be pleasant to your soul.
> **Prov 2:1-5, 9-10**
>
> Keep hold of instruction; do not let go;
>   guard her, for she is your life. **Prov 4:13**
>
> Take my instruction instead of silver,
>   and knowledge rather than choice gold;
> for wisdom is better than jewels,
>   and all that you may desire cannot compare with her.
> **Prov 8:10-11**

Becoming wise requires dedication. It does not happen overnight. It is an ongoing, lifelong pursuit. It involves persistent heeding of words of wise counsel, continued growth from experience both in making wise observations and learning from foolish mistakes, and continued alignment to the God who made the world, growing in knowledge of his ways.[19] One must choose to be wise and seek wisdom with one's whole being, but wisdom is not far, elusive or secretive. Wisdom is always present in the world. A person must always be ready to learn.

Wisdom in Proverbs is personified as a woman, fitting Proverbs' basic word picture of an ideal father instructing his son. We, as readers, are listening in on the advice.[20] The father is metaphorically instructing his son about the kind of life he should choose by appealing to the sort of woman he should be attracted to and the sort of woman he should avoid. Wisdom embodies all that the young man should pursue. By contrast, the "forbidden woman" (Prov 2:16; 5:3-14), also known as the "adulteress" (Prov 2:16; 5:20-23; 6:23-35; 7:5-27) and "folly" herself (Prov 9:13-18), though deceptively alluring, offers nothing but pain and hardship, while promising an unreliable enjoyment.

Certainly, Wisdom can be tough. She laughs at those who ignore her because she knows what is best (Prov 1:22-33). One who rejects her ways deserves to be scorned—the experience of natural consequences is a type of scorn. But for those who listen to Wisdom, life works out extraordinarily well. She is more valuable than precious metals and costly gems (Prov 3:13-20). She is to be highly prized (Prov 4:4-9). She has a unique attractiveness that sets her apart from any person or object. She is God's first act of creation and then the means by which God has made the world. When one is in touch with Wisdom, one is in touch with the agent responsible for making things the way they are supposed to be (Prov 8:1-36). She offers a simple invitation (Prov 9:1-6). Those who want to be wise must accept her invitation.[21]

In committing oneself to seeking after wisdom, one must therefore be attentive to the instructions of the wise. That is what readers find throughout Proverbs, not only sporadically in Proverbs 1–9, but especially beginning with Proverbs 10. One observes simple, pithy sayings that instruct about the good and bad ways of life. When people commit themselves to learning from that instruction, they grow wise. They learn from some of those instructions to begin to make their own observations of the created order, rooted in the fear of the Lord. They begin to see their own life experiences through that lens, renouncing their own folly and seeing what has indeed been good. Then they too can begin to see those ways that some call right actually leading to death (Prov 14:12).

From Proverbs' perspective, people who want to become wise must begin by fearing the Lord, Israel's covenant God, growing in knowledge of him.

They must cultivate a passion for wisdom, renouncing Folly and responding to Wisdom's invitation, entering into a lifelong impassioned pursuit of her. Only then can they begin to make true sense of the instructions that follow in the rest of Proverbs, beginning with chapter 10. They must always seek out and listen to the instruction of the wise. They must examine their own lives in view of that instruction. In the fear of God, under the counsel of the wise, both as written in the Proverbs and as learned directly from the wise, whose wisdom they seek, they can begin to make their own wise observations in an ever-changing world.[22] Those observations will then be filtered through a true standard because one is in touch with God and with the way he has made the world. They must then live based on those observations.

WISDOM VERSUS ETHICS

The person who is wise will be ethical. Why? Because that person knows how to distinguish right from wrong and from what does not matter. Not all wisdom is about ethics, though. Remember that ethics refers to activities that advance good or hinder harm in one's world. Sometimes wisdom involves just good, practical advice. Wisdom is about learning to live well. Ethics is only one aspect of that.

Consider this proverb:

> A gossip goes about telling secrets,
> but one who is trustworthy in spirit keeps a confidence. **Prov 11:13**

Being trustworthy is compared with being a gossip. Gossips advance harm in their world by breaking confidences or telling secrets, often damaging the people they gossip about. Trustworthy people advance good by keeping silent about issues that do not concern anyone but those who have confided in them in the first place. Gossiping is bad, immoral behavior. Being trustworthy is good. Moral people will be trustworthy people.

Now according to the proverb just quoted, a wise person will also go one step further, moving beyond the morality of trustworthiness and the immorality of gossiping to act on the proverb in a different way. Whom should one trust with special information, someone with a track record of being a loudmouth babbler or someone who knows how to keep silent, even in the most tempting moments? It would be wise to rely on the trustworthy person.

Choosing to do so would be a matter of wisdom, not of ethics.

Wisdom is much bigger than ethics. So do not restrict everything you read in Proverbs to morality and ethics. But because wisdom points out the best ways to live, and because ethics also deals with how one chooses appropriate activity, expect to learn ethics from becoming wise.

PROVERBS ARE FOR ALL WHO WOULD BE WISE, NOT SIMPLY FOR GOD'S COVENANT PEOPLE

Proverbs does not restrict its invitation to those who may become wise. Its words are addressed to all who would hear.[23] It lacks any specific overt appeal to the covenants between God and Abraham and between God and his people Israel. At least one prophetic writing in the Old Testament, 1 Kings, refers to proverbial wisdom in language that indicates that wisdom offers one way for the non-Israelite nations to be blessed in Abraham's descendants. Here is how that writing puts it:

> *God gave Solomon very great wisdom, discernment, and breadth of understanding as vast as the sand on the seashore, so that Solomon's wisdom surpassed the wisdom of all the people of the east, and all the wisdom of Egypt. He was wiser than anyone else, wiser than Ethan the Ezrahite, and Heman, Calcol, and Darda, children of Mahol; his fame spread throughout all the surrounding nations. He composed three thousand proverbs, and his songs numbered a thousand and five. He would speak of trees, from the cedar that is in the Lebanon to the hyssop that grows in the wall; he would speak of animals, and birds, and reptiles, and fish. People came from all the nations to hear the wisdom of Solomon; they came from all the kings of the earth who had heard of his wisdom.* **1 Kings 4:29-34**

Notice the mention of the proverbs, some of which presumably are a part of the biblical collection in Proverbs. Notice also that Solomon, as a wise man, made observations from the created order, being expert in both flora and fauna. His wisdom surpassed the wisdom of the wise people of the surrounding nations, but more to the point, his wisdom spread to the nations. Earlier, 1 Kings 4:20-28 had described Solomon's reign in terms resembling the Abrahamic covenant:

- A multiplicity of descendants. "Judah and Israel were as numerous as the sand by the sea" (1 Kings 4:20).

- Land. "Solomon was sovereign over all the kingdoms from the Euphrates to the land of the Philistines, even to the border of Egypt; they brought tribute and served Solomon all the days of his life. . . . For he had dominion over all the region west of the Euphrates from Tiphsah to Gaza, over all the kings west of the Euphrates; and he had peace on all sides" (1 Kings 4:21, 24).

- Blessing. "They ate and drank and were happy. . . . [A]nd he had peace on all sides. During Solomon's lifetime Judah and Israel lived in safety, from Dan even to Beer-sheba, all of them under their vines and fig trees" (1 Kings 4:20, 24-25).

The summary of Solomon's wisdom extending to "all the kings of the earth" (1 Kings 4:34) is here portrayed as a realization of the important goal of nations being blessed by Abraham's descendants.[24] Wisdom here builds bridges from God's people to the rest of the world.

The words of the writing of Proverbs itself do not make that claim. But the universal character of Proverbs, its adaptation of the Israelite covenantal language as observed earlier and the general invitation that wisdom issues to all who want to be wise fit with such a point. Wisdom does begin with a fear of God, the same God who is Israel's covenant God. So Proverbs maintains the same sense of religious exclusivity found in Torah. But Proverbs does not indicate that anyone must first come into the fold of God's covenant people to benefit from wisdom's positive outcomes of being in touch with God. Wisdom is for all people.[25] When God's people are wise, they use wisdom as a bridge to extend to those who are not God's people the benefits of coming to know their God. Through their own wise choices they demonstrate that when people trust in God with all their hearts, they have a clarity and direction in life that reliance on mere human understanding cannot produce (Prov 3:5-6).

PROVERBS AS INSTRUCTION

Let's look at a few Proverbs. The first nine chapters of Proverbs do have some useful instructions, but much of the contents of those chapters is designed to urge readers to respond to the invitations of Wisdom and the instructions of the wise parent to become wise. The collection of actual proverbs themselves begins in earnest in chapter 10. The instructions in Proverbs 10 and following rely totally on the background of chapters 1–9,[26] where wisdom is put forward as beginning with the fear of the Lord.

Proverbs 10:1 states,

> A wise child makes a glad father,
>   but a foolish child is a mother's grief.

Let's make a few observations here. Most of the proverbs consist of two lines that are in basic relationship with each other. Though some proverbs are a bit longer, those tend to be exceptions. The instruction is very simple. The two lines here appear in contrast with each other. Sometimes the second line will carry the thought of the first one step further. Sometimes the second line may express a similar thought, but with different words that intensify the thought from the first line. On other occasions, one of the lines may have a metaphor or word picture that the other explains.[27] The point of recognizing this pairing of lines is twofold: (1) simple, two-line statements with identifiable relationships between the lines are easily memorized, boosting their instructional value; (2) simple, two-line statements can never exhaust the possibilities of a topic.

Consider Proverbs 10:1 again. A wise child is contrasted with a foolish one. Wisdom brings about gladness, in contrast with folly, which brings about grief. In emphasizing the contrast, "father" appears with one line while "mother" appears on the other, not because one parent is considered wise and the other foolish but to underscore the comparison between the wise and foolish child.

What we have is a basic observation, as many proverbs actually are. The statement is not about ethics in and of itself, though it is full of implications for ethics. A child in some modern cultures might show his or her wisdom by making a good set of contacts that allow him or her to get a good summer job, for instance. That has nothing to do with ethics, though it does have lots to do with successful living. But suppose the child is showing wisdom by engaging in a moral act? What if the child is known for being kind and giving? That also is the sort of child that most parents (or at least wise ones) would delight in. Compare that with the child who is always on the verge of being in trouble with the authorities. That sort of child indeed is a grief bringer. "Oh that son of mine . . ." says the mother, lamenting the fact that he just threw a rock through the neighbor's window.

Proverbs 10:1 is a simple statement. But those who are becoming wise discover how to learn continually from such insights.[28] Some of those insights may have implications for ethics.

Consider Proverbs 10:2.

> *Treasures gained by wickedness do not profit,*
> *but righteousness delivers from death.*

This statement offers more direct ethical instruction than the first one we considered. It goes beyond the mere observation of that previous statement to advocate more purposefully righteous behavior. The topic here involves how enriching oneself through wicked, immoral means does not really work as a life strategy. The proverb we just looked at in verse 1 simply described how the parents of wise and foolish children feel about the outcome of their children's lives. The proverb in verse 2 offers a similar, simple contrast in the same way we saw the proverb in verse 1 doing, this one here between "treasures gained by wickedness" and "righteousness." But the proverb in verse 2 also offers direct consequences of both righteous and unrighteous behaviors. The former, we are told, does not profit. The latter "delivers from death." Notice how this saying emphasizes outcomes or consequences. Some cultures have a saying similar to the first line: Crime does not pay.

Such simple statements can go just so far. Some might challenge the claim being made here. After all, don't some people actually get away with evil? Or even if they don't, isn't it true that the direct penalty they do pay does not really negate the evil they have committed?

For example, some people choose to be drug dealers, knowing that they may have to go to jail, but reasoning that the money they earn running drugs will more than pay for whatever inconvenience they may eventually experience by having to go to jail for a few years. And some people don't get caught. So, they reason, it is more worthwhile selling drugs and having money to buy all sorts of things, than behaving honestly in a setting where many people struggle to make ends meet. Or, consider a second example: some students choose to cheat on an assignment or test, reasoning that they would flunk anyway, so they may as well risk doing wrong in the hope that they may actually get away with it. The fact that it is possible for some people to get away with their evil activity motivates others to participate in it.

The simplicity of various proverbs may sometimes appear to negate their truthfulness. That is when we need to realize that they are not designed to say everything. Neither are they designed to portray absolute declarations. The fact is that the world is full of evil people. But all things being equal, many of those evil people regularly suffer harmful consequences for their activity, even if all do not. Drug dealers do get caught and are sent to jail; cheaters do get caught and are kicked out of school. By contrast, those who choose what is good do not, generally speaking, have to worry about others coming after them. Their habitual consistency in doing the right thing does indeed deliver them.[29] Now, there are exceptions to both rules. An individual proverb does not aim to address exceptions to its claim. Proverbs' instructions tend to address basic leanings and inclinations. People who do the right thing generally have nothing to worry about. They sleep well at night. The wise do well to focus on the basic tendencies, rather than to hope for exceptions to those tendencies. Those who do what is right live at ease. Those who do what is wrong always face the potential of getting caught— and they often do.

The next proverb states:

> The Lord does not let the righteous go hungry,
>   but he thwarts the craving of the wicked. **Prov 10:3**

Is that true? Do no righteous people go hungry? Do all wicked people suffer? Recall what we just noticed with the previous proverb. We are again dealing with a basic observation. Casual Bible readers unaware of Proverbs' designs can unfortunately pick such statements out and treat them as religious or prophetic promises. The world of Proverbs describes general, observable tendencies. Yet those tendencies can easily be frustrated because of the imperfections of human existence. This proverb offers an observation affirmed by those who know God; God *does* provide for his righteous ones, while making life difficult for wicked people as they attempt to fulfill their evil desires or cravings. It does have implications for ethics. People who are righteous do what is moral. People who are wicked do what is immoral. But we do not have a declaration of absolutes.[30] In times of major disaster, all people, both wicked and righteous, suffer. Those are moments of extenuating circumstances. Proverbs addresses life's tendencies.

Proverbs also does not allow us to reverse the logic of its sayings. People cannot conclude that because a person may be going hungry, that person is wicked, or because a person has food in abundance, that person is an ethical person. Neither do any proverbs advocate a thought pattern that says, "I will be righteous so that God will give me food too." The words of the proverb in their context do not encourage any reversals of their logic.

Though many of Proverbs' consequences are built in to the design of life, the world of Proverbs is a God-infused world. The proverb does claim that God acts on behalf of righteous, moral people, providing for their basic needs, and that God acts against wicked, immoral people, standing in the way of their wicked desires. That is a basic observation rooted in the fear of the Lord, with an awareness of how God acts on behalf of those who do what is right. People who come to know God grow in their awareness of God's hand on their lives.

Let's look at Proverbs 10:4, our final one from this chapter:

> A slack hand causes poverty,
>   but the hand of the diligent makes rich.

The simple contrast here is between laziness and diligence. We may actually be familiar with exceptions. Some students, for example, may know of others who never seem to open their books but who always seem to get A's anyway. And there are other students who seem to hit the books continually yet struggle to get by with C's and B's. But by and large the observation holds true. People who are diligent are more prone to success, described in this proverb as financial success, than people who never really apply themselves to their work. Again, we have to be careful not to reverse the logic of the words. The proverb does not say that people are poor because they are lazy, or rich because they are diligent. The point of the words is to encourage a solid, stable work ethic. People advance good for themselves and for their world when they work hard. People promote harm on themselves and their world when they refuse to work.

Now that we have looked at four consecutive proverbs, we are also equipped to notice something else. Consider the topics we have explored so far: wise versus foolish children, the fruit of ill-gotten wealth versus well-being from righteous living, God's provision for righteous people versus his hindering the desires of wicked people, laziness versus diligence. Are any of these related? Not directly. That is the world of Proverbs. Many of the proverbs we read need not be connected directly either to what precedes or to what follows. They can be, but not always.[31] For example, the proverb in Proverbs 10:5 also addresses the same notion of diligence and laziness as in Proverbs 10:4: "A child who gathers in summer is prudent, / but a child who sleeps in harvest brings shame." But its core meaning does not grow directly out of the preceding sentence.

Proverbs can group several sayings around common topics, such as the righteous versus the wicked or the wise versus the fool, sometimes with the expectation that we as readers connect the sayings directly. And there are a number of sayings starting in Proverbs 22:17 that are part of larger developments of a topic, such as the folly of drinking too much wine in Proverbs 23:29-35. But most frequently Proverbs moves rapidly from one topic to another, sometimes revisiting a topic addressed earlier, but with few or no expectations in the words of that proverb that we as readers know the earlier saying. Proverbs jumps around from topic to topic in an almost haphazard, random manner. In that regard Proverbs appears to resemble life itself. No one ever knows what turns the events of a given day may take. The wise are prepared to live through such variety because they fear God, knowing him and the ways he has designed life to be lived. This is one reason why it is unwise to tune out the overall environment of an isolated proverb, ignoring other life possibilities its presence in the collection may suggest.[32]

Before moving on, several more issues should be addressed. To do that, we will have to jump out of order. Many proverbs do indeed offer simple observations. Many of those observations have built into them a sense of moral rightness or wrongness. So, as we saw in Proverbs 10:1, not only do disobedient children make their parents unhappy, the unhappiness of the parent coupled with the implied negative social outcome leads one to see that it is not good for children to disobey their parents. But some proverbs can talk about bad behavior in such an apparently neutral manner that they appear to approve of that behavior in their failure to condemn it. Consider the following statements about bribery:

> *A bribe is like a magic stone in the eyes of those who give it;*
>   *wherever they turn they prosper.* **Prov 17:8**
>
> *A gift in secret averts anger;*
>   *and a concealed bribe in the bosom, strong wrath.* **Prov 21:14**

These two proverbs at the very least point out occasions that show the act of bribery working. Does their failure to condemn the practice indicate their approval of it? Should one ever actually engage in the process of bribing another? The mere observation that a bribe works would seem to indicate that bribery could be an allowable act.

But now consider the following proverbs:

> *Those who are greedy for unjust gain make trouble for their households,*
>   *but those who hate bribes will live.* **Prov 15:27**
>
> *The wicked accept a concealed bribe*
>   *to pervert the ways of justice.* **Prov 17:23**

Which is which? Should one ever give or take bribes? Sometimes bribes actually work. But aren't the motives for giving or receiving them evil?

The wise know how to sort out such dilemmas.[33] There may be occasions when a gift, or even an act of kindness, ought to be considered before any request is made, rather than forthrightly making a demand, no matter how justified the demand might be.[34] But is it wise ever to be manipulative? Never, if it leads to corrupt acts, such as an unjust decision. Otherwise, probably not, which indicates that for the most part, all things being equal, the act of bribing should be avoided. Establishing a positive mood before making a request of someone may be a wise course of action, but not for crass, self-seeking motives.

Sometimes proverbs can flat out contradict each other. Consider the following, found back to back:

> *Do not answer fools according to their folly,*
>   *or you will be a fool yourself.* **Prov 26:4**
>
> *Answer fools according to their folly,*
>   *or they will be wise in their own eyes.* **Prov 26:5**

Which is it? Answer the fool, or don't answer the fool? Again, the wise know when to do what. Remember, proverbs are situational. There are some occasions when it's best to let fools spout their folly. There are other moments, however, when it would be important to speak out in response to a fool's nonsense. Those who learn from the wise also begin to learn in their own experience which piece of advice is best for which situation.[35]

Notice what we have observed from this brief exploration:

- Proverbs are simple.

- Proverbs are often mere observations.

- Proverbs are poetic, making them more easily learned.

- Proverbs may vary in the implications they have for ethics.

- Proverbs are not prophetic promises.

- Proverbs are situational more than absolute.

- A proverb's logic is not supposed to be reversed.

- Proverbs are presented sometimes randomly—just as life often appears to be.

PROVERBS COVERS A RANGE OF TOPICS: THE WISE MUST SEEK OUT ITS INSTRUCTION

Individual proverbs address a wide variety of topics. Many of those topics cover issues never dealt with in Torah. For example, though Torah might proscribe certain forms of illicit speech (e.g., lying, slander, false witness), Proverbs offers a wider range of inappropriateness beyond the legal context. Proverbs broadens that sense of illicit speech to address the gossip who reveals secrets (Prov 11:13; 20:19) and the whisperer who breaks the trust placed in him or her by revealing sensitive information (see Prov 16:28; 18:8; 26:20, 22). Proverbs comments about the folly of discussing issues without the principal players being present (Prov 25:9).

Further, many individual proverbs apply to a variety of potential topics. Consider Proverbs 10:6:

> Blessings are on the head of the righteous,
> but the mouth of the wicked conceals violence.

Very clearly this addresses the well-being of those who are righteous, who do what is right, a point important for ethics. How are people known as righteous? They are known for doing a wide range of morally good activities, while refraining from all morally bad activities. The next line, however, is much more specific, offering a variety of contrasts with the righteous: evil speech, wickedness and violence. To restrict an individual proverb to a single topic may sometimes be a mistake.

While noting that many proverbs potentially cover a wide array of behaviors, consider the list in table 5.1 only as a minimal starting point. It is certainly not exhaustive. There are other moral topics in Proverbs that may not be on this list. Those in table 5.1 are among the obvious:

Table 5.1. Array of Some Behaviors Covered in Proverbs

• honesty	• humility-pride	• evil-wickedness
• use of words	• quarreling	• greed
• alcohol consumption	• bribery	• justice
• sexual behavior	• vengeance	• kindness
• patience	• envy	• response to the poor
• anger	• generosity	• righteous
• laziness-diligence	• self-control	• violence

No chapter and verse references appear in this list. That would go counter to the spirit of Proverbs. First, Proverbs encourages its readers to become wise. The wise must diligently seek out wisdom. Second, since many individual proverbs do apply to more than one topic, any listing of verse references would potentially restrict the possibilities of wisdom that the statement advocates. Third, reading an individual proverb in its immediate context can also suggest an application of that proverb that might not be obvious when the proverb is isolated by itself.

Proverbs does not pretend to raise topics that deal with all of life, but the topics listed are clearly tilted in the direction of everyday life. Proverbs encourages its readers to think broadly, not restrictively. Those who are becoming wise know how to obtain wisdom not found directly in Proverbs' words of instruction. The possibilities of issues addressable by proverbial wisdom are as expansive as life itself.

Notice, finally, how microethical much of this is. Grand policy makers certainly should be wise. Those who wage wars, for example, should do so carefully (Prov 20:18; 24:6). But most of Proverbs' instruction addresses interpersonal interactions. People who are wise refrain from behaviors that hinder the quality of relationships they have with the people in their immediate communities, the people with whom they deal on a daily basis. Wise people are not angry with people with whom they interact. Neither are they dishonest. Neither do they gossip, talking about others behind their backs. Those are behaviors that affect the well-being of others. Attention to wisdom in interpersonal interactions is moral.

Near the beginning of this discussion, we considered Proverbs 14:12: "There is a way that seems right to a person, / but its end is the way to death," which is in a setting of proverbs that loosely address the deceitfulness of appearances.[36] We applied it to contemporary attitudes about sexuality. The possibilities of application are beyond that for those who are willing to observe. Consider how some might justify their decision to file for divorce or to get an abortion. They might seek temporary relief, failing to see the longer-term consequences of their decisions, not only on themselves but on those involved with them. None of those explicit topics are mentioned either by this proverb or any other proverb. But the one who learns how to use proverbs such as this and to think about the world in the fear of God under the counsel of the wise will see all sorts of relevant possibilities for how to apply wisdom beyond the issues specifically addressed by individual proverbs.

Individual Proverbs Reflect a Rudimentary Philosophy

According to Proverbs, those who study and observe life begin to develop an ever-expanding sense of how life should be lived. Life, as Proverbs addresses it, must always begin with and maintain a fear of the Lord. It should aim to be in touch with the way things are supposed to be, showing awareness of who God is and how his creation functions. Living that way is not about trying to attain an unachievable ideal or utopia, as, for example, the philosopher Plato advocated (whom Proverbs, for the most part, predates). Proverbs' approach somewhat resembles what one may learn from Plato's pupil Aristotle, whose philosophy is also rooted in observation. But proverbial wisdom differs sharply from Aristotle's approach, precisely in being founded on the fear of God. The possibilities of life that a person encounters in his or her limited experience may not necessarily reflect the possibilities of how all of life is designed. There is a good standard rooted in God the Creator, and discovering the order of God's design and how it applies to life is itself a lifelong pursuit. God and his creation are huge.

But Proverbs' sayings fall far short of delving into discourses on life's issues. Instead, in Proverbs we see brief, concise sayings, many of which are designed to provoke thought in a practical way. Consider the following statement:

> *A fool takes no pleasure in understanding,*
> *but only in expressing personal opinion.* **Prov 18:2**

In one short, simple set of contrasts, Proverbs introduces its readers to a practical application of a concept that Plato develops in his *Republic*, the difference between opinion and knowledge.[37] Plato talks about knowledge based on speculating about a perfect ideal. By contrast, the statement in Proverbs draws on a practical everyday observation of God's created order in which people heed or resist the influence of the wise.[38]

We often see people who think they know more than they really do spouting off on all sorts of topics, quite frequently moral topics, yet sounding sillier and sillier with every word they speak. One only need tune in to a television talk show or read the "People" section of the daily newspaper to observe such nonsense. In the process, one also observes that audiences and readers actually take seriously what such loudly confident individuals say, mostly because those individuals are famous people, celebrities, who delight in voicing opinions to an adoring audience. Folly competes to draw people into her nonsense. Proverbs 18:2 reminds us that whenever we hear people spewing out their views, we ought to ask whether they know as much as their confident words may be indicating, particularly if, from Proverbs' perspective, those words are not rooted in the fear of God and the counsel of the wise. That is especially true in the area of morality, where people often speak loudly and confidently merely to justify their own unethical behavior, without any thoughtful, ethical backing behind what they say. We have a rudimentary philosophy reflected in the proverb here, but not a highly sophisticated, step-by-step exploration into the mysteries of human thought and action.

Proverbs Go Just So Far

Proverbs cannot answer all of life's ethical queries. The wise should be among the first to know that. Other wisdom writings in the Bible address this point. The limited nature of wisdom is talked about most directly in the lengthy dialogues found in Job and in the darkly speculative flow of thought in Ecclesiastes.[39] Both of those writings, in the end, appear to point to the faith-oriented fact that some of life's queries, ultimately, are knowable and solvable only by God. People need to trust that God actually knows what he is doing.

SUMMING IT UP:
WHAT DO WE LEARN ABOUT ETHICS FROM PROVERBS?

o Proverbial wisdom offers an entirely different way of thinking from Torah.

o Wisdom ethics focuses on consequences: morally good behavior brings good consequences; morally bad behavior brings bad consequences.

o Wisdom ethics is rooted in the fear of God, in a strong ethic of relationship with God.

o Wisdom ethics stems from observations of the design of God's created order.

o The ethically wise observe how acts are morally good because their consequences advance a good that upholds the created order in theirs and others' lives, and acts are morally bad because their consequences show the order being defied or exploited to the harm of that order.

o Proverbs' wisdom is for all people. It offers a means for communicating the sensibility of God's ways to those who do not yet fear God.

How do people become ethically wise?

o by purposefully choosing to become so, seeking diligently after wisdom while rejecting the allurement of the ethically foolish ways that surround them

o by learning from the counsel of others who fear God, who are ethically wise o by heeding Proverbs' ethically wise instruction from which the wise themselves continue to learn

o by applying those instructions to their lives, growing in and from experience

When it comes to reading and understanding Proverbs, we also noted the following:

o Proverbial wisdom's ethical standards are conveyed mostly through simple, easily memorized two-line instructions.

o Proverbs' instructions move quickly from one topic to another with the same sort of randomness that people encounter in everyday life.

o Proverbs' simple statements cover a wide variety of topics.

o A proverb sometimes offers a mere observation with no direct evaluation standard in its words.

o That kind of proverb is best considered against the background of the entire collection of statements.

o Proverbial instruction tends to be more situational than absolute. Wisdom flexes with ever-changing life circumstances.

o The simplicity of a proverb does not permit its logic to be reversed.

o Individual proverbs are regularly applicable to more than one topic.

Additionally, we should keep in mind that

o Proverbs does not begin to exhaust the possibilities of life issues that could be addressed.

o Those who want to become ethically wise must continue to mine Proverbs' statements in search of their ethical wisdom, both in the fear of God and in community with other wise people.

o Though Proverbs does portray a simple, basic philosophy, its approach can go only so far. The wise know Proverbs' limitations.

Proverbs shows how moral people live good, full lives. Those who want to live good, full lives need to become wise. They need to know that wisdom is there for all who pursue it (her); they need to pursue wisdom intentionally. To pursue wisdom confidently people need to respect and trust God, the wise Creator of all. They then need to learn from the truly wise. Proverbs is full of statements from the wise. Studying its instructions on an ongoing basis is necessary for people to grow in wisdom. As people grow in wisdom, they also learn how to make their own wise observations from the created order. As wise people, they seek the advice of a wide circle of other wise people to be certain that what they have observed is valid. Wise people never become wise by themselves.

In Proverbs' ethical vision, ethics grows out of wisdom. People who are becoming wise will become ethical. They will be increasingly in tune with life's ways designed by God to work out well both for themselves and for others, continuing to learn from instruction and from observation what advances good or inflicts harm in their world. They will consider the instruction of the wise, who also fear God. They will reflect on their own experiences, with respect and trust in God. They will observe their world carefully, in the fear of God. They will embrace what advances good in their everyday interactions with others. They will flee from what advances harm. They will offer advice, wisely, to those who are willing to hear, helping others to become ethical in the process.

Becoming wise is a lifelong pursuit. So, therefore, is becoming an ethical person. The wise know that they don't know everything. But they keep on learning. Reading Proverbs again and again, with attention to the fear of God, is a good starting place. Hanging around experienced, wise people who fear God is also important. Those who become wise that way will establish a strong moral foundation. They will also know why they should behave morally. They will understand how their actions reflect the ways life was designed to be lived by God, the Designer and Creator.

Proverbs also indicates that its instruction can help readers sort out issues now, if only they are willing to submit to its wisdom. Do you want to know if committing a certain act would be right or wrong? Read Proverbs. You will find guidelines that give counsel even for activities not mentioned explicitly. Then, run your thoughts past several wise, experienced people who also respect and trust God. Do some homework. Are there harmful consequences stemming from the act? Does the act skirt around God's design, and when it does, what are its effects? Armed with all of that, you can have confidence in your choice. But the wise also know that they may still get it wrong, and so they are willing to admit a mistake and move on to get it right. Pay attention to the consequences. Morally good acts have good results. Morally bad acts have bad results. The wise study God's creation diligently to be sure they have observed correctly and thoroughly.

Reflection Questions

1. How are ethics and wisdom related?

2. How does someone become wise, especially if a person only consults his or her peers?

3. What is the relationship between fearing God as Creator/Designer and the consequences for doing certain actions?

4. What is the relationship between morality and consequences?

5. Choose an item from the list in table 5.1. How does Proverbs' sense of consequences help you think about those items? How would that sense help you think about other moral settings or actions not on that list?

FOR FURTHER READING

Bartholomew, Craig G., and O'Dowd, Ryan P. *Old Testament Wisdom Literature: A Theological Introduction.* Downers Grove, IL: InterVarsity Press, 2011.

Prophets

Ethics or Morality?

Introductory Issues

We come now to the world of prophets, a world full of moral concern. Readers are deluged with declarations of right and wrong bursting from the seams of the Bible's prophetic writings. But what sense of *ethics* do they convey? Remember our introductory points:

- Morality is simply about knowing what is right and what is wrong.
- Ethics involves both the reasoning for distinguishing right from wrong and the motivations for doing what is right and hindering what is wrong.

To begin to talk about ethics in the prophets, we would have to discern both obvious explanatory patterns for distinguishing right from wrong behavior and obvious reasons or motivations for why one should do what is right and avoid what is wrong. It is not enough just to observe the prophets' repeated moral declarations.

We will find that our exploration into prophets will be more morally than ethically illuminating. We will observe an ethical vision restricted to moral indictment. But our brief exploration will end up being useful as a bridge for the next set of writings we consider. Some of the basics we examine here will apply directly to our understanding of the person we deal with in the remaining chapters of this book—Jesus.

We have to start with some basics. We'll explore what a prophet is and what it means to be prophetic. We'll limit our observations to the opening declarations of the famous prophet Isaiah, though we will eventually touch

on other prophets' moral concerns. The patterns we will see in Isaiah do not
differ dramatically from what we would see elsewhere.

What is a prophet? Ask people on the street what a prophet is and
someone surely will say, "A person who predicts the future." When we come
to biblical writings associated with prophets, we tend to encounter something else. That could be confusing. We may have to adjust our expectations
for prophets so that they line up with what we actually see.

Limiting prophets to the role of predictors of the future can lead us to
envision people who act like soothsayers, psychics, diviners or fortunetellers.
Those are *not* prophets. In fact, according to the laws of the Torah, such
people were subject to the death penalty. Why? Those were religious practices common among non-Israelites. They were considered "abhorrent to
the LORD," providing one reason why the nations were being driven out of
the Promised Land (Deut 18:9-14). Israelite prophets did indeed declare the
future. And they frequently announced imminent judgment set to fall on
God's disobedient people. But mere future predicting was not their primary
focus. What would that be? Speaking for God.[1]

Let's look at the opening words of Isaiah, to get a sense of what this means.
Consider the following:

> Hear O heavens, and listen, O earth;
>   for the LORD has spoken:
> I reared children and brought them up,
>   but they have rebelled against me.
> The ox knows its owner,
>   and the donkey its master's crib [i.e., feeding trough]
> but Israel does not know,
>   my people do not understand. **Is 1:2-3**

Notice, first of all, who is speaking. Though these words are attributed to
Isaiah, Isaiah says "the LORD has spoken." So, when the next line declares, "I
reared children and brought them up," we should know readily that Isaiah
is not talking about his own children. The "I" speaking is none other than
God. The prophet is speaking for God, his number one job.

What sorts of things do prophets say in speaking for God? Here in Isaiah,
the prophet uses poetic, metaphoric language to declare that God's people, the

Israelites, are acting like rebellious children (think, Westernized teenagers) and worse. Apparently, they are refusing to acknowledge God as their chief caregiver. God is portrayed in the role of caring parent, who deserves respect, adoration and obedience from his children. Instead, their behavior is so outlandish that they show they do not know what even farm animals know—the one they belong to and owe allegiance to. This is the language of relationship, appealing to the basic claim God has on their lives—they are his people.[2]

What kinds of words are these? They certainly are not about the future. In fact, they are accusatory words. They reflect a kind of courtroom scene in which the heavens and the earth are called on as witnesses of Israel's general wickedness and perhaps even of violations of Israel's covenant with God.[3] Accusatory words are typically prophetic. Often as they speak for God, prophets point their fingers at God's people for not measuring up to God and his ways. They regularly sound judgmental.[4] How dare they! Because they claim to speak for God, they can expect to get away with such declarations. Accusatory words are not nice to listen to. Only those who want to be responsive to God will pay attention to them. It's no surprise, then, that some prophets suffered abuse for their words.

Notice, however, that the prophetic world also reflects our basic ethic of relationship. People who know God and want to stay in touch with him should know better. Remember another of our basic principles from chapter one: *Ethics in the Bible flows primarily out of people's healthy relationship with God.*

When people are connecting well with God, they show it with their good behavior. When they engage in bad behavior, they show that they are not at all in touch with God. When people desire to relate to God, they are responsive to God's messengers. When they are in open rebellion from God, they are not at all interested in wanting to listen to anyone claiming to speak for God. In this context Isaiah is addressing those who belong to God's people (Is 1:3) who willfully turn their backs on him. They show no interest in knowing God, responding to God or growing in relationship with him. They need to heed the words of God's prophet.

So, what is a prophet in the Bible? Someone who speaks for God. When the prophet speaks, people should listen as though God himself were speaking. Narrative writings depict other roles for prophets, most notably those of *seer*, someone a person can consult for special insight on life issues, and of *man of*

God, someone who can also perform miraculous works for the benefit of others.[5] In all cases, offering words with a divine perspective is the chief activity.[6]

What do prophets tend to speak most? Just what we have here—various words of judgment. They convey God's perspectives about what his people, and sometimes others, are doing when those people have gotten off-track. They bring accusations and often announcements of disaster to be expected based on the accusations unless those people repent (i.e., change their ways to conform to God's desires as proclaimed by the prophet). In the process they often interpret contemporaneous disastrous events, explaining how they express God's judgment on the people's behavior.[7] They may hold out the prospect of future blessing, occasionally tied to appropriate behavior.[8] The specifics of future blessing and judgment often mesh well with general ideas of the future already seen in Torah, ideas such as exile for covenantal disobedience, or the blessing of nations.[9] Let's continue our explorations in Isaiah to see how some of that appears.

MORAL INDICTMENT IN ISAIAH

Prophetic sayings and moral preaching. We've just observed Isaiah accusing Israel, God's people, of being out of touch with God, declaring that they do not know God as their true master. A new set of accusations carries over into Isaiah 1:4 with a list of biting labels:

> Ah, sinful nation,
>   people laden with iniquity,
> offspring who do evil,
>   children who deal corruptly,
> who have forsaken the LORD,
>   who have despised the Holy One of Israel,
>   who are utterly estranged!

First, notice that this is a new thought from what we saw in verses 2-3. That is typical of prophetic writings. We appear to have an arrangement of related sayings, designed in this case to work together to communicate the hideousness of the condition of God's people. One important step in learning how to follow what a prophetic writing is communicating is to notice when one saying ends and a new one begins. Doing that can sometimes be complicated, but thankfully, most modern translations do the work for readers by leaving gaps between sayings as determined by editors.[10] The key would be to look for the gaps and then figure out what the isolated saying communicates. Then a reader can try to observe how it is connected to what precedes and what follows. In this case, the nation itself is being addressed, as opposed to the heavens and the earth in verses 2-3. Isaiah indicts the nation directly in these verses.

Second, notice the continuation of accusatory language. Here, the overall charge is unspecified sinfulness applied to the nation as a whole and then in descending fashion all the way down to individuals:[11] "sinful . . . laden with iniquity . . . who do evil . . . who deal corruptly." We learn nothing specific about what people have done to earn such accusations, though the terminology resembles vocabulary associated with covenantal infractions observable in the Torah.[12] All we know is the general charge of blatant misbehavior—more finger pointing. We also see the prophet connect sinfulness and moral impropriety in the first four lines of verse 4 to being out of touch with God in the final three lines: they have forsaken and despised God and are thus "utterly estranged" (v. 4). We do see evidence of a broad ethic of relationship here, even though we have yet to see any ethical rationale except for what may be implied by the introductory declaration of verse 2: "for the LORD has spoken." We will have to be certain to note ethical rationale, if we see any. Remember that the mere discussion of morality is not the same as the discussion of ethics. Two people can have the same moral convictions but quite different ethics. We only have minimal clues to the prophet's ethics.

Isaiah's words continue in the next segment (Is 1:5-6) in words that initially appear confusing:

> Why do you seek further beatings?
>> Why do you continue to rebel?
> The whole head is sick,
>> and the whole heart faint.
> From the sole of the foot even to the head,
>> there is no soundness in it,
> but bruises and sores
>> and bleeding wounds;
> they have not been drained, or bound up,
>> or softened with oil.

Beatings? Sick heads? Faint hearts? What is going on here?

Prophets and the interpretation of events. As part of their role in speaking for God, prophets can connect events happening around them to God's activities. That appears to be what is happening here in Isaiah. God's people are said to be receiving beatings because they rebel. This picks up the introductory metaphor from verses 2-3 of God's people behaving as unruly children and connects that to what they are experiencing as coming from the hand of God.[13] The language conveys the experience of extreme hardship that is being interpreted as direct punishment from God. Why would God punish his people? Because they are doing what he does not want them to.

This is not arbitrary punishment from God. Neither is it angry vengeance. Implied, but never stated, is the kind of activity that we saw projected in Deuteronomy. There, God's people were told to expect God's corrective hand for persistent, national violations of their covenant with God. Here, Isaiah implies that the nation is undergoing severe hardship as God's disciplinary intervention for their misbehavior, inflicted with a parent-like design to get them back on track, not as law enforcement's retributive punishment. Their hardship is to be a wake-up call, which the prophet implies they need to begin heeding.

Where verses 5-6 present a condition of suffering in metaphoric terms, verses 7-9 express more specifically the various distresses the people of Israel are experiencing:

> Your country lies desolate,
>   your cities are burned with fire;
> in your very presence
>   aliens devour your land;
>   it is desolate, as overthrown by foreigners.
> And daughter Zion is left
>   like a booth in a vineyard,
> like a shelter in a cucumber field,
>   like a besieged city.
> If the LORD of hosts
>   had not left us a few survivors,
> we would have been like Sodom,
>   and become like Gomorrah. **Is 1:7-9**

The prophet refers to cities burned with fire and aliens devouring their land; they appear to be experiencing a military invasion that has left desolation and destruction.[14] Who has invaded? Isaiah does not say. One valid guess associates this with a specific invasion also described in Isaiah 36, the invasion of the forces of Assyria into the territory of Judah ruled by King Hezekiah. Let's presume for the moment that this is correct. What do we have here?

The prophet is issuing a call to respond to God based on a cataclysmic event—an invasion. How can he do that? The prophet speaks for God. The prophet is interpreting a disaster as a message from God. As a nation, God's people here should acknowledge the connection and change their ways (i.e., repent).[15] Connecting disastrous events with God's judgment is risky. In most Western cultures today, people who try to do that receive strict public condemnation. The risk of sparking offense is just as great in ancient Israel, in an environment where people who could claim to belong to God are choosing to be unresponsive to God.

Now, let's also observe that no specific invasion is actually identified. Prophetic writings can be specific when they have to be. For example, the issues addressed in Isaiah 7 and following flow from a definite situation—an alliance between two foes of Ahaz, king of Judah. How do we know? Because Isaiah 7:1 says so quite directly. What might the absence of a reference to a specific historical event imply?

The writings attributed to prophets are clearly collections of sayings. How these came together and were organized is something that cannot be determined with precision, and to explore that would distract us from our task of discerning ethics. But clearly Isaiah's sayings have been arranged in a way to make their appearance together relevant beyond their initial setting.[16] Starting with awareness of an initial setting can be important. But seeing relevance of a group of sayings beyond their initial settings is equally important as implied by their arrangement. Isaiah, as a collection, appears designed to communicate significant messages for all people who need to hear words from God that may encourage them to renew or stand fast in their commitment to God.[17]

Isaiah aims to be instructive to a broad audience. As the initial hearers would be called to respond to a message designed to correct them, so all readers receive a challenge to consider how they might be disobeying God, thus needing to respond to him. That would not be simply because they are experiencing disasters in their lives, even if disasters can serve as wake-up calls. Rather, it would be to prod people to consider the seriousness of relationship with God, who desires all connected to him to live properly. The passage here strongly shows morality as an essential aspect of relationship with God.

But we still do not know from Isaiah 1 what anyone has done wrong. And we still have not observed Isaiah communicating about how to distinguish right from wrong. And we have scant awareness from Isaiah, so far, about why right should be embraced and wrong jettisoned.

Some moral specifics. Finally, we get to some definite behaviors connected to the accusations. What we see first is a bit puzzling. According to Isaiah 1:11-13, the people are being condemned for their acts of worship.

> What to me is the multitude of your sacrifices?
>   says the LORD;
> I have had enough of burnt offerings of rams
>   and the fat of fed beasts;
> I do not delight in the blood of bulls,
>   or of lambs, or of goats.
>
> When you come to appear before me,
>   who asked this from your hand?
>   Trample my courts no more;
> bringing offerings is futile;
>   incense is an abomination to me.
> New moon and sabbath and calling of convocation—
>   I cannot endure solemn assemblies with iniquity.

What gives? According the world of the Torah, sacrifices play an essential role in God's people connecting with him. Is Isaiah suggesting something different? That could be a valid conclusion were it not for the final statement: "I cannot endure solemn assemblies with iniquity." The problem is not sacrifice. The problem is sacrificing while living improper lives filled with iniquity.[18] Sacrifice, or any other religious duty, is meaningless if it is not coming from a life that also advances good on others. That becomes even clearer from the words of Isaiah 1:15, which show that God rejects prayers coming from people whose "hands are full of blood." How are their hands full of blood? The words of Isaiah 1:16-17 speak even more clearly in the language of morality:

> *Wash yourselves; make yourselves clean;*
>   *remove the evil of your doings*
>   *from before my eyes;*
> *cease to do evil,*
>   *learn to do good;*
> *seek justice,*
>   *rescue the oppressed,*
> *defend the orphan,*
>   *plead for the widow.*

The evils of perpetrating injustice and oppression, along with the evils of failing to act decisively for the fatherless and widows, are raised to the level of blood guiltiness. What a remarkable comparison. The collection of sayings began with generic accusation and moved to a description of judgment being meted out through a disastrous foreign invasion. It has just connected all that to an incomplete religiosity that has neglected the proper treatment of its society's weaker members. Isaiah has compared God's people to Sodom and Gomorrah (v. 10), cities known for being "wicked, great sinners against the LORD" (Gen 13:13). Isaiah makes that connection, not because God's people are guilty of any stereotypical immorality associated with those cities, but for their failure to address the weak in their midst. We have an impassioned declaration of the importance of helping the weak that reinforces what we have seen in Torah.

Notice the strengthening of the expectation that those in touch with God should be known for their good moral behavior. Prayers and sacrifices alone do not count; they do not suffice to show that someone is validly connected to God. But notice also that we have no stated rationale for why any of this is wrong, other than what God says in his teaching (v. 10—in Hebrew, his *tôrâ*). The main stated rationale appears to stem from God having spoken. This swerves very closely to the ethical approach known as divine command theory, an approach briefly discussed in chapter one. Israel is wrong chiefly because God, through the prophet, has said so.

Those who care about God should listen carefully to the prophetic word. But what is the sense of right and wrong here based on? Must one wait for a word from God in order to determine what is right or wrong? There is more here than initially meets the eye. We have already observed strong echoes with the world of Torah: a lawsuit motif suitable for the violation of a covenant (v. 2); the language of covenant relationship implicit in the words *my people* (v. 3); the sense of a divine intervention consequence for disobedience (v. 5); references to festivals and sacrifices (vv. 12-14); the concern for justice for the oppressed, the fatherless and the widow (v. 17); and even the references to Sodom and Gomorrah (v. 9 and, differently, v. 10). Isaiah assumes an awareness of those issues without ever directly quoting Torah. The word, even the concept of, *commandment* is entirely absent. But what we have here does not make sense apart from an awareness of basic points also found in Torah. Isaiah's words imply that God's people are wrong because they are in violation of their covenant with God.

The rest of the chapter. Isaiah offers much more than condemnation. Isaiah 1:18-19 provide a measure of hope, again in covenantal-type language.[19] For the first time we see a future prediction, one predicated on the response of the people. The people can decide to repent and experience goodness that resembles the blessings articulated in Torah, or they can stay as they are and experience negative consequences that resemble covenantal curses articulated in Torah. Isaiah 1:21-26 list further misbehaviors: murder (v. 21); theft (v. 23); bribery (v. 23); harm to the widow and fatherless (v. 23). None of that should surprise those who know the Torah. The language of Isaiah 1:29 implies idolatry, not a direct moral problem as we have been defining morality but a major infraction for those in covenant relationship with God. Positively, verses 26-27 mention righteousness and justice. Within another set of future predictions, Isaiah 1:26, 29-31 also hold out hope for the repentant. This projects the same sense of God's covenant faithfulness found in Torah. The future is not a surprising one—judgment for the rebellious (v. 28) and deliverance for those responsive to God.

Overall the passage has urged those who belong to God to examine their lives, to repent from their wickedness and to look forward to eventual final deliverance. It is intensely moral. But has there been any ethics? We have seen here the elements of our ethic of relationship: people who are in touch with God are expected to show it with their good, moral behavior; when people act immorally, they show that they are out of touch with God and receive deserved, severe prophetic condemnation. Yet we have seen no specific articulation of how right should be distinguished from wrong, only implications based on what they should know from their covenant with God.

SUMMING IT UP:
THINKING THROUGH WHAT
WE HAVE BEEN OBSERVING

- A prophet's main job is to speak for God.

- A large portion of that speaking uses the language of accusation and judgment—the prophet is a finger pointer.

- Announcements of judgment can be tied both to current and future events.

- Prophetic accusations can reflect an intense sense of morality.

- When a prophet does predict the future, the prediction need not be surprising.

- A prophet's message can reflect standards and patterns also known from the Torah.

Now, let's make some more observations.

A glimpse into the future, and concern with pride. Isaiah 2:1-4 is introduced as the "word" that Isaiah "saw" for the people of Jerusalem. That word involves "days to come"—a period yet to happen for the prophet. Let's listen in:

In days to come
    the mountain of the LORD's house
shall be established as the highest of the mountains,
    and shall be raised above the hills;
all the nations shall stream to it.
    Many peoples shall come and say,
"Come, let us go up to the mountain of the LORD,
    to the house of the God of Jacob;
that he may teach us his ways
    and that we may walk in his paths."
For out of Zion shall go forth instruction,
    and the word of the LORD from Jerusalem.
He shall judge between the nations,
    and shall arbitrate for many peoples;
they shall beat their swords into plowshares,
    and their spears into pruning hooks;
nation shall not lift up sword against nation,
    neither shall they learn war any more.

First some basics. "The mountain of the LORD's house" is a reference to the place where the temple in Jerusalem is situated. It is in a more elevated section known as the hill or mountain of Zion. So in metaphoric language the prophet is projecting a global prominence for the God whose temple is in Jerusalem, such that "all the nations shall stream to it," that is, to Jerusalem, to learn from God and "walk in his paths."

This begins an entirely new segment in the arrangement of sayings within Isaiah, a segment with a clear future orientation that runs through the end of Isaiah 4.[20] We will not proceed much beyond the verses quoted here, although we will have to make some important observations about Isaiah 2:5-22.

The future as projected here affects all nations, not just the people of Israel. It coordinates well with basic goals for God's people envisioned in the Torah, reflecting the ultimate blessing of all nations through Abraham's descendants (Gen 12:3).[21] The reader familiar with the Torah would not be surprised to read a statement expecting all nations benefitting from association with the God of Israel. People from all nations at some unspecified moment will desire to learn the "ways" of God and to "walk in his paths" (Is

2:3). Though the next statement applies that to legal mediation from God, the overall context suggests more than legal direction.[22] From the God of Jerusalem people in the world can expect "instruction"—*tôrâ*. That instruction does include God acting as judge or arbiter between nations, but the overall outcome of God's *tôrâ* fosters peace. When people in the world learn from the God of Israel, they will not need to go to war against each other ever again.

Global peace is certainly a major ethical ideal. Isaiah projects that as possible only when the whole world seeks after God to learn his ways. Isaiah does not say that the people of the world will learn *the* Torah. Rather, in turning to Israel's God, they will acquire an unspecified instruction, teaching one would expect to be in tune with what also appears in Torah. It is by virtue of seeking out and calling on the God of Israel that people are said to be receiving that. The content of that teaching is never stated. So once more we have a sense of morality without any specific guidance for how that morality can be learned, apart from connection with God. The general ethic of relationship is affirmed, without details as to what that ethic involves.

Glimpsing briefly at Isaiah 2:5-22, we see something quite different. Those verses project a sense of judgment. The judgment stems from the "house of Jacob," God's people, having embraced the ways of foreigners: divination, soothsaying, accumulation of wealth and horses (for military protection), and idolatry.[23] What is responsible for all that activity? Pride, a problem not only for God's people but for all humanity. The vocabulary of haughtiness, pride and loftiness directly appears nine times in verses 11-17. People have elevated themselves above God. That is a clear relational affront to God, one that prompts words that include the people of Israel with the ultimate judgment reserved for all nations. That moment is known eventually as "the day of the LORD," a day (Is 2:11, 12, 17, 20) when finally all who elevate themselves above God will be "brought low" (Is 2:17). When will that day occur? Isaiah does not specify, in the same way that the projection of world peace in Isaiah 2:1-4 is also not specified.

Pride and its avoidance might offer a subtle clue to understanding Isaiah's sense of right and wrong.[24] *Does this activity elevate me above God or does it elevate God over me?* If pride and its avoidance play that role, they do so in only a limited sense, since one still needs help to discern what is genuinely self-elevating or God-elevating. The persistent interest in pride that one can see throughout Isaiah probably reflects Isaiah's vision of God that he received when called to his prophetic ministry, a vision in which he "saw the Lord sitting on a throne high and lofty" (Is 6:1). At the very least, pride is a chief indicator that one is not close to God. Can people consistently do what God wants if they act as though they, and not God, are at the center of their lives?

The items in the list we've considered previously—divination, soothsaying, accumulation of wealth and horses—are addressed by the Torah. Curiously Torah hardly addresses pride.[25] Wisdom writings such as Proverbs, however, do.[26] Isaiah shares an additional cluster of common issues with wisdom. To that we turn, briefly.

Wisdom in Isaiah 5? Isaiah 5 begins with a sort of parable, expressed as a love song for God and his vineyard. It describes how God's people, having shunned God's care for them, have abandoned him for their own ways, enacting bloodshed instead of justice and provoking cries from afflicted people instead of producing righteousness. Beginning in verse 8, we see a series of woes pronounced on God's people for their misbehavior. Some of those woes make sense against the background of Torah's instructions: accumulation of others' land inheritance (v. 8), succumbing to bribery in judicial proceedings (v. 23), caring for justice and righteousness (v. 16). But others do not reflect issues at home in Torah: drunkenness and lavish parties (vv. 11-12, 22); haughtiness (v. 15), calling good evil and evil good (v. 20), people being wise in their own eyes (v. 21). Where else have we seen such concerns? Proverbs, in the world of wisdom.

Consider the expression from Isaiah 5:11: "Ah, you . . . / who linger in the evening / to be inflamed by wine." The only other place in the entire Hebrew Bible talking about "lingering" and "wine" together is Proverbs 23:29-30: "Who has woe? . . . / Those who linger late over wine, / those who keep trying mixed wines."[27] Isaiah isn't quoting Proverbs. But the vocabulary here in Isaiah certainly reflects identical concerns, with identical vocabulary, to Proverbs. The same can be said about Isaiah 5:21: "Ah, you who are wise in your own eyes." Compare that with Proverbs 3:7: "Do not be wise in your own eyes; / fear the LORD, and turn away from evil." The importance of distinguishing good from evil is also common in the world of Proverbs (e.g., Prov 11:27; 12:2; 14:22; 17:13), though Proverbs never addresses people mixing the two up. Haughtiness and pride, already observed to be important concerns for Isaiah, are also important wisdom issues (Prov 6:17; 8:13; 11:2; 15:25; 16:18-19; 18:12; 21:4, 24; 29:23).

With these clear allusions to the concerns of Torah and Proverbs, Isaiah appeals to an expansive sense of right and wrong God's people should be familiar with from other sources.[28] Isaiah definitely reflects a strong interest in morality. But the writing itself does not encourage developing active thought patterns for learning to distinguish right from wrong.[29] Its interest in ethics is minimal, even if its interest for morality is quite high.[30]

And that is proper. Prophets speak for God. They point the finger at God's people for not living up to the standards they are supposed to know as God's people, especially from the Torah.[31] Those who claim to be in touch with God would do well to heed what prophets say about what lack of connectedness to God looks like. The world of the prophets, at least based on Isaiah, would strongly affirm the atmosphere of the ethic of relationship that we have observed elsewhere. But missing from this world has been the strong sense of how to distinguish right from wrong and why one should do it. We saw that sense in the overt relational-covenantal language of the Torah (i.e., God has shown mercy to you, you should show mercy to others; you shall be holy, for God is holy; God has blessed you, you should bless others) and in the ongoing reminder of Proverbs 1–9 to acquire wisdom in the fear the Lord, the Designer of the world. Prophets assume their hearers should agree with their basic standards of right and wrong. God has spoken! Prophets also assume their hearers should want to be connected to God, and would know how to do that. People who care about knowing God respond to God's word. People who do not, despise it.

IMPORTANT MORAL ISSUES FOR PROPHETS

Special emphases. Prophets are notorious for emphasizing certain themes that are often grouped under the banner of "social justice," issues such as: regard for the poor, the widow, the fatherless, the alien; the accumulation of wealth at the unrighteous expense of others; the distortion of justice in favor of the wealthy and powerful, to the harm of the less wealthy and powerless. We have seen elements of those issues already in Isaiah, elements that also are important for Torah (and sometimes Proverbs). The same issues appear elsewhere in Isaiah as well as in prophets such as Amos 2:6-7; 4:1-3; 5:10-15; 6:1-7; 8:4-6; Micah 2:2, 8-9; 3:1-3, 9-11; 6:9-12; 7:3; or much less so in Hosea 11:7-9. It is probably no accident that, according to the opening verses of each of those writings, Isaiah, Amos, Micah and Hosea would have been contemporaries. Incidents of a particular kind of unjust land abuse seem to have been prevalent in the eighth century B.C.E., probably not as a widespread macroeconomic failing within the entire land but a more localized, microeconomic problem centered in specific major cities.[32] The need for mercy to the weak and for evenhanded prosecution of justice would have been strong where there was clear abuse.[33] The importance of caring for the poor persists in prophetic writings beyond this period, calling God's people to maintain a persistent microethical responsibility, as opposed to enacting grand, macroethical policy changes.[34]

Related to those issues, but also much more comprehensive, is the attention given to the people's leaders. Unrighteous leadership is addressed not only in the writings mentioned previously but also at length in sayings found in Jeremiah and Ezekiel. With this issue comes a more macroethical concern. As the leaders go, so the people. The leaders themselves are to be microethical, but their effect is much greater than their mere interpersonal interaction.

Though generally not with the same frequency, prophets also address accusations to the nations at large, regularly calling them out by name. Isaiah, Jeremiah, Ezekiel and Amos each have lengthy sections where nations are held accountable for their misdeeds, generally for basic standards of humaneness, their mistreatment of God's people or for their elevation of their status over God.[35] Obadiah, Jonah, Nahum and Habakkuk each predominately address judgment against specific nations.

All prophets have in common a strong message of judgment. Prophets are finger pointers. That is not all they do. A common pattern within most prophetic writings is a movement from accusation and judgment to messages of hope and restoration.[36] We do have lots finger pointing—and hope. What we find in the prophets coordinates well with what we have seen much less intensely in the Torah. God is aiming at some sort of global restoration.

Conclusions. So why are we looking at prophets? For one, they issue strong sets of moral messages. Those who belong to God are accountable to God for their behavior. Even non-Israelites are declared to be responsible for living up to general standards of humaneness. Further, prophets show that events are proceeding to fixed ends. Isaiah, for example, projects a moment of global peace—and other such moments that we did not examine.

What we have here though is a bridge within our exploration into biblical ethics. We will find that the kind of activity that urges people to connect with God is also typical of what we'll see in chapter seven, where we will encounter Jesus. We will actually see him portrayed in prophetic terms, both as a miracle worker and as a finger pointer. We should not be surprised to see Jesus strongly advocating a divine sense of right and wrong that stands at odds with what some in society let people get away with. We should not be surprised to see a strong emphasis on mercy—God's people must care for the socially disenfranchised. And we should not be surprised to see people respond to Jesus with anger for accusing them of misbehaving.

But we will also see Jesus as much more than that. He will emerge as a herald of a new, more defined program in God's restoration of global order, the program taking shape under the title "the kingdom of God." When we see Jesus as a herald of that program, we will see prophetic accusation combined with prophetic anticipation. When the weak are being trampled, they need to be rescued now, in view of the final rescuing to come. When people are being given up for lost, they need to be restored to God now, in view of the final moment of restoration to come. When someone rebels, that person needs to submit to God now, in view of the judgment to come. These senses of mercy, restoration and judgment will be important factors for understanding Jesus as we encounter him in the Gospels according to Luke and Matthew. As we read, we will discover that those writings promote the kingdom program with *ethics,* not mere morality. It is to that vision that we now turn.

Reflection Questions

1. What makes prophetic moral indictment sound obnoxious?

2. What would make someone responsive to such words?

3. Compare a wisdom approach to ethics with prophetic moral indictment.

   - What sort of circumstances would make one approach more effective than the other?

   - What leads people to gravitate to one approach over the other?

FOR FURTHER READING

Wright, Christopher J. H. *Old Testament Ethics for the People of God.* Downers Grove, IL: InterVarsity Press, 2004.

7

Reversal and Exemplar

Jesus and the Kingdom in Luke

Introductory issues

As we enter the world of Luke, let's recall, again, some basic principles.

- Ethics refers to how a person distinguishes right from wrong behavior.

- Ethics is also concerned with the reasons for why a person should choose what is good and abstain from what is not.

Let's also remember that biblical ethics involves more than merely identifying statements that address moral issues. Rather,

- Biblical ethics is concerned with how the writings themselves advocate distinctions between right and wrong, and what motives exist for choosing right and condemning wrong.

- Biblical ethics must always start from an understanding of the Bible's own messages based on the individual writings' purposes, agendas and ideologies.

In this chapter we will explore how the Gospel of Luke encourages distinguishing right from wrong behavior.[1] We will also explore why, according to Luke, someone should choose right over wrong. We will run into limitations here, as we have elsewhere. Luke does not exist to advance an ethical system. Its purpose is to portray the life of the significant, central figure of the New Testament, Jesus.

We will also see that where ethics in the Old Testament has tended to look to the past—creation, deliverance from slavery in Egypt—we will find ethics in the New Testament looking to the future, to the *kingdom* in the Gospels or to *salvation* in Paul. Before probing how Luke's portrayal of Jesus does that, we first have to address some important issues.

What is a Gospel? The word *gospel* comes from an Old English word, *godspel*, that combines two words: *god*, meaning "good," and *spel*, meaning "news." It is used to translate the Greek word *euangelion*, which also means "good news." News is event centered, often a simple declaration: "We won!"—the game or perhaps the battle.

New Testament writers used the expression "good news" to declare the outcome of the events surrounding Jesus, who throughout the New Testament is regarded as the one who takes God's world-reordering program begun with Abraham to a new and fresh level. Stories about Jesus were recorded in writings eventually known as "Gospels"—good news accounts about Jesus that described selected aspects of what he said and did. The New Testament has four such accounts, usually abbreviated as Matthew, Mark, Luke and John, after those traditionally considered to be their authors. In the Gospels themselves the news is a variant of "The kingdom of God has come near to you" (Lk 10:9). The Gospels address the basic circumstances associated with that news, focusing on Jesus, the bringer of God's kingdom, that ultimate expression of God's reign over the earth and its inhabitants.

For much of the twentieth century, scholars approached the Gospels' genre as a literary invention of the first followers of Jesus, the early Christians. Scholarship in the last two decades of the twentieth century, however, has successfully shown how the Gospels, rather than being Christian inventions, are Christian adaptations of a well-known type of literature, the Greco-Roman *Life* (Greek—*bios*; Latin—*vita*), a form of biography.[2]

Unlike our biographies, which attempt to give detailed accounts of all aspects of the life of their subjects, Greco-Roman biographies would focus on representative words and deeds, presented in a loosely chronological fashion. While our biographies often explain how a certain person achieved greatness and what hurdles he or she had to overcome in doing that, Greco-Roman biographies were more interested in showing who their subjects were and why those people were worth celebrating, perhaps even following in some way. They often served a morally instructive purpose so that those who read them could learn proper ways of living based on how the subject of the *Life* was said to have lived. Regularly, a Greco-Roman biography would focus with more detailed chronology on the way its subject's life ended, sometimes to explain the difficult circumstances of an unusual death, and sometimes even to show how the death reflected the essential elements of the subject's life as the writer has portrayed it.[3]

What we find in the New Testament's Gospels basically reflects that pattern. Luke unquestionably gives us episodic snatches from Jesus' life rather than a blow-by-blow chronology. We certainly have representative words and deeds. Luke definitely celebrates a core set of ideas about Jesus. And his description of the end of Jesus' earthly existence, the most drawn-out sequence, does indeed bring to a climax a set of issues about Jesus that has also appeared throughout the writing.

Further, just as other *Lives* sometimes provide moral guidance, Luke is both religiously and morally instructive. Its words aim not so much to convert its readers to faith in Jesus as to affirm them in their conversion and help them to be better followers of the one they have devoted their lives to.[4] The first followers of Jesus in the Gospels were known as "disciples"— learners. Luke's language addresses people who would want to align themselves with those disciples.

Understanding Luke, then, requires that we trace how the writing presents Jesus' words and deeds to portray its own outlook of who Jesus is and why Jesus is worth celebrating and his agenda worth adhering to. That means suspending what we may know about Jesus from general knowledge. It also means not dragging into Luke issues that we may know about Jesus from other writings in the New Testament that Luke never appeals to in the story. We will want to focus entirely on what Luke aims to communicate. We will place ourselves at Luke's mercy, letting Luke guide us through the deeds and words of Jesus. We will think in terms of "Luke says" rather than "Jesus says," seeking principally to understand Luke's portrayal of Jesus, not merely Jesus.[5] We should expect a strong religious or pious dimension to that portrayal. Closely tied to that will be challenges to the reader to respond to the fullness of what Jesus stands for, not in piety alone but in the ethical vision that emerges from that. One major feature we will discover is that Luke portrays Jesus as an exemplar, a point that we will explore a bit later.

More than a teacher. Scholars of the Gospels have long noted how readers' preconceived ideas of Jesus often compete with the images of Jesus portrayed by the Gospels.[6] Jesus looms as such a large figure in general popular awareness that people often impose their ideals onto him, rather than observe how each Gospel actually portrays him. Among the many images to which people regularly reduce Jesus are two related concepts that focus on Jesus' words, at the expense of his deeds: that of philosopher and that of moral teacher, advancing an agenda of love.[7]

No Gospel ever portrays Jesus as a philosopher.[8] We rarely see Jesus as a Socrates who relentlessly probes the faulty reasoning of others, in the process discovering a more accurate way. We do see situations where various people test him, and where he comports himself with extraordinary wisdom. And on some occasions Jesus does question people. But we never see him addressing the crowds, or even his disciples, about great philosophical questions of life: Who am I? How do I exist? What should be my destiny? We do see a number of pithy sayings, but not exhaustively reasoned comments. And those sayings do not generally address philosophical subjects but rather the program that he claimed to have been advancing—the kingdom of God.[9] The Gospels never show the crowds perceiving Jesus as a philosopher.

The Gospel of Luke certainly does affirm Jesus' role as teacher, as opposed to philosopher. At least twenty-eight times throughout its pages we see Jesus either teaching or being addressed as a teacher. What we tend to see in Luke, though, is not someone instructing others in the way they should live morally or challenging people with a new philosophy of life. Rather, we often see Jesus speaking with a definite prophetic edge, frequently pointing a judging finger at others. He is concerned with people being out of touch with God and his program. Jesus' most frequently addressed topic in Luke, as in other Gospels, is God's restoration program: the kingdom of God.[10] When he teaches, Jesus advances a divine intervention program connected with God's reign over the world, not any kind of philosophical system.

The second faulty image, Jesus as the great teacher of love, likewise falls apart under scrutiny. True, he did make some striking comments about love, some of which we will explore in chapter eight on Matthew. But those comments do not capture the essence of who Jesus was and what he promoted. He never once, in any Gospel, said that *all people* should love each other. In one Gospel, the Gospel of John, Jesus told his disciples to love one another as proof to an unbelieving world that they were his disciples.[11] And in two other Gospels, Matthew and Mark, Jesus spoke the words "Love your neighbor as yourself," though those words, as we have already seen in chapter four, were not invented by Jesus. They appear in the Torah, in Leviticus 19:18. Jesus was quoting, not speaking afresh.

In Luke Jesus never quotes the words "Love your neighbor as yourself." Those words are only spoken by someone who was coming to "test" Jesus (Lk 10:23-27). The word *love* is used by Jesus just four times in Luke, three of those in close proximity within a section where he is instructing his disciples: "Love your enemies, do good to those who hate you, bless those who curse you, pray for those who abuse you" (Lk 6:27-28); "If you love those who love you, what credit is that to you? For even sinners love those who love them" (Lk 6:32); "But love your enemies, do good, and lend, expecting nothing in return" (Lk 6:35). In one other usage, he criticizes a group called Pharisees for neglecting the "love of God" (Lk 11:42). That small cluster hardly displays a core message, even if those words do offer challenging, deep thought.

When we fixate on words from Jesus, we can also fool ourselves into thinking that everything Jesus ever said is found in the Gospels, something that one Gospel certainly declares to be impossible (Jn 20:30-31; 21:25). Then we can assume that whatever subject we do not see Jesus addressing must be unimportant to life. "Jesus never taught about that," people say. Or "Jesus taught more about this topic than about that." So what! We are at the mercy of the Gospels. We see one set of words from Jesus and not others, because each Gospel conveys its own special set of ideas about him. Ethical insight will come from close attention to those unique emphases. There are all sorts of moral topics that no Gospel ever shows Jesus addressing—for example, rape or spousal abuse. Should disciples of Jesus remain morally neutral about those for lack of words from Jesus about them?

Relying merely on topics addressed by Jesus to determine moral views swerves too closely to divine command theory. That would be valid only if Luke, or any other Gospel, portrayed Jesus as a figure who aimed to establish an ethical system based on his sayings. In this chapter we will see that Luke does no such thing. An exploration into the other Gospels would yield similar results. Remember, it's not right just because Jesus said so. Jesus said so because it's right. Why is it right? Answering that will help us uncover the ethical emphases of each Gospel.

The major problem with all of these ways of thinking is that they elevate Jesus' words over his deeds.[12] Gospels, as Greco-Roman biographies, present selected words and deeds. Both should be considered as part of each Gospel's overall picture of Jesus. That is easier to do in Luke than in Matthew, where we can get so drawn into his sustained blocks of teaching that we miss the point of the rest of the Gospel. It is why we are probing Luke before Matthew, even though Matthew is prior in the table of contents. By establishing our biography-reading patterns with Luke, we can better perceive what Matthew is doing. As we work our way through both Gospels, we will try to learn from what Jesus did, as well as what he said.

LUKE'S STORY OF JESUS

So, how does Luke portray Jesus? The basic story structure is quite simple, falling into four broad sections. The first, an introduction spanning Luke 1:1–4:13, alternates between stories about the birth and early years of John the Baptizer, a prominent predecessor to Jesus, and about Jesus himself. Subsequent sections follow a loose chronology organized around broad geographic movements. Starting in Luke 4:14, Jesus is shown interacting with people in the territory of Galilee. A third section of the Gospel begins in Luke 9:51, when Jesus embarks for Jerusalem from Galilee. The final section begins in Luke 19:29 with Jesus' entry into the city of Jerusalem, relating momentous events that lead, in that city, to the end of his earthly life.

Beyond Jesus' geographical movements, Luke displays several important thematic concerns. The first activities in the Gospel (Lk 1:5-23) take place in the central worship structure for Jewish people, the temple in Jerusalem. The last moment of the Gospel (Lk 24:53) refers to continued activities in the same place. Other moments of worship dot the Gospel's landscape. At regular intervals, people praise God—specific words of praise abound especially in the first two chapters. In this Gospel, more than in any other, Jesus is shown praying or teaching on prayer. The Holy Spirit is also referred to in Luke more than in any other Gospel. That Spirit both guides and empowers Jesus. This writing has a uniquely clear, positive God focus.[13] That focus itself teams up with numerous reversals of expectation and inversions of social outcomes that abound throughout the writing.[14] Certainly something more than mere geographic movement from Galilee to Jerusalem is going on. In fact, the movement eventually to Jerusalem, coupled with statements about its significance (Lk 13:31-35), point to that city as the place of his ultimate destiny, where Luke's picture of Jesus comes most sharply into focus.[15]

Luke introduces Jesus as the great one, who is to advance God's plan to remake the world in a new and fresh way. Yet Luke principally portrays Jesus as the humble one who is to be exalted.[16] That exaltation takes place ultimately in the final events of the Gospel, with Jesus' bodily resurrection from the dead and then ascension into heaven. That exaltation begins to happen within the Gospel as various individuals see who Jesus is. Luke makes a point of showing the renowned Jesus in quite unglamorous settings. Though forecast initially as a great king, Jesus is born into lowly circumstances. An angel declares to his mother, Mary, that "He will be great, and will be called the Son of the Most High, and the Lord God will give to him the throne of his ancestor David. He will reign over the house of Jacob forever, and of his kingdom there will be no end" (Lk 1:32-33).

Yet Mary is portrayed as an unwed mother at the time of his birth (Lk 2:5-6).[17] The baby Jesus is placed in a feeding trough for animals. He is first visited by humble shepherds.[18] His mother offers the poor person's sacrifice for Jewish ritual purification after birth (compare Lk 2:24 with Lev 12:6-8). The great one does not appear to be very great at all. Further, he ministers throughout Galilee to all sorts of socially questionable people: sick, poor, lepers, demon-possessed, Gentiles, Samaritans, women, tax collectors, "sinners."[19] He continues the same kinds of activities as he moves toward Jerusalem, while in Jerusalem he is thoroughly humiliated by being crucified, receiving public shame and scorn (Lk 23:34-46). Then, in a stunning reversal three days later, he is shown having been raised bodily from the dead (Lk 24:1-9). After significant postresurrection encounters with his disciples (Lk 24:13-49) he is taken up into heaven (Lk 24:50-51), receiving the ultimate in exaltation. All throughout the Gospel, in fact, we witness Jesus being either elevated or denigrated by various people or groups of people. This is a story about the elevation of Jesus. It is an elevation from God's perspective, and all in this story who have God's perspective elevate him with their own words and deeds. It is also a story filled with moments when Jesus is belittled by those who refuse to recognize his greatness.

Evaluation standards are called into question throughout the Gospel. From its inception we see social expectations turned inside out. Those expectations appear to be contrasted with a God perspective. Those portrayed as wanting God's perspective see Jesus appropriately. Those portrayed as resisting God's perspective see him inappropriately. To set us up for such a contrast, Luke appears to pull out from beneath us our own rug of social expectations.

Highlights from Luke's introduction: Luke 1:1–4:13. Consider the opening scenes. We are introduced to a childless, honored figure; a righteous, old male priest named Zechariah.[20] An angel appears to him, declaring that his prayers are about to be answered and that at last his wife would conceive and bear him a son. Zechariah questions how that could be since both he and his wife are old. The angel rebukes him with an accompanying sign: he will be mute until the events the angel has foretold come to pass. After the priest returns home, his wife conceives a child and then hides herself.[21] In the very next scene the same angel appears to an unimportant, young virgin named Mary.[22] When he declares that she is about to conceive a son, she questions how that could happen, since she was a virgin. Note, she is allowed to ask a question. Not fair!—but then this Gospel does challenge expectations of propriety. Certainly her question is of a somewhat different nature from Zechariah's, but she still gets to ask one, unlike him. She receives an answer and then accepts the plan. Thus we have it: the old, honored male priest questions God's messenger and gets taken down; the young, less-honored woman questions God's messenger, gets an answer, accepts the plan and gets raised up. And, reinforcing the atmosphere of reversal of expectations, she is shown soon after praising God with language full of contrasts between high and low status people:[23]

> [God] has looked with favor on the lowliness of his servant . . .
> He has shown strength with his arm;
>   he has scattered the proud in the thoughts of their hearts.
> He has brought down the powerful from their thrones,
>   and lifted up the lowly;
> he has filled the hungry with good things,
>   and sent the rich away empty. **Lk 1:48, 51-53**

We are served notice as readers. We should expect any sense of social ordering, propriety or valuation that we may have to be challenged by Luke's story of Jesus.[24] Luke sets up a contrast between what people value and what God values. What God values is all that matters. Throughout the story, people's values are routinely reversed. Those who accept their place before God or his agents, thus lowering themselves, get elevated; those who question their place before God or his agents, thus elevating themselves, get lowered.

Jesus arrives on the scene as God's unique agent. Responding to him and responding to God are equivalent.[25]

Of course there is more than this pattern of reversal. There is the positive God focus already mentioned. Even that positive focus encourages people to place themselves beneath God. In this atmosphere, what God has planned will indeed take place. Jesus is God's agent for that. John the Baptizer is the forerunner to this agent. When John is born, his father affirms that his name indeed should be John and is consequently enabled to speak once more. With this measure of elevation, Zechariah

> was filled with the Holy Spirit and spoke this prophecy:
>
> "Blessed be the Lord God of Israel,
> > for he has looked favorably on his people and redeemed them.
> He has raised up a mighty savior for us
> > in the house of his servant David,
> as he spoke through the mouth of his holy prophets from of old,
> > that we would be saved from our enemies and from the hand of all who hate us.
> Thus he has shown the mercy promised to our ancestors,
> > and has remembered his holy covenant,
> the oath that he swore to our ancestor Abraham,
> > to grant us that we, being rescued from the hands of our enemies,
> might serve him without fear, in holiness and righteousness
> > before him all our days." **Lk 1:68-75**

We learn again to anticipate a story about a kingly "savior" from the "house of . . . David" who will revive the Abrahamic promises declared in the Scriptures.[26] Equipped with that perspective, we see Joseph setting out to Bethlehem as a descendant of David. We see Mary, not merely an unwed pregnant woman but a woman who has conceived a baby miraculously through the Holy Spirit, never having had sex with a man. In this Gospel surface appearances are often unreliable. One must recognize Jesus for who he truly is, since he does not appear to meet the expectations of everyone in his story.

When the baby Jesus himself is dedicated in the Jewish temple in Jerusalem, he receives words of affirmation that he is God's "Messiah," God's "salvation" and a "light for revelation to the Gentiles and for glory to [God's] people Israel" (Lk 2:26, 30, 32). Mary is told, "This child is destined for the falling and the rising of many in Israel, and to be a sign that will be opposed so that the inner thoughts of many will be revealed—and a sword will pierce your own soul too" (Lk 2:34-35). The readers themselves see people "rising" and "falling" throughout this story, based entirely on how those people either humble themselves or elevate themselves before Jesus.[27]

Highlights from Luke's part two—Jesus in Galilee: Luke 4:14-9:50. Let's jump ahead to Jesus' first publicly recognized moment as portrayed by Luke, his appearance on the sabbath at the local synagogue in his hometown, Nazareth. There we observe Jesus reading the following words from the scroll of the prophet Isaiah:

> The Spirit of the Lord is upon me,
>   because he has anointed me
>   to bring good news to the poor.
> He has sent me to proclaim release to the captives
>   and recovery of sight to the blind,
>   to let the oppressed go free,
> to proclaim the year of the Lord's favor. **Lk 4:18-19**

He then declares, "Today this scripture has been fulfilled in your hearing" (Lk 4:21). The time of reversal has begun.[28] People in positions of lowly status can expect elevation. And yet the hearers in the synagogue ultimately reject that announcement, forcing Jesus to a nearby cliff, where they try to throw him over. The incident sets the tone for what follows.

After a series of extraordinary deeds, Jesus appears by the Sea of Galilee, teaching from a boat. What he taught receives no coverage. His encounter with the boat's owner, Simon Peter, does. Taking Jesus' suggestion to fish in deeper water, he is astounded by the overwhelming catch of fish he and his companions land. Falling "down at Jesus' knees, [Peter said], 'Go away from me, Lord, for I am a sinful man!'" (Lk 5:8). What has Peter done here that would be considered sinful? Nothing.[29] But with that response Luke portrays Peter's sudden awareness of Jesus' surpassing greatness in orchestrating the miraculous catch. Peter knows his place before Jesus, his own unworthiness to be in Jesus' company. Jesus responds by elevating him: "Do not be afraid; from now on you will be catching people" (Lk 5:10). Those who acknowledge their own worthlessness in comparison to Jesus receive affirmation. That becomes a recurring pattern for Luke's story of Jesus.

 In the very next scene a leper lowers himself before Jesus.[30] He "bow[s] with his face to the ground and beg[s] him, 'Lord, if you choose, you can make me clean'" (Lk 5:12). Jesus heals him, a form of elevation. Soon after that, Jesus calls a tax collector named Levi to follow him. Levi then invites Jesus to a party at his house, attended by a "large crowd of tax collectors" (Lk 5:29). That draws a negative reaction from a notorious religious group, the Pharisees, who complain about the company that Jesus keeps. Jesus has elevated a man who belongs to the category of people the Pharisees denigrate. We have a power struggle over who is worthwhile to God and who is not. Luke portrays Jesus' perspective as the correct one, but the Pharisees refuse to acknowledge that his sense of proper association is better than theirs. Jesus remarks that he has "come to call not the righteous but sinners to repentance" (Lk 5:32). In scenes immediately following, Pharisees continue to question Jesus' authority to do what he does. Luke consistently portrays Pharisees as those who see themselves as better than Jesus.

After choosing twelve disciples to be his special agents, apostles, Jesus begins teaching them with a shocking message of reversals. The poor, the hungry and the mourners, he proclaims, are all blessed, while the rich, the full and the happy are to incur woe (Lk 6:20-21, 24-25). The disciples should love their enemies, bless those who curse them, pray for those who abuse them, turn the other cheek to those who strike them, give to all who ask of them (Lk 6:27-31).

 In the next scene a group of Jewish elders approach Jesus on behalf of a Gentile centurion to ask Jesus to heal that centurion's beloved slave. "He is worthy of having you do this for him," they say, "for he loves our people, and it is he who built our synagogue for us" (Lk 7:4-5). According to their values, the centurion's use of his wealth as their benefactor qualifies him to receive mercy from Jesus.[31] But the centurion himself sends other messengers to say, "Lord, do not trouble yourself, for I am not worthy to have you come under my roof" (Lk 7:6). The worthy centurion recognizes Jesus' superiority, calling himself unworthy. In the end he receives both a healed slave and special commendation from Jesus for his faith. In the very next scene Jesus revives the son of a poor widow, once more elevating someone in an intensely weak situation (Lk 7:11-17).[32]

Later, in Luke 7:36-50, Luke portrays a setting where a Pharisee named Simon invites Jesus to his house for a lavish meal, but fails to show him the proper courtesies of hospitality for honored guests.[33] While there, a woman identified only as a "sinner" visits the meal, performing extravagant acts that go beyond mere devotion: weeping, bathing Jesus' feet with her tears, drying them with her hair, kissing his feet, anointing his feet with ointment.[34] Simon inwardly criticizes Jesus for not knowing what type of woman is doing such things to him. Jesus, knowing Simon's thoughts, then tells a story, the point of which eventually puts Simon in his place for not seeing the woman the same way that Jesus has. In the end the woman is commended for showing such great love, motivated by her awareness that Jesus has forgiven her.[35] She receives a public declaration from Jesus that her sins indeed have been forgiven.

The social dynamics here are intense. The woman enters as a sinner and remains a sinner as far as Simon and those like him are concerned. But from Jesus' perspective she enters as one who knows Jesus has forgiven her, showing extremely humble forms of devotion. She leaves with a public affirmation that God has given her the highest elevation—forgiveness of her sins, which are never described, only said to have been many. The Pharisee gets taken down in his attempt to see himself as better than Jesus. The sinner is elevated in her humiliating expressions of devotion. The guests question who Jesus is to be able to pronounce forgiveness, activity that should not surprise those who are really in the know.

The reversals continue. We learn at the beginning of Luke 8 about formerly demon-possessed women, not male disciples, who are financially supporting Jesus (Lk 8:1-3).[36] In the middle of that chapter, Jesus tells a series of parables, the point of one being that

> nothing is hidden that will not be disclosed, nor is anything secret that will not become known and come to light. Then pay attention to how you listen; for to those who have, more will be given; and from those who do not have, even what they seem to have will be taken away. **Lk 8:17-18**

He declares that his true kindred are not his physical family but those who hear and do God's will (Lk 8:21). He astonishes his disciples by calming a raging storm on the sea (Lk 8:22-25). He has mercy on a demon-possessed man and then is banished from the territory for sending the demons from the man into a herd of pigs (Lk 8:26-39). He openly commends the faith of a woman healed from a prolonged hemorrhage, after that woman had secretly tried to touch him (Lk 8:43-48). He raises a little girl from the dead after being told that coming to her would be futile and being laughed at publicly when he states that she was only sleeping (Lk 8:49-56). These all defy expectations in some manner.

A bit later, after Peter declares that Jesus is "the Messiah of God" (Lk 9:20), Jesus "sternly ordered and commanded them not to tell anyone, saying, 'The Son of Man must undergo great suffering, and be rejected by the elders, chief priests, and scribes, and be killed, and on the third day be raised'" (Lk 9:21-22), an inverted notion—one would expect the declaration of Jesus as Messiah to be shouted abroad. And one should certainly not expect the Messiah to be rejected. The words that follow this continue the startling nature of this scene:

> If any want to become my followers, let them deny themselves and take up their cross daily and follow me. For those who want to save their life will lose it, and those who lose their life for my sake will save it. What does it profit them if they gain the whole world, but lose or forfeit themselves? Those who are ashamed of me and of my words, of them the Son of Man will be ashamed when he comes in his glory and the glory of the Father and of the holy angels. **Lk 9:23-26**

Association with the Messiah should mean association with glory. Instead, Jesus associates himself with shame, which is what the cross signifies to the Roman culture Luke's Gospel initially addresses.[37] Those who follow Jesus must themselves enter into a reversal of expectations. And yet the reader is also given a glimpse of Jesus in an honored state, when in the next scene Jesus is praying on a hilltop with three of his disciples and "the appearance of his face changed, and his clothes became dazzling white" (Lk 9:29). Two men, Moses and Elijah, are seen talking to him, appearing "in glory and . . . speaking of his departure, which he was about to accomplish at Jerusalem" (Lk 9:31). His departure? At the end of the Gospel, Jesus leaves by being taken up into heaven.[38] Once more Luke affirms that Jesus is indeed far greater than he often appears to be to others in his story.

Highlights from Luke's part three—Jesus' journey to Jerusalem: Luke

9:51–19:28. Soon after this, Luke's Gospel shifts to a segment known as the "travel narrative," in which Jesus sets out for Jerusalem, the place from which his departure is to be accomplished. The segment has an even higher concentration of reversals of expectations and inversions of social situations.

After debriefing with seventy of his disciples whom he had sent out to declare the nearness of the kingdom, Jesus tells his disciples how privileged they are to have heard and seen what they had about Jesus. Out of that, a lawyer tests, or challenges, Jesus' loftiness with a question: "Teacher, ... what must I do to inherit eternal life?" (Lk 10:25).[39] Jesus responds with a question, "What is written in the law? What do you read there?" (Lk 10:26). When the lawyer answers by quoting the commands to love God and neighbor, Jesus responds, "You have given the right answer; do this, and you will live" (Lk 10:28). The lawyer had been trying to get the better of Jesus, and resenting that Jesus had turned the tables on him asks, "And who is my neighbor?" (Lk 10:29). Jesus responds with a parable whose hero is most unexpected, a Samaritan (archenemies of Jews), who stops to help a bleeding victim of roadside robbers after having been neglected by two other, more honorable travelers.[40] When asked, "'Which of these three, do you think, was a neighbor to the man who fell into the hands of the robbers?' [The lawyer] said, 'The one who showed him mercy.' Jesus said to him, 'Go and do likewise'" (Lk 10:36-37). What a reversal! The lawyer initially tries to put Jesus in his place with his test, exalting himself over Jesus. Instead he gets taken down. The parable cements the reversal, advancing an unlikely hero, a Samaritan, whom the lawyer cannot even mention, and whom he is then told to emulate.[41]

Next, as Jesus and his disciples "went on their way" to Jerusalem, they end up in the house of two women, Mary and Martha. Mary is sitting at Jesus' feet, the position assumed in that culture by male learners.[42] Martha is involved in the meal preparation, the traditional female role. In another typical inversion of social roles, Mary is commended over her sister Martha (Lk 10:41-42).[43] The cultural sense of propriety for Luke's world is being challenged yet again.

When people denigrate Jesus by accusing him of being empowered by the prince of demons (Lk 11:14-26), he confronts his accusers, declaring their eventual doom (Lk 11:29-32). Jesus then challenges all people who fail to see properly who he is, and thus what God is doing and wanting in the world; when people see improperly, they reveal their own inner moral and spiritual

darkness (Lk 11:33-36).[44] After Pharisees criticize him for eating with unwashed hands, he responds by pronouncing woe both upon them and upon
lawyers who question him (Lk 11:37-54). Soon after, he contrasts God's perspectives on money with popular notions (Lk 12:13-34). He shows mercy to
an old, crippled woman, and then puts a synagogue leader in his place when
he criticizes Jesus for healing on the sabbath (Lk 13:10-17). "When he said
this, all his opponents were put to shame; and the entire crowd was rejoicing
at all the wonderful things that he was doing" (v. 17). Jesus exalts the humble
and humbles the exalted, based on how they respond to him.

Those thoughts are expressed directly soon after this, when Jesus is invited
to the home of a Pharisee to eat. He notices the guests positioning themselves
for the most honored seats, and dares to challenge his hosts with a parable,
which echoes words from Proverbs 25:6-7, how it would be better to take a
lower seat and be asked to come higher than to take a more honored seat and
be asked to come lower.[45] He summarizes the advice with a prophetic pronouncement that declares what we as readers have been seeing throughout
this Gospel: "For all who exalt themselves will be humbled, and those who
humble themselves will be exalted" (Lk 14:11). The statement moves beyond
mere table etiquette. Knowing one's place before God is the key issue.[46] But,
as we have seen throughout the Gospel, knowing one's place before Jesus,
God's special agent, is equivalent to knowing one's place before God.

Luke continues to show Jesus reversing expectations with his teaching
that those who cannot repay should be those invited to banquets (Lk 14:12-
14), and with his parable about the lowly being welcomed to a banquet that
the original invitees had insultingly refused to attend (Lk 14:15-24). Those
who want to be disciples should know that following Jesus is reputationally
expensive, requiring a reversal in the expectations of public honor: they
must choose Jesus over family (Lk 14:26); they must "carry the cross" (Lk
14:27), a clear association with shame; they must give up their possessions
(Lk 14:33) as part of counting the cost of following him.

When Pharisees complain that he welcomes "tax collectors and sinners,"
Jesus responds with three parables that show the joy in God's presence when
the lost are found, when sinners repent. The final parable in this series itself
contains all sorts of reversals of expectation[47]—a son dishonoring his father
by asking for his inheritance early; the father surprisingly giving it; the son
squandering the inheritance and choosing to return home in shame, willing

to be treated by his father as a hired hand; the father, instead, having a party to celebrate the son's return; the son's older brother insulting his father for so treating his younger brother; the father accepting that insult, urging him to consider why there must be a celebration (Lk 15:11-32). In the end the opponents appear as the obvious targets of criticism. They should be rejoicing instead of complaining. In exalting themselves over Jesus, they find themselves lowered—though they are also challenged to change their minds, or repent, and embrace the same attitude about repentant tax collectors and sinners as the father in the parable displays to his returning son.

They ridicule Jesus for his comments about the dichotomy between serving God and serving money. He puts them in their place: "You are those who justify yourselves in the sight of others; but God knows your hearts; for what is prized by human beings is an abomination in the sight of God" (Lk 16:15). Their sense of valuation is radically out of touch with God's.[48] Luke follows this encounter with an unusual parable about a rich man and a poor man—one of the characters, Lazarus the poor beggar, is actually named.[49] In a complete reversal of fortune, Lazarus, who used to sit at the rich man's gate, is carried by angels to "to be with Abraham" (Lk 16:22), while the unnamed rich man finds himself in "Hades, where he was being tormented" (Lk 16:23). When the rich man asks for Lazarus to go back and warn his brothers about their eventual fate, he is told that "Moses and the prophets" (i.e., the Scriptures) should suffice (Lk 16:29). According to Jesus' words, the socially important must rethink what really matters from God's perspective.

Meanwhile, others receive challenges from Jesus. Disciples must never lead others astray with their behavior. Neither must they restrict how much forgiveness they offer others. They must forgive and forgive and forgive (Lk 17:1-6). They must consider themselves to be on the same level as "worthless slaves" (Lk 17:10), not expecting any special privileges for living the moral, God-pleasing lives Jesus' words here encourage.[50] When Jesus shows mercy by healing a group of ten lepers, social outcasts indeed, only one of them returns to thank Jesus, a Samaritan whom Jesus elevates, while criticizing the others for failing to do so (Lk 17:11-19).

After defying the kingdom expectations of some Pharisees (Lk 17:20-21), Jesus tells a parable about a Pharisee and a tax collector (Lk 18:9-14), where yet again he turns social expectations inside out. The Pharisee prays in a manner that elevates himself over all, including the tax collector. The tax collector, by contrast, refuses even to look up while praying, beating his breast in anguish as he calls on God for mercy. He, rather than the Pharisee, is commended, since "all who exalt themselves will be humbled, but all who humble themselves will be exalted" (Lk 18:14), the second time we see those words. Knowing their place before God, and by extension Jesus, becomes essential for those who would follow Jesus.[51]

This scene is followed in quick succession by a series of incidents where Jesus elevates children as models for receiving the kingdom (Lk 18:15-17); challenges a rich ruler to sell all and follow him (Lk 18:18-23), declaring how money and possessions hinder entrance to the kingdom (Lk 18:24-30); warns his disciples of his imminent shame (Lk 18:31-34); heals a blind man crying out for mercy to the elevated "Son of David" (Lk 18:35-43); and feasts in the house of a wealthy, repentant tax collector named Zacchaeus, who initially shows a measure of humility toward Jesus by trying to glimpse him from a tree branch and who, having been accepted by Jesus, later shows the extent of his repentance by declaring his intention to spread his wealth to the poor and repay with extra interest those whom he had defrauded (Lk 19:1-10).[52]

In this last incident Jesus again receives criticism for being "the guest of one who is a sinner" (v. 7), criticism that he meets by pointing out that Zacchaeus "too is a son of Abraham" just as they would claim to be. He also underscores his role as Savior of the lost, with Zacchaeus the rich sinner offering yet another example of Jesus' rescuing of others.[53] Once more, those who elevate themselves over Jesus are corrected, while others they would want to denigrate are elevated by virtue of knowing their place before Jesus.

Highlights from Luke's part four—Jesus' departure in Jerusalem: Luke 19:29–24:53. Jesus finally arrives in Jerusalem, where he is initially acclaimed as the great "king who comes in the name of the Lord!" (Lk 19:38). When some Pharisees, appalled by the acclamation, order Jesus to correct the crowds, Jesus instead corrects them (Lk 19:39-40). That, followed by Jesus' acts of judgment in the temple (Lk 19:45-46), sets up a series of conflicts with Jewish leaders in the city of Jerusalem. The leaders try to get the better of Jesus by attempting to make him look foolish before the crowds. Instead, Jesus increases his stature each time by foiling their attempts to ensnare him, eventually criticizing them openly (Lk 19:45–20:47). He then, in typical fashion, elevates a poor widow who contributes all she had to the temple treasury, a contrast to those who give only out of their abundance (Lk 21:1-4). People's sense of order continues to be challenged by Jesus, who offers an alternative evaluative pattern.

The words of the story move the life of Jesus to a cataclysmic event—his crucifixion. Jesus' opponents refuse to see him as the great one that Luke has shown him to be. They seek not merely to kill him but to destroy his reputation at the same time. Consequently, they readily accept the offer of one of Jesus' disciples to betray him (Lk 22:1-6). Luke has been foreshadowing Jesus' death throughout. Recall the following: Simeon's words to Mary, Jesus' mother in Luke 2:34-35; the attempt of his hometown acquaintances to kill him (Lk 4:16-30); and his own words immediately following Peter's declaration of Jesus as God's Messiah (Lk 9:22).[54] Thus the Passover meal Jesus celebrates with his disciples at this point of the story takes on extra significance in view of his imminent death. The bread that he breaks with them at the end of the meal is his "body, which is given for [them]," while the "cup that is poured out for [them] is the new covenant in [his] blood" (Lk 22:19-20). Even as Jesus declares that he is being betrayed by one of his own, however, his disciples respond by arguing which of them is the greatest. That prompts Jesus to challenge a major aspect of Roman social order, the sense of greatness fostered by the patron-client system:

> The kings of the Gentiles lord it over them; and those in authority over them are called benefactors. But not so with you; rather the greatest among you must become like the youngest, and the leader like one who serves. For who is greater, the one who is at the table or the one who serves? Is it not the one at the table? But I am among you as one who serves. **Lk 22:25-27**

Once again Luke portrays Jesus offering a competing sense of order and valuation from that posed by the social world of his readership.[55] And with those words he offers himself as a model, a pattern setter, an exemplar. Further, Jesus, according to Luke, sees what he must go through as a necessary humiliation to fulfill what was written about him in the Scriptures: "For I tell you, this scripture must be fulfilled in me, 'And he was counted among the lawless'; and indeed what is written about me is being fulfilled" (Lk 22:37).[56]

The events of the story take Jesus through abandonment by his disciples

(Lk 22:54-62) and mockery and shame at the hands of various important groups of people: temple authorities who refuse to recognize Jesus as God's agent (Lk 22:62-65), the ruler Herod (Lk 23:8-11), and eventually the Roman soldiers and other people present at the crucifixion site (Lk 23:35-38). Further, in a strange twist of events, Luke also depicts an ironic conversation between Jesus and the two criminals who were being crucified with him. One criminal, himself a thoroughly shameful man undergoing the public humiliation of crucifixion, begins to make fun of Jesus. The other criminal defends Jesus, noting Jesus' innocence, in contrast to their obvious guilt. That same criminal then calls on Jesus to save him. In spite of the public humiliation of being crucified, he receives a spectacular promise from Jesus (Lk 23:43). The scene stunningly portrays Luke's reversals. A man who had lived a shameful life, in his dying breath, acknowledges his place before Jesus and receives the promise of Paradise itself. The crucifixion may look like a shaming event, but to one who knows his place before Jesus, it is a moment of elevation.[57]

Luke's story does not end here. When women go to anoint Jesus' body with spices two days later, they find the stone of the tomb where he had been laid rolled back. Angelic messengers greet them with the words, "Why do you look for the living among the dead? He is not here, but has risen" (Lk 24:5). Jesus has apparently reversed death. The news creates uncertainty among his disciples. Jesus appears to two of them who are traveling home in the aftermath (Lk 24:13-32), and even those two do not recognize him until he breaks bread with them. Jesus appears to another group of disciples and has to eat food in order for them to see that he is not a ghost (Lk 24:33-43). In view of this uncertainty, Jesus then opens their minds to understand what he has to say, commissioning them to proclaim "repentance and forgiveness of sins . . . in his name to all nations" (Lk 24:44-49).[58] He leads them toward the town of Bethany, and, while blessing them, is carried up into heaven (Lk 24:50-51). The story concludes with the disciples worshiping Jesus and blessing God in the temple (Lk 24:52-53). In the typical fashion of a Greco-Roman *Life*, Luke has ended his story by displaying the essence of Jesus—humiliated by those who refused to recognize him for who he actually was, the great King, but exalted by God in his resurrection and ascension, and thus worshiped by those who know him for who he truly is.

Luke has portrayed Jesus as the great one, for those who will acknowledge his greatness. He was projected as a saving King but born into a lowly setting. He ministered to the lowly, many of whom acknowledged his greatness. He continually turned inside out popular attitudes of evaluating others. He was himself challenged by many who thought of themselves as greater, was definitively humiliated through crucifixion—and then raised, bodily, from the dead and taken up to heaven, the ultimate in exaltation. Jesus is the humble one who is to be exalted.

JESUS AS PROPHET

The pattern of Jesus as the humble one to be exalted is shaped by other important images. Jesus as the promised Messiah, the king of Israel who is to restore the fortunes of Israel, is a significant notion that Luke applies at the beginning of his Gospel, in contrast to the pattern that emerges in the unfolding story (from the Gospel's introduction, e.g., note Lk 1:32-33, 68-75; 2:11, 29-32, 38). It is important to the background of the humble One to be exalted because his kingliness is not always readily transparent to people in Luke's story. John the Baptizer expects Jesus to be the Messiah (Lk 3:16-17; 7:18-19). Various figures acknowledge him as the Messiah (Lk 9:20) and Son of David (Lk 18:38-39), Israel's former great king. Those declarations are part of the picture of Jesus being exalted while interacting with the general populace in the unfolding story. Mockingly, in his death, he is declared as king, most prominently with the sign placed on his cross. But apart from these passing moments, Luke does not feature Jesus' royalty. He does show Jesus declaring the arrival of "the kingdom of God," reshaping expectations of what the kingdom looks like with how he portrays Jesus behaving.[59] That declaration is in line with another, more prevalent portrayal of Jesus as prophet.

The image of prophet adds a special edge to Jesus as the humble one to be exalted. The main role of a prophet is to proclaim God's words (see chap. 6). Part of that proclamation involves God's assessment of what his people are doing. Prophets can declare that evaluation verbally, but also in acts that reinforce verbal declarations. Prophets sometimes perform wondrous signs that corroborate their position as God's agents, occasionally even predicting aspects of the future.[60]

Luke's first public portrayal of Jesus underscores Jesus' role as prophet, his appearance in his hometown synagogue in Nazareth (Lk 4:16-30).[61] After reading a passage from the scroll of the prophet Isaiah, a passage declaring good news for the poor and the oppressed, Jesus makes an amazing claim: "Today this scripture has been fulfilled in your hearing" (v. 21). He speaks with the assurance of a prophet and goes on to say, "no prophet is accepted in the prophet's hometown" (v. 24), connecting his expected rejection with the legacy of Israel rejecting its prophets. The villagers respond by trying to kill him.

That crowds perceive him as a prophet is clear from the response in Luke 7:16, after Jesus mercifully restores to life a widow's dead son in the village of Nain: "A great prophet has risen among us!"[62] Simon the Pharisee questions Jesus' prophetic credentials when Jesus allows the "sinner" woman to kiss and anoint his feet: "If this man were a prophet, he would have known who and what kind of woman this is who is touching him—that she is a sinner" (Lk 7:39). Reports to Galilee's ruler Herod proclaim Jesus as "one of the ancient prophets" come back from the dead (Lk 9:8). When warned later that Herod was seeking to kill him, Jesus again applies the prophetic label to himself: "Go and tell that fox for me, 'Listen, I am casting out demons and performing cures today and tomorrow, and on the third day I finish my work. Yet today, tomorrow, and the next day I must be on my way, because it is impossible for a prophet to be killed outside of Jerusalem'" (Lk 13:32-33). The soldiers of the temple leaders taunt Jesus as a prophet: "Now the men who were holding Jesus began to mock him and beat him; they also blindfolded him and kept asking him, 'Prophesy! Who is it that struck you?'" (Lk 22:63-64). When the resurrected Jesus is walking with two of his disciples, those disciples refer to "Jesus of Nazareth" as "a prophet mighty in deed and word before God and all the people" (Lk 24:19).

Prophetic teaching. Recognizing the prophetic dimension of Jesus illumines Jesus' words and deeds in Luke. Prophets have a legacy of speaking with an edge (see chap. 6). By speaking for God, they aim to express God's views about what his people are doing at the moment. When God's people are doing badly, prophets point an accusing finger; God's people should know better. They are held to high standards by being connected covenantally to God. When God's people fail to do what their connection to God requires of them, they should expect criticism. They should also agree with the criticism and repent in response.

We find such dynamics from the first "prophet of the Most High" (Lk

1:76), whom we encounter in Luke, John the Baptizer, Jesus' herald. His initially recorded words are quite harsh:[63]

> *You brood of vipers! Who warned you to flee from the wrath to come? Bear fruits worthy of repentance. Do not begin to say to yourselves, "We have Abraham as our ancestor"; for I tell you, God is able from these stones to raise up children to Abraham. Even now the ax is lying at the root of the trees; every tree therefore that does not bear good fruit is cut down and thrown into the fire.* **Lk 3:7-9**

Luke shows the hearers accepting the criticism. They respond, "What then should we do?" (Lk 3:10).[64] John answers significantly: "Whoever has two coats must share with anyone who has none; and whoever has food must do likewise" (Lk 3:11). Notice how he appeals to the world of morals, especially in helping the poor and disadvantaged. That would be evidence of repentance, turning away from evil and turning toward God, doing God-pleasing activity. Those connected to God are expected to be merciful to the disadvantaged. John's are the words of a prophet, who is also identified as "Teacher" (Lk 3:12).

Thus, when we see Jesus arriving on the scene aligning himself with the fate of the prophets and performing prophetic signs of mercy, we should not be surprised that he also teaches with an authoritative prophetic edge. He can say, "Blessed are you who are poor" (Lk 6:20) and "Woe to you who are rich" (Lk 6:24) because he speaks for God as God's messenger. When he speaks of moral issues, he speaks in a manner that cuts to the heart of the guilty among God's people. Though Jesus is a teacher in Luke, he is a prophetic one who declares God's perspectives on people, challenging the way his people valuate others. Jesus' declarations of social reversals and his elevation of the lowly have prophetic force. The prophetic orientation supports Jesus' ultimate declaration that those who respond to him receive from him what only God can give, forgiveness, pointing to his being more than a prophet.[65] He is one with whom no one is really worthy of associating; positive response to him is often equated with positive response to God.[66] He speaks for God in a way that no one else ever could.

Jesus' prophetic agenda: The kingdom of God. While Luke does portray Jesus making declarations with strong moral import, Luke shows much more than that. Jesus, as prophet, proclaims the onset of God's ultimate work in the world, the kingdom of God. Consider Luke's initial descriptions of Jesus. Having astounded the crowds of Capernaum with his teaching, his demon exorcisms and his healings, he denies their request for him to stay with them: "I must proclaim the good news of the kingdom of God to the other cities also; for I was sent for this purpose" (Lk 4:43). Jesus must declare that the moment is at hand for the disorder in the world to be reversed. God's reign is to break out in their midst. In Luke, Jesus' deeds and words point to the arrival of that moment. When he pronounces blessing on the poor, it is not just to establish a different sense of social order but to announce their entrance into the domain of God's reign: "yours is the kingdom of God" (Lk 6:20). The poor can expect elevation in God's order, overturning the degradation they currently experience. As he travels through "the cities and villages" of Galilee, he brings "the good news of the kingdom of God" (Lk 8:1).

But that kingdom's arrival, though imminent, is also distant. Jesus' disciples must be ready to wait patiently for its eventual fruition (Lk 8:10-15). Luke shows his disciples participating with Jesus in the spreading of the news of the kingdom's imminence (Lk 9:2; 9:11), both in words and in miraculous deeds. Then Luke more overtly points to aspects of the kingdom that will not come to pass without an ultimate, cataclysmic intervention. The kingdom will eventually come with the glory of the Son of Man and "the glory of the Father and of the holy angels" (Lk 9:26), though only a few of his disciples at that point are allowed a glimpse of that kingdom (Lk 9:27).

Thus, there are aspects of the kingdom that are projected for the lives of Jesus' disciples now, even if the kingdom in its fullness is part of the not-yet of human experience. Luke shows Jesus oscillating between those two aspects of the kingdom in the travel section of the Gospel (Lk 9:51–19:28). On the one hand, its imminence requires focused, unrivaled attention on the part of those who want to be disciples (Lk 9:60, 62), who themselves are commissioned to spread the news of its imminent arrival (Lk 10:9-11). On the other hand, the coming of the kingdom is also more distant, something that disciples should pray for (Lk 11:2). On the one hand, when Jesus defends himself against charges that he exorcises with satanic authority, he declares, "if it is by the finger of God that I cast out the demons, then the kingdom of God has come to you" (Lk 11:20). On the other hand, instead of worrying over what they will eat or wear, disciples should seek God's kingdom first of all (Lk 12:31-32), as though its arrival is further off. On the one hand, the kingdom can even be compared to a mustard seed, small and insignificant, which eventually grows into a large bush (Lk 13:18-19), or a handful of yeast that gradually makes its way through a batch of dough (Lk 13:20-21). On the other hand, the kingdom will come at a final, future, ultimate moment at which all people will be held accountable before God (Lk 13:28-29). Though the kingdom is said to be "among" them (Lk 17:20-21), there is also the expectation of a moment of final, future, cataclysmic accountability (Lk 17:22-37).

Awareness of the oscillation between the now-ness of the kingdom and its not-yet-ness helps to account for the apparent stridency and urgency of Jesus' words in Luke.[67] For example, when questioned about people who had died at the hands of Pilate, with their blood being used to desecrate a sacrifice they were in the process of making, Jesus responds,

> *Do you think that because these Galileans suffered in this way they were worse sinners than all other Galileans? No, I tell you; but unless you repent, you will all perish as they did. Or those eighteen who were killed when the tower of Siloam fell on them—do you think that they were worse offenders than all the others living in Jerusalem? No, I tell you; but unless you repent, you will all perish just as they did.*
> **Lk 13:2-5**

The kingdom is coming in earnest. Those concerned with the coming program of God must respond—now! That response involves repentance, a turning away from what displeases God and a turning to God and what pleases him. It is why Jesus insists that the crowds count the cost of following him, telling them that they must forsake family, reputation and possessions to become one of his disciples (Lk 14:25-35).[68] Further, this increased urgency appears to accompany the impending moment of Jesus' departure. Jesus the prophet pleads all the more earnestly.

The acted message. Prophets not only declare messages that show God's assessments of his people. They often act out aspects of those messages.[69] For example, Jesus' unusual activity in driving out people selling things in the temple (Lk 19:45-46) is regularly regarded as symbolic of judgment.[70] But in an overall sense, Luke shows a prophetic Jesus enacting a core message. Jesus certainly declared the onset of the kingdom of God. Part of that declaration involved the hope of elevation of the downcast. That Jesus himself repeatedly shows mercy to the weak and accepts those who repent, no matter what their background, corroborates what he also declares. Jesus himself is the great one before whom others should humble themselves. In Luke's Gospel many do that and receive a measure of elevation, a form of down payment in the coming kingdom. In addition to that, Jesus appears in humility, associating with outcasts and inferiors, eventually enduring abject mockery, shame and humiliation in his crucifixion. Then he rises from the dead and subsequently ascends to heaven. His life embodies a core message. Jesus the great is the humble one to be exalted. His prophetic life serves as the grounding for the ethics that emerges from the story, ethics rooted in Jesus as exemplar.[71]

JESUS AS EXEMPLAR

Popular Christian religion has embraced the slogan What Would Jesus Do (WWJD)? That slogan comes from a Christian novel written at the end of the nineteenth century, but it does not accurately reflect what New Testament writings convey. What Jesus would do and what his eventual followers can do are potentially two sets of completely different acts. There are some things that only Jesus could do. In Luke that includes miraculous activities such as healing blind people or restoring dead people to life, hardly the kind of activity regularly expected of or enacted by anyone. What might Jesus have done had he seen a bleeding, dying man lying by the roadside? Would he have touched him and healed him, unlike the Samaritan of his parable who could only tend the wounds of the robbers' victim and bring that man to an inn?

 More to the aim of our exploration here, let's recall a point from the beginning of this chapter. We must be careful not to fabricate a Jesus in our own image, enacting our own personal ideals. We can easily invent that Jesus by reconstructing fuller historical scenarios for settings described with limited detail by Luke. For example, we might insert an emotional quality to Jesus' actions where Luke offers none. Did Jesus really say "I love you" to the little children he welcomed (Lk 18:15-16), as a children's Bible storybook once declared? We can also easily invent a Jesus for our own particular contemporary culture and get this Jesus to agree with our own questionable perspectives. Would Jesus really approve of our political views over those of our opponents (whether politically right or left)?

Instead, we must be readers of Luke, not creative writers who subtly invent our own story to reflect our ideals. As readers of Luke we would aim to plug into what Luke's words convey about Jesus and his relevance, understanding Luke's writing as first-century biography. What Jesus *would* do is not a question the words of Luke's story point us to.

A better slogan might be WWJWMTD—What Would Jesus Want Me to Do? Though it does not completely do away with the kind of subjectivity that WWJD is prone to, it does more actively encourage people to revisit the words of New Testament writings. Those writings offer various suggestions for answering that question. Luke's answers are closely tied to the life of Jesus, not as an example but as an exemplar.

An *exemplar* refers to a pattern or paradigm that could be applied by analogy to a variety of similar life situations.[72] We have been observing Luke's special pattern of the life of Jesus: he is the humble one to be exalted. Luke does not portray Jesus urging his followers to do exactly as he did. Instead, Luke shows a pattern of living: Jesus, the anticipated King in the line of David miraculously conceived but being born into humility to a poor, unwed mother; Jesus performing astounding miracles but mostly for the benefit of the poor and humble; Jesus heading for Jerusalem, the city of his destiny, becoming more urgent and even more strident in showing the contrast between God's ways and people's, all the while extending himself to the sinners and outcasts; Jesus challenging the authorities and then being thoroughly humiliated by them in his trial and crucifixion; Jesus, rising from the dead and, after spending time with his followers, being taken up into heaven.

How does this pattern instruct disciple readers? All who would connect with God in his kingdom must exalt Jesus by humbling themselves before him, which is the same as humbling themselves before God. All who humble themselves before Jesus, and thus God, will be exalted, both in this world and in the world to come. All who exalt themselves over Jesus (treated equally to exalting themselves over God) will be humbled. Luke is urging humility before Jesus, equated with humility before God. Only the humble before Jesus enter the kingdom, both in its now-ness and its not-yet-ness. Only those humble are in a position to do the kingdom acts Jesus advocates. Ethical behavior is an essential aspect of kingdom acts, even if it isn't the only aspect.

In Luke, good ethics starts with people placing themselves below Jesus.

People who do that then enter into the life of acceptance from Jesus, a life that ultimately leads to entrance into the kingdom when it comes in its fullness. We have an ethic of relationship here also. People must come to know God through knowing Jesus. That flows out of a humbling posture aptly conveyed in the following words: "If any want to become my followers, let them deny themselves and take up their cross daily and follow me" (Lk 9:23). One who follows the example of Jesus would aim to get crucified; one who follows the exemplar of Jesus would embrace the daily life of shame that may come from defying the practices and values set in place by the controlling social order, especially when that order denigrates those whom God accepts, devalues what God champions and elevates to importance what may actually compete with God's values.[73] Following Jesus means recognizing his superiority over all others, even to the point of personal humiliation for so doing. It also means valuing what he values, even if that defies what others value. Luke advocates the pattern of disciples lowering themselves before Jesus as one that leads them to lower themselves for the benefit of others, a pattern with strong ethical import. That is the pattern that Luke strongly depicts Jesus declaring with his prophetic words and modeling with his prophetic acts.

ETHICS IN LUKE

The limited sphere of ethics in Luke. At last we can focus on the ethical vision in Luke. We have been glimpsing aspects of that throughout the bulk of this chapter in touching on certain moral points in Luke's presentation of Jesus—for example, people repenting in response to Jesus, Jesus' acceptance of repentant sinners, Jesus' deeds of mercy to people in needy weakness, or Jesus' elevation of the poor and devaluing of the rich. Before we launch into a fuller treatment of the ethics, let's also remember that the advancement of ethics is not the principal emphasis of the Gospel of Luke. A presentation of the life of Jesus is. We have not observed a worked out system of ethical thought applicable to all aspects of daily life and defensible with sustained argumentation from the writing itself. But the writing projects an ethical vision. Luke fits within the genre of the Greco-Roman *Life*. Moral instruction is a major purpose for such works.[74] Luke indeed shows us moral instruction. The Gospel also provides basic principles that indicate the kind of grounding we would expect from ethics: both a sense of how to determine right from wrong and a motivation for choosing what is right and refraining from what is wrong.

Ethics in Luke begins with people first of all becoming disciples. That requires repentance, turning away from the evil in one's life and turning toward God and the good that he wants. That is what Jesus eventually tells his disciples to convey to others, worldwide: "repentance and forgiveness of sins . . . in his name" (Lk 24:47).

Recall words relevant to this that Luke displays earlier in the Gospel:

> *If any want to become my followers, let them deny themselves and take up their cross daily and follow me. For those who want to save their life will lose it, and those who lose their life for my sake will save it. What does it profit them if they gain the whole world, but lose or forfeit themselves? Those who are ashamed of me and of my words, of them the Son of Man will be ashamed when he comes in his glory and the glory of the Father and of the holy angels.* **Lk 9:23-26**

Let's proceed carefully here. Those words are not addressed directly to the readers. In the Gospel, Jesus speaks them to his disciples in the aftermath of Peter's declaration of Jesus as the Messiah. Those identified as "followers" are those in the Gospel who actually followed Jesus; they went where he went, slept where he slept, ate where he ate. No reader can do that, since Jesus is no longer around to follow in that way. And yet there is an expectation that the disciple reader should learn from the story about Jesus. The open-endedness implied by the words "If any want to become my followers," along with the words being directed no longer to the disciples in private (Lk 9:18) but more publicly "to them all" point to that.[75] Denial of self, rather than advancement of self, is a necessary step in connecting with Jesus.[76] So also is a daily taking up of one's cross—not the bearing of burdens, as is often conveyed in Western, guilt-oriented cultures, but the daily renunciation of self-aggrandizement.[77] The cross is an object of extreme shame in the Greco-Roman world. Self-denial and willing association with shame have been part of the story of Jesus all along. They are part of the exemplar.

Both with repentance and self-denial, people must recognize their place before Jesus. He is great. They are not. That basic recognition is regularly the starting point when people in Luke's Gospel become disciples. It is the implied starting point for the disciple reader. For such readers, Jesus is the King.

They are the subjects. But Luke does not portray a king in the standard way that disciples in the story would recognize:

> *The kings of the Gentiles lord it over them; and those in authority over them are called benefactors. But not so with you; rather the greatest among you must become like the youngest, and the leader like one who serves. For who is greater, the one who is at the table or the one who serves? Is it not the one at the table? But I am among you as one who serves.* **Lk 22:25-27**

Here, as the leader of his disciples, Jesus instructs them to follow his model. He has served others; so must they. The prelude to this scene, Jesus' blessing of the Passover bread as his "body given for them" and the cup of wine as the "cup that is poured out for them as the new covenant in [his] blood," points to the cross as his definitive act of service, where he is also thoroughly humiliated. Yet three days after the experience of the cross, he is also raised from the dead and after a time taken up into heaven. Disciple readers should take note. They need to recognize Jesus as one worthy of association, one to whom they must give full allegiance, one whom they must come to know. In so doing, they also take onboard his standards that elevate others as more important than themselves, even when those standards result in association with shame. The ethic of relationship here is costly. It is also personally elevating, since a person receives immediate acceptance from Jesus, regardless of prior background, and final acceptance at the kingdom's fullness.

Valuations of others. One who is associated with Jesus must not recoil from those Jesus associates with. It should not be a problem that his mother is not married at the time of his birth (Lk 2:5-6), that his first bed is an animal feeding trough (Lk 2:7), that the first people to visit him are lowly shepherds (Lk 2:15-16), that his mother offers the poor person's sacrifice for her postchildbirth ritual cleansing (Lk 2:22-24). One who is linked with Jesus should delight in the fact that his first proclamation is that he has come

> to bring good news to the poor . . .
> to proclaim release to the captives
>   and recovery of sight to the blind,
>   to let the oppressed go free,
> to proclaim the year of the Lord's favor. **Lk 4:18-19**

He interacts with people possessed by unclean demons who cause those whom they possess to do strange acts and utter loud cries (Lk 4:33-37). He elevates common fishermen to be his own followers (Lk 5:1-11). He touches people covered with leprosy (Lk 5:12-13). He goes to parties attended by crowds of tax collectors (Lk 5:27-32), among the most despicable of socially questionable characters. These are only some of the beginning encounters between Jesus and others. Luke shows Jesus eagerly associating with shameful people, not to present Jesus badly but to enhance his reputation as the one who restores the world first by reversing the rejection of the marginalized. Those who belong to Jesus must also delight in acts that restore people to right connections with God and to whole, fruitful and fulfilling living.[78]

That involves seeing others in a manner that goes beyond superficial evaluation. Those who rate others based on social standing or usefulness miss the point. Those who see the futility of such standards in view of who Jesus is, understand more fully what Jesus is about (Lk 7:1-10). People who resist Jesus' perspective write others off, as does Simon the Pharisee, who fails to see a woman showing extravagant love to Jesus as anyone other than a sinner (Lk 7:39-47). How people see Jesus affects what they do. People who fail to see Jesus and his ways properly show that they are filled with evil. People who see the way they ought to from God's perspective become filled with goodness (Lk 11:34-35). Rather than complaining about sinners claiming any acceptance from God, disciples should rejoice when people repent (Lk 15:1-32). God does, as do the angels in heaven (Lk 15:7, 10). What people tend to prize, God despises (Lk 16:15).

Having Jesus' view of others encourages people to offer mercy to those who are weak, to help them out in their weakness. It does not condone morally illicit activity, but it does extend a helping hand to enable people to break from that activity. There are no lost causes in humanity, except for those who insist that they are superior to the ways of Jesus, and hence, the ways of God. And even they can receive acceptance if they repent in humble submission to Jesus. Jesus declares the arrival of the kingdom of God, the moment when the wrongs in the world are to be righted and God's reign established once more over the earth. The initial arrival of that kingdom signals the beginning of the restoration of a broken humanity to a divinely supported wholeness, a restoration that still awaits its total completion at the coming of the Son of Man (Lk 21:25-31), who has been crucified and raised from the dead, and then taken into heaven.

Major themes with ethical connections. Several issues emerge as prominent moral themes within Luke's Gospel. To probe their ethics, we ought first to recognize that they all grow out of or are consistent with the overall sense of revaluing others from God's perspective, which itself calls for people to place themselves and their personal valuing perspective beneath God. This, further, is in view of the coming kingdom, which is about the restoration of order, the dramatic reversal of the harm so present in the world. An issue in Luke is not important merely because Jesus talked about it. Rather, Luke shows Jesus talking about it because it is part of the overall set of messages that Luke aims to make known to its readership. The ethics support the teachings.

Absorbing the attitudes belonging to these issues is essential to knowing Jesus, and hence knowing God through Jesus. Those who wish to connect well with God need to learn how these kinds of attitudes are close to the heart of God, and what God is doing in reversing the wrongs in the world at the arrival of the kingdom.

Forgiveness. A major theme with ethical implications in the Gospel concerns how one should view the misdeeds of others.[79] Jesus fully accepts all who repent of their misdeeds, a point illustrated throughout the Gospel. Numerous stories and sayings indicate that others should grant the same forgiving acceptance to the penitent. Jesus has come, after all, "to call not the righteous but sinners to repentance" (Lk 5:32). He instructs his disciples to be careful about how they evaluate others, urging them to forgive as the basis of expecting forgiveness from others (Lk 6:37). God is kind to the "ungrateful and the wicked" (Lk 6:35). They must also "be merciful, just as [their] Father is merciful" (Lk 6:36). The sinner woman who anoints Jesus' feet becomes a model of love for Jesus because she is aware of how much Jesus has forgiven her (Lk 7:36-50). Jesus', and thus God's, acceptance of those who seek his forgiveness provides a model for the forgiveness they are to extend to others (Lk 11:4). That same sense of acceptance is championed in the three parables of Luke 15, each of which proclaims joy in heaven for repentant sinners; the last of those chides those who refuse to accept the penitent (Lk 15:32). Jesus cautions his disciples against letting their behavior cause others to sin. He then instructs them to rebuke others who sin repeatedly, forgiving them each time they repent and beg forgiveness (Lk 17:3-5). Jesus himself urges his Father to forgive those crucifying him, instead of pronouncing condemnation against them (Lk 23:34). In the end, the resurrected Jesus charges his disciples to proclaim "repentance and forgiveness of sins . . . in his name to all nations" (Lk 24:47).

Supporting this is a sense of what Jesus, and hence God, deems important. God's perspectives contrast strongly with human standards that seek perpetual punishment for wrongdoing. Forgiveness does not mean letting the unrighteous off the hook, encouraging offenders to say something they don't really mean in order to gain standing. People's awareness of their place before Jesus, and hence before God, is always portrayed as a sincere awareness. But people who are thus in touch with God are also in touch with their own personal shortcomings, shortcomings that are primarily immoral. God bears no grudge against them when they repent. They should bear no grudge against others.

Upholding the unimportant. Consistent with forgiveness are moments that advocate upholding others normally deemed unworthy of attention. Jesus instructs his disciples to love their enemies, to pray for them and to turn "the other cheek" to those striking them (Lk 6:27-29). They should instead do good to them (Lk 6:35). Even some enemies have inherent weaknesses that cause them to be enemies in the first place, requiring disciples of Jesus to show them the same mercy they have received from God (Lk 6:36).[80] Disciples must extend this mercy to all who are weak. That is certainly what we see Jesus doing throughout the Gospel; for example, in healing a hemorrhaging woman, raising a widow's son from the dead or accepting repentant sinners. When challenged by a man skilled in the Torah to explain who the neighbor is whom he should love as himself, Jesus responds with a parable that portrays an unlikely hero, a Samaritan, showing mercy to a dying, bleeding victim of robbers. The lawyer is urged to do the same (Lk 10:37). Anyone in need of mercy whom he meets is the neighbor he should show love to. Disciples who know their own irrelevance in light of Jesus' greatness readily perform such deeds. They are to consider themselves "worthless slaves" for having done just what they ought, not people whom others should commend (Lk 17:7-10). Those who know their place before God are exalted (Lk 14:8-11), who are not dismissive of others as though beneath them (Lk 18:10-14), who accept children and enter the kingdom with childlike acceptance (Lk 18:15-17). Luke prompts the reader to ask, How could anyone who knows his or her place before God ever treat others as beneath him or her? Disciples of Jesus should react to all weak people with uplifting mercy, even when they find their settings and perspectives personally revolting. That should also include people they have major disagreements with. Jesus dined even with resistant Pharisees (Lk 7:36; 11:37; 14:1).

Wealth. Closely related to helping others in their weakness is the prominent treatment that Luke gives to the subject of wealth. Jesus, in Luke, offers continued challenges to those with money and possessions, and ongoing hope to those who have none. Those who have are charged with a responsibility to assist those who do not.

Much of this reflects specific issues relevant to the Roman social environment for which Luke appears to be tailored. The Roman patron-client system of reciprocation is contrasted with Jesus' instructions for his disciples to give to those who cannot do good in return or to lend to those who cannot repay, even to enemies (Lk 6:30, 33-35).[81] That same system is challenged directly with the story about the healing of the centurion's servant (Lk 7:1-10). The centurion's clients, the synagogue elders, try to broker a deal with Jesus, the honored healer, based partly on the centurion's benefactions in building their synagogue. The centurion, by contrast, sends others to declare his unworthiness to have Jesus associating with him, regardless of any worthiness his use of money might allow him to claim. When Jesus teaches about not inviting to dinner those who can return the favor but instead inviting the poor (Lk 14:12-14), the implied challenge to that same system is clear. Luke 22:25 records Jesus directly referring to "benefactors," a mainstay concept to the whole system, as examples for how the disciples should not conduct themselves.

Similarly, greed and wickedness provide examples for how not to be clean on the inside:

> Now you Pharisees clean the outside of the cup and of the dish, but inside you are full of greed and wickedness. You fools! Did not the one who made the outside make the inside also? So give for alms those things that are within; and see, everything will be clean for you.
>
> But woe to you Pharisees! For you tithe mint and rue and herbs of all kinds, and neglect justice and the love of God; it is these you ought to have practiced, without neglecting the others. **Lk 11:39-42**

The love and justice of God flow from a pure, inner regard for others, the opposite of greed and wickedness. Luke shows Jesus returning to the same point, only without reference to money, in Luke 12:1-5. Both issues, proper use of money and being inwardly pure, stem from people being rightly connected to God, valuing God's perspectives over human acclaim. The parable appearing soon after, in Luke 12:13-21, implies the same. Disciples should seek richness toward God, not mere human wealth. That means, among other things, valuing others and valuing life from God's perspectives, doing what God wants, especially in helping the poor. People cannot serve both God and money (Lk 16:1-14).

How does a person know what God wants? Accompanying some of the comments on wealth are perspectives learned from the Scriptures, both from Torah and from the Prophets. Recall the parable of Lazarus and the rich man; the rich man is told that his brothers can avoid his fate by heeding "Moses and the prophets" (Lk 16:31). That implies the high standards of the Scriptures about the need for God's people to care for the poor and disadvantaged.[82] Those same standards are also implied in Jesus' exhortation to the rich ruler not merely to keep the commandments but to sell all his possessions for the benefit of the poor and to follow Jesus (Lk 18:18-22). They are heralded in the repentance of Zacchaeus, the rich tax collector, who pledges larger portions of his wealth for the poor than what Torah legislates, and who is commended as a lost son of Abraham who is now saved (Lk 19:1-10).

God is establishing his kingdom through Jesus. His new reign begins in the now of Jesus' world and comes to fruition at the coming of the Son of Man. The poor receive a place in the kingdom (Lk 6:20). Because of God's regard for those who belong to his kingdom, those who belong ought not worry about the basics of life or any material matters, but must "strive for [God's] kingdom" (Lk 12:22-31), selling what they own and giving alms (Lk 12:32-34). Participation in the kingdom can be so costly it could even demand severing family ties and giving up possessions (Lk 14:15-24, 25-35). Many of these statements coincide with the increasing urgency and stridency of the travel section of the Gospel, as Jesus moves to Jerusalem, the scene of his humiliation and departure. Monumental moments require monumental commitments.

SUMMING IT UP:
JESUS' ETHICS IN LUKE

o Ethics in Luke begins with people knowing that they are beneath God. In Luke, people show that by lowering themselves before Jesus. Acknowledging oneself as beneath Jesus is the starting point. This is an ethic of relationship. Jesus accepts all who come to him in this way. As people know God and his acceptance of them through Jesus, they can accept others.

o People who know their place before Jesus are in touch with their personal moral shortcomings. They know that his greatness makes them unworthy of associating with him because they know how they have misbehaved and have continued to do so.

o People who acknowledge their moral shortcomings before Jesus, and thus before God, must repent, turning away from the evil and embracing God's sense of good, with a commitment to perform God-pleasing deeds. The Torah is an implied source for learning some of what specifically pleases God. So also is the strengthening sense of God's moral superiority.

o People who know their place before Jesus must follow his exemplar. He is the humble one to be exalted. They, therefore, must humble themselves before him, denying themselves, taking up their cross daily in willing association with what others might devalue but that God values, even as Jesus, on his own literal cross, experienced full mockery and shame. That especially includes people others denigrate.

o People who so behave because they believe will receive exaltation from God by being part of his kingdom, which is now but not yet, and available to all who humble themselves before Jesus in belief, regardless of their background. Jesus has not only been shamefully crucified, he has been raised from the dead and taken into heaven. The kingdom will come in its fullness. Shame will be reversed.

o One major ethical point emerging from all this is that others are more important than oneself. There are no unimportant people. There are no lost causes. No human is not worth helping. All human life is dignified. Thus, enemies must be forgiven and the unimportant upheld. Pursuit of wealth is to be replaced with the pursuit of meeting others' needs.

o Positively, ethics in Luke emerges out of a higher regard for others than for oneself. Others' needs are to be identified and addressed.

Consider the second to last principle. Some ethicists recognize that many immoral behaviors stem from people diminishing the personhood of others they deem as beneath them in some way. Some people go so far as to deny the personhood of another in order to justify treating him or her subhumanly: "He's just an animal" or "It's just a blob of cells." Luke's "Life of Jesus" teaches that people who know God and are in touch with his ways do not deny the personhood of others in order to justify their behavior against them. People in relationship with God through Jesus must aim to uphold all human life because that's what God has done in establishing his kingdom through Jesus. This is a microethical responsibility, governing people-to-people contact. It is not a responsibility that addresses all spheres of human existence. But it does go a long way in promoting good and hindering harm in the world.

Consider further the final principle. What happens when people seek to meet others' needs ahead of their own? What would be the implications for doing that with regard to hot-button issues such as sexual activity outside of marriage, abortion or divorce? People who, in all their interactions with others, aim to treat them as better than themselves advance good in their world. They reflect the kingdom they belong to. The ethical vision from Jesus that this Gospel projects champions the reversal of people's tendencies to debilitate their world. Jesus has established the pattern in his life and crucifixion, his resurrection and ascension. He will enact the ultimate reversal when the kingdom comes in its fullness.

Reflection Questions

1. What sense of ethics is reflected by a kingdom that ultimately reverses the world's condition?

2. How does the exemplar of Jesus reflect kingdom reversals?

3. How does the exemplar of Jesus shape how people should respond to practitioners of bad behavior?

4. Consider the final points in the summary:

   • there are no unimportant people—all human life is dignified

   • others are more important than oneself

      • Choose a hot-button moral issue (e.g., sexual behavior, abortion, divorce, substance abuse, gambling, war)

      • How do these final points offer helpful, clarifying perspectives to the issue?

      • Why, according to this ethical vision, should right be done and wrong avoided?

      • What sort of people do you tend to write off, and how would the ethics of Jesus address that?

FOR FURTHER READING

Burridge, Richard A. *Imitating Jesus: An Inclusive Approach to New Testament Ethics*, pp. 227-83. Grand Rapids: Eerdmans, 2007.

Green, Joel B. *The Gospel of Luke*. Grand Rapids: Eerdmans, 1997.

Hays, Richard B. *The Moral Vision of the New Testament: A Contemporary Introduction to New Testament Ethics*, pp. 112-37. San Francisco: HarperCollins, 1996.

York, John O. *The Last Shall Be First: The Rhetoric of Reversal in Luke*. Journal for the Study of the New Testament 46. Sheffield, UK: Sheffield Academic Press, 1991.

PERFECTION, MERCY AND IMITATION

Jesus and the Kingdom in Matthew

INTRODUCTORY ISSUES

Let's begin as we did with Luke and rehearse once more our basic principles:

- Ethics refers to how a person distinguishes right from wrong behavior.
- Ethics is also concerned with the reasons for why a person should choose what is good and abstain from what is not.

And once more, let's distinguish biblical ethics from the mere identification of biblical morality:

- Biblical ethics is concerned with how the writings themselves advocate distinctions between right and wrong, and what motives exist for choosing right and condemning wrong.
- Biblical ethics must always start from an understanding of the Bible's own messages based on the individual writings' purposes, agendas and ideologies.

We will find moral teachings leaping off the pages of the Gospel of Matthew, coupling clear instructions of right and wrong behavior with dire, ultimate consequences for failure to enact them. The urgency to obey can easily lead readers to bypass the deeper supporting reasons and motivations for those behaviors. We'll aim to be careful readers of Matthew, certain not to impose on the writing any expectations or assumptions that might blur the ethical vision the writing projects.

Points in common with Luke. Though the table of contents of any Bible places Matthew ahead of Luke, we are doing the reverse. One reason is to highlight the importance of absorbing a Gospel's presentation of Jesus in its entirety before exploring its ethics, something we did with Luke. A second grows out of that: it is easy to let stereotypes of Jesus dominate our views of Jesus in a particular Gospel. Consider the stereotype discussed in chapter seven, that of master teacher. In Luke we noted that Jesus' teaching activity is prominent, but not dominating. When he teaches, he does so with a prophetic edge, challenging the crowds and his opponents with the realities of the imminent kingdom. When we come to Matthew, however, we *do* see a dominating teacher, whose teachings are collected in identifiable, lengthy sections. If we started with Matthew, we would potentially reinforce whatever elements of the Jesus-as-master-teacher stereotype we may carry with us. Reading Luke first helps us to see Jesus as more than a teacher.

It's important to note that Matthew also fits within the basic literary genre of the Greco-Roman *Life* or *bios*. We are reading a form of biography. Readers uncertain of what that means should consult the discussion in chapter seven. Here, let's recall that a *Life* is a collection of selected words and *deeds*.[1] Though Matthew features words from Jesus' teaching, he also shows representative deeds. We will better understand Matthew if we consider the entire emerging portrait of Jesus before dwelling on featured parts.[2]

Further, let's recognize how flexible a *Life* can be. We will observe that Matthew follows the convention of other ancient biographies by grouping representative words and deeds around thematic points.[3] Chronology is often loose in *Lives*.[4] When we see in Matthew clusters of words moving freely from topic to topic with no noticeable logic to their flow, we should not assume that those words were all presented together on that specific historical occasion. We will observe Matthew interrupting the basic story line with groups of sayings that may have begun with the specific historical moment that Matthew declares, but that clearly also give way to other related sayings that may or may not have been spoken at that moment.

In Luke we observed major storytelling techniques that consistently emphasized reversals of expectation. Though we will see some identical moments of reversal in Matthew—Jesus is the same subject, after all—we will not see them with nearly the same intensity. Instead, we will see two other major techniques, repetition and comparison. Repetition needs only to be observed by readers.[5] Comparison requires further explanation.

Matthew abounds with comparisons, some being more significant and drawn out than others.[6] Sometimes we see comparisons of Jesus with various figures—Isaac, Israel, Moses, David, Jonah, John the Baptizer, Solomon, the queen of Sheba, Jeremiah. Sometimes Jesus compares one entity with another—the righteousness of scribes and Pharisees with that of disciples; the "kingdom of heaven" with a field or a mustard seed; the cares of the Gentiles with what disciples should be concerned with. Sometimes in the story one person or entity is considered less than the other by comparison, not to put down the less but to elevate the greater. Many of the simple comparisons make sense in a story that features Jesus' teaching. Comparison is a good teaching technique. Matthew's storytelling sometimes connects Jesus to the overall legacy of Israelite history, with more drawn out comparisons to groups such as Israel and to people such as Moses and David.[7] They help communicate that what God does through Jesus advances what God has been doing all along.

Luke's "Life of Jesus" portrays a life pattern, an exemplar that informs the story's ethics. As we proceed through Matthew, however, we will see a related, more common concept: imitation.[8] In a writing that emphasizes comparisons, some figures should be imitated and others not. Some of what is to be imitated will involve morality, and ultimately ethics, but much actually will not, even though it may be important for a developing Christian. For example, Jesus declares the blessedness of the disciple who is "meek" (Mt 5:5) while later identifying himself as meek or humble (Mt 11:29), an attribute that Matthew's narration also applies to Jesus as he enters Jerusalem (Mt 21:5). Jesus' meekness is to be imitated as a positive moral quality. In other places, imitation does not have any direct moral bearing. Jesus goes about healing and casting out demons (Mt 4:23-24) and then authorizes his disciples to do the same (Mt 10:1), not to promote kindness or any other virtue, but to demonstrate the imminence of the kingdom of God.

As we saw in Luke, so we will see in Matthew. Neither Gospel portrays Jesus as being all about ethics or morality. We will see significant moral teaching much more drawn out in Matthew than in Luke. But that morality will fit within a broader picture of the presentation of Jesus as part of its identifiable ethical vision.

If ethics is not the main point of Matthew, Jesus is. That is what we would expect from a Greco-Roman *Life*. Luke portrays Jesus as the humble one to be exalted, a pattern worth tracing because it supports an ethical exemplar. Though a *Life* need not have a unifying focal image, we should not be surprised if we do find one in Matthew also. In Matthew we will see Jesus as the Messiah, the teacher of Israel. The messianic focus makes this image less directly related to ethics than Luke's. As we work our way through Matthew we might sometimes feel tension between describing the focal image and teasing out the ethics it supports.

Before exploring that portrait, let's observe that the kingdom of God features even more prominently in Matthew than in Luke. Matthew mentions the kingdom directly thirty-seven times, compared to Luke's thirty-two. The kingdom, as we have seen, refers to God's ultimate restoration of the world, a restoration begun with the birth of Jesus and to be culminated at his second coming. The kingdom shapes the ethical vision generated by Matthew. Matthew mostly refers to the "kingdom of heaven" rather than the "kingdom of God."[9] In fact, Matthew is the only writing in the entire Bible to use the words *kingdom of heaven*. Why? The writer, as a good Jew, minimizes his use of the word *God*, probably also for a Jewish-Christian reader.[10]

MATTHEW'S PRESENTATION OF JESUS

Some initial thoughts. The Gospel of Matthew begins with a simple, broad declaration: "An account of the genealogy of Jesus the Messiah, the son of David, the son of Abraham." It assumes lots of prior knowledge on the part of its readers. What's a Messiah? Who was David? Who was Abraham? One well-versed in the Old Testament, or the Scriptures for a Jewish reader, would know David and Abraham. David was Israel's greatest king, one to whom God had promised a perpetual monarchy for his descendants (see 2 Sam 7:8-16). Abraham was the father of the nation, the one to whom God promised land, descendants and blessing so that through him and his descendants the entire world would be blessed (see chap. 2).

One well-versed in the Scriptures would not necessarily know what *Messiah* means. That's because the Old Testament never refers to it by that term.[11] It is an important Jewish concern that develops in the second temple period of Jewish history, a period that begins in the sixth century B.C.E. It becomes especially significant in the first century B.C.E.[12]

So to what does the title "Messiah" refer? It comes to express the hope for many, but not all, Jewish people that they will finally be delivered from their exile among the nations to their restored land, at a point in time when the wrongs of the world will be righted and the wicked will be judged. Expectations for the Messiah and the kingdom can go together. If the concept of kingdom has implications for ethics, we can also expect the same for the concept of Messiah.

Some, but not all, hopes of Messiah referred to a ruler in the line of David, satisfying God's promise that David would never lack an heir to the throne, a promise suspended by the exile of the people of Judah from their land in the sixth century B.C.E. That Davidic ruler would not only be a restorer of the nation but would also be involved in judgment against the ungodly.[13] Other messianic images referred to one involved in prophetic deeds of mercy, such as healing, restoring sight to the blind, releasing captives.[14] Some hopes envisioned a teacher, who sometimes is reflected as a priest, and sometimes as a prophet and a priest.[15] The concept has multiple expectations associated with it. And though the Davidic restorer may be the foremost, those other images also help us understand Matthew.

Now let's return to our opening line. With it, Matthew introduces Jesus as the restoring King who will gather *all* his people from exile and bring about the promised Abrahamic blessing of all nations. Matthew portrays Jesus as the Messiah in ways that would affirm its Jewish-Christian readers in the decision they have made to become followers of Jesus.[16] In Matthew Jesus fills out several messianic images, the initial being that of a judging Davidic king who restores and elevates Israel. As the story unfolds, we discover that though judgment is coming, Jesus first offers an extraordinarily high moral standard of living, tempered with mercy. He does that both as teacher and healer. Perfection and mercy are two major foci of the ethics we will see here.

Tracing highlights through the basic story. We'll now work our way through the rest of the story, dwelling on moments relevant to ethics. The ride might sometimes feel a bit bumpy as we skip over less ethically relevant scenes. But it helps first to observe how elements of Jesus' ethics fit within the flow of Matthew's story.

We have already noted Davidic and Abrahamic issues. Matthew tells a series of opening stories that also introduce other important aspects of Jesus relevant to ethics. In the first Jesus is announced as a Savior. A righteous man named Joseph learns that his fiancée has become pregnant, apart from him. While contemplating severing the engagement, he is visited by an angel. The angel discloses the miracle of his fiancée's virginal conception, declaring that her son is to be named Jesus—the Greek name for Joshua, meaning "the Lord saves"—since Jesus will "save his people from their sins" (Mt 1:21). Though in historical context that might refer to God's people being delivered from the consequences of their historical sinfulness, in this Gospel it comes to refer to individual forgiveness from God himself.[17] Sinfulness and immorality overlap significantly. We have here a signal that people can expect help from Jesus in dealing with their immoral imperfections.

Matthew's narration then amplifies that signal when the virginal conception of Jesus is said to "fulfill what had been spoken by the Lord through the prophet: 'Look, the virgin shall conceive and bear a son, / and they shall name him Emmanuel,' / which means, 'God is with us'" (Mt 1:23). The first of a string of passages that quote prophetic utterances that Jesus is said to fulfill, this one underscores that he, Jesus, is the presence of God.[18] That presence, as we'll see, is to continue with disciples and will offer significant encouragement for the moral life expected of them. That presence also informs the story's ethic of relationship. Jesus is *with* those who follow him. God is therefore with them.

The next scene depicts a noteworthy comparison between the dastardly King Herod and what Jesus, as Messiah, is projected to be: one "who is to shepherd [God's] people Israel" (Mt 2:6). Herod kills God's people to destroy kingly rivals.[19] Jesus will shepherd them with compassion, as we see frequently in the story, offering a point both of comfort and moral imitation for the readers. Jesus is worth getting to know.

The story jumps then from Jesus to John the Baptizer, who comes announcing the imminence of the kingdom and its judgment (Mt 3:1-12). That introduces one of Matthew's major themes: recompense, or judgment.[20] It has important implications for ethics, reminding readers that God holds people accountable for their moral imperfections. As the Gospel story progresses we learn of a delay of that judgment, which blends well with Matthew's concern for mercy. People have an opportunity to get their lives together. Jesus offers hope for those who choose his ethical ways.

As the story focuses more directly on Jesus, Matthew summarizes his general activity:

> *Jesus went throughout Galilee, teaching in their synagogues and proclaiming the good news of the kingdom and curing every disease and every sickness among the people. So his fame spread throughout all Syria, and they brought to him all the sick, those who were afflicted with various diseases and pains, demoniacs, epileptics, and paralytics, and he cured them. And great crowds followed him from Galilee, the Decapolis, Jerusalem, Judea, and from beyond the Jordan.* **Mt 4:23-25**

That hardly conforms to expectations of a judging king, bringing back his people from exile. But it does point to Matthew's overall purposes. The writing shows how all of the activities of Jesus fit a broad messianic profile, not a narrow one. Jesus heals people, fixing what is broken in the world. If the wrongs of the world are righted at the arrival of the kingdom, then healing belongs to that, signaling that the kingdom certainly is at hand. How that is significant to ethics in Matthew will soon become clear. But perhaps more significant for Matthew than acts of healing are the moments beginning in Matthew 5—Jesus teaching.

Chief among Matthew's features are the five definable blocks of teaching, collections of sayings that revolve around basic, identifiable themes. We'll point each of these out as we come to them, but dwell on only three of them—Jesus does teach much more than ethical material. The first block spans Matthew 5–7 and over the centuries has come to be known as the Sermon on the Mount. Though we will walk through that in more detail later in this chapter, we can make some basic observations now that help us understand Jesus better.

The words of this first block of teaching invite an important comparison between Jesus and Moses.[21] Jesus first ascending a mountain and then sitting down evoke images of Moses on Mount Sinai, receiving the law. Jesus intensifies some of those laws in Matthew 5:22-48 by contrasting what his disciples may have heard about the laws with what he says about them. What Jesus offers goes beyond the direct words of Moses, as great as Moses is.[22] Jesus the Messiah is a teacher, establishing his ways of thinking as something new, but consistent with the old.

At the same time, let's also note that in the entirety of the Gospel, Matthew discourages us from seeing Jesus as just a Jewish teacher or rabbi. Jesus does refer to himself as *the* teacher (Mt 23:10; see also Mt 10:24-25;

23:8; 26:18), but throughout the story, only those who are opposed to Jesus, or are outside of the circle of disciples, call him "teacher."[23] And the only person in Matthew ever to call Jesus "rabbi" is Judas, at his betrayal. People who are aligned with Jesus call him "Lord."[24] Though Matthew shows us someone who teaches with unusual authority (see Mt 7:28), he shows us someone who is more than a teacher. He is the Messiah. When we consider the ethics supporting what Jesus teaches, we will have to consider how his teaching fits within a sense of judgment and restoration that kingdom expectations encourage.

From this point forward in the story we see alternating clusters of words and deeds. Jesus' words in the first teaching block have just affirmed the role of the Law or Torah in the life of the disciple. In his first deed described after the teaching, Jesus heals a leper and then tells him to do what the Law commands (Mt 8:4). We learn that Jesus does what he teaches, unlike some of his opponents, whom he later condemns for failing to do so (Mt 23:2-3). We can trust what he teaches, important for accepting his moral instruction. In the scenes that follow we also learn about other healings (Mt 8:5-17), about his authority over the elements (Mt 8:23-27) and over evil spirits in the world (Mt 8:28-34). We have more than a teacher here. But his authority and control reinforce something more that Jesus offers: mercy.

Consider the role of mercy in the cluster of deeds that we next see. Jesus connects his ability to heal a paralyzed man to his authority to forgive sins (Mt 9:1-8). Then he calls a tax collector to follow him as a disciple and goes to a party in the tax collector's home attended by other lowlifes, drawing criticism from religious leaders (Mt 9:9-12). Jesus' response is significant: "Those who are well have no need of a physician, but those who are sick. Go and learn what this means, 'I desire mercy, not sacrifice.' For I have come to call not the righteous but sinners" (9:12-13).

Jesus, metaphorically, is a healer of the sinful. Jesus, the one with authority to forgive sins, welcomes repentant sinners as an act of mercy. That is utterly important for the ethical vision in this Gospel. Let's see how.

Two episodes later, Jesus is hailed by two blind men as the "son of David" from whom they can expect "mercy" in granting them sight (Mt 9:27-31).[25] He is a merciful restorer, one who aids the weak and fixes the broken, whether they be sinfully or physically infirm. Matthew significantly combines healing and forgiveness as acts of mercy. The arrival of the kingdom involves righting the wrongs of the world, whether external, physical wrongs or internal sinful ones. Jesus is saving his people from their sins by restoring them to rightness and wholeness.

Those are important observations for the emerging ethics. The first teaching block is filled with hope and foreboding. It begins with promised blessing for those experiencing the world's brokenness (e.g., the "poor in spirit" or "those who mourn"). But it also conveys tough realities. Jesus teaches moral standards of perfection: "Be perfect, as your heavenly Father is perfect" (Mt 5:48).[26] Throughout the teaching section he warns of judgment for not living up to those standards. In his conclusion he declares,

> *Not everyone who says to me, "Lord, Lord," will enter the kingdom of heaven, but only the one who does the will of my Father in heaven. On that day many will say to me, "Lord, Lord, did we not prophesy in your name, and cast out demons in your name, and do many deeds of power in your name?" Then I will declare to them, "I never knew you; go away from me, you evildoers."* **Mt 7:21-23**

If the standard is perfection and the consequence for not meeting that standard is denial of the kingdom, then what hope is there? The deeds of Jesus demonstrate powerful mercy from the one who forgives, who also taught his disciples both to forgive and to pray for forgiveness (Mt 6:12). Jesus himself extends mercy to all who ask it from him. He fixes the broken.

Those who hear the teaching of Jesus learn quickly of their own moral brokenness. The standards of the kingdom may be high, but all are welcome to receive mercy from Jesus and then submit to them.[27] And submit to them they must, or else they are not truly his disciples. In view of their own moral failures, disciples need ongoing help and acceptance from Jesus, who offers forgiveness, modeling what he teaches his disciples also to do. Those who receive mercy must show mercy. They must imitate Jesus.

We also learn that disciples of Jesus are allowed to be works in progress. When instructing his disciples not to worry about life the way those who have no connections with God do, he chides them gently as those with "little faith" (Mt 6:30). He applies the same term after he delivers them from a raging storm (Mt 8:26). Being little-faith ones becomes a term applied three more times in this story (Mt 14:31; 16:8; 17:20), each moment conveying the sense that his disciples should continue to grow. They need to have full faith, and that would come from understanding more completely who Jesus is.[28] That reinforces our ethic of relationship. Disciples connect to God through Jesus, the presence of God. Disciples grow in their relationship with God by growing in their faith in Jesus, who is with them. Growth in moral performance is part of that increase in faith.

One key to understanding Jesus' ethics is to observe his Davidic links, not simply to the historical David but to the messianic "son of David."[29] The scenes that span the end of Matthew 9 through the end of Matthew 11 subtly connect restoration promises from the prophet Isaiah with Davidic ones from Ezekiel 34. Jesus has "compassion" on the leaderless people, who "were harassed and helpless, like sheep without a shepherd" (Mt 9:36). His initial response to seeing that is to empower his twelve key disciples, the apostles, to heal and to cast out demons, going out with the message that the kingdom is at hand. Like teacher, like pupil. That begins a set of instructions about spreading the message of the kingdom's imminence (Mt 10:1–11:1). Since this second teaching block has limited use for our exploration of ethics, we will skip over it to continue observing how Matthew fills out the messianic son of David image even more.

In the sequence following this teaching section, John the Baptizer, who preached a message of impending judgment, sends his disciples to ask Jesus whether he really is the Messiah (Mt 11:3). No ultimate moment of judgment had come. Jesus responds by pointing to his deeds, and the deeds of his apostles: "Go and tell John what you hear and see: the blind receive their sight, the lame walk, the lepers are cleansed, the deaf hear, the dead are raised, and the poor have good news brought to them. And blessed is anyone who takes no offense at me" (Mt 11:4-6).

Jesus is a messianic restorer of broken people, first.[30] It's a different sort of messianic Davidic role.[31] His response gives way, eventually, to the following significant invitation:

> *Come to me, all you that are weary and are carrying heavy burdens, and I will give you rest. Take my yoke upon you, and learn from me; for I am gentle and humble in heart, and you will find rest for your souls. For my yoke is easy, and my burden is light.* **Mt 11:28-30**

Judgment will come, we eventually learn, at another coming of the Messiah (Mt 16:27–17:8; 25:1-46). Something other than judgment must happen as a first stage. Jesus is restoring people to God before restoring the world. At the end of Matthew 11, Jesus the Davidic shepherd king invites all who are weary and weighed down to come under his light burden and easy yoke, and learn from him, the humble and gentle one. Matthew eventually links that gentle humility, first declared as a blessed way to live (Mt 5:5), to Jesus' Davidic royalty when Jesus rides into Jerusalem in Matthew 21:5.[32] These words encourage readers to accept Jesus' ways for themselves. Included in that is Jesus' ethical model of gentle humility, to be imitated as part of what they are to learn.

In the next scenes in Matthew 12 we see what the "easy yoke" and "light burden" look like morally. Pharisees criticize Jesus for allowing his disciples to gather food on the sabbath—work! Jesus defends their practice in two ways. First, he compares himself to scriptural figures David and the temple. He is greater than both. Second, he gives insight into how to live when two important values conflict, in this case sabbath practice and food gathering. Jesus' answer is to exercise mercy, quoting again (see Mt 9:13) from Hosea 6:6: "I desire mercy and not sacrifice." The practice that advances mercy always wins. That same sense of mercy carries over into the next scene (Mt 12:9-13), where doing good triumphs over sabbath rest.[33] Jesus' words and deeds show disciples one way to learn how to distinguish between competing values, which is important to ethical reasoning. They also illustrate how showing mercy to others is an easy burden to carry.

The scenes that follow in the rest of chapter 12 significantly establish Jesus as a more honored authority than Pharisees. The scenes build to the "sign of Jonah" that compares the prophet Jonah's three days and nights in the belly of a great fish with Jesus' expected three days and nights in the grave. That sign points to his resurrection, when he will indeed be fully vindicated as the restoring Davidic Messiah (Mt 12:38-42).[34] These are important to affirm Jesus, the "son of David" as a valid, ethical standard bearer.

Matthew's third block of teaching follows this cluster of episodes that portray Jesus' messianic credentials. It consists of parables about the kingdom (Mt 13:1-53), some of which help to shape ethical expectations. The first parable declares that a good response to the message of the kingdom should "bear fruit." Fruit, metaphorically, can include moral deeds, though in this parable it clearly also implies a wide range of activities that show a disciple's faithfulness to the kingdom and its King. Fruit bearing contrasts in the parable with giving up after being hindered by the devil, by troubles and persecutions or by the anxious pursuit of wealth (Mt 13:1-23). The troubles accompanying the anxious pursuit of wealth were also talked about earlier in Jesus' teaching (Mt 6:19-34). Money and worldly anxieties clearly compete with kingdom morality.

From the next parable we learn that subjects of the kingdom and pretenders will live side by side in the world until the final day of judgment (Mt 13:24-30, 36-43). That has implications for Matthew's interest in moral development. Sometimes disciples are indistinguishable from outsiders. Morally underdeveloped disciples must aim for kingdom perfection and are given time to grow up, but those who are pretenders will be found out when the kingdom comes in its fullness. Though parables about mustard seeds and yeast may point to a delay of the kingdom's ultimate arrival (Mt 13:31-33), a parable about a catch of fish declares a final reckoning (Mt 13:47-50), based on people's moral goodness or badness. This again repeats the theme of judgment, important to the emerging ethical picture that requires perfection.

In Matthew 14, after feeding a crowd exceeding five thousand, Jesus walks on top of the sea to his disciples, who are struggling to row to the other side. Surprisingly, Peter is enabled to do the same, until his fear overcomes his faith in Jesus (Mt 14:22-33). Disciples receive an object lesson to increase their "little faith," also important to moral development. They should know better, but they are allowed to grow and learn in his presence. Jesus rescues them, even in their failings. They can always count on his presence for help, a point Jesus himself makes with his final words at the very end of the story.[35] We may infer that when it comes to living up to the standards of moral perfection, disciples must depend on Jesus, the reliable presence of God.

In Matthew 15, confronted once more by Pharisees who are upset that his disciples do not heed their version of purity traditions, Jesus minimizes those traditions by declaring "it is not what goes into the mouth that defiles a person, but it is what comes out of the mouth that defiles" (Mt 15:11). Inner cleanliness leads to moral behavior, unlike outer cleanliness. People perform immoral deeds—"evil intentions, murder, adultery, fornication, theft, false witness, slander" (Mt 15:19)—because they are evil within. External, visible cleanliness or uncleanliness is irrelevant to the internally impure. Perfection must begin on the inside.

As if to illustrate the point, Jesus then heals the daughter of a Canaanite woman who calls on him for mercy (Mt 15:21-28).[36] She accepts his comparison of her to a "dog" but persists in her faith in Jesus.[37] Even externally unclean Gentiles can be clean on the inside, in contrast to outwardly clean Israelites whose deeds may reveal their actual inner evil. The set of stories encourages any disciple readers struggling with their own impure, moral imperfections. Jesus accepts all people based on their persistent faith, for which this woman becomes a model, just as a Gentile centurion previously had been (see Mt 8:5-13).[38]

A series of encounters gives way to the great moment in Matthew 16:13-20, when Peter openly confesses Jesus as the Messiah. Jesus first affirms Peter and then must rebuke him when Peter objects to Jesus' forecast of his eventual rejection and death in Jerusalem, to be followed by his resurrection on the third day. Jesus challenges his disciples with the words, "If any want to become my followers, let them deny themselves and take up their cross and follow me" (Mt 16:24). From this we learn that associating with the Messiah now means associating with shame—the cross. It requires self-denial, loss of life, the removal of whatever hinders someone from following the Messiah.[39] Those are important words for disciples and disciple readers since following Jesus does not lead first to a life of ease and glory. That has implications for ethics. Jesus shows himself to be trustworthy when physically present. Disciples must continue to trust him, even when the perfect morality demanded by following Jesus brings hardship. The story encourages that trust as it progresses to the death and resurrection of the Messiah, events of which we are reminded two more times (Mt 17:22-23; 20:18-19).

That trust is also important in view of the inevitable judgment that we learn definitively has been postponed.[40] Jesus declares that he, the "Son of Man is to come with his angels in the glory of his Father, and then he will repay everyone for what has been done" (Mt 16:27). We now know that there will be a second coming of this Messiah. The transfiguration scene in Matthew 17:1-8 certifies that coming by depicting Jesus suddenly radiant in his full messianic glory.[41] At a future point people will be held accountable for their deeds, and if those deeds are immoral, they can expect repayment.

But as we have seen throughout this story, disciples can receive mercy now from calling on Jesus, who allows those with little faith to grow, even morally.

Matthew's fourth block of teaching comes a few scenes later (Mt 18:1–19:1). It focuses on the moral issues of humility and forgiveness, important points for disciples who gather as the church after Jesus' resurrection, and also important for ethics. We first learn that disciples are to be humble, like children (Mt 18:1-5). But they must also esteem children, a lesson Jesus repeats soon after (Mt 19:13-15). Jesus provides a model to imitate by welcoming them himself. Jesus also emphasizes the perfection of childlike purity and innocence, condemning with harsh words those who destroy that both in others and in themselves (Mt 18:6-14).

After these child-focused lessons, Jesus outlines a procedure for dealing with someone in the "church" who "sins against" another disciple (Mt 18:15-20). He teaches that one who persistently resists correction for inflicting moral harm against another is to be placed outside the community as someone now in need of rescuing.[42] Though that may sound harsh, Jesus promises his special presence among his disciples, which affirms the community's due process against church members who have harmed another member. But in the lesson that follows, when asked how often one should forgive when sinned against by another in the church, Jesus declares that disciples must forgive, and forgive, and forgive (Mt 18:21-35). He then illustrates that with a parable that speaks of forgiveness as an act of mercy that must come from the heart.

After this teaching segment, some Pharisees test Jesus with a question about the permissibility of divorce. Jesus declares that when it comes to marriage the created order trumps laws designed to regulate the breaking of that perfect order through divorce (Mt 19:3-9). Divorce is a concession to moral hardheartedness, not an excusable legal option. We receive insight into another principle of ethical reasoning that disciples are encouraged to imitate, the priority of creation intent.

A brief encounter with a young man soon after is also ethically significant. When asserting his righteousness not only in keeping the Ten Commandments but in loving his neighbor as himself, the young man is disappointed when Jesus tells him what the standards of perfection demand: "If you wish to be perfect, go, sell your possessions, and give the money to the poor, and you will have treasure in heaven; then come, follow me" (Mt 19:21). Being rich, he is unwilling to do that. Following Jesus requires absolute commitment beyond moral performance, something the man finds difficult. Participation in the kingdom is not about enjoying the fine things of life but about responding to Jesus, who can make personally costly demands even to help others in need. Kingdom ethics are all consuming, as the words of Matthew 19:23-30 affirm.

Then on his way to Jerusalem, where he discloses for a third time that he will be crucified and raised, two of his disciples make a bold request for special honor in the kingdom. Jesus responds with a lesson about perfect service, which should be at the heart of their lives as disciples. He is about to model that in the cross as one who has come "not to be served, but to serve, and to give his life a ransom for many" (Mt 20:28). For disciples, life is to be about serving others, not themselves. We learn more about how Jesus the Messiah will save his people from their sins. His crucifixion will be a means of delivering them in their greatest need. His disciples are then told to imitate that same attitude of service. As if to reinforce the point, the next scene depicts Jesus healing two blind men who call on him as the "Son of David" to show them mercy.

After this, Jesus enters Jerusalem humbly, while the crowds hail him as the son of David (Mt 21:1-11), again modeling his prior teaching about humility. He pronounces judgment against the Jerusalem leadership (Mt 21:12-22). They challenge his authority (Mt 21:23–22:33). When his opponents ask Jesus about the greatest law, Jesus responds by quoting two, that of loving God with all of one's heart, soul and mind, and that of loving one's neighbor as oneself (Mt 22:39). For the third time in this writing Jesus quotes this second law, elevating the moral importance of loving one's neighbor (see Mt 5:43; 19:19).

In the words of Matthew 23 Jesus condemns the hypocrisy of teachers who have resisted him. His disciples learn that they must never be like scribes and Pharisees who

- fail to practice what they teach (Mt 23:3, 13, 15, 23, 25, 27, 29, unlike Jesus in Mt 10:24-25)

- load others with heavy burdens (Mt 23:4, unlike Jesus in Mt 11:30)

- love honor, exalting themselves (Mt 23:5-12, unlike Jesus in Mt 12:15-21)

- discourage people from the kingdom (Mt 23:13-15, unlike Jesus in Mt 11:28-30)

- teach ignorance (Mt 23:16-22, unlike Jesus in Mt 5:1–7:29; 10:1–11:1; 13:1-53; 18:1–19:1)

- neglect weighty matters of the law (Mt 23:23-24, unlike Jesus in Mt 9:13; 12:7)

- neglect inner purity and righteousness (Mt 23:25-26, 27-28)

- destroy God's servants (Mt 23:29-36, as they will also try to destroy Jesus).

Jesus' life has clearly offered an imitative example that counters the sort of behavior coming from people who consider Jesus as a rival.

The final teaching block follows in Matthew 24–25, addressing the imminent destruction of the Jerusalem temple and the return of Jesus, who refers to himself as the "Son of Man." Two parables in the middle illustrate how disciples should faithfully anticipate that return (Mt 25:1-13, 14-30). The last words of the section depict the final judgment, with people in the world being held accountable for their deeds, including the moral treatment of disciples in need (Mt 25:31-46).[43]

Events now proceed steadily to the crucifixion. Jesus has a farewell Passover supper with his disciples (Mt 26:17-30). During that supper he establishes, with bread and wine, an ongoing commemoration of his death. The wine points to his blood that he will pour out "for the forgiveness of sins" (Mt 26:28), a direct reference to the cross. That, ultimately, is how he will save his people from their sins. Through betrayal and injustice he is condemned to death on a cross, and severely mocked (Mt 27:27-44), ironically as a helpless "King of the Jews" (Mt 27:37).

Matthew intensifies that irony by showing how the crucifixion confirms the very same Davidic messianic credentials his opponents had hoped to destroy. Matthew narrates the crucifixion with language from Psalm 22, a psalm attributed to David.[44] In that comparison, Jesus suffers literally and intensely the extremes experienced by his forebear David. He is a true son of David, and more, who three days later rises from the dead. When he does rise from death, the sign of Jonah comes to pass (see Mt 12:38-40; 16:1-4). That seals his messianic qualifications.

When he appears to his disciples in Galilee after his resurrection (Mt 28:17), Jesus declares his full messianic authority and sends his disciples out with the charge to make more disciples from the entire world, baptizing them and "teaching them to obey everything" he has commanded them (Mt

28:20).[45] They are guaranteed the support of his spiritual presence in that endeavor. He will be with them "always, to the end of the age" (Mt 28:20).

What has he taught them to obey? To find out, the readers must go back to the beginning, now with ears to hear from the risen Messiah, Jesus. That would include revisiting Jesus' deeds, since he taught by example. It would especially include his words. Jesus taught, according to Matthew, not as a Jewish teacher or rabbi but as Lord. And though he is compared with Moses, he is both fulfiller of Moses' law and one with authority in his own right, the bringer of new things based on old. How do ethics emerge from Jesus' words and deeds? It is to that task we now turn.

Ethics in Matthew

The messianic portrait. Though forecasting judgment, Matthew highlights Jesus as a gentle, compassionate Davidic Messiah who offers a light and easy yoke, requesting his followers to learn from him (Mt 11:28-30). As Messiah he heals, restoring the broken. He also teaches. His favorite topic? The kingdom. We also learn that he is a Messiah for all people, Jew and Gentile. Through this "son of Abraham" (Mt 1:1) all nations are to be blessed (Mt 28:19-20), and we see that begin to happen at significant points in the story (Mt 8:5-13; 12:18-21; 15:21-28). All are invited to become disciples, learning what Jesus has commanded. Matthew introduces the Messiah as Emmanuel, the presence of God (Mt 1:23). We observe his enabling presence, which aids his disciples at key moments of powerlessness (Mt 8:23-27; 14:22-33). He promises ongoing presence with his disciples whenever they gather (Mt 18:15-20) and as they make more disciples (Mt 28:20). They can count on his presence to help them, even in their imperfections, until the age ends and the kingdom comes in its fullness.

This Messiah offers mercy throughout the account to all who call on him (Mt 9:13; 9:27; 12:7; 15:22; 17:15; 20:30-31), connecting that mercy to the forgiveness of sins (Mt 9:13; 18:33), and teaching his disciples of the blessedness (Mt 5:7) and weightiness (Mt 23:23) of mercy. He announces the arrival of the kingdom, healing people as part of that kingdom declaration. He rescues "people from their sins" (Mt 1:21), forgiving them (Mt 9:6), giving his life a "ransom for many" (Mt 20:28), pouring out his "blood of the covenant . . . for the forgiveness of sins" (Mt 26:28). He rises from the dead, in full affirmation of his messianic stature. He will return, but at that return the time for mercy will end, and *then* the judgment and full kingdom restoration will begin (Mt 25:31-46). Judgment will be extreme and final, based on people's deeds.

Until that moment, Jesus' disciples are to make more disciples, teaching them to obey what he had commanded them. Jesus is the restoring Davidic Messiah who establishes the kingdom both now and in finality when he comes to judge and to restore the world. He has begun to rescue his people from their sins, not by military triumph but by offering mercy to all who come to him to fix their brokenness, and then by forgiving them through the cross. In this ethical vision Jesus the Messiah both models ethics and makes ethics possible.

Ethical specifics. *Becoming disciples of Jesus.* Ethics in Matthew begins when people become disciples of Jesus. We learn that being a disciple is both a costly commitment and a light burden, but connection to Jesus, the crucified, resurrected Messiah, is required. This is an ethic of relationship. Matthew has depicted Jesus as the presence of God, "God with us." Knowing Jesus means knowing God. In knowing Jesus the disciple receives merciful acceptance from him, including the forgiveness of sins. With regard to morality, disciples are now committed to the life of perfection that Jesus teaches, a life in which they must grow from "little faith" into great faith in Jesus, whose resurrected presence remains with them. Moral perfection is a lofty goal, but it is the ongoing challenge for which the ever-present Messiah offers continued, merciful help.[46]

Changing the inner person. Jesus teaches that a person's words and deeds show what he or she is really like on the inside. In one place he declares that the person who is pure in heart will be the one to see God (Mt 5:8). In another, preference of money over God is a matter of the heart that affects how someone perceives good and evil (Mt 6:19-24). Elsewhere, one must be clean inside before showing it on the outside (Mt 23:25). Jesus in Matthew shows ethical perfection flowing from the inner person to outward performance.

Consider Matthew's depiction of farming and shepherding metaphors. In Matthew 3:8-10, John the Baptizer declares that people show true repentance by their fruit. People's true inner character appears in what they actually do. In Matthew 7:15-20 Jesus compares false prophets to wolves clothed as sheep whose deeds reveal their true identity. In Matthew 12:33-37, which combines points from Matthew 3:7 and Matthew 7:15-20, Jesus ties what a person says to what flows out of a person's inner core. In Matthew 13:23 Jesus compares the behavior of the one who accepts the word of the kingdom to fertile soil producing good crops. Each comparison shows that a person's words and deeds emerge from the heart.[47] Good hearts lead to good words and deeds, bad hearts to bad ones.

Recall the scene in Matthew 15:1-20, when Jesus fields criticism for his disciples eating with unwashed hands. He teaches the crowds, "It is not what goes into the mouth that defiles a person, but it is what comes out of the mouth that defiles" (Mt 15:11). "What comes out of the mouth," he explains, "proceeds from the heart, and this is what defiles. For out of the heart come evil intentions, murder, adultery, fornication, theft, false witness, slander" (Mt 15:18-19). People do evil because their hearts are evil. How provocative!

Look at fornication, an item on the list. Jesus indicates that people have sex outside of marriage because they have evil hearts. That would offend all sorts of people who would assert their personal goodness while engaging in unmarried sex. What sort of person would not be offended? A true disciple of Jesus, who teaches moral perfection. The list of Matthew 15:18-19 is not troubling for people who know God and God's perspectives. It matches standards found in the Ten Commandments and other laws. So Jesus, who has already declared that he has come to fulfill the Law (Mt 5:17), reflects that Law in his moral standards, while challenging people to consider why they do evil. Jesus indicates that people who inflict harm in their world do so out of damaged hearts. Those hearts need repair so that good may proceed from them.

How does one become clean on the inside? Matthew implies that true disciples of Jesus become different by being genuine disciples. True disciples surrender to him and his ways, which are moral, rooted in the Torah and sometimes surpassing it. Not everything Jesus teaches connects to the Torah, but nothing that he teaches undermines it. The commitment of being a disciple implies a life-changing association with Jesus, not as teacher but as Lord.[48] He is a teacher with a plus, one with authority, unlike other teachers (see Mt 7:29). With "all authority in heaven and on earth" given to him in the aftermath of his resurrection (Mt 28:18), he sends out his disciples to make more disciples, promising his ongoing presence. Following him means much more than adhering to the Ten Commandments and other morally instructive laws (Mt 19:16-22). It requires total commitment that could demand hardship, even loss of life (Mt 8:19; 10:38; 16:24-

26). However, he offers a yoke that is easy and a burden that is light.[49] He is worth coming to know.

Kingdom restorative mercy, kingdom judgment. A disciple of Jesus the Messiah comes under the reign of God. Jesus brings the kingdom of God, which we learn is here now, but also not yet. Jesus heals as part of his preaching that the kingdom is at hand (Mt 4:23-25; 9:35). His casting out demons by the Spirit of God, which Matthew regularly equates with healing (Mt 4:24; 12:22; 15:28; 17:16-18), demonstrates the kingdom's arrival (Mt 12:28).[50] He sends his disciples out also to cast out demons and to heal (Mt 10:7-8). Jesus cites healing and restorative activities as evidence that he indeed is "the one who is to come" and that John the Baptizer need not look for another (Mt 11:2-6).

Healing and demon exorcism reflect that God is asserting his reign on earth through his Messiah. Jesus performed them often in response to pleas for him to show mercy (Mt 9:27; 15:22; 17:15; 20:30-31) and sometimes prompted by his compassion (Mt 9:36; 14:14; 15:32; 20:34). But Matthew portrays healing principally as an expression of the kingdom, not as an ethical end in itself. The kingdom could be thought of by some Jewish people as a moment of judgment and national restoration.[51] Matthew points to acts of physical restoration, a fixing of brokenness, to indicate that the Messiah Jesus is launching the reign of God in the world. There is subtle support here, not for healing itself as necessary kingdom practice but for the extension of mercy to broken people, of which healing is a powerful expression that God indeed was beginning to exert his reign.[52] Active response to the needs of others grows out of powerful kingdom activity. Post-Easter disciples do not receive the same authorization for healing that the pre-Easter disciples did when they were commissioned and sent out. But they do have Jesus as an imitative figure, responsive to people's cries for mercy. They can show mercy.

Matthew shows Jesus linking merciful behavior to the kingdom. Jesus declares that those who extend mercy to others are blessed (Mt 5:7), and then himself extends mercy by healing those who cry out to the Son of David for mercy (Mt 9:27; 15:22; 17:15; 20:30-31). He teaches that people who forgive those who offend them are extending them mercy (Mt 18:33). He calls sinners to himself and then associates with them as an act of mercy that he compares to a physician helping the sick (Mt 9:13). All of this is kingdom activity. Helping people out of their brokenness is important to the kingdom, which in its fullness promises total deliverance from the wrongs of the world. Disciples of Jesus should embrace restorative deeds of mercy, imitating Jesus.

Accompanying kingdom activity is a strong sense of accountability. Recall the tough words of John the Baptizer, who announces Jesus as the one coming to judge with fire (Mt 3:11-12). Recall also the words (Mt 16:27-28) that introduce Jesus' transfiguration in Matthew 17:1-8: judgment is coming based on deeds, a judgment later depicted in Matthew's final teaching block as the moment "when the Son of Man comes in his glory, and all the angels with him" (Mt 25:31).

Matthew overflows with recompense language—people will be judged based on their own words and deeds. In one place we learn that those who do not forgive those who offend them cannot expect to receive God's forgiveness (Mt 6:14-15). Elsewhere Jesus teaches that those who claim allegiance to him, even who do miracles in his name, but do not do the will of God will not enter the kingdom when it comes in its fullness (Mt 7:21-23). The will of God? That refers to the perfect morality that Jesus had just been teaching about in Matthew 5–7. In another setting Jesus states that people's words disclose what is in their hearts, so that if their hearts are evil, so will their words be. At the judgment they have to "give an account for every careless word" they utter (Mt 12:35-37). Elsewhere, a parable illustrates that those who accept the kingdom message but who do not clothe themselves properly, a metaphor that includes moral deeds,[53] are themselves subject to removal from the kingdom as illegitimate subjects (Mt 22:11-14). In his last teaching segment Jesus declares that those for whom helping needy disciples is not natural behavior are likewise subject to judgment (Mt 25:45-46).[54] Those associated with the kingdom are expected to do proper kingdom deeds. Moral imperfection has dire consequences.

So, does this challenge the points made earlier in this book that people should not behave morally to avoid eternal punishment? Yes and no. Yes, because Matthew clearly shows that people who fail to act well will suffer for it, while disciples who do act well can expect a reward.[55] No, because within the scope of the entire Gospel rewards and punishments push disciple readers to embrace a lifestyle of proper moral activity. Good performance is all or nothing, not a balancing act where good or bad outweighs the other. It flows from knowing Jesus and thus God through him. Growing dependence on God's mercy is part of that.

When the resurrected Jesus commands his disciples to go and make more disciples, he tells them to teach those new disciples "to obey everything I have commanded you" (Mt 28:20). Disciples must obey Jesus. Yet Matthew also indicates that disciples will struggle in the process. Jesus instructs his disciples to pray for forgiveness (Mt 6:12). He teaches that wheat and weeds will exist together in the kingdom, and it is only the job of the angels at the judgment to root up the weeds (Mt 13:40-42). Sometimes the two are indistinguishable, though in the end the true disciple becomes known. Later Jesus also says that although people by themselves might struggle with letting go of what they must in order to follow him, with "God all things are possible" (Mt 19:26). Those who call on the same Jesus who extends mercy to others in their need can expect that mercy when they need forgiveness. And there is the key. Disciples know the standards of the Messiah—perfection (Mt 5:48). They can live up to those standards and experience blessing (Mt 5:3-12). They also know they regularly fail to meet God's standards. The more sensitive they are to his standards, the more they know they need God's mercy. When they cry out for mercy, they can expect to receive it and in some way be enabled to do what's right. The resurrected Messiah has promised his presence with them until the end of the age.

We must keep the deeds of Jesus next to his words. Jesus offers willing help to the cries for mercy. At various points in the story he mercifully associates with lowlifes such as tax collectors and sinners, who require their own healing as well (Mt 9:12-13). As a result, "the tax collectors and the prostitutes" enter the kingdom ahead of those who resist Jesus and his ways because they have responded to the call to repent and to receive mercy (Mt 21:31-32).

Disciples of Jesus know both the seriousness of the kingdom and its joys. They experience ongoing mercy from Jesus, who is with them. In imitation of Jesus and in response to his teaching, they extend restorative mercy to people in need, knowing that final restoration will come with the kingdom's fullness. As the merciful, they will receive mercy (Mt 5:7). They enter the kingdom as those who are "poor in spirit" (Mt 5:3), aware of their own minimal self-worth before God. In a world of people opposed to God and his ways, they should also expect to suffer various forms of persecution for living out the kingdom's moral standards, being blessed with the kingdom in the end (Mt 5:10). The kingdom and its King make strong demands on the lives of disciples. The stakes are high, but so are the rewards. Jesus himself has paved the way, both in his own suffering and in his vindication through the resurrection.

All of this stems from being disciples of the Messiah Jesus, who embraces a life of merciful service to rescue his people from their sins. In that mercy, the first are last and the last first (Mt 19:30; 20:16). Disciples are to rethink what matters most, embracing a regard for others ahead of their own honor, imitating Jesus who came "not to be served but to serve, and to give his life a ransom for many" (Mt 20:28). That service takes shape most vividly in the cross, by which Jesus offers the "blood of the covenant, which is poured out for many for the forgiveness of sins" (Mt 26:28). His resurrection points to his authority to do and to demand what he does. He exercises that authority in sending out his disciples to make more disciples. His disciples are to act mercifully because they have received powerful mercy in being rescued from their sins.

Jesus' teaching, and ethics: the Sermon on the Mount. Finally we can consider the highly celebrated first block of teaching known as the Sermon on the Mount. Typical of biographies, we have a collection of words, probably uttered on more than one occasion. It's not really a sermon. But Matthew does present the words in a well-organized structure, even if individual sayings do not always connect smoothly with what precedes and follows. The entire unit has an introduction (Mt 5:3-16), then a core set of teachings, concluding with an invitation to respond (Mt 7:13-27).[56]

The introduction itself has one set of sayings beginning with the words "Blessed are" and another group beginning with "You are": *beatitudes,* from the Latin word *beatus,* meaning "blessed," and "similitudes" (as in "similar") because disciples are compared to salt and light. As introductory words they set the tone, providing indirect rather than direct moral teaching.[57] For example, "Blessed are the poor in spirit" does not declare "Become poor in spirit." It states that those who already are poor in spirit are blessed. Poverty in spirit, or humility, can be a necessary starting point for becoming a disciple as Jesus declares in Matthew 18:3-4, or it can be an exemplary quality that Jesus applies to himself (Mt 11:29).[58] Here it appears with other statements of blessing that are contrary to what people normally do to achieve satisfaction in life.[59]

Consider the topics:

- "poor in spirit"—embracing abject humility
- "those who mourn"—grieving over their own wretched condition
- "meek"—willingly suppressing the right to exert personal power
- "those who hunger and thirst for righteousness"—longing for morally right activity in a crooked world
- "merciful"—those extending themselves to others in their needy weakness
- "the pure in heart"—those who are morally clean on the inside
- "peacemakers"—those who solve disputes nonviolently
- "those persecuted for righteousness's sake"—putting up with criticism from others for having stood up for God's sense of rightness

These words offer no viable plan for getting ahead in life. They do address worldly troubles, many of which exist because of the moral evil of others. They also promise blessing, not necessarily in this world but in the kingdom that is to come. Those who do the will of Jesus' Father in heaven may sometimes suffer from doing that will. Jesus the Messiah's assurances of blessing encourage disciples to persevere in doing what is right, as does his imitative model. The reality of a kingdom future offers a significant motive for Jesus' ethics in Matthew, a future eventually assured by the resurrection of the crucified Messiah.

A different kind of ethical motivation appears when Jesus compares disciples to salt and light. Jesus indicates that their behavior should make the world better and point the world to God.[60] If neither their words nor their deeds do so, they are as worthless as flavorless salt and hidden lamps in a dark room. All these introductory words set the table for the meal that follows. Disciples can heed Jesus' more explicit teaching, much of which is moral, because they are both aiming for outcomes beyond this world, while simultaneously helping to change it.

In Matthew 5:17-20 and Matthew 7:12 a concern with both the Law and the Prophets brackets the core teaching in between. That core presents a variety of sayings, some of which are connected to Law or Torah, some to the practice of piety, some to concerns with money and the affairs of daily survival in the world, some to criticizing others' shortcomings and some to prayer. Much of this, but not all, connects to morality, to activities that either advance good or hinder harm in the world. For example, prayer may be excellent activity for disciples, especially because it keeps them connected to God, necessary for a biblically ethical person. But it asks *God*, not people, to intervene so that good may be advanced on the world. And though contributing financially to the poor is itself morally good, the discussion where it appears accents not the goodness of that act but its privacy. It's not for others to know about publicly, but only for God to know "in secret."

The material in Matthew 5:21-48 is directly moral, and grows out of Jesus' statements that he has come to fulfill the Law and the Prophets, not to abolish them.[61] He is concerned that disciples uphold what the Scriptures point to, encouraging proper behavior that exceeds the righteousness of the scribes and Pharisees (Mt 5:20), a high degree of righteousness indeed! In demonstrating that, Matthew offers a series of sayings in which Jesus contrasts Torah-linked words that his own hearers have at some time heard with what *he* says. Often referred to as antitheses, these contain rich moral teaching that encourages disciples to think more expansively about laws. They don't replace laws with Jesus' views. Rather, they intensify or amplify certain laws.[62]

Thus,

- Disciples must not merely refrain from murder. Anger and insult also destroy lives and relationships.[63] Disciples should make it right with another they have offended in those ways (Mt 5:21-26).

- Disciples must not merely refrain from adultery. Lustful (or covetous?) glances are just as bad, and disciples should do what they can to keep themselves from being entangled in anything like that activity.[64] (In contemporary terms, true disciples don't look at porn, ogle suggestive magazine covers or check out potential "hot" sex partners.) Lust is just as destructive to marriage as adultery is (Mt 5:27-30).

- Divorce is also connected to adultery. Disciples who divorce and remarry both commit adultery and force their former spouses to do the same when they remarry (Mt 5:31-32). Elsewhere in Matthew, when questioned as to why laws regulating divorce existed in the first place, Jesus points to the created order of one husband with one wife as the divinely intended standard (Mt 19:3-9), making divorce a divine concession to human stubbornness and also effectively prohibiting polygamy.[65] Legality is not the same as morality!

- Truth telling is so important that one need not swear great oaths in order to assure one's honesty. Teaching about the potential silliness of oaths is repeated in Matthew 23:16-22. People should do what they declare they will, period (Mt 5:33-37).

- Though laws point out fitting punishments for those who do evil, disciples should not demand those punishments. They should accept the evil perpetrated against them in a nonretaliatory manner, instead doing positive deeds for the benefit of the evil person (Mt 5:38-42). Perhaps Jesus himself demonstrates this in his submission to crucifixion.[66] That attitude would provide an ethical model worthy of imitation.

- The love disciples are to show their neighbors must extend beyond their friends to all, including their enemies, who may not be a part of their normal circle of associates. That's what God does (Mt 5:43-48). Those who do that show how they are truly his children. (Note how Mt 5:45 and Mt 5:9 are similar on this point.) This is the first application of the command to love, which is implied in an altered form in Matthew 7:12, but which is also directly appealed to in Matthew 19:19 and Matthew 22:39.[67] Merciful love becomes an important ethical standard for Matthew.

Notice how microethical this teaching is.[68] For example, turning the other cheek when being struck (Mt 5:39) can only be done by an individual in response to evil she or he is receiving directly. What should a man do if he sees someone next to him being struck? Jesus' words do not really advocate noninvolvement when evil is being enacted against adjacent people—unless those people have an agreement to stand together and not allow what happens to one affect the other. So "turn the other cheek" is not presented as ideal social policy.

None of the points of right behavior promoted here in Jesus' teaching are particularly novel.[69] Other teachers from that culture advocated similar moral standards. But we do find two significant principles that begin to move us from morality to ethics. First, note how Jesus upholds the Torah. He does so by citing a sampling only of laws that affect how others should be treated. He offers no exhaustive treatment of the Torah's multiple laws. Second, he uses individual laws as starting points, not to establish a new law but to encourage disciples to think deeply about what laws point to. He does not state "You shall not be angry" to be added to "You shall not murder." He uses the law against murder to urge disciples to avoid all forms of activity that destroys others. He assumes the rightness of a law and then moves beyond it.

How, according to Jesus, can a person learn right from wrong? The Torah is a great starting place. But the Torah is not the finishing place. Jesus offers a model for doing even more than what a law might say. He challenges disciples to be alert to all forms of potentially destructive behaviors, using laws as launch points for considering new possibilities of curbing bad behaviors and replacing them with more constructive ones.

In this first teaching block, Matthew shows Jesus addressing more than laws. The instructions of Matthew 6:1-18 deal with practicing piety (v. 1) and address morality mostly by criticizing the performing of pious deeds for public acclamation. And in the midst of the discussion on prayer we find these words: "For if you forgive others their trespasses, your heavenly Father will also forgive you; but if you do not forgive others, neither will your Father forgive your trespasses" (v. 14). It connects to Jesus' prayer: "Forgive us our debts, as we also have forgiven our debtors" (v. 12). Forgiveness is a major moral act, and failure to grant it is a major moral fault. Precisely because disciples are connected to God who forgives, they should be experts in forgiveness. No one should expect forgiveness from God while neglecting to forgive others.[70] God forgives all who ask him for it. But those who ask God for forgiveness and then refuse to extend it to others show that they do not understand God's forgiveness. God forgives as an act of mercy, a point repeated elsewhere in another teaching on forgiveness (Mt 18:21-35). Extension of mercy is a major moral responsibility for disciples.

The segment from Matthew 6:19-34 offers important moral challenges to disciples worried about money and security. We have already seen that concern in the parable explained in Matthew 13:22, in the aftermath of a rich man's refusal to sell all, give to the poor and follow Jesus (Mt 18:23-26), and in Jesus' denunciation of Pharisees (Mt 23:25). The desire for money is an inner evil that prevents a person from seeing the needs of the world. It gets in the way of serving God, and leads to the anxiety and worry typical of those who do not know God. That thought is repeated in Matthew 13:22, where worries about "the cares of the world" along with the "lure of wealth" are shown to stifle good reception of the kingdom message. They hinder disciples from performing the righteousness that belongs to the kingdom.[71]

Rather than teaching passive contentment with what they have, though, Jesus teaches his disciples to seek actively God's kingdom and the right-eousness that belongs to it. Both the pursuit of money and the anxious pursuit of security hinder people from being ethical. Both interfere with how a person is connected to God. Instead of being people of little faith, they should increase their confidence in God, who will help them be the kind of people who do the good that he desires.

The final segment of morally relevant teaching appears in Matthew 7:1-5.[72] There Jesus warns disciples against judging others while overlooking their own faults. That would be hypocrisy! He repeats the warning later, when condemning Pharisees in Matthew 23. Hypocrisy invites God's judgment against them at the end of the age. Only when disciples are honestly in touch with their own faults can they ever properly address the faults of another. Such self-awareness would change both what one says and how one says it. The moral standard is perfection. Disciples who know that know they don't measure up. Circumspectly judging others' imperfections is consistent with a context that promotes forgiving mercy.

Matthew concludes the core teaching section with the famous words known as the Golden Rule: "In everything do to others as you would have them do to you; for this is the law and the prophets" (Mt 7:12). This captures the essence of performing the law, reflecting a regard for well-being bene-ficial to anyone. Torah taught the Israelites to learn mercy from their legacy as slaves and foreigners in Egypt (Ex 22:21; 23:9; Lev 19:34; Deut 24:17-18). By urging Israelites, as former aliens, to love aliens as themselves, Leviticus 19:34 connects love of neighbor (Lev 19:18) with merciful concern for the weak. This is a merciful love that addresses people's needs.

Jesus does the same here. There is scarcely any difference between showing the same regard for a neighbor's needs as one's own and loving one's neighbor as oneself. That is the essence of what the Torah and Prophets in-struct. That's the same sort of love Jesus has already taught them to show to their enemies in Matthew 5:43-48. It is repeated in Matthew 19:19 and Matthew 22:39. In the last instance, "law and the prophets" are said to "hang" on love of God and love of neighbor together in a similar way that the Golden Rule is said to here.

The teaching block concludes by urging all who hear Jesus' words to put them into practice (Mt 7:24). Disciples of Jesus must perform moral deeds that flow out of their new connection to God as disciples of Jesus. Those who do not do the kinds of deeds Jesus has just taught about cannot enter the kingdom. That's not because entry is performance based. Rather, being a disciple is performance based. A true disciple has come under the reign of God, eager to do what Jesus, the Lord Messiah, commands.

Has there been an ethical core to this? Not exactly. No single concept summarizes the moral teaching here, not even the strong accent on mercy that addresses brokenness. Various topics do actually reflect something that needs to be fixed: anger, lust, divorce, unreliability, vengeance, hatred of enemies, performance of piety to impress the public, money and anxiety, hypocritical judgment, failure to pray, neediness. However, the passage lacks a consistent vocabulary of brokenness.

Still, the words do offer an overall kingdom pattern. They point to the kind of fixed-up world that one should expect in the kingdom's full restoration. In the end the Sermon on the Mount encourages disciples both to think deeply about how the law promotes the welfare of others and how they must proceed wisely within a broken world, in dependence on God. That is what God's reign offers the disciple of Jesus now, in view of the kingdom's eventual complete arrival. Disciples of Jesus heed these teachings in response to Jesus' authority. He is more than just another teacher.

Mercy, righteousness and the law. Throughout the Gospel we see an emphasis on mercy. We have already explored how it informs people's morality. Mercy also helps disciples read the Law, the Torah.[73] Though the Torah teaches more than mercy, mercy helps disciple-readers learn what to pick up from laws.

Consider three key places where Jesus addresses laws:

- When criticized for allowing his disciples to work on the sabbath, Jesus explains that needy circumstances should override legal requirement; mercy takes precedence over sacrifice (Mt 12:1-8).

- When criticized for allowing his disciples to eat with unwashed hands, Jesus first criticizes the Pharisees' immoral use of one law to dodge family responsibilities taught by other laws, and then makes a pronouncement that elevates internal, moral purity over external ritual purity (Mt 15:1-11).

- When accusing Pharisees of hypocrisy, Jesus notes that they practice minutia from the Law such as tithing spices, while neglecting "weightier" matters such as "justice, mercy and faith" (Mt 23:23-24).[74]

In all three of these instances, we see teaching and practice that shape what Jesus said in Matthew 5:18 about performing the least stroke of the law. Though Jesus claims to uphold all laws, he clearly emphasizes some kinds over others. Those laws that help advance the well-being of other people are the more significant. Learning from those laws is at the heart of kingdom living. Merciful love is a filter, more than an interpretive principle. Advancing the full well-being of others is what really matters. Disciples must not strain out gnats while swallowing camels (Mt 23:24).

That concept can help disciples decide between all sorts of competing righteous standards, not simply law-related ones.[75] For example, if rigid truth telling in a particular situation would actually endanger someone's life, then the merciful rescuing of another would take precedence.[76] Even social and political standards should never supersede the merciful rescuing of others, no matter how well-intentioned those standards may have initially been.[77] Disciples of Jesus, who belong to the kingdom, learn from what Jesus did and said that God's righteousness favors helping others, even if that help defies other competing standards.

Matthew may portray Jesus as the Lord Messiah who teaches, but what he teaches is not right just because he, the Lord, says so. He says so because it is right. He assumes the rightness of Torah, encouraging his disciples to expand their ethical vision beyond what Torah says. He also launches the kingdom. The restoration offered in the kingdom also coordinates with what Torah teaches. Jesus emphasizes mercy as a kingdom value, helping to fix the broken and strengthen the weak now, in view of the final fix to come. His instruction on merciful love emphasizes helping people in their need.

SUMMING IT UP:
MATTHEW'S ETHICAL VISION OF JESUS

o Ethics in Matthew begins when people become disciples, submitting by faith to Jesus as the Lord Messiah. That privilege extends to all people from all nations.

o Jesus, as Messiah, rescues people from their sins, ultimately through the cross. Just as he healed the physically infirm, Jesus cures the sinfully sick. Disciples must grow in faith that Jesus, in his mercy, can save them from their sins and change them on the inside, where true moral behavior originates.

o Jesus has established God's reign or kingdom. His resurrected presence helps disciples to live rightly until "the end of the age," when the kingdom comes in its fullness. This too is an ethic of relationship. Disciples know God better by continuing to depend on Jesus, the presence of God.

o Disciples must learn from the Messiah, both from what he said and in imitation of what he did. Jesus taught moral perfection and God's judgment against all human immorality. Disciples must be morally perfect. Jesus modeled mercy in his deeds, especially the cross, extending forgiveness to all who followed him. Disciples must imitate that mercy in forgiving and serving others. His most common teaching topic? The kingdom.

o Kingdom morals promote mercy, the fixing of the broken, now, in view of the final fix at the kingdom's full arrival. Disciples should seek that kingdom and its righteousness above all else. That will make the world better in its current state of brokenness.

o A kingdom sense of right and wrong upholds Torah's basic moral framework. Jesus taught his disciples to think deeply about weightier laws that extend merciful benefit to others, which take precedence over laws and practices that do not. Matthew's story points its readers to decide right from wrong with kingdom questions such as, Will this uphold righteous mercy, or will it weaken it? and Will this break or will this fix?

Matthew does not offer as focused an ethical vision as Luke. But the ethics emerging from Matthew are not dramatically different. According to both *Lives* of Jesus, people must respond to God by responding to Jesus the Messiah (or Christ), who brings God's kingdom. In that kingdom disciples experience God's restoration of the world now and help to advance it, while anticipating the final restoration coming when the crucified, resurrected Jesus returns. Jesus has begun something new, without abandoning Torah's basic moral standards. People who come in contact with Jesus become aware of their own deep moral shortcomings. Responding positively to Jesus leads both to total acceptance from him and to a clearer sense of how to behave properly. What he taught in both word and deed encourages that sense. His acceptance of disciples encourages them to extend merciful help to the morally, spiritually and physically needy. Jesus' life offers a guiding pattern or imitative model connected to the shame of the cross. The cross and the resurrection influence how disciples are to live, even if the particulars of their significance vary from one writing to the other. Doing Jesus' good may lead to personal shame, but it turns to ultimate glory at the fullness of the kingdom. Each Gospel portrays those points uniquely, but each also shows how what Jesus offers is good, and promotes goodness in others.

Reflection Questions

1. How does awareness of the kingdom, headed by the crucified, resurrected Messiah, affect a person's sense of right and wrong?

2. What sort of people does Matthew encourage its readers to become?

3. In what specific ways does Jesus in Matthew perform moral behavior to be imitated?

4. Consider the "kingdom questions" in the summary: Will this uphold righteous mercy, or will it weaken it? and Will this break, or will this fix?

   • Choose a hot-button moral issue (e.g., sexual behavior, abortion, divorce, substance abuse, gambling, war)

   • How do the "kingdom questions" bring clarity to the issue?

   • How do the "kingdom questions" encourage people to consider both why an activity is right or wrong, and why people may struggle with it in the first place?

For Further Reading

Burridge, Richard A. *Imitating Jesus: An Inclusive Approach to New Testament Ethics*, pp. 187-225. Grand Rapids: Eerdmans, 2007.

France, R. T. *The Gospel of Matthew.* New International Commentary on the New Testament. Grand Rapids: Eerdmans, 2007.

Hays, Richard B. *The Moral Vision of the New Testament: A Contemporary Introduction to New Testament Ethics*, pp. 93-111. San Francisco: HarperCollins, 1996.

Talbert, Charles H. *Matthew.* Grand Rapids: Baker Academic, 2010.

———. *Reading the Sermon on the Mount: Character Formation and Ethical Decision Making in Matthew 5–7.* Grand Rapids: Baker Academic, 2004.

9

TRANSFORMATION IN PRACTICE

Paul and 1 Corinthians

INTRODUCTORY ISSUES

The world of Paul is an exciting world. Paul knows God's promises to Abraham. He knows the expansion of those promises through the prophets (see Rom 1:1-4; 4:13; 9:4-5; 15:8-12).[1] He shows how that program comes to fullness in the crucified, resurrected and returning Jesus. As we will see him explain, the death and resurrection of Jesus bring people into a closer connection with God never before possible. In Paul's ethical vision, good behavior flows directly out of that growing relationship. By responding to God in that relationship, people come to know God deeply.

Paul, who identifies himself as an apostle, is not part of the Gospels' stories. He never claims to have seen Jesus as he walked the hills of Galilee or even as he was crucified in Jerusalem. According to his own accounts, he came to believe in Jesus as the Messiah, or Christ, sometime after the events of the resurrection and the ascension. He states in 1 Corinthians that the resurrected Jesus did appear to him as though he, Paul, were an untimely birth, untimely because he was so busy persecuting believers in Jesus he failed initially to recognize who Jesus actually was (1 Cor 15:3-9).

Paul is a Jewish man who never abandons his Jewish roots. Rather than thinking of him as changing religions, from Judaism to Christianity, we should regard him as someone who, when he saw the risen Jesus, recognized Jesus as the Christ, the promised Jewish Messiah through whom God is to complete his program to change the world.[2] Paul is a deep thinker, well versed in the Old Testament Scriptures. His Jewish roots inform his theology, especially his views about who God is and what he is doing in the world. That in turn drives his ethics.

In Paul we see a profound merging of theology with morality.[3] His theology indicates why people should behave properly. Paul declares that God has acted in the world in ultimate ways by sending his Son, Jesus the Christ, who was crucified and raised bodily from the dead. The death and resurrection signal the beginning of the end. They are transforming events that, explains Paul, profoundly change the lives of those who believe in Jesus, even as those people await their final transformation at the coming of Jesus. Because the end is a righteous end, a restored world with a restored creation, believers in Jesus are empowered to live in the present age in ways that reflect the restored order. Those ways necessarily include proper moral activities. This strongly resembles what Jesus, in the Gospels, called the kingdom.

Paul, as an apostle, was an itinerant preacher, the head of a team that traveled through the eastern part of the Roman dominated Mediterranean world spreading the good news about Jesus, God's Son, who was crucified and raised from the dead.[4] As people believed the message about the crucified, resurrected Jesus, Paul formed them into communities known as churches. Thinking of churches as communities of believers in Jesus may appear a bit unusual for people today who have gotten used to thinking of church either as an event ("I am going to church"), a building ("We're meeting in the church") or an institution ("The church says"). The actual meaning of the word *church* is "assembly," indicating a gathering of people.

Paul, as a Jewish man, extends the message about the crucified, resurrected Jesus to non-Jewish people, Gentiles. He pursues that task as his special commission from the resurrected Jesus himself, a point to which he alludes in various places, including Romans, as we will see in chapter ten. The commission is unusual because Jewish people normally separated themselves from Gentiles.[5] Paul sees it as directly connected to the ultimate goal of global restoration God forecast in his promises to Abraham that in him "all the nations shall be blessed" (Gen 18:18; 22:18; see also Gen 12:3). Paul proclaims that that global blessing is being extended to all people, Jew and Gentile, through the crucified, resurrected Jesus. He roots his proclamation firmly in the expectations of the Scriptures, in line with the plan of God.

No one knows exactly how many believing communities, or churches, Paul established. But at least five of these are reflected in the titles eventually assigned to letters that Paul wrote to help those communities through various issues arising while he was absent from them, involved in his missionary work elsewhere. The letters known as 1 Corinthians, 2 Corinthians, Philippians, 1 Thessalonians and 2 Thessalonians were all sent to the towns of Corinth, Philippi and Thessalonica, respectively. Paul also founded churches in the region of Galatia (hence Galatians) and in Ephesus, also being a facilitator for churches being started in the region of that city (hence Ephesians). As we will learn in chapter ten, Paul did not found the church in Rome.

Thirteen letters in the New Testament state that they come from Paul.[6] Though the table of contents lists them after the Gospels, the letters all appear to have been written well before any Gospel.[7] Paul never quotes one in his letters. He never says, "Do what Jesus taught," even though some of his letters show that he knows words that come from Jesus.[8] Paul never says, "Do what Jesus did," even though he does appeal to aspects of the crucifixion of Jesus as an exemplar, in much the same way we saw Luke advocating.[9] We will see evidence of both of those in 1 Corinthians.

Paul's letters are not arranged in the order they were written. Rather, they seem to be organized according to their relative length.[10] Romans, the first entry, is the longest, with 1 Corinthians, appearing after Romans, the next longest. That is important to recognize since Paul wrote 1 Corinthians before he wrote Romans. We are considering 1 Corinthians before Romans because it precedes Romans in its time of writing. More pertinent, we find in 1 Corinthians ideas that receive fuller treatment in Romans, ideas that are worth getting used to in the more practical environment we see in 1 Corinthians.

First Corinthians appears in part to be Paul's response to a letter sent to him by the groups composing the church in Corinth—there may have been several groups, each meeting in different homes, limited in size by the amount of space available in them.[11] Additionally, he has received a report from people associated with a woman named Chloe, a woman known to them (1 Cor 1:11).[12] The report and letter reflect a list of issues and questions about the Corinthians' faith in Jesus that Paul must address in the letter that he writes in response.

There are at least nine major issues that appear in his letter, along with other related subissues. One or more of those come from the reports from Chloe's people (1 Cor 1:11; 5:1).[13] Other issues stem from queries about which they, as a church, have written Paul (1 Cor 7:1). Most of those issues have direct connections to moral dilemmas. Our approach here will be to address each obvious, morally relevant issue one by one. In the process we will discover that Paul not only has distinct religious emphases. Many of his religious or theological views also reflect elements of profound ethical reasoning. Paul has an ethical vision.

The issues appear as follows:

1. divisions over their spiritual mentors (1 Cor 1:10–4:21)

2. sexual immorality (1 Cor 5:1–6:20)

3. marriage (1 Cor 7:1-40)

4. food sacrificed to idols (1 Cor 8:1–11:1)

5. women and head coverings (1 Cor 11:2-16)

6. divisions from their practice of their sacred meal (1 Cor 11:17-34)

7. divisions from their pursuit of spiritual gifts (1 Cor 12:1–14:40)

8. the resurrection of the dead (1 Cor 15:1-58)

9. collecting money for the poor among the "saints" in Jerusalem (1 Cor 16:1-4)[14]

Six of these nine have strong ethical import in the way that Paul discusses them: issues 1-4 and issues 7-8. Paul addresses each at length. The others do have ethical implications, but without the same extensive treatment. In the following discussion, we will focus on what is most relevant for understanding Paul's ethics.

Reading 1 Corinthians as someone else's mail. As we explore each issue, let's keep in mind that we are reading a letter.[15] The fancy word for letter is *epistle*, which tends to hide the fact that when reading 1 Corinthians, and indeed when reading any epistle in the New Testament, we are actually reading someone else's mail. The letter claims to have been written to "the church of God that is in Corinth" (1 Cor 1:2) by Paul and Sosthenes (v. 1), perhaps a member of the Corinthian church (see Acts 18:17). None of us was there when this letter was written, sent and initially read. It was not written to us.

That is often difficult for readers to acknowledge, especially when they have a high regard for biblical writings. We, as readers, can too easily assume when we see in letters words such us *we* and *us*, that we are actually the people being talked about, or that words such as *you* and *your* indicate statements directly aimed at us. That cannot be true. It's not our mail.

We've had to make similar distinctions before. When exploring the Torah, we needed to keep in mind that the words there were aimed at God's covenant people, the Israelites. When words such as those found in the Ten Commandments declared "You shall not commit adultery," *you* referred directly to the Israelites, God's covenant people who accepted those words as part of their covenant with God. When exploring Proverbs, we needed to be aware that in the beginning of that writing we were listening in on a conversation between an ideal father and his son. The words "let your heart keep my commandments" were not aimed at us but at the son the father was addressing. When exploring the Gospels, we had to keep in mind that words that Jesus spoke were, in the context of those stories, aimed at his disciples or at the crowds, both groups of which were there, present at the events. Thus, when Jesus declared, "Blessed are you who are poor," he was addressing the disciples and crowds in his hearing at that moment. In all instances, we as readers must carefully build bridges from the worlds of the biblical texts to our own particular settings. Some bridges are easier to build than others, but the chasm from the world of the writings must be bridged, not leapt over.

The same must hold true for the epistles. Sometimes that will be easy. When Paul writes, "For it has been reported to me by Chloe's people that there are quarrels among you" (1 Cor 1:11), it is easy to realize that he is addressing quarrels existing among an identifiable group of people at a different place and time from ours. But when Paul writes, "we have the mind of Christ" (1 Cor 2:16), it may not be as easy. Paul appears there to be including both himself and the Corinthian believers in that word *we*. *We* should probably be extended to apply to any who believes in the crucified, resurrected Jesus. Nevertheless, we have to realize that we as readers living in the twenty-first century are not being addressed directly with those words. This letter was not written *to* us. But, as is true with most of what we read on a regular basis, it is certainly *for* us.

Even with material outside the Bible we regularly discern how to learn from writings that are not written to us directly. Exit signs are there for us to note so that we know ways to leave when we need to. They are not ordering us to leave the building each time we pass them. Remember that we are approaching biblical ethics first as a descriptive task, then a prescriptive one. We will need first to describe what Paul tells the Corinthians, instead of directly appropriating to ourselves the instructions that Paul offers them.

In doing that let's also note that we are reading only one side of a discussion. Paul makes a number of assumptions on the part of his readership. For example, he knows who Chloe is. So do the Corinthians he is addressing. We do not. We have to investigate. Did she live in Corinth or Ephesus?[16] Was Chloe a good person or bad, a mild person or a controlling one, a younger woman or an older widow? If we knew her, would we smile when we heard her name, or would we roll our eyes? We can only guess at her reputation. But the Corinthians receiving this letter did know about her. Paul has no need to explain anything about her or her people. Thus, when reading a letter we will find that some items will have obvious clarity, while others will appear more obscure. That is the hazard of reading someone else's mail. However, if we want to discern Paul's ethical vision more clearly, we'll have to explore the scenarios that the words address. Paul only reveals those aspects of his ethics that apply to the situation at hand.[17]

ISSUE 1: DIVISIONS OVER THEIR SPIRITUAL MENTORS (1 COR 1:10–4:21)

After his basic letter opening, Paul begins with a common plea for unity. It is a plea similar to those found frequently in the everyday moral dialogue of his era and culture: "Now I appeal to you, brothers and sisters, . . . that all of you be in agreement and that there be no divisions among you, but that you be united in the same mind and the same purpose" (1 Cor 1:10).[18] Paul does uniquely ground the commonplace topic of unity in "the name of our Lord Jesus Christ," but that indicates the source of Paul's authority to make his request in the first place. Those words alone do not provide any true hint of Paul's ethical argumentation.

Paul addresses a situation in which the Corinthian believers in Jesus are competing with each other about who offers the best spiritual input. Though Christ is mentioned, and also Cephas (a way of saying "Peter" in his birth language, Aramaic), the actual struggle appears to be between those who continue to look to Paul and those who look to a man named Apollos.

Who was Apollos? We are reading someone else's mail. By sleuthing elsewhere in the New Testament, particularly Acts 18:24-28, we learn that Apollos was a highly educated Jewish man from Alexandria. When straightened out in his knowledge of faith in Jesus, he embarked from the port city of Ephesus, where he had been staying, to the city of Corinth, where he was received by the church. As an educated man, he would have been trained in rhetoric (i.e., speechmaking). He seems to have been a highly persuasive speaker, so effective that he even outshone Paul, who downplays his own speaking abilities (1 Cor 2:1-5).[19]

That persuasive ability has had such an effect in Corinth that some believers had begun to choose sides between Paul and Apollos, as though the two men were actual competitors.[20] This becomes clear from what Paul eventually says in 1 Corinthians 3:4-9. He addresses the folly of that attitude by portraying himself and Apollos as members of the same team, each playing his own unique role toward the advancement of the faith:

> *What then is Apollos? What is Paul? Servants through whom you came to believe, as the Lord assigned to each. I planted, Apollos watered, but God gave the growth. So neither the one who plants nor the one who waters is anything, but only God who gives the growth. The one who plants and the one who waters have a common purpose, and each will receive wages according to the labor of each.* **1 Cor 3:5-8**

Note. This rationale comes in chapter 3. Paul begins to address the problem in chapter 1. The fact that he and Apollos are colaborers on the same side is only a pragmatic, secondary point, made after he has developed his core argument. What is the focus of that core point? Wisdom. Believers in Corinth are foolishly making bad decisions about the wrong sort of issue. They have created an immoral situation because their flawed thinking is totally out of phase with God's wisdom, available to them through faith in Jesus.

Paul initially dismisses the nonsense of the Corinthians' dispute: "Has Christ been divided? Was Paul crucified for you? Or were you baptized in the name of Paul?" (1 Cor 1:13). But he does not dwell on the nonsense. Instead, he cuts to the heart of the matter:

> For Christ did not send me to baptize but to proclaim the gospel, and not with eloquent wisdom, so that the cross of Christ might not be emptied of its power. For the message about the cross is foolishness to those who are perishing, but to us who are being saved it is the power of God. For it is written,
>
> "I will destroy the wisdom of the wise,
>> and the discernment of the discerning I will thwart."
>
> Where is the one who is wise? Where is the scribe? Where is the debater of this age? Has not God made foolish the wisdom of the world? For since, in the wisdom of God, the world did not know God through wisdom, God decided, through the foolishness of our proclamation, to save those who believe. **1 Cor 1:17-21**

Paul contrasts the wisdom of the unconverted world with the wisdom of God. The wisdom of the world values eloquence, which reflects an elite education.[21] It values those who score debaters' points in their speeches. It leads to writing off others who do not measure up to the accepted standards of smartness determined by cultural elites. That sense of wisdom is blind to God and his ways, especially as displayed through the crucified Jesus. It leads both to the rejection of God and to the rejection of God's people who live by God's wisdom. Based on that form of wisdom, not only does the message about Jesus that the Corinthians have believed look bad (1 Cor 1:18-25), both they (1 Cor 1:26-31) and Paul (1 Cor 2:1-5) do as well.[22] And yet, that is the kind of faulty wisdom they are applying.

Central to what Paul proclaims is the cross of Christ, which astoundingly brings life to those "who are being saved." Great speech makers look good by their elitist standards. The cross does not. Crucifixion is a shaming event.[23] It is not only a form of execution; one of its main functions in the Roman culture that employed it was to smear the reputation of the one being crucified, while elevating the power of Rome. Who would want to associate with the legacy of one who was so publicly humiliated? Only those who are able to see beyond the shame, to see the power of God at work in Christ do that. The cross as endured by Christ displays God's power and wisdom. It, along with the resurrection, forms the basis on which God works to change the lives of those who believe: "we proclaim Christ crucified, a stumbling block to Jews and foolishness to Gentiles, but to those who are the called, both Jews and Greeks, Christ the power of God and the wisdom of God"

(1 Cor 1:23-24). That is the sort of wisdom that should be guiding their evaluations of others.

Paul is not focusing on the fact that there are divisions within the Corinthian church. He is faulting the reason for that division—a failure to understand God's wisdom in Christ. In contrast to those who have embraced God's message of the cross, those who are "perishing" see differently, whether Jews or non-Jews, here called Greeks. They can't get beyond the shame of the cross. Thus, Christ crucified is a "stumbling block" to unbelieving Jews and "foolishness" to unbelieving Greeks. By appealing to the cross in this way, Paul is associating the Corinthian believers' rationale for division with the thought patterns of those who refuse to believe:

> But God chose what is foolish in the world to shame the wise; God chose what is weak in the world to shame the strong; God chose what is low and despised in the world, things that are not, to reduce to nothing things that are, so that no one might boast in the presence of God. He is the source of your life in Christ Jesus, who became for us wisdom from God, and righteousness and sanctification and redemption, in order that, as it is written, "Let the one who boasts, boast in the Lord."
> **1 Cor 1:27-31**

Here we have the beginning of insight into Paul's ethical reasoning. The Corinthian believers' disunity is unethical. Why? Because it is based on reasoning standards that totally criticize their very basis for existing as a community in the first place.[24] The cross, with the resurrection, is a transforming event, not a shameful one.[25] It changes the lives of those who believe. By having faith in God based on the crucified Jesus, the Corinthian believers have experienced God's power and wisdom. They are different people from those who do not believe. But the wisdom of God is at odds with the wisdom of the unbelieving world. The Corinthian believers, argues Paul, must evaluate others in a manner that is consistent with the power and wisdom of God at work in their lives.

One of the chief results of faith in Christ is the receiving of God's Spirit. Through his Spirit, God is at work directly in the lives of those who believe. The Spirit of God is the agent of the new covenant, which upgrades the covenant of the Torah.[26] God's Spirit resides in those who believe. They can know God closely by responding to God's Spirit, obtaining the special insight to evaluate positively from God's perspective when others might be dismissive (or to evaluate negatively from God's perspective when others might be accepting).

> *For what human being knows what is truly human except the human spirit that is within? So also no one comprehends what is truly God's except the Spirit of God. Now we have received not the spirit of the world, but the Spirit that is from God, so that we may understand the gifts bestowed on us by God. And we speak of these things in words not taught by human wisdom but taught by the Spirit, interpreting spiritual things to those who are spiritual. Those who are unspiritual do not receive the gifts of God's Spirit, for they are foolishness to them, and they are unable to understand them because they are spiritually discerned. Those who are spiritual discern all things, and they are themselves subject to no one else's scrutiny.*
>
> *"For who has known the mind of the Lord*
> *so as to instruct him?"*
>
> *But we have the mind of Christ.* **1 Cor 2:11-16**

The main ethical problem is not the existence of division itself, but the basis of the division—their failure to see God at work in both of his servants, Paul and Apollos. That failure conflicts with the fact that they have God's Spirit within them, giving them "the mind of Christ."[27] Talk about neglecting a close relationship! Were they to let God's Spirit influence their thoughts, they would not be applying the standards of the unconverted to evaluate the work of God. Paul goes on to explain that both he and Apollos are on the same team, but with different roles. Were the Corinthians in tune with God through his Spirit who dwells in them, they would see God using both Paul and Apollos (1 Cor 3:5-9). Failing to see what God is doing has led them to focus on the wrong standards, giving way to their immoral divisions.

There are other issues associated with this particular problem, as becomes clear in the rest of chapters 3 and 4. Remember, we are reading their mail. They already know about those issues. We can only infer them from what Paul says. Apparently, people in the church are being stirred up by certain self-styled-opinion leaders, people who claim to know better about those the Corinthian believers should appeal to for their spiritual guidance.[28] Paul takes them on subtly with his caution about people building God's community of believers with the right kind of material

(1 Cor 3:12-21), a sacred community inhabited by God's Spirit (1 Cor 3:16-17). He then comes more to the point when he urges the Corinthian believers not to judge him with improper standards (1 Cor 4:3-5). That language of judgment and discernment underscores the point that the believers in Corinth are making improper distinctions about the wrong sort of issue. Were they properly in touch with God and his wisdom through his Spirit they would not be experiencing the particular type of division they were at that point. Were they more mindful of the effects of the cross and the resurrection they would see the world entirely differently. They would see that true wisdom is associated with God changing lives through the cross and the resurrection. Failure to connect well with God, who is at work in them through Christ and his Spirit, leads to their immorality. We have a profound ethic of relationship here.

ISSUE 2: SEXUAL IMMORALITY (1 COR 5:1–6:20)

The second basic issue reflects a depth of thought that we will have to probe carefully. It relates well to the first. Both issues deal with improper arrogance that some in Corinth are showing (1 Cor 4:18-19; 5:2).[29] In having divisions over their spiritual mentors, some Corinthian believers are making arrogant judgments and distinctions based on faulty reasoning patterns about an issue that does not matter. In this next topic, sexual immorality, some are arrogant while refusing to make judgments and distinctions about an issue that does matter. Paul has to explain how making proper distinctions between good and evil fits with the destiny of all who believe in Jesus (1 Cor 6:1-4).[30] He shows careful ethical reasoning here. We'll have to follow his words closely to see both how he distinguishes right from wrong and what he presents as rationale and motivation for doing what is right and refraining from what is wrong. If we are not careful, we can easily overreact, either misappropriating his instructions or dismissing them.

Paul clearly states the issue:

> It is actually reported that there is sexual immorality among you, and of a kind that is not found even among pagans; for a man is living with his father's wife. And you are arrogant! Should you not rather have mourned, so that he who has done this would have been removed from among you? **1 Cor 5:1-2**

We have here a form of incest, "a man . . . living with his father's wife." The response of the Corinthian believers is shocking. They are arrogant, boasting about the man or perhaps in spite of him.[31] Paul tells them that instead of being arrogant, they should have been mourning over that man's misbehavior.

Paul's expression "father's wife" probably comes from the Torah (see Lev 18:8; 20:11; Deut 22:30; 27:20). There, it refers to a stepmother, not a physical mother. It probably means the same here. But what other particulars can we associate with this situation? That is difficult to determine. We're reading their mail. Is the man's father still living, so that the son is committing both adultery and incest?[32] In that case, Paul's directive to expel the offending man would parallel what Roman law demands. Or suppose something like the following.[33] An older widower marries a younger second wife and then dies. Why can't his son marry that second wife? Though awkward, it would not be illegal in many cultures today, as it would be for the Roman, Jewish and Greek cultures of Paul's day. So which is it?

And why would the Corinthians be arrogant? Perhaps the offending man's social position is so attractive that they were delighting in it, overlooking his behavior.[34] Or perhaps some believers in Corinth had an overinflated view of the liberation brought to the world through Jesus, an issue Paul may be addressing in 1 Corinthians 6:12.[35] Why not celebrate such freedom?[36] After all, the woman is not really his mother. See the difficulties of reading someone else's mail?

Regardless of the uncertain particulars, the fact remains that the man and his father's wife are unmarried. By having sexual relations outside of marriage, they are committing sexual immorality. No matter where one reads in biblical literature, any sex between unmarried people is unacceptable for those who belong to God. Paul eventually explains why in chapter 6 when addressing a man having sex with a prostitute. But immediately, Paul calls the Corinthian believers to task for their arrogance in view of one who is committing an act that should have put them into mourning.[37] It is sad when a person who claims to belong to God openly participates in behavior that is completely out of phase with God's sense of moral rightness.

Paul's initial instruction to the Corinthian believers is for them to dismiss the offender from their assembly. That sounds harsh. Remember, we are reading their mail. Paul is not mandating that to be the practice for all Christians at all times, everywhere in the world.[38] But the supporting rationale or warrant, for Paul's directive speaks volumes about his ethics, ethics that clearly transcend the situation he is addressing. His first reason sounds proverb-like, such as what we saw in the world of wisdom (see chap. 5): "Do you not know that a little yeast leavens the whole batch of dough?" (1 Cor 5:6). The saying resembles an aphorism common to many Western cultures: one rotten apple spoils the whole barrel. It indicates that their tolerance of someone so flagrantly displeasing God could lead to a whole host of other destructive behaviors. Tolerating the moral corruption of one leads inevitably to the moral corruption of others, weakening moral standards altogether and thus harming the church community.

Paul builds on the leaven metaphor, advising them to "clean out the old yeast so that [they] may be a new batch" (1 Cor 5:7). What he says after this, however, is quite startling. He declares that they "really are unleavened" (v. 7). Already unleavened?

That exposes a central feature of Paul's thought world: "you are . . . therefore be!"[39] We will see it elsewhere both in 1 Corinthians and in Romans. It is rationale initially hard to grasp for readers unfamiliar with it. Paul's point is that the death and resurrection of Jesus bring about profound changes in the lives of those who believe. They are transforming events. Through no effort, merit or training on their own, they have been made righteously pure based entirely on Jesus' crucifixion and resurrection. That transformation should shape how they know God and his ways. Paul declares that they should be unleavened because they already are unleavened. What does leaven refer to here? The morally impure man. Paul states that they should remove that man because they are a morally pure community, made up of transformed people. On what does he base that point? "For our paschal lamb, Christ, has been sacrificed" (1 Cor 5:7).

Here from two related Torah festivals, the Passover and the Feast of Unleavened Bread, Paul fashions a word picture about the effects of the crucifixion of Jesus on the lives of those who believe. In the original Passover, sacrificing the paschal lamb brought about ultimate deliverance from destruction of the firstborn and from slavery in Egypt; in the original Festival of Unleavened Bread the Israelites celebrated an immediate, hasty departure with leaven free bread (see Ex 12–13). The death of Jesus, followed by his resurrection, provides both deliverance from morally destructive living and transformation of personhood, making believers in Jesus pure before God.

They should be morally pure because they are morally pure, part of a community that is morally pure: "let us celebrate the festival, not with the old yeast, the yeast of malice and evil, but with the unleavened bread of sincerity and truth" (1 Cor 5:8).

Paul imposes a definite sense of right and wrong here. He does not explain directly where he gets that sense from. Many of his specifics mentioned both in 1 Corinthians 5:1 and in 1 Corinthians 5:9-11 are connectable both to the Torah and to legal conventions of the Corinthian culture.[40] Without appealing to concrete sources of standards, he expects the Corinthian believers to have that sense of right and wrong automatically because they are connected to God through Jesus. That connection makes them morally pure because Jesus has died on their behalf. That relationship obliges them to continue to live in "sincerity and truth." Paul never imposes any set of regulations on the Corinthian believers. He has not yet quoted a law, though his expression "father's wife" indicates that he knows laws from Torah that apply to this topic. In 1 Corinthians 5:13 he eventually quotes Deuteronomy 17:7, "Drive out the wicked person from among you," but that only solidifies his request. It does not establish it. Something other than Torah has become more prominent. His appeal instead is grounded in the effects of the cross and resurrection of Christ.

That is an important point to dwell on. Readers who assume that the Bible is a collection of rules or that Christianity is merely about doing what the Bible says should take note. Incest and the accompanying arrogance are wrong here, not because they violate a rule or an expressed standard, but because they fly in the face of the work of Christ. Expelling the offending man instead of living in arrogance is right, not because it conforms to a rule but because it upholds the holiness, or purity, of the community, a holiness created through the cross of Christ.[41]

Paul widens the discussion beyond incest to include a variety of evils, pointing out that he had previously instructed the Corinthian believers not to associate with a host of morally disobedient people. In doing that Paul is also careful to point out that he is talking about the behaviors of the Corinthian believing community, not the vastly greater number of other Corinthians who do not believe in Jesus. God's business is to judge those outside of the faith. The Corinthian believers' business is to judge their fellow believers in their faith community on issues that really matter to God. The moral behavior of those who believe is exactly one of those issues. As a community of believers in Jesus, they have a responsibility to uphold each other in righteous living standards.

Holding unbelievers accountable for their immorality is God's business, not the business of believers in Jesus. Unbelievers are not in touch with God and demonstrate that in the various morally inappropriate behaviors they perform. But Paul expects believers in Jesus to be a community of morally upright people. He is not addressing a group of individuals but a collective that is to be responsible for itself, reflective of God's work in them. They have been made pure. Practitioners of illicit behaviors are engaging in activities that are totally contrary to the ways of God. He lists some of those: "sexually immoral or greedy, or . . . an idolater, reviler, drunkard, or robber" (1 Cor 5:11). Believers should not associate with other believers who embrace such behavior.[42] They are a community made pure by the death of Jesus.

This expectation that they distinguish right from wrong behavior is what connects the issue of the man living with his father's wife to the unfortunate fact that some Corinthian believers are taking fellow believers to court in civil lawsuits (1 Cor 6:1-11).[43] Instead, they should be settling their disputes among themselves. Believers are holy, saints, righteous through the effects of the cross and resurrection. They, of all people, should have a heightened sense of right and wrong. Among them theoretically they should have the best arbiters over issues involving other believers in Jesus. Instead they are taking their cases before the "unrighteous." The unrighteous? This may be Paul carrying further the thoughts from 1 Corinthians 5:6-8, that the believers have been made pure. By contrast, then, the unbelieving judges and court officials are impure, out of touch with the true and living God and thus God's sense of rightness.[44] Or Paul may actually be referring to the reputation of the Corinthian courts, which were notoriously corrupt and biased in favor of the elite.[45] How can the righteous go to the unrighteous for a ruling intended to harm another believer? Either way they are diminishing the pure standing of their community.

Paul expects that his readers know that judging the world is part of the future destiny of believers and so does not elaborate: "Do you not know that the saints will judge the world? And if the world is to be judged by you, are you incompetent to try trivial cases? Do you not know that we are to judge angels—to say nothing of ordinary matters?" (1 Cor 6:2-3). Instead, he compares that future judging activity with what they should be doing now. If they will be involved in grave judgments in the future—the world, angels— then why can't they handle matters that by comparison are trivial? Why do they pass off their responsibilities onto "those who have no standing in the church?" (1 Cor 6:4)—unbelievers, outsiders. They should know better be- cause of what the death and resurrection of Jesus has done for them.

They should be exercising the wisdom that is theirs because they know Christ. "Can it be that there is no one among you wise enough to decide between one believer and another?" (1 Cor 6:5). Paul alludes to his previous thoughts from chapters 1–4. Believers in Jesus should be wise with God's sort of wisdom. They have the mind of Christ. Through God's Spirit they are in touch with the very thoughts of God. That people are not stepping up to exercise their wisdom in Christ is disturbing. They should be distinguishing right from wrong, the basic activity of ethics, which is also the basic activity of knowing God.

Paul proposes an alternate morality, rooted eventually, we will see, in the exemplar Jesus (1 Cor 11:1). Believers should not assert any personal rights against another member of the church, which is what a civil lawsuit amounts to.[46] They should instead forebear, willingly letting others wrong them if need be (1 Cor 6:7), not retaliating. That is especially true for life in God's holy, pure community, the church. As believers in Jesus, they are all family together.[47] Believers should be in solidarity with one another, not antago- nizing one another. To do that before the unbelievers running the civil courts is utterly shameful (1 Cor 6:5).

In fact, Paul labels the activity of those who enter into such lawsuits against their Christian "family" members as "wrong" (1 Cor 6:8), in the same category as those who practice the kinds of illicit behavior he has been talking about, and continues to talk about, in this section (1 Cor 5:9-11; 6:9- 10):[48] "Do you not know that wrongdoers will not inherit the kingdom of God?" (1 Cor 6:9). He is not threatening them with loss of kingdom par- ticipation. The flow of thought points to how out of touch with God and his ways they themselves are. How can they, who claim to belong to the kingdom, condone activities that are contrary to the ways of the kingdom? People who know God should know better. He is shaming them (1 Cor 6:5) to get them to realize how they need to live in accordance with what they are.

Paul's list in 1 Corinthians 6:9-10 is instructive: "Do not be deceived!

Fornicators, idolaters, adulterers, male prostitutes, sodomites, thieves, the greedy, drunkards, revilers, robbers—none of these will inherit the kingdom of God." As do the previous lists in 1 Corinthians 5:10-11, this one focuses on practitioners of illicit activities, not the activities themselves.[49] These lists highlight immoral people who are characterized by their performance of immoral, God-displeasing activities. Paul does not offer any explicit rationale for what makes these practitioners immoral. That's not his purpose here. Rather, Paul wants the Corinthian believers to realize how the effects of the cross and the resurrection transform them, making them different sorts of people both from God's perspective and from their own experience. Note the words that immediately follow: "And this is what some of you used to be. But you were washed, you were sanctified, you were justified in the name of the Lord Jesus Christ and in the Spirit of our God" (1 Cor 6:11).

People who belong to God through Jesus are transformed people. They are no longer identified by any activity that may have characterized their preconverted lives. A thief who converts to Christianity is not a Christian thief. She or he is a Christian. Thievery no longer defines that person's existence. Converts are washed, therefore they should be washed. They are sanctified, therefore they should be sanctified. They are justified, therefore they should be justified. Paul does not explain those terms here. He alludes to their effects. The Corinthian believers are different people through their connection with "the Lord Jesus Christ" and "the Spirit of [their] God." What God has done to them through both Jesus and his Spirit requires them to live morally and uprightly. That has also been a constant point throughout this section.

Paul returns to the topic of sexual immorality in a quite unusual way, quoting two slogans that appear to be favorites among the Corinthian believers:

> "All things are lawful for me," but not all things are beneficial. "All things are lawful for me," but I will not be dominated by anything. "Food is meant for the stomach and the stomach for food," and God will destroy both one and the other. The body is meant not for fornication but for the Lord, and the Lord for the body. And God raised the Lord and will also raise us by his power. **1 Cor 6:12-14**[50]

Notice what Paul does here with the slogans. He accepts their premises and then qualifies them. Why is that important? He is applying wisdom in distinguishing right from wrong. The use of wisdom, based on godly observation, again emerges as an important aspect of Paul's ethics. Regardless of any rights that people may consider themselves free to exercise, those who are wise know that some activities actually lead to bad outcomes. Sexual activity with a person one is not married to is one of those activities.

What are the bad outcomes? Paul declares that unmarried sex is not beneficial. How? That becomes clear from his second citation of the slogan: "I will not be dominated by anything" (1 Cor 6:12). He explains in verses 15-20 how unmarried sex is a form of domination, an explanation uniquely framed for the believer in Jesus. His points would not satisfy people outside of communities of faith, even if elements of them are relevant.

Before explaining himself more fully, Paul cites one more slogan with implications for illicit sexual activity: "Food is meant for the stomach and the stomach for food" (1 Cor 6:13), both of which God will destroy.[51] The slogan assumes that physical activity has only physical effects, which will come to nothing when a person dies. Some in Corinth place promiscuous sexual activity, often associated with the lavish meals of the elite, in the same category.[52] Paul counters by declaring Jesus as Lord of all. Believers in Jesus must realize that their eventual resurrection makes physical existence an eternal reality. Life now is not about pursuing physical gratification. "The body is meant not for fornication but for the Lord, and the Lord for the body" (1 Cor 6:13). Their bodily existence needs to be approached responsibly, since their destiny is always to live in bodies. Just as Jesus was raised bodily from the dead, so will they be. Paul will revisit that point in chapter 15. Here, he begins to introduce the notion that their bodily existence in the future should affect their bodily behavior in the present.

Here we also have an ethic of relationship. Those who believe in Jesus, Paul instructs, are uniquely connected to God by knowing him. By virtue of Jesus' death and resurrection, God's Spirit dwells within them (1 Cor 6:19); their bodies belong to the Lord. But equally true, the Lord has a regard for their bodies. This is not one-sided. This reflects mutual interaction between the Lord and between those who believe in him. Believers do not own their bodies. They "have been bought with a price," becoming responsible for making God look good with how they conduct themselves in their bodies (1 Cor 6:20). Through his death and his resurrection, Jesus has purchased them. He owns them. They are answerable to him. They are one with him (1 Cor 6:17).

Jesus so fully owns their bodies that they must not release control of their bodies to any other mastery. Paul explains how that can happen in the context of a man having sex with a prostitute, a blatant act of sexual immorality, which has been an ongoing concern throughout this segment (1 Cor 5:9, 11; 6:9).[53] Their bodies are "members of Christ" (1 Cor 6:15)—they are his body parts. How could they try to unite one of Christ's body parts to a prostitute? He affirms Genesis's view of sex as a bonding act. He appeals to Genesis 2:24 in the Torah, which portrays marriage as a man becoming "one flesh" with his wife as part of the divinely established order. Paul declares that a man becoming temporarily one flesh, or bonded, with a prostitute is the equivalent of giving her control over his body. He is being dominated by her, to whom he has no belonging at all, when he should be dominated by Christ, the actual owner of his body. Thus for the believer in Jesus, fornication, sex between two unmarried people, is a blasphemous violation of Christ himself, a sin against the body since it yields what belongs to Christ to the control of another who has no right at all over that body. They should "shun fornication!" (1 Cor 6:18).[54]

This rationale is aimed at those who believe in Jesus. Those who do not would probably find it dissatisfying. His comments touching on the created order are relevant to those outside of the faith in declaring that unmarried sex defies how God has established life to be. People engaging in unmarried sex are handing control of their bodies over to people with whom they have no legitimate belonging, an unbeneficial act indeed. But he is not addressing the grand ethical issue of sexual morality for humanity. Rather, he is explaining to the Corinthian believers how their tolerance of sexual immorality is so out of phase with their faith in Christ. His explanation appeals to their relationship with God through Jesus, whose death and resurrection have transformed them into different people from what they were before they believed. That death and resurrection have made them pure. They should be pure. They should grow wise, knowing right from wrong, because they are in touch with the source of right and wrong.

They also have the Scriptures. Though Paul has been careful throughout not to appeal directly to those writings for legal sanctions, he ultimately does indicate that part of his sense of who God is, what he has done and how he wants his creatures to behave is connected to what people can read in the Torah as Scripture.[55] Though here Torah's regulatory force may not be prominent for believers in Jesus, the Torah, as part of the Scriptures, remains an authoritative informing source for the basic contours of God, his plans, his likes and his dislikes.

ISSUE 3: MARRIAGE (1 COR 7:1-40)

Paul begins to deal with issues that the Corinthian believers themselves have raised with him: "Now concerning the matter about which you wrote . . ." (1 Cor 7:1). His topic, however, remains close to the preceding one. Where chapters 5 and 6 discuss sexual immorality, chapter 7 begins with a discussion of sexual morality, alluding to some of the points made in the previous chapter about bodily ownership and the one-flesh nature of sexual activity. Those concepts undergird the morality that emerges in this section.

The surprise for many first-time Bible readers raised under negative Western stereotypes is that Paul discusses sexual activity between a husband and a wife as a requirement. Uninformed assumptions about the Bible tag its writings as antisex. More accurately, the writings are anti-unmarried sex and pro-married sex. That is true whether one is reading in the Torah, in Proverbs, in the Prophets, in the Gospels or in Paul.

Paul is actually correcting antisex attitudes. Apparently, some Corinthian believers thought that God preferred no sexual contact between a man and a woman, though why exactly is not entirely clear.[56] We are reading their mail. "Now concerning the matter about which you wrote: 'It is well for a man not to touch a woman.' But because of cases of sexual immorality, each man should have his own wife and each woman her own husband" (1 Cor 7:1-2).

Note how Paul quotes their slogan. Some of them think that a man should not touch a woman, a euphemism for sexual activity.[57] Paul disagrees. Though he does validate people being called to lives of sex-free singlehood (1 Cor 7:7-8, 32-35), he never even intimates that as the divinely favored goal for all believers in Jesus. Rather, the state of marriage and the state of celibacy are gifts from God (1 Cor 7:7), which both have their moments requiring the moral exercise of self-control (1 Cor 7:5, 9). He does eventually discuss how all who believe in Jesus, married or not, must live in ways that acknowledge God's ultimate plans for the world affirmed through the death and resurrection of Jesus (1 Cor 7:17-24, 29-31).[58] That discussion has implications for moral practice, but it only indirectly touches on how people can advance good or hinder harm in their world. Before Paul begins that discussion, he addresses marriage as the antidote to sexual immorality. In order to keep from displeasing God, Paul says, people who want to have sex should get married (1 Cor 7:2), and people who are married should have sex, lots of it (1 Cor 7:3-5).

Paul advocates a strong sense of mutuality between a husband and wife.

> Each man should have his own wife and each woman her own husband. The husband should give to his wife her conjugal rights, and likewise the wife to her husband. For the wife does not have authority over her own body, but the husband does; likewise the husband does not have authority over his own body, but the wife does. **1 Cor 7:2-4**

This language echoes the discussion from the previous chapter, a discussion that itself had drawn on the language of Genesis 2:24: "Therefore a man leaves his father and his mother and clings to his wife, and they become one flesh." The husband is not lord of his own body. Rather, his wife is. Likewise the wife is not lord over her own body. Rather, her husband is. Though Christ is still Lord over both of their bodies as declared in 1 Corinthians 6:15-20, their being married allows them a form of joint ownership.[59] Special concerns related to that divided ownership are what Paul addresses later in the chapter (see vv. 32-35). The implication here is that married sex is belonging sex, in line with the created order. Unmarried sex is a surrender to uncontrolled passion (1 Cor 7:5, 9), a surrender that is out of place for those who believe in Jesus.

Paul's view of marriage is so high that he does not think it should be dissolved. In supporting that, he appeals directly to teaching that he knows comes from Jesus, one of the few places in his writings where he directly attributes the earthly Jesus as the source of his statements: "To the married I give this command—not I but the Lord—that the wife should not separate from her husband (but if she does separate, let her remain unmarried or else be reconciled to her husband), and that the husband should not divorce his wife" (1 Cor 7:10-11). Again, note his language of mutuality. Neither the husband nor the wife is to initiate separation. As the next statement indicates, Paul is clearly talking about believers in Jesus. A married couple professing to belong to Jesus has no business getting divorced.

Paul advocates a similar policy for those cases when one is married to an unconverted spouse. He has no words of Jesus to which he can appeal, but considers his own authority valid. He reasons based on the positive spiritual effects that maintaining the marriage relationship can have both on the unbelieving spouse and on any children the couple may have (1 Cor 7:14). He roots his appeal in the benefits that come to those with faith in the crucified, resurrected Jesus, benefits that in some way carry over to unbelievers in their family.[60] People who are married should stay married. In those situations when the unbelieving spouse wants out, however, Paul says "let it be so" (v. 15). Why? "In such a case the brother or sister is not bound. It is to peace that God has called you" (1 Cor 7:15). Note the overall rationale. God has called those who believe in Jesus to a life of peaceful relationships with others.[61] That peace is designated as a God-pleasing value. That, by implication, may also be one reason why divorce between two believers is not an option. It would be an abandonment of their calling in Christ to pursue peace.

Twice in the section Paul overtly declares that one who marries does not sin (1 Cor 7:28, 36). In both instances he seems to be referring to a man trying to decide when, or perhaps whether, to marry a woman to whom he is engaged. Paul's language in v. 36 is worth observing: "If anyone thinks that he is not behaving properly toward his fiancée, if his passions are strong, and so it has to be, let him marry as he wishes; it is no sin. Let them marry." Improper behavior toward a fiancée? He may be referring to a young man keeping his fiancée dangling with his dithering.[62] He may be referring to a special social or spiritual arrangement.[63] Or quite realistically he may be referring to unspecified inappropriate sexual activity that has aroused the person's sexual passions.[64] Again, we are reading their mail.

Paul advises marriage for such a man with strong sexual passions "not behaving properly toward his fiancée" (1 Cor 7:36).[65] Interestingly, later in the letter (1 Cor 13:4-5), he says that love does not behave improperly ("is not . . . rude"), using the same word there as he does here in 1 Corinthians 7:36. Marriage is the only moral, divinely acceptable sphere for a man and woman to pursue their sexuality. Ultimately, Paul's advice for the man to marry is driven by a strong sense of love—not romantic desire but a regard for another that transcends one's own desires. It is a concept that he first mentions explicitly in the next section.

ISSUE 4: FOOD SACRIFICED TO IDOLS (1 COR 8:1–11:1)

Here we have an issue that at first glance seems to have nothing at all to do with ethics. Rather, it appears to involve matters of religious and social practice. It addresses believers in Corinth who are participating in festivities connected to the facilities of pagan temples.[66] It involves eating the meat from an animal that has been offered as a sacrifice to a pagan god or goddess, first at temple banqueting facilities (1 Cor 8:7-13) and then in private homes after the meat has been purchased in local markets (1 Cor 10:23-30). We might initially think that some of that activity, especially in a pagan temple, would be inconsistent with being a Christian. But how would such activity have anything to do with advancing good or hindering harm in one's world?

We actually have an example of an activity that falls into the category of "this does not matter, morally." Eating food at pagan festivals is not really a moral issue, even if that food comes from an animal sacrificed to a pagan deity. Food is food. Something else seems to be going on here, something that, in the Corinthians' culture, does potentially advance harm on others in their world. In this section we will see that the central issue is how people should pursue what they regard as their own personal rights, rights that they are free to embrace, but rights that, when pursued, might harm others.[67] Our clue that a morally neutral issue has implications for ethics comes from the opening statement of the section: "Now concerning food sacrificed to idols: we know that 'all of us possess knowledge.' Knowledge puffs up, but love builds up" (1 Cor 8:1).

Paul contrasts knowledge with love. The Corinthians' knowledge leads some to reason along the following lines:

> *We know there is only one true God. We worship that God. What unbelievers worship is not a god(dess) at all. It is make-believe. When they offer an animal sacrifice in a festival for the god(dess), eating the meat from that sacrifice poses no problem at all. That food comes from an offering made to a nothing. That's what our knowledge informs us.*

Paul initially agrees with that logic. Though later on he will point out a major flaw, indicating that they do not know as much as they claim (see

1 Cor 10:14-22), he does indicate a degree of correctness to their thought pattern, especially because of their relationship with the exclusive "one God, the Father, from whom are all things and for whom we exist, and one Lord, Jesus Christ, through whom are all things and through whom we exist" (1 Cor 8:4-6).

The first problem with their thinking that an idol is nothing (1 Cor 8:4) is that "It is not everyone . . . who has this knowledge. Since some have become so accustomed to idols until now, they still think of the food they eat as food offered to an idol; and their conscience, being weak, is defiled" (1 Cor 8:7).[68] Their knowledge gives them such an inflated view of their grasp of reality that they fail to notice how exercising that knowledge might cause problems for someone else. Those problems clearly stem from much more than points of religious belief. Those claiming knowledge are actually encouraging those with weak consciences[69] to reembrace elements from the worldview and its accompanying lifestyle they had turned from by having come to faith in Christ in the first place.[70] By exercising their right to join the banqueting festivities, putting themselves first, they are not acting in love. "Knowledge puffs up, but love builds up" (1 Cor 8:1). Food is not the problem. A misuse of their liberty, or more properly rights, to eat it is.

> But take care that this liberty of yours does not somehow become a stumbling block to the weak. For if others see you, who possess knowledge, eating in the temple of an idol, might they not, since their conscience is weak, be encouraged to the point of eating food sacrificed to idols? So by your knowledge those weak believers for whom Christ died are destroyed. But when you thus sin against members of your family, and wound their conscience when it is weak, you sin against Christ. Therefore, if food is a cause of their falling, I will never eat meat, so that I may not cause one of them to fall. **1 Cor 8:9-13**

Note that the "weak believers for whom Christ died are destroyed," all because those with knowledge are exercising their right to eat the meat in the pagan temple. Paul puts them in touch with three significant realities. First, their personal behavior can have catastrophic effects on others. Second, those others are, in this instance, those for whom Christ died. Third, because of Christ's death and resurrection, they are all united with Christ so that in some way Christ is also harmed by their behavior, damaging how they know

God through him. Because they love God and are known by him (1 Cor 8:3), their special relationship with God places them under high obligation to advance the well-being of others so connected. Selfishly asserting their rights to the harm of fellow members of Christ's family is a direct sin against Christ himself (1 Cor 8:12). The solution? Suspend their personal rights for the advancement of the well-being of others.[71] That's what love does; love builds up (1 Cor 8:1). Paul portrays love in action when he says, "if food is a cause of their falling, I will never eat meat, so that I may not cause one of them to fall" (1 Cor 8:13).

Here Paul illustrates a significant ethical activity, love. He advances this as the chief, relational pursuit of believers. They belong to Christ. So do other believers. They love God and are thus known by him. So are other believers. Their relationship to God through Christ requires that they live in an appropriately caring manner to others with the same connection.

With what first appears as a mixed agenda that also defends his own authority as an apostle, Paul elaborates in chapter 9 on instances when he has suspended his own personal rights for the advancement of others and for the promotion of the good news about Jesus.[72] He chooses to remain unmarried, though he has the right to be married (1 Cor 9:5). He also chooses not to be paid by the Corinthian believers for his services to them, even though Paul has the right to such a claim (1 Cor 9:6) and advocates that others who do similar work for them should be paid.[73] In fact, he stifles his own personal preferences whenever he can for the sake of advancing the message about Christ, becoming "all things to all people, that [he] might by all means save some" (1 Cor 9:22). He then subtly shifts his emphasis from the Corinthians' needing to curb their liberties for the sake of others to their needing to consider how they might actually be harming themselves (1 Cor 9:24-27), living in laxness that could lead to all sorts of inappropriate physical behaviors (1 Cor 10:1-13).[74] He shows the Corinthian believers that they do not know as much as they claim. Their participation in the pagan festivities is actually participation with demons (1 Cor 10:20-21), activity totally at odds with those who participate with Christ in the Eucharist (1 Cor 10:14-22).[75]

Paul returns to the topic of the Corinthians' freedom to embrace their rights in the final segment of this section. He addresses the scenario of someone being invited to a meal where leftover food from the idolatrous sacrifices is being served, having been purchased in the markets. Paul cites the same wisdom slogans we have seen earlier (in 1 Cor 6:12): "'All things are lawful,' but not all things are beneficial. 'All things are lawful,' but not all things build up. Do not seek your own advantage, but that of the other" (1 Cor 10:23-24). Eating the food may be permissible, it may be claimed as a right, but is it helpful? More to the point, does it build others up? Paul revisits the thoughts of 1 Corinthians 8:1-13, where he connects love with advancing the welfare of others. As believers in Jesus they have a responsibility to put others ahead of themselves. He goes on to say that if someone they are eating with expresses concern that the food was offered in sacrifice to an idol, they ought not eat it. Why? Because that person is unsure about the propriety of the food, bothered in conscience (1 Cor 10:27-29). Continuing to assert their right to eat could damage the worried fellow believer. Otherwise, they are free to eat it. Food is food, granted to them by God, who is over all things and lets them have what they have (1 Cor 10:25-30).

Paul's conclusion to the section summarizes his points, with ethical import.

> *So, whether you eat or drink, or whatever you do, do everything for the glory of God. Give no offense to Jews or to Greeks or to the church of God, just as I try to please everyone in everything I do, not seeking my own advantage, but that of many, so that they may be saved. Be imitators of me, as I am of Christ.* **1 Cor 10:31–11:1**

The principle for exercising freedom, especially in regard to activities of questioned neutrality, is to "do everything for the glory of God." Everything they do should result in enhancing God's reputation, which is what *glory* refers to. Because they belong to God, their deeds should make God look good. This again is the ethic of relationship. God does not look good when their activities cause others to wipeout in their faith. God does not look good when their activities cause them to wipeout in own their faith. God's reputation will be enhanced if they look out for others ahead of themselves. That's what Paul does. That is what Jesus did, an implied reference to Jesus giving his life for the sake of those who believe. Paul portrays both himself and Jesus as exemplars. They offer the same instructive pattern for living out that kind of love.[76] Those who inconvenience themselves by saying no to a questioned activity so that someone else's well-being can be advanced are engaging in God-pleasing activity.

Before moving on, let's make one final observation from this section. Religiously, the issue of a believer in Jesus participating in the festivities of a pagan god would seem to be a no-brainer. What business, some might ask, do believers in Jesus have doing that? Notice that Paul does not offer a terse *no* and move on. His discussion spans three chapters. Something more than rules keeping is going on here. Something more than enforced power moves is happening. This clearly is not "the Bible says" mentality. Paul wants the Corinthian believers to think. He wants them to take a well-considered, intentional approach to their choices in life, making God look good in all they do. God looks good when those who belong to him advance the welfare of others ahead of their own. That is at the core of what God has done in offering Jesus, the crucified, resurrected One. Their behavior should reflect how they know God.[77]

Issue 7: Divisions from Their Pursuit of Spiritual Gifts (1 Cor 12:1–14:40)

We observed in the previous section Paul for the first time mentioning love as an ethical responsibility for his readers: "love builds up" (1 Cor 8:1). In this section Paul discusses love more concretely.[78] We will see that as Paul describes love, he echoes issues previously discussed in the letter. Love emerges as a key behavioral component to Paul's ethical vision for those who believe in Jesus.

The core of this section addresses how the Corinthian believers are pursuing spiritual gifts. Those clearly are not ethical concerns. Spiritual gifts, as portrayed here, appear to be special endowments given by God to those who believe in Jesus. In 1 Corinthians 12:8-10 Paul offers a partial listing of those endowments, most of which reflect supernatural activity:

- utterance of wisdom
- utterance of knowledge
- faith
- gifts of healing
- working of miracles
- prophecy
- discernment of spirits

- various kinds of tongues

- interpretation of tongues

Paul does not explain what any of those mean.[79] We are reading their mail. He appears to assume that his readers know what they mean, as though at least some of these have been a part of the normal interaction between the Corinthian believers and him.

Paul does address problems that have arisen within the Corinthian church in their pursuit of those gifts. Some have come to regard one of those gifts as so much higher than others that all are being made to feel that they must seek that gift from God to avoid feeling spiritually inferior.[80] That has produced a divisive situation where some believers have elevated themselves over others, merely because of their giftedness. Paul's first point is that what they do have, they have as a result of the Spirit who has gifted them. Second, he elaborates how there must be a diversity of giftedness in order for there to be true unity in their believing community.[81] The Spirit has given those gifts "for the common good" (1 Cor 12:7).

With that second point, he mirrors the kind of discussion found frequently in the writings of Greco-Roman moral philosophers. He even draws on the same kind of metaphor found in many of those same philosophers—the body.[82]

> For just as the body is one and has many members, and all the members of the body, though many, are one body, so it is with Christ. For in the one Spirit we were all baptized into one body—Jews or Greeks, slaves or free—and we were all made to drink of one Spirit. **1 Cor 12:12-13**

Though Paul draws on a commonplace, he takes it to a new level. The body is not merely an example of how diversity advances unity. It is an expression of who Christ is. The believers in Corinth aren't merely part of a community. They are all part of Christ. This is the same radical ethic of relationship that we began to observe in 1 Corinthians 8:12. Paul does not advocate a view that says "do your own part for the sake of the team." He advocates that they all function in accordance with their Spirit-endowed abilities as being part of Christ himself. Unity is necessary because they all belong to Christ through God's Spirit. With the body metaphor, Paul also goes on to point out how honor and importance actually should be viewed. "The members of the body that seem to be weaker are indispensable" (1 Cor 12:22).[83]

But the advancement of Spirit-empowered unity and regard for those with less impressive gifts are not enough. Paul has a "more excellent way" to show them (1 Cor 12:31). He unfolds that in a passage that is probably the best known segment in all of Paul's writings—his praise of love.

Paul does not present love as a gift endowed by God's Spirit, but as a requirement for all who believe, regardless of their gift.[84] It is an ongoing responsibility for eternity, even when the need for giftedness ceases at the dawn of the coming age (1 Cor 13:8). Any function that a believer performs without love becomes useless and obnoxious. Paul's opening comments in 1 Corinthians 13:1-3 refer directly to various gifts he has already mentioned in 1 Corinthians 12:8-10, 28-30: tongues, prophetic powers, understanding all mysteries and all knowledge, faith. The real problem among the Corinthian believers is that they do not know how to love.

That becomes clear when Paul describes what love does.

> Love is patient; love is kind; love is not envious or boastful or arrogant or rude. It does not insist on its own way; it is not irritable or resentful; it does not rejoice in wrongdoing, but rejoices in the truth. It bears all things, believes all things, hopes all things, endures all things. **1 Cor 13:4-7**

Most English translations mask two important points here. In the first place, love is described by action words. Paul isn't communicating that love *is* patient. He states that love *shows* patience. Love patiences, if such a word could exist. The same is true with all of the other words in verses 4-6. Love kindnesses. Love does not boast or show arrogance or show rudeness. Paul portrays love as an activity, not as a mental state.

The second observation is that five of the negative action words of verses 4-6 connect to major issues from earlier in the letter. "Love is not envious." The Corinthian believers had been quarreling in envious division over their spiritual mentors (1 Cor 3:3). "Love is not . . . arrogant." They had shown arrogance in their divisions over spiritual mentors (1 Cor 4:6), in their responses in spite of the man living immorally with his father's wife (1 Cor 5:2), and in their pursuit of food offered in sacrifice to idols (1 Cor 8:1). "Love is not . . . rude."

Some of the believing men in Corinth who were not treating well the virgins to whom they were engaged were being just that (1 Cor 7:36). "Love does not insist on its own way." Yet their pursuit of rights in eating meat looked like selfish insistence (1 Cor 10:24), which was contrary both to Paul's own life orientation (1 Cor 10:33) and ultimately to that of Jesus (1 Cor 11:1). "Love does not rejoice in wrongdoing." But their participation in lawsuits against each other (1 Cor 6:7-8) demonstrates that they have been doing just that.

This indicates that near the moral core of most of the Corinthian believers' problems has been their failure both to understand what love is and to recognize its importance for their lives. They have been mistreating each other, in a major microethical breakdown. People who love others do not form divisive parties based on trivial matters. People who love others do not participate in sexual immorality or brag about the sexually immoral in their community. People who love others know how to treat the opposite sex well. People who love others place meeting others' needs ahead of their own personal rights. People who love others seek after those others' good ahead of their own.

Thus, love emerges as a major, microethical guiding principle for Paul's ethical thought in this letter, with Christ's own self-giving act in the cross becoming an implied pattern for that (1 Cor 11:1).[85] Paul applies that principle in the passage that follows by urging the Corinthian believers to seek after gifts that actually help others, instead of themselves.[86] Those who speak in tongues only edify themselves. They should, rather, desire gifts that build up others, gifts such as prophecy, since "those who prophesy build up the church" (1 Cor 14:4). The believers in Corinth should strive for the well-being of others ahead of their own.

ISSUE 8: THE RESURRECTION OF THE DEAD (1 COR 15:1-58)

The final item for consideration likewise pulls together thoughts scattered throughout the letter. The discussion of the resurrection of the dead underscores that Paul does more than advance a mere philosophy. He ties his thought into the overall plan of God—God's restoration of the whole earth, which has been under a sentence of death since the disobedience of Adam (1 Cor 15:21-22). That sentence, proclaims Paul, is reversed through Jesus, who himself has been raised bodily from the dead. What is striking for our discussion here is that Paul ties the reversal of death directly to morality. The resurrection plays a major role in his ethics.

The crux of the problem that Paul must address is that some Corinthian believers were denying the resurrection of the dead. What does that mean? The resurrection of the dead is a specific, future event when those believers who have died come back to life in new bodies. It is a cornerstone of traditional Christianity, too often undervalued by many today, who instead restrict the outcome of Christian faith to a mere existence in "heaven" after death. Faith in Jesus points to a future, bodily existence at a very specific future time, when the world also will be remade and the created order fully restored. That's what Paul's language points to in 1 Corinthians 15:20-28.

Why some Corinthian believers were denying the resurrection is uncertain.[87] It probably reflects the tendency articulated by some philosophers to regard physical, bodily existence as an inferior existence. Any bodily existence after death would then be a step backward, since the physical was thought to get in the way of appreciating what life is about.[88] By the same token, physical enjoyment would be only for the here and now, so that one should aim for physical satisfaction before it is taken away. Paul has already tackled thinking of that sort in 1 Corinthians 6:13-14. In that passage Paul challenged attitudes that dismissed restrictions on physical activity with the false claim that physical existence, being finite, is irrelevant. When he opposed those attitudes there, he referred directly to the same issue he deals with here—the resurrection of the dead. Paul challenges such attitudes here in this section even more directly.

Paul portrays the bodily resurrection of believers as central to faith in Jesus. That event, he points out, is one reason why Jesus has been raised. He is first, to be followed by others at his coming (1 Cor 15:20-24). At the foundation of Paul's proclamation is that "Christ died for our sins . . . and that he was raised on the third day" (1 Cor 15:3-4). Paul proclaims both Jesus' death and his resurrection, not merely his death. Those events are in accordance with what the Scriptures (i.e., the Old Testament) point to. Both events are supported by physical proofs—he was buried after his death and seen after his resurrection.[89] Without his resurrection, his death is meaningless: "If Christ has not been raised, your faith is futile and you are still in your sins" (1 Cor 15:17). But because Christ is risen, those who believe in him must expect also to be raised bodily from the dead at his coming (1 Cor 15:20-23).

Paul pulls his letter together with his discussion of the resurrection.[90] He began by handling the problem of factions within the Corinthian church.

His solution to their factions appealed directly to the crucifixion of Jesus. He ends the major discussions of his letter by addressing their denial of a foremost piece of teaching belonging to faith in Jesus, the resurrection of the dead. He begins to solve that issue by appealing to the resurrection of Jesus.

What does this have to do with ethics? As part of a series of concise comments, Paul first appeals to his own struggles in Ephesus, probably metaphorically referring to his fight against his own personal, immorally hedonistic tendencies.[91] That fight would be senseless if there were no bodily resurrection. Then he declares, "If the dead are not raised, 'Let us eat and drink, for tomorrow we die'" (1 Cor 15:32). He is quoting from Isaiah 22:13, a context that criticizes the refusal of the people of Judah to repent of their covenantal faithlessness.[92] In that passage they were being asked to turn away from their evil and reconnect humbly and contritely with God, in view of the invasion of the Assyrians. Instead, they responded hedonistically. Paul makes a similar connection here. Blatant hedonism is out of touch with the purposes of God. People who know God know what he is doing in the world.

To underscore the point, Paul appears to quote a common saying that is attributed to the playwright Menander: "Bad company ruins good morals" (1 Cor 15:33).[93] A denial of the resurrection only encourages associating with the hedonistic lifestyle of elitist Roman Corinth with its food, drink and sexual excesses, a lifestyle that Paul corrects once more, urging his readers: "Come to a sober and right mind, and sin no more; for some people have no knowledge of God" (1 Cor 15:34), something about which they should be ashamed.[94] Notice how, in one shot, Paul connects a denial of the resurrection both to immoral living and to a lack of knowledge about God, ironic in view of the knowledge in which some in Corinth had boasted (1 Cor 8:1-6).

In the context of 1 Corinthians 15, Paul indicates that denying the resurrection of the body leads naturally to hedonism, a life focused on physical pleasure, a life also reflected within the Corinthian community (see 1 Cor 6:12; 8:8-9; 10:23). With no sense of any future bodily existence, people aim for all the gratification they can get while still possible, before it is taken away. But since God has launched a plan for the world that culminates with the bodily resurrection of the dead and the reversal of the curse on the earth, believers in Jesus should live in accord with that plan. Bodily existence after death at the dawn of the coming age belongs to their destiny. It is a righteous destiny. They should live now in a manner that coordinates with that destiny.

Faith in Jesus is not merely about the here and now. It is about partici-pating in God's unfolding plan of restoring the world. The beginning of that end commences with the crucifixion and resurrection of Jesus. It comes to its finality at the coming of Jesus, when the dead are raised in a body that is "imperishable" (1 Cor 15:53). Believers in Jesus live in the in-between time.[95] They are to persevere in unswerving faithfulness (1 Cor 15:58), living now in a manner that reflects the final outcome of their faith. That final outcome also includes a righteous, moral existence.

SUMMING IT UP: PAUL'S ETHICS SO FAR

What initially appeared to be a random collection of advice based on a list of items Paul has been presented with has turned out to reflect an overarching, sophisticated ethical vision, even if Paul does not develop that in a systematic, step-by-step manner. Here is what we can begin to see taking shape.

o Ethics in Paul begins with the death and resurrection of Jesus. Those events signal that God is bringing his global restoration program to completion, climaxing in the eventual return of Jesus. Those who believe in Jesus are part of that program. They should live like it.

o The death and resurrection of Jesus are transforming events. They alter the lives of those who believe, changing them now in preparation for the yet-to-come final transformation.

o The death and resurrection of Jesus bring believers into a new community inhabited by God's Spirit, where they are all directly a part of Christ through his Spirit, who also inhabits each individual. God has a new, special relationship with those who believe, who, in response, can know him closely. Through God's Spirit, believers have the mind of Christ, offering them a wisdom that defies the thought patterns of the unconverted world. Through the provisions of God's Spirit, they can live in churchly unity.

o The death and resurrection of Jesus make believers righteously pure. Therefore they and their faith communities should be righteously pure. That includes sexual and marital matters.

o The death and resurrection of Jesus connect believers closely to God. They belong to Christ. They are to enhance God's reputation by how they behave.

o The death and resurrection of Jesus are liberating events. Believers in Jesus are free.

o Believers in Jesus need to exercise their freedom wisely and responsibly. That they can engage in a certain activity does not mean that they should. Some activities are not beneficial. Some dethrone Jesus as lord of their lives. Some actually hurt others. Some are impure. Some lead to outcomes that make God look bad, showing they do not know him as well as they should.

o The Scriptures (i.e., the writings of the Old Testament) offer guidance and instruction for believers to learn both about God's plans for the world and about his likes and dislikes. They do so as instructional sources, not regulatory ones. They are not to eclipse the significance of what has happened through Jesus' death and resurrection.

o In the same vein Paul's own words and opinions can have authoritative force, just as Jesus' can, but again, with the same restrictions just mentioned about the Scriptures.

○ Love is a major guiding principle to help believers in Jesus do what is morally right. As transformed people, they should treat others as more important than themselves, going so far as to deny themselves their own rights when that advances the well-being of others. Paul aims to live that way, following the pattern of Jesus shown in his death on their behalf. They belong to a new community. They must care for that community. Jesus has died for them.

These items emerge from considering the letter of 1 Corinthians as a whole. They are not part of a point-for-point treatise. Paul does have a definite sense of morality, declaring some kinds of activities right and others wrong. Behind his moral teaching is a strong sense of ethics, stemming from people being in close connection with God. That connection is possible through the death and resurrection of Jesus, which shape how they can know God. Ethics, in Paul, begins with the acts of God through Jesus. Ethics emerges as believers allow God to work in them through his Spirit, reflecting their belongingness to Christ and to each other. God has intervened in the world through Jesus. God continues to intervene in the lives of believers, transforming them as they respond to him. Paul describes this process more purposefully in his letter to the Romans.

Reflection Questions

1. How should having "the mind of Christ" affect the way people respond to what is going on around them? Think of specific situations when exercising the mind of Christ could bring a problem-solving perspective.

2. How should being made pure by the death and resurrection of Jesus affect people's sexual behavior inside and outside of marriage?

3. What should guide people to know whether they can exercise their personal rights to be involved with behavior that others might deem inappropriate?

4. How should love as Paul describes it affect people's attitudes toward work, sexual relationships, community interactions, responses to those not from their communities?

5. How should the resurrection of the dead affect believers' behavior?

For Further Reading

Ciampa Roy E., and Brian S. Rosner. *The First Letter to the Corinthians*. Grand Rapids: Eerdmans, 2010.

Thiselton, Anthony C. *The First Epistle to the Corinthians*. Grand Rapids: Eerdmans, 2000.

Winter, Bruce W. *After Paul Left Corinth: The Influence of Secular Ethics and Social Change*. Grand Rapids: Eerdmans, 2001.

TRANSFORMATION EXPLAINED

Paul and Romans

INTRODUCTORY ISSUES

Chapter nine introduced some basic aspects of Paul's ethical vision. Though Paul never focused on ethics in 1 Corinthians, ethical patterns emerged in the ways he addressed various moral issues in the church. Proper moral behavior must be normal for those who believe in Jesus. Why? They are transformed people, changed by God through the death and resurrection of Jesus. They have been brought into close relationship with God, who is bringing his global restoration program to completion in Jesus. Righteous, ethical living is part of that restored order, just as much as unrighteous, unethical behavior reflects a world out of touch with God.

Let's go back to our basics one final time:

- Ethics refers to how a person distinguishes right from wrong behavior.

- Ethics is also concerned with the reasons for why a person should choose what is good and abstain from what is not.

The kind of behavior that ethics is concerned with generally is behavior that advances good or hinders harm in one's world.

What have we seen in Paul so far?

- The transformation of believers' lives through the death and resurrection of Jesus makes them wise and pure, facilitating and demanding discernment between what is right, what is wrong and what does not matter. Because the Spirit of God lives within those who are transformed, those people have the mind of Christ, enabling them to know God closely and to make wise distinctions between right and wrong. They also have a heightened sensitivity to what the Scriptures communicate about God's likes and dislikes.

- Believers in Jesus should live righteously because they have been made new. They are also newly owned by Jesus. Those two points provide strong ethical motivation.

- Love offers the kind of guiding standard that is the essence of advancing good on the world. That love is shown in our exemplar: the crucified, resurrected Jesus.

In Romans we will see more of the same, with more profound theoretical explanation. Before exploring how Romans does that, let's first deal with some other important issues.

1. Be prepared to expand your view of Romans. Ethics in Romans? Popular preaching sometimes casts Romans as a writing that explains how to get forgiveness from God, how to go to heaven after dying and how to get saved. Romans actually has a broader view of those issues. The word *forgiven* occurs only once, in a quote (Rom 4:7) from the Psalms. Paul's more common word is *justified*.[1] Though justification clearly includes forgiveness, it's a much deeper concept, as we'll see. Paul never talks about heaven as a destination for the afterlife. He only uses the word twice in Romans (Rom 1:18; 10:6), to refer to the dwelling place of God, the abode of Christ. And though he talks about eternal life, he does not discuss it as the afterlife (see Rom 2:7; 5:21; 6:22-23) but as some other related outcome associated with the end of the age, which believers participate in now, in some way.[2]

Paul *does* talk about salvation in Romans, not merely as the moment of people getting saved by converting.[3] Consider this: "Salvation is nearer to us now than when we became believers" (Rom 13:11). Salvation, for Paul, points to the final righting of all the wrongs in the world, the total global makeover that happens at the return of Jesus.[4] Much of Paul's language about salvation is future-program oriented. It swerves closely to the concept of *kingdom* found in the Gospels. Salvation begins with Jesus' death and resurrection and is completed when he returns. It offers reasons for living ethically. Believers enter into salvation now, by faith, but God continues to work in them now, saving them from their immoral tendencies when they

call on him. He will continue to work in his people up through the final
moment of salvation at Jesus' return.

As we move our way through Romans, let's be prepared to go where its
words take us. And then enjoy the surprises.

2. Romans is a letter. Understanding Romans as a letter is required for
understanding its ethics. Paul is the stated author. He is addressing "God's
beloved in Rome" (Rom 1:7), also known as "saints" (i.e., believers in Jesus)
living in the empire's capital city. How many might that include? Who
knows? But certainly a small number compared with the approximate one
million who inhabited the city at the time it was sent.[5] A guess?—perhaps
no more than one thousand, distributed across an array of house-based
churches.[6] That's not much. And they have become believers not because of
anything that Paul has done but through the activities of others. How do we
know that? Again, we are reading their mail. They would know their own
circumstances. But Paul also directly declares, "I want you to know, brothers
and sisters, that I have often intended to come to you (but thus far have been
prevented)" (Rom 1:13). So why is he writing them? He says initially that he
wants to visit them to "reap a harvest" among them as he has elsewhere
among non-Jewish people. That's not very clear.

At the end of the letter Paul discloses more. He announces his intention
to visit them on his way to Spain, where he desires to proclaim the good
news about Jesus (Rom 15:24). He has already been doing that all over the
eastern part of the empire (Rom 15:19). He now wants to go west, to Spain,
where no other Christian missionary has gone, visiting the Roman believers
on his way (Rom 15:20, 23-24). After spending some time with them, he
wants "to be sent on by [them]" (Rom 15:24). What does that mean? It may
point to people accompanying him to his ship, standing on the dock and
waving goodbye as he sails. But more likely implied is his hope that they
support the venture, including finances since Paul travels with a group of
people.[7] To do that they would at least need to agree with what he stands for
and what he promotes. What does he stand for? What does he promote?
That's what the letter in part appears to present.[8]

Paul must explain himself to people who do not know him because some
out there like neither him nor what he does.[9] He implies that when he asks
the believers in Rome to pray "that I may be rescued from the unbelievers
in Judea, and that my ministry to Jerusalem may be acceptable to the saints,

so that by God's will I may come to you with joy and be refreshed in your company" (Rom 15:31-32).

Paul expects trouble on two fronts. First, unbelievers in Judea may oppose him stiffly, even violently. Second, the believers in Jerusalem may actually reject his ministry to Jerusalem, a reference to money that Paul has been collecting from non-Jewish believers in Jesus for the poor among the believers there (see Rom 15:25-28). What's going on here?

Paul's comments reflect issues that he assumes his readers know. He's writing to them, not us. Why would Jewish unbelievers in Jesus be disturbed about Paul? We can begin to guess. Paul travels among Gentile people, inviting them to belong to the people of God. Regular Jews don't do that, especially those connected to Pharisees, as Paul was initially.[10] They try to stay away from Gentiles, whose company would defile them. One ancient Jewish writer put it this way: "To prevent our being perverted by contact with others or by mixing with bad influences, he [i.e., Moses] hedged us in on all sides with strict observances connected with meat and drink and touch and hearing and sight, after the manner of the Law."[11] God's covenant people need protection from outsiders. The laws of the Torah provide just that.

Now along comes Paul, who traffics with Gentile people, even eating with them, and worse to some, destroying the integrity of God's people by claiming that Gentiles can belong *without having to become Jewish!*[12] That would release them from obligations of Torah's laws, which belong to Israel as God's covenant people. Paul proclaims that with the death and resurrection of Jesus the Messiah, God has initiated a new way, what some prophets anticipated as a "new covenant." We'll soon explore how Paul does that in Romans, and how it is important to ethics.

Paul's reputation for telling people not to keep the laws of Torah is damaging. It opens him up to the false charge of promoting a behavioral free-for-all, a charge he mentions in Romans 3:7-8. He can also be accused of defiling God's people by improperly mixing with Gentiles.[13] No wonder he anticipates trouble. No wonder he also has to explain himself carefully in this letter.

Closely related to Paul's tainted legacy is the money he brings for the poor among the believers in Jerusalem. Since it comes from Gentile converts, accepting it would require Jewish believers to grant status to people they had been keeping their distance from all their lives.[14] Only those who understand what God has accomplished in the death and resurrection of Jesus would have no problem with that money. Paul seems to be praying that the believers in Jesus in Jerusalem would all be receptive to that perspective.

Romans functions partly like a personal letter of recommendation, even with character references. (Note how in Romans 16 he refers to people whom he already knows in Rome.)[15] Paul appears to be explaining essentials of his ministry so that the believers in Rome themselves would be willing to come on board with it, in spite of his tainted legacy.[16] While Paul does declare that the Torah's legal code no longer applies, he also carefully explains issues from the Torah that do. And as he does that, he starts to speak the language of ethics.

3. Is there a moral difficulty among the Roman saints that Paul is helping to resolve? This final question flows from the previous discussion of Romans as a letter. Because the letter unfolds like a general treatise on the gospel, the good news about Jesus, it's harder to discern specific situations it may be addressing for the believers in Rome. Yet part of Paul's "eagerness to proclaim the gospel to [the 'saints'] also who are in Rome" (Rom 1:15) seems to relate to a controversy stewing in their midst. He doesn't wish to convert them. They already are "saints" (Rom 1:7), "God's beloved." Rather, part of the point would be to explain to them how the gospel can help them out with a moral difficulty of theirs.

What difficulty? Romans 14:1-3 declares:

> Welcome those who are weak in faith, but not for the purpose of quarreling over opinions. Some believe in eating anything, while the weak eat only vegetables. Those who eat must not despise those who abstain, and those who abstain must not pass judgment on those who eat; for God has welcomed them.

Quarreling? Despising? Judging? This sounds like a genuine, immoral argument, and it's based on food.[17] Why food? We know that food is important to those concerned with upholding the Torah. Remember Leviticus 11 and Deuteronomy 16? They both offer explicit details about food that would be considered clean and unclean for God's covenant people to eat. Add to that the complications of the sort we have already seen in 1 Corinthians 10:23-30, where meat left over from sacrifices in an idol's temple was sold in the markets, meat that would certainly be unclean for those concerned with

Torah's standards. Some in Rome seem to think they can eat anything they want. Others, identified by Paul as those "weak in faith," eat only vegetables, not because they are vegetarians but because vegetables are always "clean" from Torah's perspective. It's a common Jewish solution.[18] When in doubt about the meat, eat the vegetables.

This sounds like an argument growing out of concerns for the relevance of Torah's laws for believers in Jesus—note the purity language of Romans 14:14, 20. Some, not necessarily restricted to Jewish believers in Jesus, apparently think that they must uphold such laws. Paul refers to them as "weak in faith." Why? We'll examine that later. For now, just note that the situation is causing an immoral rift. In addressing that problem, Paul actually applies points he has made in the earlier part of the letter about the gospel. He is communicating to the Roman Christians how life is different for those who believe in Jesus. Central to that is how believers should be behaving (i.e., what is right, what is wrong and what does not matter), the subjects of ethics. At the end of this letter from Paul to the Roman Christians we are observing a direct, practical demonstration of some of the deep ethical theory found in its earlier parts.

THE LETTER ITSELF

Let's try to follow the letter's basic flow of thought.[19] In doing that we should be able to see how ethics is close to the core of what Paul is communicating. Ethics is not the central topic. Rather, Romans shows how, for both Jew and Gentile, the death and resurrection of Jesus finalize God's program of restoring the world that has been so long dominated by sin.[20] While upholding Israel as God's people, that restoration now includes non-Jewish people (Gentiles) in new ways. That program, radically advanced by the death and resurrection of Jesus, will come to completion at the return of Jesus, which is also the completion of salvation. Since salvation begins with the defeat of sin through the cross and resurrection, and ends with the total remaking of the imperfect world, ethics is a necessary part of it. In Romans' ethical perspective believers in Jesus are to be now what they are already (because the cross and the resurrection made them that), even if they aren't that yet (because the world hasn't been remade yet).[21] That is, they are to live righteously in salvation now, being saved now from the effects of sin, in view of the righteousness that awaits them at salvation to come; God has made them right with him, now, through the death and resurrection of Jesus.

Introduction: The "gospel" or good news (Rom 1:1-17). Paul begins
Romans in an unusual manner. Most letters in the Greco-Roman world state
the writer's name, followed immediately by the names of the addressees and
then by a greeting. That's chiefly what we saw in the first two verses of
1 Corinthians, where Paul and Sosthenes are identified as the writers, the
"church of God in Corinth" as the addressee and "Grace to you and peace
from God our Father and the Lord Jesus Christ" serves as the greeting.

Not so with Romans. Here Paul first introduces himself in verse 1, then
elaborates both on his personal call and his message, "the gospel," rooted in
the crucified, resurrected Messiah, Jesus, before identifying his addressees
six verses later. This is highly unusual, and with it Paul tips his hand about
his core concerns.[22] Within those six verses, Paul declares that the purpose
of his ministry is "to bring about the obedience of faith among all the Gentiles" (Rom 1:5). He does not promote a behavioral free-for-all, contrary to
rumors about him.

Paul has just identified an ethical concern: "the obedience of faith." Obedience refers to people conforming to explicit standards. Standards generally come from authoritative people, writings or other recognized sources.
Notice how Paul declares that he advances the "obedience of faith," as opposed to the obedience of something else, such as the Torah.[23]

What is the "obedience of faith"?[24] That is what we can expect the rest of
the letter to explain. From the opening, we know that it is closely connected
to Jesus, the Christ (i.e., Messiah), descended humanly from David and
raised bodily from the dead. The events of Jesus' death and resurrection are
at the core of the good news or gospel that Paul proclaims. Paul states in
Romans 1:16-17 that he is not ashamed of that news, first, because the powerful events associated with it indicate the beginning of the end, "salvation,"
which leads to the final righting of wrongs in the world. But second, that
news also reveals God's righteousness, which certainly includes God's standards of moral rightness.[25] Among other things, the gospel shows how much
morality is a part of God's character and God's plans for the world now, and
the world to come. In talking about righteousness, Paul is using the vocabulary of ethics, a vocabulary that abounds in this letter.[26]

Paul ties that vocabulary directly to how one comes to know God and
then relate to God. God's moral rightness is revealed "through faith for faith;

as it is written, 'The one who is righteous will live by faith'" (Rom 1:17). Faith, as we will see, reflects ongoing response to God in relationship with him.[27] People who initially respond to God through the gospel come to know his moral rightness. Those who continue to respond to God through Jesus increasingly incorporate that moral rightness into their daily lives. This points to a profound ethic of relationship. People's ongoing response to God's work in their lives drives Paul's ethical vision.

The unfolding argument: Step 1—Unrighteousness from unfaith (Rom 1:18-3:20). Though the good news reveals God's righteousness (Rom 1:17), human unrighteousness leads God to reveal his wrath (Rom 1:18). How so? Paul follows a very Jewish train of thought in stating that people act immorally because they refuse to acknowledge God, whose existence is very plain in the creation he has fashioned.[28] Those people, instead, make up their own gods and religious systems (Rom 1:18-23). God displays his wrath in the present by letting people live their lives without him, with all of the moral messiness that always follows. It's as though God is saying, "All right. You think you can live without me. Then go ahead. And enjoy sinking in the mud your resulting behavior makes."

Here is the negative aspect of our basic ethic of relationship that we have been observing all along. People who are out of touch with God show it with their bad behavior. Paul lists a series of moral misdeeds as activities symptomatic of being out of touch with God. Though he begins by elaborating on specific sexual activity, he eventually enumerates a broad list that includes the obvious, such as murder, and the more subtle, such as gossip.[29] He concludes his list with the following observation: "They know God's decree, that those who practice such things deserve to die—yet they not only do them but even applaud others who practice them" (Rom 1:32). Paul does not offer instruction here about what makes these wrong. Neither do his words accuse the Roman Christians of doing any of these. Instead he makes the general point that people who refuse to acknowledge God show it with their bad behavior.

While Romans 1:18-32 describes what happens when people refuse to acknowledge God, chapter 2 takes the surprising turn of drawing Jewish people into the overall indictment against human unrighteousness. Jewish resistant hearts (Rom 2:5, 29) are just as subject to God's judgment as Gentile ones (Rom 1:21, 24). Boasting in knowing right from wrong so well that one can confidently judge the misbehavior of the godless is of no value if the one judging also commits the same kinds of misdeeds.[30]

> But if you call yourself a Jew and rely on the law and boast of your relation to God and know his will and determine what is best because you are instructed in the law . . . You that boast in the law, do you dishonor God by breaking the law?
>
> **Rom 2:17, 23**

Any Jew would know both the Israelite heritage of covenantal disobedience and various contemporary mess-ups. Knowing the laws as written in the Torah is no antidote to disobeying them. What matters is obedience from the heart (Rom 2:15, 29), with praise from God, not people (Rom 2:29). In fact, when it comes to consistent, righteous living, there is no ethnic advantage to being a Jew, says Paul, since all people, whether Jew or Greek, are under sin's power (Rom 3:9). He builds to the declaration that *all* have sinned (Rom 3:23).[31] Even doing the Law's requirements cannot make someone right before God (Rom 3:20). So if participating in the Law of God, what is written in the Torah, does not put a person at an advantage over the godless, then what does?

The unfolding argument: Step 2—Righteousness from faith (Rom 3:21–5:11). Beginning with Romans 3:21, Paul concisely explains how the death and resurrection of Jesus disclose God's righteousness "for all who believe" (Rom 3:22).[32] The written, contractual standards of the Law certainly do portray God's righteousness, which includes God's sense of moral right and wrong.[33] But much more so do the death and resurrection of Jesus. Those events provide "redemption" (Rom 3:24) or liberation from the life of being relegated to the dominating power of sin (Rom 3:9) that places people under God's wrath (Rom 1:18, 24, 28).[34] Jesus has been "put forward as a sacrifice of atonement by his blood" (Rom 3:25), a clear reference to his death on the cross as God's means of redemption and for dealing with people's sinfulness, removing its guilt and defilement from them:[35] Christ "was handed over to death for our trespasses" (Rom 4:25); "Christ died for the ungodly" (Rom 5:6); "While we were still sinners Christ died for us" (Rom 5:8).

That sacrifice of atonement, says Paul, shows God's righteousness because he had previously "passed over" sins committed by others in the past, dealing with those sins through the death of Jesus instead of directly judging the guilty parties.[36] We don't have to read very far into the history of the Israelites, who complain in the wilderness (Ex 14:11-12; 15:23-24; 16:2-3; 17:2-3), or worse, who sacrifice to an idol (Ex 32:1-6), to see God passing over sins. Even prior to that we saw God showing mercy to Cain the murderer, still continuing to bless Abram with wealth even though he had advised his wife to say that she was his sister, using Moses as the leader of his people even though he had murdered an Egyptian. Instead of destroying people for wrongdoing, God put up with them, showing "forbearance" (Rom 3:25). Rather than ignoring sin, he dealt with it through the death of Jesus. He does the same for people in the present (Rom 3:26). Quite remarkably, all who place their faith in this crucified Jesus are justified from their sins.

Justified? That is a hard term to define because Paul uses it in an unusual way. At the very least it refers to people being acquitted by God of their wrongdoing. As Paul continues to appeal to the concept, he points to people being made right with God.[37] That happens, not because of anything they have done or could ever do, but because of how God has dealt with their sin in the crucified, resurrected Jesus. In making people right with him, God sees those who believe in him through Jesus as having guilt-free, right standing with him, with no sense that there is anything wrong ever to be counted against those who have so believed. That's powerful. Here then is the essential second step in his argument. Faith in the crucified, resurrected Jesus makes people right with God, despite all their known moral and religious wrongs. It is an undeserved gift (Rom 3:23). It underscores what we have seen all along, that people cannot earn standing with God by doing good, but that doing good comes from their standing with God. Here we learn that that standing is possible only because of Christ.

As Paul continues, righteousness based on the crucified, resurrected Jesus rules out the possibility of any boasting in any righteous status stemming from living up to the Law's (Torah's) written, contractual commands or any other standards (Rom 3:27-28).[38] That, says Paul, makes God to be God of both Jews and non-Jews (Rom 3:29-30), since the law belonged only to Israel. It is also consistent with how God has always acted. Proof? Abraham. He "believed God, and it was reckoned to him as righteousness" (Rom 4:3, quoting Gen 15:6). Paul refers to a scene we have already explored in chapter 2. He points out that God regarded Abraham as righteous before Abraham ever had to respond to any command. God's command for Abraham to become circumcised happened in Genesis 17, well after God had reckoned Abraham as righteous because of his faith in him in Genesis 15. Paul describes a righteousness that God deems, attributes or ascribes (the technical word is *imputes*) to Abraham, stemming from his faith, before there was any covenant with Israel demanding righteous deeds.

In explaining Abraham the way he does, Paul also sets up his ethical discussion in Romans 14 concerning obedience to commands about food and celebration of special days (such as keeping the sabbath).[39] Remember Romans 14:1—"Welcome those who are *weak in faith*." Here, in Romans 4, Paul talks about how Abraham didn't "weaken in faith" when promised a son at an old age through a barren wife. Rather, he "grew strong" in his faith (Rom 4:20, anticipating Rom 15:1), becoming "fully convinced" (Rom 4:21, anticipating Rom 14:5, 22) that God would do what he had promised. The significance of that moment is not only for Abraham, says Paul, but for "us who believe in him who raised Jesus our Lord from the dead, who was handed over to death for our trespasses and was raised for our justification" (Rom 4:24-25).

The death and resurrection of Jesus change how God relates to people who believe. Those who believe have "peace with God" (Rom 5:1), who, because Jesus died for them and rose from the dead, is no longer wrathful toward them but fully reconciled with them (Rom 5:9-11). The death and resurrection of Jesus also change or transform those who believe. They are justified, made so completely right with God by God that Paul can eventually say that God has no charge against them (see Rom 8:33). That lays the foundation for the ethics we will now begin to see.

The unfolding argument: Step 3—Righteous living in the new order of the Spirit (Rom 5:11–8:39). Romans 5:11–8:39 gets to the heart of Paul's ethics.[40] We'll carefully probe relevant specifics. We'll find Paul explaining how the death and resurrection make ethical living possible. We'll see that the gospel provides not only guidance to distinguish right from wrong behavior and motivation to do the right and to avoid the wrong, but something no other ethical system offers—both the power to overcome the strong personal tendencies to do wrong and the power to live rightly. As we'll see Paul explaining, the events of the death and resurrection establish a new order of living, with Christ in charge. Believers in Jesus are transferred into that new order. They experience God's work in their lives through his Spirit as they continue to respond to him. The death and resurrection not only change people, they empower them to live ethically. In knowing God, believers look to God to change them, working his resurrection power and righteousness within them. It is *not* about believers striving on their own to conform to moral standards, laws or rules of any sort. That doesn't work, as we'll see Paul explaining.

Paul has just introduced faith in God through the crucified, resurrected Jesus as God's way for establishing human righteousness. He now begins describing the two dominions (like kingdoms) that currently exist in the world. The first has endured since the beginning of humanity, originating with "the one man" Adam (Rom 5:12-14). Through that man sin entered the world (Rom 5:12), passing to all people and dispensing death. Notice Paul using the word *sin* in a way similar to how that term first appears in biblical writings, in the Torah.[41] Recall from Genesis 4:6-7 how God warned Cain: "Why are you angry, and why has your countenance fallen? If you do well, will you not be accepted? And if you do not do well, *sin is lurking at the door; its desire is for you, but you must master it*" (italics added).

Likewise here in Romans, sin appears as a controlling power at work in all people throughout the world. We first saw such a usage in Romans 3:9: "all . . . are under the power of sin." In Romans 5:21 Paul states that sin has "exercised dominion in death," ever since its entry into the world through Adam. Sin is the power that dominates all people in the world, controlling God's original dominion. Sin's controlling influence over people leads them into unethical acts that not even the existence of Torah's covenantal standards can overcome. In fact, Paul declares that violation of Torah's standards increased with the giving of Torah (Rom 5:20), with the result that sin, as a power, exercised dominion in death.

By contrast, God has established a new dominion through the crucified, resurrected Jesus. In that dominion God's grace abounds through Jesus (Rom 5:15), bringing justification (Rom 5:16) and life (Rom 5:18) to all who believe. Those who believe will eventually be made completely righteous (Rom 5:19), even as they allow grace to reign in their lives now because they have been justified, or made right with God already, through the crucified, resurrected Jesus (Rom 5:21). These words actually point to the lifestyle of transformed, ethical living under the influence of God's empowering grace. How?

Paul elaborates further on what he means in Romans 6–8. He begins by addressing the ethical practicalities of being right with God through Jesus' death and resurrection. If the vast quantities of human sinful activity were matched by God showing an increase in his grace toward humanity, then why shouldn't believers in Jesus continue under sin's dominating power, since they can always count on God's grace through Jesus?

Paul answers that in Romans 6 by describing the new dominion established through Jesus. Jesus' crucifixion and resurrection have transferred all who believe in him from the control of sin's power to the realm where Jesus reigns.[42] Believers have changed their citizenship. Prior to conversion they had been under sin's reign. They now live under a new monarch.

How did that transference take place? Paul explains that in the Roman Christians' conversion, indicated by their baptism, they were thoroughly connected to Jesus in his death (Rom 6:3-4). As Jesus died, so in some very real way had they. But just as Jesus had been raised bodily from the dead, so they have now become those who live "in newness of life" (v. 4). That newness of life necessarily involves righteous living. Here we have ethics—believers in Jesus doing what is right, morally, because they have been made right with God through the death and resurrection of Jesus. They have been freed from the domination of sin through the death of Jesus and given new life in his resurrection. When sin had been the official monarch of their lives, they lived immorally. Now they have a new ruler. To continue to answer to sin would be just as ridiculous as someone who has changed nationality continuing to submit to his or her former country of citizenship.

Paul explains, though, that life stemming from the resurrection is not complete until God's final act of salvation, the bodily resurrection from the dead of all who believe in Jesus (Rom 6:5). Here we have the same tension of thought that we have seen elsewhere in the New Testament—the now and the not yet. Because of Jesus' resurrection, believers in Jesus experience newness of life now (Rom 6:4), while awaiting the complete newness of their own resurrection in the not yet.

Consider the implications for ethics. Believers in Jesus must live now what they will be—morally right now, in view of the righteousness that is to come. They are no longer entrapped sinners; they are newly made human beings. Note Paul's comments in Romans 6:6-8:

> *We know that our old self was crucified with him so that the body of sin might be destroyed, and we might no longer be enslaved to sin. For whoever has died is freed [Greek, "justified"] from sin. But if we have died with Christ, we believe that we will also live with him.*

Sin is no longer a rightfully ruling power over those who believe in Jesus. Jesus has died and been raised, freeing them from sin's power. Believers in Jesus are so identified with Jesus in his death and resurrection that they too have died and have experienced a measure of resurrection. They now belong to a stronger controlling influence stemming from the resurrection, a powerful influence that leads to moral living. Because of that, they are to "consider [themselves] dead to sin and alive to God in Christ Jesus" (Rom 6:11).

Romans 6:11 is a "you are" statement.[43] The readers are urged to bear in mind what they are—dead to sin and alive to God in Christ. The words in Romans 6:12 declare a "therefore be": "Therefore, do not let sin exercise dominion in your mortal bodies, to make you obey their passions." They must *be* dead to sin. Paul is dealing deeply with behavioral motives, an important concern in ethical discussion. He is addressing people who submit to sin instead of to God, placing their unrighteous bodily urges under sin's control.[44] That leads to unethical activity. Believers are not to do that because they have a new master, Jesus, who in his death and resurrection has broken the controlling power of sin. They are not to present their bodily members—their hands, their feet, their mouths—to sin so that immoral behavior results. Rather, they are to "present [themselves] to God as those who have been brought from death to life, and present [their] members to God as instruments of righteousness" (Rom 6:13). Why? They belong to a new world order infused by God's grace (Rom 6:14) that has overcome the tyranny of sin. They are dead to that power and alive to God; therefore they should be so.

Paul is describing a lively, intentional ethic of relationship. As an aspect of knowing God, believers are actively to hand themselves over entirely to God to be used by him to do righteous, moral deeds, as though saying, "Here are my hands, God; please use them. Here are my feet, God; please use them. Here is my mouth, God; please use it." That involves a major faith interaction with God. Here, we can see how obedience comes from faith. People enter into the new dominion through faith, being made right with God through the crucifixion and resurrection of his son Jesus. People live within that dominion through faith, offering themselves to God, who through his grace enables them to live rightly, doing righteous deeds, in the new, resurrection life he gives them. Righteousness in the gospel is through faith, for faith (Rom 1:17).

This is not authoritarian morality—"do it because you have to." This is a liberating ethics—"do it because you are now free to be what you are being remade to be." No one who belongs to the dominion of God can say about his or her own bad behavior anything like "I can't help it. I was made this way." Everyone who belongs to God through Jesus has been made new through the resurrection of Jesus and therefore can behave rightly, as those who are new.

Paul encourages this with a metaphor of competing masters (Rom 6:16-23). Sin, as master, exercises horrible control that leads to death. By contrast God, through Christ, has set people free from that tyrannical slave master, sin (Rom 6:18) to a completely better way of life. They are now set free to do what is morally right, as slaves of righteousness.

Paul offers an ethical motivation: "For the wages of sin is death, but the free gift of God is eternal life in Christ Jesus our Lord" (Rom 6:23). He speaks not of the wages of sinning as an activity but of sin as a master. The tyrant sin pays people in death every time they submit to its reign.[45] Why would anyone choose to serve that master? Submitting to sin leads to immoral activity. Everyone who submits to sin dies a little each time. By contrast, God offers life in Jesus. Each time a believer responds to Jesus as Lord, doing what is right, that person experiences life in a manner that more and more reflects God's sense of rightness, while the believer increasingly knows God as the gracious life-giver.[46] Paul says that "the advantage you get is sanctification. The end is eternal life" (Rom 6:22). Performing moral activity in submitting to Christ now offers a foretaste of the fully restored life received at the return of Jesus.

The transformation of believers in Christ is so effective that the power of the death and resurrection makes them "obedient from the heart to the form of teaching to which [they] were entrusted" (Rom 6:17). Their new connection with God leads them almost automatically to perform moral activity. Here, we begin to see how Paul could have written earlier in the letter about

Gentiles who "do instinctively what the law requires" and "show that what the law requires is written on their hearts" (Rom 2:14-15).[47] In transforming believers God places Torah's requirements onto their hearts, giving them moral direction in their "newness of life" (Rom 6:4) without their having to know laws. Paul explains further how that happens in Romans 7–8.

Romans 7 begins a segment with complicated details, yet one that can be explained with simple, clear reference points. Paul is clarifying the role of Torah's covenantal obligations, its laws, in view of the cross and the resurrection. Quite startlingly, Paul indicates that those obligations are no longer binding on believers in Jesus. How so? Those obligations belong to an old order. Believers in Jesus have died to that order, being transferred to the new dominion presided over by Christ.

Paul begins to explain the point with an analogy from marriage; in everyday life a wife is free to marry another husband only when her first husband has died. "In the same way, my friends, you have died to the law through the body of Christ, so that you may belong to another, to him who has been raised from the dead in order that we may bear fruit to God" (Rom 7:4). He explains further that "we are now discharged from the law, dead to that which held us captive, so that we are slaves not under the old written code but in the new life of the Spirit" (Rom 7:6). "Discharged from the law"—those are strong words. Torah is no longer legally binding on believers in Jesus.

Paul's language reflects the Old Testament's hope of a new covenant in which God will place his law on the hearts of his people (Jer 31:33), leading them to obedience through his Spirit (Ezek 36:26-27).[48] A new program has begun in Christ. That program upgrades the Torah-based covenant with a "direct intervention of God through his Spirit" covenant. God now directly influences the righteous living of those who continue to respond to him in Christ. This is an ethic of relationship stemming from an ongoing, lively, dynamic interaction with God, who steps in to work in the lives of those connecting with him in faith.

Paul points out why that is necessary. The law does not work. To make his case Paul uses the commandment "You shall not covet" in a way that also implies the uselessness of any law or rule for morality. He quotes the commandment in Greek, rather than Hebrew, in the process challenging a chief virtue of his culture's moral philosophical world, self-control.[49] The com-

mandment could be translated "Do not act on your passions."[50] That is what
moral philosophers of Paul's day regularly said, instructing people instead
to be self-controlled. Paul explains how that commandment, and any similar
law, encourages rather than curbs misbehavior. Urging a person just to say
no to an immoral act that the person feels deeply and strongly hard-wired
to perform does not work. The human flesh is too weak by itself to resist the
power that sin exerts on it. In fact the flesh is so inclined toward evil that the
mere suggestion of not doing something that sin-dominated flesh is driven
to do feeds the passion instead of restraining it.

Consider, for example, New Year's resolutions. People often direct them
at their personal bodily desires and cravings. And so few people actually
keep those resolutions because they are aimed at curbing what their bodies
feel driven to do. Paul describes something similar to that happening
morally. Though the regulations of Torah may themselves be "holy and just
and good" (Rom 7:12), they are powerless to keep someone from doing
wrong. Torah's words may point out sin (Rom 7:13; also Rom 3:20). The best
that awareness can do, courtesy of the reign of sin that "dwells within" (Rom
7:20) is to create a divided person, with the immoral bodily tendencies a
person feels driven to act out overruling what the person knows to be
wrong.[51] "For I delight in the law of God in my inmost self, but I see in my
members another law at war with the law of my mind, making me captive
to the law of sin that dwells in my members" (Rom 7:22-23).

That is not the way life should ever be for those who belong to God
through Jesus. Such a weakness leads a person who knows not to do an evil
to do it anyway because of her or his fleshly inclinations (Rom 7:13-24).
That's because sin at work in people's lives is more powerful than the words
of the law, or of any personal moral standard someone is determined to live
out. Sin can even use the law against itself, bringing death. The believer who
lives that way has returned to the dominion of sin, instead of living under
the dominion of Christ.

By contrast, the death and resurrection of Jesus have released God's
Spirit into the lives of those who believe. In the cross and the resurrection
"God has done what the law, weakened by the flesh, could not do" (Rom 8:3).
He has dealt with sin "so that the just requirement of the law might be
fulfilled in us who walk, not according to the flesh but according to the
Spirit" (Rom 8:4). God is able to intervene directly in the lives of those who

believe in Jesus to keep them on track in their lives in Christ. Not the exact commands of the Law but its "just requirement," its orientation toward righteousness, is facilitated and enabled in the lives of believers by God's Spirit, whom everyone who believes in Jesus receives (Rom 8:8-10).[52] Believers who live under the control of their unrighteous bodily inclinations, their "flesh," are living in the ways that lead to death; "but if by the Spirit [they] put to death the deeds of the body, [they] will live" (Rom 8:13).[53] By responding directly to the Spirit of God who dwells within them, those who believe in God through Jesus receive an enlivening that enables them to overcome sinful tendencies inherent in their bodies. God works in them directly by his Spirit to keep his people on track *when they respond to his Spirit within them*. Paul is describing further practicalities of what he has already declared in Romans 6:23.[54]

This is rich ethics, based on people growing in knowing God. God directly guides those who believe in him in the ways of rightness by what he does on their hearts through his Spirit. Further, he enables them through his Spirit to overcome sin in their lives. It's as though each time someone responds to that enabling, that person experiences a measure of life that reflects the fullness of life such people will receive at their own resurrection (Rom 8:11). This contrasts with the measure of death someone experiences when succumbing to unrighteous bodily urges.

Paul, of course, is well aware that he is not describing the possibility of present-day perfection. He knows that no one on earth can experience complete perfection until Christ returns to finalize his salvation. That salvation is the ultimate goal of the work of God in the world, work that has moved forward significantly through the death and resurrection of Jesus.

In Romans 8:18-27 he revisits a thought initially expressed in Romans 5:2-4, where he had presented the moral changes brought about in those who rejoice in sufferings while living in the hope of that salvation: sufferings produce endurance, which shapes character, which engenders hope, which is satisfying because of God's love at work in their hearts through his Spirit. In Romans 8:18-27 he discusses the present moral and physical imperfections in believers and in the creation as both groan under the load of global decay and disorder, awaiting "the glory about to be revealed to [them]," "the freedom of the glory of the children of God," "the redemption of [their] bodies" (Rom 8:18, 21, 23). Even God's Spirit groans with them through this

(Rom 8:26-27). Paul points out that being "conformed to the image of [God's] Son" (Rom 8:29) is part of God's foreordained plan for those who love him. He is referring to people becoming like Jesus' in his resurrected, glorified, heavenly state, not his earthly life.[55] In the meantime believers can be assured that in spite of their own imperfections and difficulties, God will continue to love them (Rom 8:31-39).

People who are transformed by the death and resurrection of Jesus must act like it, morally. But believers in Jesus are allowed to be works in progress. Moral living flows from people's relationship with God. Those who know God should not fear that their relationship with him is destroyed by moral lapses: "Who will bring a charge against God's elect? It is God who justifies. Who is to condemn? It is Christ Jesus, who died, yes, who was raised, who is at the right hand of God, who indeed intercedes for us" (Rom 8:33-34). God loves those who have responded by faith to what he has offered them in Jesus (Rom 8:35-39). He continues to love them, in spite of their mess-ups. But as part of the deliverance he has enacted, based on the crucified, resurrected Jesus, he not only makes them right with him, he gives them new lives, enabling them through his Spirit to live the way he has remade them to live. God continues to extend himself to his people *as they present themselves to him* (Rom 6:13). He gives them life through his Spirit now, in view of the ultimate life they receive at the return of Jesus, when believers are remade so thoroughly that committing moral wrongs would be impossible.

Faith in God through the crucified, resurrected Jesus allows no room whatsoever for any type of moralism. It's a denial of that faith to say, "Be good . . . because God says so." It's a denial of that faith to say that it's all about keeping rules of any sort. The cross and the resurrection of Jesus make believers right with God. They should be righteous because they are righteous. And they are righteous already, even if they are not yet. Obedience comes from faith—faith in God who transforms people's lives through the crucified, resurrected Jesus, and through his Spirit who, as a result, now dwells within them.

The unfolding argument: Step 4—Israel and the new sense of the people of God (Rom 9–11). Romans 9–11 are not as informative ethically.[56] Remember, ethics forms only part of Paul's concerns in this letter. In discussing a new order of God in the world, Paul must explain how that order connects to what God has been doing previously in the world through Israel, especially since many Israelites, or Jews, of Paul's day had not responded to Jesus as their Messiah or Christ. These chapters convey a necessary aspect of what Paul promotes about Christ among Gentiles. They address how failing to see God's righteousness in Jesus as the crucified, resurrected Messiah leads to an improper Torah-focused religion out of sync with God's ways (Rom 9:30–10:4).[57] But they are not as necessary for our discussion on ethics.

Paul shows how what God has done through the Messiah fulfills, rather than counteracts, what he has been doing all along with the people of Israel. Israel's complete turning to God is an eventual, expected outcome (Rom 11:26). Through Jesus, God has extended his direct outreach to all peoples, just as he had promised to do in the Scriptures. That has strong implications for how believers in Jesus are to live harmoniously in their faith communities (see Rom 14–15), regardless of whether their background is Jewish or Gentile. In case any would be inclined to say that God has abandoned Israel in favor of non-Jewish believers in Jesus, Paul points out that "the gifts and the calling of God are irrevocable" (Rom 11:29). God has not forsaken his covenant with Israel as his people. God never abandons his people, whether Israel or those "in Christ." But, Paul concludes, God's ways and plans for the world are too deep to be fully comprehensible by people who haven't seen them brought to completion yet (Rom 11:33-36).

The practicalities of ethics for those in Christ (Rom 12–15). Paul has disclosed core ethical basics in the first part of his letter. They emerge directly from the effects of the cross and the resurrection. We must take care never to separate those basics from the specific practicalities mentioned in these chapters. To do so would be to create a moralism and a ground for boasting that opposes the very gospel that Paul has declared.

Paul's language throughout evokes what he has said earlier. He begins with general advice that builds to his more pointed discussion of food issues in chapter 14.

> *I appeal to you therefore, brothers and sisters, by the mercies of God, to present your bodies as a living sacrifice, holy and acceptable to God, which is your spiritual worship. Do not be conformed to this world, but be transformed by the renewing of your minds, so that you may discern what is the will of God—what is good and acceptable and perfect.* **Rom 12:1-2**

These words repackage points Paul has made earlier in the letter.[58] Recall, for example, how in chapter 6 Paul urged his readers no longer to "present [their] members to sin as instruments of wickedness, but present [them]selves to God as those who have been brought from death to life, and present [their] members to God as instruments of righteousness" (Rom 6:13). Here in chapter 12, Paul urges each of his readers to present his or her entire body to God. What's the difference? None, really. Paul is portraying faith activity rooted in the cross and the resurrection, exhibiting how righteousness is "through faith for faith" (Rom 1:17). People who believe in Jesus are to continue to connect with God by offering themselves to be his instruments for performing righteous acts in the world.

Recall as well the words from Romans 2 about the inadequacy of knowing God's will from the Torah, knowledge which itself does not keep the knower from improper behavior: "But if you call yourself a Jew and rely on the law and boast of your relation to God and know his will and determine what is best because you are instructed in the law. . . . You that boast in the law, do you dishonor God by breaking the law?" (Rom 2:17-18, 23).

Paul's words in Romans 12:2 about knowing God's "good and acceptable and perfect will" contrast directly with the boastful words of those claiming to know God's will and God's best from God's Law (Rom 2:18). The way offered in Jesus is better than the way offered in Torah precisely because it facilitates believers living God's ways through a close connection with God. Implied in Paul's words in Romans 12:2 is a sense that even specific content about good, God-pleasing behavior comes to people who know God through the crucified, resurrected Jesus.[59] Here we see hints of previous points about Gentiles "doing instinctively what the law requires" because it is "written on their hearts" (Rom 2:14-15) and of believers in Jesus now being "obedient from the heart to the form of teaching to which [they] were entrusted" (Rom 6:17). People in active faith contact with God through Jesus know his ways through that contact, with transformed minds that renounce the foolish, unrighteous behavior of the unbelieving world. They would be those who, with their minds "consider [them]selves dead to sin and alive to God in Christ Jesus" (Rom 6:11), who "live according to the Spirit," who thus "set their minds on the things of the Spirit" (Rom 8:5).[60]

Believers in Jesus are called to interact with one another in faith communities. Romans 12:3-8 portrays that life by describing metaphorically how they belong to "one body, in Christ," with each being, "individually . . . members one of another" (Rom 12:5), exercising various divinely endowed abilities for the sake of that "body." Though his topic does not directly address ethics, Paul begins his discussion by appealing to the influence of a transformed mind, relevant to ethics: "I say to everyone among you not to think of yourself more highly than you ought to think, but to think with sober judgment, each according to the measure of faith that God has assigned" (Rom 12:3). The specific abilities they do have come from their faith connection with God. Awareness of that should lead to proper moral attitudes in practicing those abilities.[61]

In Romans 12:9-21 Paul enumerates specific activities that fall directly into the realm of morality. He does so with a list of loosely related pieces of moral advice given in short, crisp "sentences," a common way of presenting simple moral advice in Paul's culture.[62]

> *Let love be genuine; hate what is evil, hold fast to what is good; love one another with mutual affection; outdo one another in showing honor. Do not lag in zeal, be ardent in spirit, serve the Lord. Rejoice in hope, be patient in suffering, persevere in prayer. Contribute to the needs of the saints; extend hospitality to strangers.*
>
> *Bless those who persecute you; bless and do not curse them. Rejoice with those who rejoice, weep with those who weep. Live in harmony with one another; do not be haughty, but associate with the lowly; do not claim to be wiser than you are. Do not repay anyone evil for evil, but take thought for what is noble in the sight of all. If it is possible, so far as it depends on you, live peaceably with all. Beloved, never avenge yourselves, but leave room for the wrath of God; for it is written, "Vengeance is mine, I will repay, says the Lord." No, "if your enemies are hungry, feed them; if they are thirsty, give them something to drink; for by doing this you will heap burning coals on their heads." Do not be overcome by evil, but overcome evil with good.* **Rom 12:9-21**

Notice how most of these items affect how believers should interact with other people. These are microethical concerns. Notice further that much of this focuses on harmony and on advancing the well-being of others: sincere love (vv. 9-10); showing honor to others (v. 10); contributing to the economic needs of fellow believers (v. 13); showing hospitality to strangers (v. 13); being kind to those who wrong or even harm them (vv. 14, 17, 19-20);

being empathetic toward others, whether they are joyful or sorrowful (v. 15); living harmoniously with one another (v. 16); hanging out even with those who might be socially inferior (v. 16); living peaceably with all people (v. 18); overcoming evil with good instead of retaliation.

From where does Paul get these moral standards? They appear as random good advice. Much of it has direct implications for the discussion about quarrels in Romans 14.[63] So, he is partly setting up his discussion of that topic. One piece of advice (Rom 12:14) resembles words from Jesus that we have seen in Luke 6:28 and Matthew 5:44 about blessing rather than cursing persecutors, though Paul does not say directly that he knew them from traditions about Jesus.[64] The advice in verses 19-20 comes straight from an identifiable, important source—the Scriptures. In verse 19 he quotes a line from Deuteronomy 32:35 and in verse 20 he quotes from Proverbs 25:21-22. He quotes these as informing sources, rather than legal ones.[65] Paul regularly advocates learning from the Scriptures. But he refrains from appealing to the Scriptures in ways that give them the same covenantal force as the Torah has for Israel. Paul is not establishing a moralistic alternative of Torah-like laws. Rather, he is portraying specifics of a developing sense of right and wrong that is very much at home in an environment that advocates being deeply in touch with God.

He picks up the thread of the usefulness of the Scriptures for moral instruction after a segment where he advocates obedience to governing authorities, a piece of instruction common within Paul's culture.[66] The new order they belong to, after all, does not put them above governmental authorities, who are established by God to maintain order (Rom 13:1-7). In Romans 13:8, however, Paul discusses moral specifics by quoting from the Ten Commandments:

> Owe no one anything, except to love one another; for the one who loves another has fulfilled the law. The commandments, "You shall not commit adultery; You shall not murder; You shall not steal; You shall not covet"; and any other commandment, are summed up in this word, "Love your neighbor as yourself." Love does no wrong to a neighbor; therefore, love is the fulfilling of the law. **Rom 13:8-10**

Paul lists four laws from the Ten Commandments offering obvious moral sanctions, those prohibiting adultery, murder, theft and coveting. He indicates that these and other laws do have usefulness. But he incorporates them within a more general standard, that of love. Rather than focus on obeying specific commandments from the "holy and just and good" Torah (Rom 7:12), Paul advances a summarizing "word"—"Love your neighbor as yourself."[67] That "word" also comes from the Torah as the second half of a law prohibiting vengeance (see Lev 19:18). Here Paul appeals to those words in an instructive manner. Those words, says Paul, convey the essence of what commands in Torah aim for—love. He provides a measuring device for love: it does no wrong to a neighbor. Notice that we have a direct ethical principle. Anything that wrongs another is unloving and hence immoral. Adultery, murder, theft and coveting harm others. (Remember that coveting is not mere desire but a controlling desire that easily becomes the first step in outward wrongdoing.)[68] By opposite reasoning, anything that advances the well-being of others is moral. Love is just that activity.

Why should love be that standard? Paul says that love "fulfills" the Law. Here, he gives the practical demonstration of how the Law's "just requirement" is "fulfilled in [those], who walk not according to the flesh but according to the Spirit" (Rom 8:4).[69] When believers are in submission to God's Spirit, they love. When they love, they do what individual laws of the Torah advocate. Torah is useful as informing Scripture, even if its covenantal obligations change in the death and resurrection of Jesus. Love is what God has been pressing for all along in his prior covenantal activity.[70]

Love has been mentioned earlier in the letter as what God has both poured into believers' hearts through his Spirit (Rom 5:5) and demonstrated in the death of Christ for people while they were still "sinners" (Rom 5:8). Believers are mentioned in passing as those who love God (Rom 8:28). But significantly, God is said to persist in his love that he shows to all who belong to him (Rom 8:35-39), regardless of their life circumstances. God has shown preferential love to Israel in choosing them as his people (Rom 9:13). Fittingly Paul calls on believers to love one another sincerely (Rom 12:9-10). Love points to activity in concert with God's, who acts most supremely in love through Jesus, crucified and raised, and through his Spirit at work in believers' lives. When believers love, they show that they know God and his love.

We'll see Paul apply that same standard of love in Romans 14 when discussing food issues. But before we can get there, let's finish out Paul's thought in Romans 13. In addition to showing the usefulness of the Law's words about love as morally instructive Scripture, Paul returns to the key issue of God bringing his plans for world restoration to completion. Awareness of that restoration should drive believers to live morally in the present:

> *Besides this, you know what time it is, how it is now the moment for you to wake from sleep. For salvation is nearer to us now than when we became believers; the night is far gone, the day is near. Let us then lay aside the works of darkness and put on the armor of light; let us live honorably as in the day, not in reveling and drunkenness, not in debauchery and licentiousness, not in quarreling and jealousy. Instead, put on the Lord Jesus Christ, and make no provision for the flesh, to gratify its desires.* **Rom 13:11-14**

Paul sees the moment of God's global restoration drawing near. How should believers in Jesus prepare for that? By living morally. Why? Because their future in that restored world is a righteous one. Their lifestyle now must reflect what they become at the return of Jesus. Paul portrays moral generalities with the metaphoric language of night and day. Because they belong to the day, they should perform honorable daylight activities. They should "lay aside the works of darkness," immoral activities such as reveling, drunkenness, debauchery, licentiousness, quarreling and jealousy.

One of the last two items is significant for the Romans, as we're about to see. But all six items on the list show what happens when people give in to uncontrolled, unrighteous passion.[71] Quarrelling over issues in heated arguments, with raised voices and heightened emotions does not reflect a life under the control of the Lord Jesus Christ (v. 14). It, like drunken orgies or like unmarried sex, stems from a surrender to the power of sin, which dominates the realm of the flesh and hinders people from doing what is right, even when they know better. Remember the mess of Romans 7:7-25? That's never the way life in Christ is to be lived.

Instead, Paul urges his readers to "put on the Lord Jesus Christ, and make no provision for the flesh, to gratify its desires" (v. 14). What does that mean? He is restating in fresh metaphoric terms what he has already said in chapters 6 and 8.[72] He revisits the realities of their transformation. They must live what they have become through the crucified, resurrected Jesus, renouncing what they have been. Connecting with God through Jesus is the alternative to domination by those fleshly, bodily inclinations that lead to immoral deeds. It is another way of stating how they should be living by God's Spirit, in a close bond with God through Jesus. This is an ethic of relationship through and through. They are to deepen their relationship with God, not nurture any immoral, fleshly inclinations they feel drawn toward.[73]

THE PRACTICAL APPLICATION: RIGHT LIVING, NOW, AMONG A UNITED PEOPLE OF GOD

We've just seen Paul list contentious quarreling as immoral activity of "darkness." He proceeds to address an actual quarrelsome dispute among the saints in Rome (Rom 14:1). Who would be quarreling? Those who are weak in faith, with others who are not specifically identified and who are not necessarily strong, the opposite of weak.[74] What would be the source of the dispute? Paul refers to food. "Some believe in eating anything, while the weak eat only vegetables" (Rom 14:2). We've noted this situation earlier in this chapter.[75] Paul has just connected angry quarreling with a passion-dominated life, the opposite of one that is living out the effects of the cross and the resurrection (Rom 13:13-14). He is now placing their current dispute in the same category. Their quarrel is immoral. Each party to it harms the other: those abstaining are wrong to judge the eaters; those eating are wrong to despise the abstainers (Rom 14:3). Paul shows how this particular clash also reveals people out of step with what God has done in Christ.

This looks like a dispute over the applicability of the written covenantal requirements of the Torah. Those who appear to be appealing to the Law as covenantally binding are identified as the weak. Isn't that ironic. They are the ones whose behavior conforms to the Scriptures. Definite laws prohibit the eating of certain foods. "It's in the Bible," they could say. They of all people should have a right to quarrel. Isn't truth on their side? And yet Paul refers to them as weak. We could see weakness in one sense. After all, if it is merely the existence of a law that keeps someone from doing wrong, that person has a lot of growing up to do. However Paul calls such people not merely "weak" but "weak in faith." Why weak *in faith*?

Recall Paul's earlier discussion about Abraham, in Romans 4.[76] There, Abraham was portrayed favorably as one who had clung to God's promises, in spite of the difficult circumstances hindering the fulfillment of those promises. Rather than "weaken in faith," "he grew strong in his faith, . . .

being fully convinced that God was able to do what he had promised" (Rom 4:19-21). Paul would like to see the same sort of faith in his readers. What do some of his readers need convincing of? That God has established his righteousness in a new order for the world through the death and resurrection of Jesus, an order that signals restoration now in view of a restoration to come. That is what Paul has been explaining so carefully earlier in the letter. There he also clearly declared how as part of that new order they have been "discharged from the law, dead to that which held [them] captive, so that [they] are slaves not under the old written code but in the new life of the Spirit" (Rom 7:6). Those who realize that also know that there is no longer any requirement to heed commandments from the Torah as legally binding. But each must become "fully convinced" about that in his or her own mind (Rom 14:5, 15, 22-23).

To advocate living under the authority of Torah's laws or regulations, even a moral code of any kind, is to be weak in faith. In fact, it is a tacit denial of the gospel, an admission that the death and resurrection of Jesus do not make any substantive difference in the present life of a believer. Such people need to become strong, fully convinced of how life is now different because of the gospel, by which God makes people right with him. A strengthening sense of God's righteousness emerges directly from a continuing, active knowledge of God through the crucified, resurrected Jesus.

A necessary aspect of being "fully convinced" is learning what God wants, God's "good, acceptable and perfect" will (Rom 12:2). How do people do that? By fully attaching themselves to God, metaphorically presenting their body "as a living sacrifice" (Rom 12:1). Those people actively let their minds be transformed, forsaking the standards of the unconverted world around them.

What major behavioral standard emerges from such a process? Love. That, as Paul has just explained in Romans 13:8-10, is the practical fulfillment of the Torah's instructions, the outcome of living by the Spirit (Rom 8:3-4). What do food regulations have to do with love? Nothing. Believers in Jesus are free to eat whatever they want. Except—if another believer does not have the same conviction and is "injured" by what is being done, then the believer who is convinced that eating the food is okay should abstain, not because there is a law against it but to remove a stumbling block from the one being harmed.[77] Food laws, and even laws mandating celebrations such as a weekly sabbath (see Rom 14:5-6), are no longer binding issues for believers in Jesus; those laws belong to the old, now-abolished order. Yet the obligation to love remains (Rom 13:8), not as a covenantal duty but as the outgrowth of the Spirit at work within them, fulfilling the Law's just requirement (Rom 8:3-4). Love fulfills what individual commands point to (Rom 13:8, 10). So, though some believers may know they are free to eat formerly prohibited foods, they should refrain from doing what harms other believers in their midst who cannot yet claim the same freedom. The requirement to abstain from unclean foods would come from love, not from any biblical regulation. Hear the difference in ethics between Torah and Paul?

> *If your brother or sister is being injured by what you eat, you are no longer walking in love. Do not let what you eat cause the ruin of one for whom Christ died. So do not let your good be spoken of as evil. For the kingdom of God is not food and drink but righteousness and peace and joy in the Holy Spirit.* **Rom 14:15-17**

Believers in Jesus are free to do what they want on any day of the week, free even from resting on Saturday, the sabbath (Rom 14:5-6). In addressing disputed activities that appear to be morally neutral, Paul instructs that believers are free to do them, *as long as they hurt no one.* But if the activity, when practiced, actually advances harm, leading to "the ruin of one for whom Christ died," then it is immoral. This is quite close to Paul's point from Romans 13:8-10 about morally instructive commandments from Torah: if an act causes harm to another, it is wrong; it is not love. If believers focus on loving others, they will enact what the Law points to. Paul consistently advocates believers looking out for the well-being of others ahead of their own as an aspect of God's perfect will (Rom 12:2). God always wants his people to love others, never to harm or despise them. Whatever form that love may take proceeds from people staying in close connection with God through Jesus.

Paul points out that believers are accountable to God through the Lord Jesus Christ (Rom 14:7-12). Their practices about food, special days or any other disputed matter should reflect private convictions for honoring God (Rom 14:5-6). They must not be imposed on others. Judging is God's ultimate prerogative, not theirs (Rom 14:10-12). Judging another brother or sister with no authority to do so is an affront to Jesus as Lord. Their quarrels, rooted in a disregard for others' legitimate convictions, indicate that they are not as in touch with God as they think, recalling Paul's earlier points about Torah-based judging in Romans 2.[78]

People who are connected to God through Jesus must grow in knowing God. If they do eat food that others regard as unclean or do any other disputed activity that others prohibit, they must do so because they are positively convinced that God wants them to do it. Only then can they be considered strong in faith (Rom 15:1). They don't perform disputed practices because everyone else is doing them or approving of them. That would too closely resemble being "conformed to this age" (Rom 12:2). The mere eating of previously prohibited foods does not make a person strong. In fact, it may even be wrong (!)—"for whatever does not proceed from faith is sin" (Rom 14:23).[79] If that sounds strange, recall Paul's opening arguments, our previous steps 1-2.[80] When there is no faith, there is a mess (Rom 1:18-32). When there is faith, there is righteousness because of the death and resurrection of Jesus (Rom 3:21–4:25). Paul promotes obedience that comes from faith in God, based on the work of the crucified, resurrected Jesus.

What about people who persist in appealing to the Law's regulations? How should believers who act under the full conviction of God's approval respond to those people? Paul advises, "We who are strong ought to put up with the failings of the weak, and not to please ourselves" (Rom 15:1). They are to hang in there with them and help them along, instead of pursuing their own preferred way of living.[81] Why? Living merely to please oneself is not love. Instead, Paul continues, "each of us must please our neighbor for the good purpose of building up the neighbor" (Rom 15:2). Love looks out for the betterment of others, even at one's own expense.

Paul's support for that activity here rests not on a written principle but on the gospel itself, on Jesus' own willing offering of himself for the benefit of others:[82] "For Christ did not please himself; but, as it is written, 'The insults of those who insult you have fallen on me'" (Rom 15:3). Jesus' death and resurrection are transforming events. They also provide an exemplar. Jesus' death offers a pattern of loving service, even when that means suffering harm at the hands of others. One person insulting another who is doing what God wants is insulting God. Jesus bore such insults against God, not to please himself but to help others. In one sense it is the ultimate demonstration of not repaying "evil for evil" (Rom 12:17) and of overcoming "evil with good" (Rom 12:21). Paul does not make that connection directly, but it is implied by the wider context.

The strong in faith must put up with insults, if any be hurled in the food wars. They too should aim to please others, not themselves.[83] Further, Paul also implies that the complainers are failing to see God's explicit work in people's lives. They too must stop insulting God by denying his work in others. Those who care about their relationship with God should care about that.

But Paul does not see the acts of Christ as independent niceness. Rather, he sees them as being in line with what is portrayed in the Scriptures (i.e., the Old Testament). He quotes from Psalm 69:9 as a word to support the rightness of Christ's activities.[84] He considers that to be important because "whatever was written in former days was written for our instruction, so that by steadfastness and by the encouragement of the scriptures we might have hope" (Rom 15:4). The Scriptures disclose God's plans for the world (Rom 1:2; 3:21). But they also disclose God's sense of rightness.[85] That sense has been conveyed astoundingly in the events of the gospel (Rom 1:16-17; 3:21), matching how the Scriptures portray God's views of rightness and wrongness.

Paul has said already that God's love is shown supremely in Christ dying for the ungodly (Rom 5:6-8). He has also said that love fulfills the law (Rom 13:10). That is a point he has learned from reading the Law, not as a document of covenantal obligations but as informing Scripture shaping his awareness of Christ's acts.[86] Though the Law's covenantally binding force is officially over for those who belong to God through Christ (Rom 7:6), that Law should still inform believers in Jesus. The Law belongs to the Scriptures, which are meant to communicate to people about God and his ways. It is a point that Paul has made very carefully, lest believers in Jesus fall into the trap of an outdated covenantal obligation or create a new one because "the Bible says so."

As the readers live in love, they live in the fulfillment of the Torah's moral standards. They also match the pattern of Jesus, a pattern in line with the plans disclosed in the Torah and the rest of the Scriptures. When they love each other, they conform to God's final concerns for the entire world, concerns that appeal to all people, Jew and Gentile alike (Rom 15:7-13). The cross and the resurrection point to a necessary solidarity between all believers in Jesus, who, whether Jew or Gentile, look for the final act of God to right the wrongs of the world. It's why Paul wants Roman believers in Jesus to stop quarreling and to get along with each other. It's why he wants the believers from his Gentile churches to contribute to the financial needs of their Jewish fellow believers in Jerusalem, and why he wants those Jerusalem saints to accept the contribution. It's why he would like the believers in Rome to send him on his way to Spain.

SUMMING IT UP: ETHICS IN ROMANS

Though Romans does not focus on an ethical system, Paul projects an ethical vision that shows believers in Jesus acquiring a clear sense of right and wrong. Where does that sense come from?

- o responding to God by faith in the crucified, resurrected Jesus

- o experiencing the transformation produced by the cross and the resurrection

That transformation

- o places believers into close relationship with God by making them right with him

- o breaks the controlling, dominating power of sin in a believer's life, the reason people are unethical in the first place

- o brings believers into a new order, governed by the resurrected Lord Christ

- o frees them to live more and more the way God wants them to as they submit to him

- o provides God's Spirit, who enlivens believers to overcome evil bodily passions

- o advances God's righteous requirements as believers respond to God's Spirit

- o begins the restoration in believers that is completed at the coming of Jesus

- o draws believers into harmonious solidarity with the wider community of God's transformed people, where proper behavior begins to be talked about and worked out.

As we have seen throughout the Scriptures, righteous standing before God can never be earned by performing good deeds. In the gospel it comes only through the work of Christ, through his death and resurrection. Accordingly, doing good does not originate with human effort to conform to authoritative standards. It should flow now from God's work in those who have responded and continue to respond by faith to God and what he has done through the crucified, resurrected Jesus, living in dynamic interaction with him through his Spirit. Believers should offer themselves to God, renouncing the evil standards of the unconverted while renewing their minds, doing actively what God has enlivened them to do. This is an ethic of deep relationship with God; believers are to grow in that relationship, knowing God more. Doing good is both possible and necessary because believers have newness of life through the resurrection of Jesus.

So, how, concretely, do believers learn the specifics of right and wrong? Paul appeals to several overlapping informing sources: the mind, the Spirit, the Scriptures and the exemplar of Christ. In all of that, love emerges as a chief moral guide. Let's briefly consider these, one by one:

Mind. Paul, in Romans 12:2, urges the saints to be "transformed by the renewing of [their] minds" so as to discover how God wants them to live.[87] He implies that their minds are renewed when they present themselves to God in an ongoing act of faith (Rom 12:1-2), simultaneously rejecting the immoral standards prevailing in the unconverted world. That would contrast with the misuse of the mind by those who refuse to acknowledge God (Rom 1:20-25).[88] It would coordinate with Paul's desire for his readers to apply the release from the power of sin brought about through the crucifixion of Jesus and the newness of life advanced through his resurrection. Paul's readers should "consider [themselves] dead to sin and alive to God in Christ Jesus" (Rom 6:11), similar to how God will consider them to be righteous (Rom 4:23-25). That act of the mind calls for continued awareness that life in Christ encompasses totally different standards and influences. All throughout Romans Paul encourages his readers to engage their minds. Note the frequency of words such as *consider* or *reasonable* (Rom 2:3; 4:19; 6:11; 8:18; 12:1; 14:14), or *mind, understanding, think* (Rom 1:21, 28; 2:21; 7:23; 8:6-7; 11:20; 12:2-3; 12:16; 14:5; 15:14).

How people think affects how they relate to God. Believers must learn to think properly about God's work in Christ and its effects on their lives. The life of the mind in Christ merges with the life of the Spirit, on whom Paul urges his readers to set their minds (Rom 8:5-6).[89] That's the opposite of setting the mind on the flesh, aiming to satisfy immoral bodily inclinations.

Spirit. Believers receive life by God's Spirit (Rom 8:5, 12-14), given to all who belong to Christ (Rom 8:9). As they respond to God's Spirit, they experience that life. The way of the Spirit is opposite to the way of the flesh, dominated by immoral bodily inclinations. Believers' new lives require them to live by the Spirit, whose ways fulfill Torah's just requirement (Rom 8:3-5). They should respond to God's Spirit, through whom they can overcome evil bodily passions (Rom 8:13), who bears "witness with [their] spirit that [they] are children of God" (Rom 8:16). Paul speaks of this naturally, not mystically, implying that believers gain a sense of moral rightness by responding to God's Spirit. The result is God's law written on their hearts (implied by Rom 2:14-15, 29), with love being the Spirit's practical outworking.[90] The Spirit solidifies the ethic of relationship.

Scripture. Throughout Romans, Paul has been depending on the Scriptures commonly known now as the Old Testament. Learning from the Scriptures matters. Many of Paul's thoughts in this letter rely on them. Though technically much of what he quotes could be said to come from the Law (i.e., the Torah), Paul mostly identifies those as words of informing Scripture to help him explain God's plans, not as words of law.[91]

Paul scarcely quotes commandments. When he quotes one in Romans 7:7, he points out its weakness as regulation, not its value in advancing any behavioral standard. He quotes four commandments in Romans 13:8-10 as worthwhile, instructively. But he minimizes that by showing how Torah's instruction to love (Lev 19:18) yields the same results as those commandments. That point connects with his earlier comment that those who live by the Spirit fulfill the Law's "just requirement" (Rom 8:4). The role of Scripture is to instruct, not regulate, as shown in his moral use of quotations from Deuteronomy 32:35 and Proverbs 25:21-22 (see Rom 12:19-20).

Scripture plays a foundational role in presenting God's plans and purposes. It also teaches what God likes and dislikes. "Whatever was written in former days was written for our instruction, so that by steadfastness and by the encouragement of the scriptures we might have hope" (Rom 15:4). Paul does not treat the Scriptures as a regulating source. Instead he shows he learns from them. Surely Scripture plays a role in shaping the mind away from the standards of the world to God's point of view (Rom 4:23-24). As an apostle commissioned by Christ (Rom 1:5), he also offers his own authoritative moral advice (Rom 12:9-21), some of which comes from Scripture and some of which resembles words from Jesus. He expects all that advice to be treated in the same way as Scripture.

Exemplar. This does not become explicit until Romans 15, when Paul concludes his discussion of the quarrels over food. He has learned of love from the Scriptures. He has also seen love in action through Christ who, instead of pleasing himself, bore insults against God in his death. He reinforces that exemplar by quoting the Scriptures. When believers in Rome live to help others instead of themselves, they will not only be ethical. They will reflect their relationship with the one who has given them newness of life in his own death and resurrection. They will also advance harmony within their community. Just as Christ's death for the weak (Rom 5:6) reconciles God to people (Rom 5:1-11), so following the exemplar of Christ's putting up with insults will advance harmony and reconciliation within the Roman believing community.

Conclusions. The ethic of relationship here depends entirely on God's interventions in people's lives through the crucified, resurrected Christ and through his Spirit. It is not based on any moral code. As people respond to God's interventions, they enter into a lively relationship with him, receiving the life and empowerment to live as God has remade them to live. God will intervene again to remake the world at the completion of salvation. In the meantime life for believers is to be characterized by God-empowered love, which seeks others' well-being ahead of their own.

People do not deserve those interventions. They can never be good enough to earn them or strong enough to live successfully by their own effort. God provides that life in his kindness and grace (see Rom 3:24; 5:20). People must respond to that grace in faith. God is restoring order to the world through Jesus, in line with his promise to Abraham. He restores order to the lives of those who continue to respond to him through the crucified, resurrected Jesus. That is good news.

SUMMING IT UP: PAUL'S ETHICAL VISION

We have seen in both Romans and 1 Corinthians a common starting point: the gospel or "good news" about Jesus, the Christ, who was crucified, raised from the dead and who is coming again to bring about final salvation. In both letters those gospel events lead to the following:

o People must respond to God, based on this Jesus. That response is called faith. It is how they enter into relationship with God.

o People must continue to respond to God, based on this Jesus. That also is faith. It is how they are to continue in relationship with God, knowing him.

o The cross and the resurrection of Jesus are transforming events through which God changes and continues to change people who respond to him in faith.

o People of faith are changed people who are always letting God change them. God is the one who makes them ethical as they respond to him.

o Jesus is Lord over the lives of people with faith in God. He must reign over them in the new life he gives through his resurrection. The ongoing change in the lives of people of faith is a process stemming from responding to God, who has made them new in Christ.

o That change process is captured by the expression "You are . . . therefore be." People of faith must align themselves with the change God has worked in them. In 1 Corinthians we saw "be pure, as you already are pure through Christ" (1 Cor 5:7, my paraphrase); in Romans we saw "you are dead to sin and alive to God in Christ, therefore live as dead to sin and alive to God in Christ" (Rom 6:11-12, my paraphrase).

o That change reflects both an *already* and a *not yet*. Believers are to be what God has made them already in Christ; they are also to be what they have not yet become but what God will eventually make them to be. That is *salvation*, Paul's counterpart to *kingdom* in the Gospels, which is already, but not yet.

o The Holy Spirit is God's agent of change. People of faith live by the Spirit, who gives them the life they need to live as God wants them to live. The ethical life is thoroughly dependent on people of faith continuing to respond in faith to God's work in their lives through Christ and his Spirit. They continue to know God through his Spirit in them.

o The Holy Spirit guides the thought life of people of faith. There is a close connection between the world of the mind and the world of the Spirit. People of faith must allow God's Spirit to probe them deeply to root out thought patterns reflecting the ungodliness of the unconverted, replacing them with new patterns reflecting God's ways to live.

o That is important, in part, because the ethical world of Christ is a world of freedom. Believers in God through Jesus are free to live as God would have them to live, not *contractually* bound by any moral code, including the laws of the Torah.

o Love is one key moral concept by which people of faith are to live. It often involves suspending their own rights and freedoms for the well-being of others. It builds others up, instead of harming them. It flows naturally from the work of the Spirit in the lives of people of faith. People made new in Christ, responsive to God's Spirit, are to ask a question like the following to help them know right from wrong: To what extent will this act build others up, and to what extent will it harm them? Love itself is an obligatory act, not a virtue. It is a micro-ethical concern, affecting interpersonal behavior.

o Love is practiced principally in communities of people of faith. Those communities are to support one another in their pursuit of God, which includes growing in ethical awareness.

o Love is advocated by the Scriptures, Paul's word for the Old Testament. One who practices love fulfills what the Law communicates morally. People of faith continue to learn specifics of that love from the Scriptures.

o Love is also typified in the exemplar or pattern of Jesus, whose own suspension of rights in his death serves as a model for how people of faith are to live.[92]

Does this capture every aspect of ethics found in Paul's letters? No. But those who absorb these points are well on their way to grasping the uniqueness of how the cross and the resurrection thoroughly change the lives of those who believe in God. Paul's spectacular contribution to ethics is to show how God now works directly in the lives of those who respond to him through Jesus. This is antimoralistic. People do not become ethical on their own by conforming to an imposed standard. They are transformed people, made right with God through the death and resurrection of Jesus. They live not by willpower but by the power of the cross and the resurrection. They think. They let the Spirit work in them, also learning from the Scriptures and other legitimate sources, including the exemplar of Jesus. They present themselves to God actively, so that God, through his Spirit, can enable them to live rightly, overcoming their strong desires to do wrong. Further, when they fail, and they will, they have ongoing acceptance from God, based on Jesus, crucified for their sins, raised to give them life and righteous standing with God, coming again to change them forever.

Reflection Questions

1. What is the gospel, and how does it inform moral living?

2. How does attention to the gospel help someone avoid performing the advice of Romans 12:9-21 moralistically (i.e., merely following a list of do's and don't's or doing it just because it says so)?

3. How does people presenting themselves to God lead to moral living?

4. How does Paul's discussion of sin-dominated flesh help to explain moral issues such as arguments, angry outbursts, addictions, unmarried sexual behavior or any other improper bodily inclinations you can think of?

5. What can transformed living look like in the home, at work, in neighborhoods, in church, in any other association or interpersonal interaction?

FOR FURTHER READING

Burridge, Richard A. *Imitating Jesus: An Inclusive Approach to New Testament Ethics*, pp. 81-154. Grand Rapids: Eerdmans, 2007.

Hays, Richard B. *The Moral Vision of the New Testament: A Contemporary Introduction to New Testament Ethics*, pp. 16-59. San Francisco: HarperCollins, 1996.

Keener, Craig S. *Romans.* Eugene, OR: Cascade Books, 2009.

Sampley, J. Paul. *Walking Between the Times: Paul's Moral Reasoning.* Minneapolis: Fortress Press, 1991.

CONCLUDING THOUGHTS

What Can We Do with All of This?

Some people have surprised me with their responses to this book project. They have asked, "Are you dealing with . . . ?" naming the questioner's favorite moral topic. I reply, "No, I am not dealing with topics. That's the whole point of the book. Instead of focusing on *what* the Bible says about topics, I want people to consider *how* various parts of the Bible encourage its readers to *think*, which they can apply to any topic." I then explain further how a focus on topics encourages moralism, which is really soft legalism. People so often prefer approaching the Bible as a unitary document to be scanned for rulings of faith and practice, an incomplete activity that obscures the Bible's various, mutually enhancing ethical visions.

"Yes," a follow-on response would often begin, "but I think having direct words to guide me about what is right in a specific situation is really useful." I agree. As a regular Bible reader I frequently come across statements with moral implications springing from the pages, hitting me between the eyes. Often statements I have read days earlier break into my life at just the right moment. Sometimes they bring me up short, and other times they encourage me in something that I was already doing. The words of the Bible can do that. And they should.

So how do we derive special relevance from our explorations here? Let's distinguish between how to use the Bible in life, how to use the Bible in ethics and how to observe the ways that various biblical writings encourage us to think ethically. This book has been about the last of those three. It has focused on learning to discern the unique, big-picture ethical vision that different parts of Scripture contribute to a multifaceted, mutually reinforcing, overall vision. That is an approach that appears to have been eclipsed by the first two uses of the Bible just mentioned.

Consider, for example, Scripture's prophetic function in the lives of people of faith, which is often the preferred, popular method for using the Bible in life. It stems from people's appropriate understanding of the Bible as the Word of God. We explored the prophetic world briefly in chapter six. People with a high respect for the Bible as Scripture let its words get to them. That's good. That often leads some to do extraordinary acts, many of which are quite moral. But if in answer to the question, Why are you doing that? the *only* response is, Because God said so in his Word, then the person may be unaware of the ethical vision the biblical writing projects. Occasionally such a person may even unwittingly and unfortunately inflict harm in the name of God by acting on a statement without understanding it, or its literary and cultural settings. In extreme examples, some have tried to justify slavery, prejudice or the mistreatment of women from their poor readings of the Bible.

Throughout this book we have seen that Scripture does more than snap people to prophetic attention. Scripture often encourages its readers to think broadly and deeply about its words. (Though not considered in this book, see Psalm 1:2.) This book has been about listening to the voices of thoughtful reason embedded in Scripture and discerning the ways of life that they project. When we hear them and catch their vision, we find an inseparably close connection between what they encourage readers to do and to be, and whom they encourage readers to know deeply. Biblical writings link good behavior to God, who has made the world, who is remaking the world and with whom people are to grow in close relationship. Relationship with God is to lead to microethical activity, directed toward people in a person's immediate vicinity.

Torah expresses that through the covenant between God and Israel. That covenant reflects God's mercy, holiness and love, also expecting Israel to show mercy to others, to reflect God's holiness, and to love God loyally, just as God loves them. That covenant is to lead to the promised blessing of the world through the descendants of Abraham.

Proverbs urges people to "fear," or highly respect, God, the maker of a good, ordered creation with consequences for upholding creation's design, for defying it or for manipulating it maliciously. Those who know, and thus respect, Israel's God know that he has established the world through wisdom, in an ordered manner that makes sense because it reflects how God overcomes the disorder within the world. They come to expect the world to work a certain way because of their high regard for God who has reliably made it that way.

The Gospels present Jesus the Christ, the one who establishes God's restorative kingdom and through whom people are now to connect with and thus to know God. In Luke Jesus reflects God's greatness, a greatness apparent only to those willing to recognize their place before Jesus. In Matthew, Jesus is the presence of God, and a promised ongoing presence to help disciples with the task of living rightly as they advance God's kingdom in their world.

Paul goes even further. He explains how God, through the death and resurrection of Jesus and through his Spirit, transforms people into those who by thus knowing him advance good, not harm, in their world. That behavior reflects the final changes to come at the return of Jesus. People in touch with God through Jesus have God at work in them. They are brought into close relationship with God through Jesus as their Lord. The more they come to know God the more readily they respond to God's work within them through his Spirit.

Covenant, consequences, kingdom, transformation—we have explored four distinct ethical visions, each of which deals closely with people learning good from knowing God. Readers who ignore these biblical approaches (and other approaches not explored in this book) hazard the trap of treating Scripture as a moral constitution to be scanned for rulings. That may sometimes even lead them to advocate inappropriate standards and practices, or to force statements to address topics to which they really cannot apply.

Discovering obvious, pertinent statements from the Bible, if any can be found, might not be a bad place to start. However, it would be a bad place to finish. Again, instead of focusing on *what is said* about a topic, we should consider *how* Scripture encourages us *to think* about it, also considering how a growing relationship with God shapes the way people should live.

Torah's laws encourage people to think about how a given activity upholds God's created order, how it extends God's mercy, how it reflects God's holiness, how it extends God's blessing. Instructive laws within the Torah not only point to potential areas of moral activity, but also they sustain those senses of created order, mercy, holiness and blessing. In thinking how Torah can help evaluate the morality of an activity, consider questions such as the following:

- How do Torah's laws encourage people to think about a certain activity? What aspects of God's covenantal activity in Torah do relevant laws express?

- How does the activity support or damage the creation order?

- How does the activity foster extending mercy to the weak?

- How does a sense of God's holiness affect how people should think about the activity?

- How does engaging in an activity extend God's blessing to others?

The individual wise instructions of Proverbs encourage people to think about the God-designed consequences of their actions, to consider the wider implications of what they are engaged in and to learn from those who have succeeded in God's wise ways. An individual proverb may have direct relevance to a particular moral issue with which a reader may be concerned. But equally profound is Proverbs's sense of how to discern right from wrong based on wise observations of the created order in action. These observations, in turn, are also to be affirmed by others with recognized godly wisdom. Activity with helpful, people-affirming consequences is probably good activity; activity with harmful, denigrating consequences is probably bad. God's wise design assures the consistency of that way of reasoning. In thinking how Proverbs can help evaluate the morality of an activity, consider questions such as the following:

- What wise advice does Proverbs offer about an activity in question? How does that advice reflect Proverbs's concerns with God designed consequences?

- What good consequences can wise people observe from others entering into this activity?

- What bad, harmful consequences can wise people observe from others entering into this activity?

Jesus' words and deeds of the kingdom in the Gospel according to Luke advocate thinking about and thus treating others with a full regard for their humanity, reversing people's tendency to put others beneath them. When people recognize what they really are before Jesus—lowly, unworthy of his acceptance—they are in prime position to see the worthwhileness of others; they refuse to depersonalize anyone. Acts are deemed ethical based on whether they affirm or denigrate another's humanness. In Matthew, Jesus encourages people to consider and then engage in acts of mercy and restoration that reflect God's kingdom that is to come. Jesus also teaches perfection, offering a measuring stick against which people can evaluate their own behavior. People who learn from Jesus' words and deeds in Matthew know that they need his mercy. Further, as they receive mercy, they can also advance merciful love in their world by determining to be involved with what heals and restores others to wholeness, rather than with what breaks them. That would be true even if others try to break them in response. In thinking how the Gospels can help evaluate the morality of an activity, consider questions such as the following:

- What specific words or deeds from Jesus, if any, appear to address the activity in question? What aspects of God's kingdom do those words reflect?

- How does this activity advance the humanness of the person or people involved? Does it put others down and leave them as damaged goods, or does it elevate them?

- How does this activity foster kingdom wholeness? Does it heal and restore, or does it break?

Paul shows how God, through the powerful events of the cross and the resurrection, as well as through his Spirit, changes people to become more and more the way they will be at the return of Jesus. Because they will be totally changed at the return of Jesus, they should live now what they are to become, with Jesus as Lord of their lives. Part of that change involves God directly fostering a sense of right and wrong through his Spirit at work in the minds of believers. Through his Spirit God also empowers people to overcome their bodily trained tendencies to live immorally. Love, a regard for others' well-being that transcends one's own, reflects what Torah and the rest of Scripture point to. It is displayed in the exemplar of Jesus. Love emerges from God's work in believers through Christ. Love becomes a key moral activity in which believers should strive to be involved, displaying the change that God brings about within them. In thinking how Paul's letters can help evaluate the morality of an activity, consider questions such as the following:

- What instructions, if any, pertain to the activity? How do those instructions fit with God's transformation of believers brought about through the death and resurrection of Jesus?

- How can transformed people function effectively in that activity, with Jesus as their Lord?

- How does entering into the activity reflect the final transformation to take place at the coming of their Lord, Jesus?

- How does God's Spirit foster proper behavior for that activity?

- How should people's love for others direct their thoughts and acts as they consider involvement in the activity?

Each of those approaches encourages a host of possible good, uplifting behaviors. Further, each offers basic reasoning patterns that help people begin to sort out various ethical dilemmas they may be facing. Those who want to learn ethical living from the Bible would do well to let each of the Bible's multiple approaches shape how they think. The approaches may also uncover a host of wrongs and hurts that need to be processed, both for the benefit of the one doing wrongly and for the one receiving the wrong. The manner in which those hurts and wrongs are addressed may make one approach to ethics more immediately and emotionally pertinent than the others, which can be good to recognize. For example, people who might bristle at being labeled as fools for their behavior may be more responsive to an approach that accepts their humanness, in spite of their folly. Or people who are reluctant to admit potential failings before God may be more receptive to an approach that shows how harmful consequences are regularly associated with the activity they are engaged in.

Before closing, let's consider one final point. None of this is meant to be figured out by lone individuals. The rightness and wrongness of some activities are obvious—extramarital sex being one of the more prominent examples that we have observed repeatedly. Often real-life dilemmas involve varying factors, both good and bad, that are best processed in the company of others who care about being deeply in touch both with God and with core ethical messages from Scripture. People who want to do what is right need to learn to listen to the perspectives of others, a point emphasized by many Christian ethicists.

Each of the four approaches to ethics has encouraged this. Torah is given to a nation, not to individuals. It is to be lived out in the home and community where people look out for one another, having been blessed by God. Proverbs declares that people can only become wise from a multitude of wise counselors, people who have processed life successfully, with respect for God. Jesus in the Gospels addresses disciples who are to encourage one another in communities, where he also promises always to be present. Paul addresses transformed people who have the mind of Christ gathering in church communities inhabited by God's Spirit. Right living isn't meant to be figured out alone.

We need a sharpening perception of the Bible's ethical vision. We foster that sharpening by discussing biblical perspectives with others who respect those perspectives, which also encourages us to live them out. These discussions can teach us where we might be right or wrong, especially when we also include alternative voices in our discussions rather than just the ones we think will agree with us. They give us fresh insight into how God can be at work. And instead of treating ethical issues in the hypothetical and the abstract, we learn from others' lives about the actual benefits of right and the actual harms of wrong. That awareness helps us avoid spouting insensitive moral rulings that harmfully alienate others rather than help them. It encourages us to be ethical in the ways we stand for what is right and against what is wrong.

SUMMING IT *ALL* UP:
PARTING ADVICE

Consider this parting advice:

o Begin with moral statements from the Bible whenever they can be found. Often there will be none.

o Deal with any statements both in their literary and cultural contexts, discerning what might apply from what really cannot.

o Let the core points of each biblical-ethical approach shape your thinking about the issue, fitting relevant statements, if any, within the approach where they are found.

o Be comfortable with letting one particular approach emerge as more helpful than the others for clarifying action with some issues in some circumstances.

o Remember that the Bible's ethics are more concerned with microethical relationship than with macroethical policy.

o Use this book as a springboard to begin discussions with other people of faith, and grow from there.

o Don't ever separate God from the ideas you discuss.

o Let discussions about the Bible's ethics deepen your faith and others' faith in God, whom you should be understanding more and more from what you read in the Bible.

o Learn good from knowing God and do it, encouraging others to do the same.

The Bible's multi-image ethical vision fosters a world of wholeness necessary for the thriving of humanity. It invites people to enter into close relationship with the true and living God, acquiring from that relationship an increasing concern with advancing good and hindering harm in their world. As people grow in their relationship with God, they find their lives becoming more whole. They live more the way God designed them to live in the first place. They also live more the way God will redesign them to live in the world to come. Learning good comes from knowing God precisely because that is part of God's plan for people. People are supposed to be good. The Bible's ethical vision shows us how.

Notes

Chapter 1

[1]Richard Hays makes this the first of four important steps in using the Bible in ethics. The second, he explains, puts texts together for achieving some sense of coherence on a subject. The third develops an application framework. Fourth, that framework is applied in a coherent fashion to contemporaneous issues. In this book we will probe the writings a bit more to determine their ethical thought patterns, which will allow for the presentation of various systems that can be seen as mutually reinforcing and, from there, potentially applicable. This will appear more like Hays's first step, while moving into his second step in each segment of literature, with the hermeneutical (step 3) assumption that the voices being considered should be listened to seriously. Step four is left to the responsibility of ethically interested communities who have explored the descriptive frameworks explored here. Richard Hays, *Moral Vision of the New Testament: Community, Cross, New Creation. A Contemporary Introduction to New Testament Ethics* (New York: HarperCollins, 1996), pp. 3-7.

[2]Reflected in this paragraph is the multiplicity of issues surrounding scholarly discussion of the Bible and ethics. For a useful survey of these, see Brian Brock, *Singing the Ethos of God: On the Place of Christian Ethics in Scripture* (Grand Rapids: Eerdmans, 2007). In his first five chapters (pp. 3-95) he explores basic scholarly approaches found in contemporaneous uses of the Bible in ethics: (1) "Reading Self-Consciously: The Hermeneutical Solution," which focuses on how biblical texts have been used unethically to suppress others as the path to learning correct behavior; (2) "Reading Together: The Communitarian Solution," which aims to read texts in the contexts of a diverse community, listening to multiple perspectives before concluding what to learn ethically from texts; (3) "Focusing Reading: The Biblical Ethics Solution," which considers the issues of critical methodology from the first chapter, but aims to discern the basic contours of the Bible's modes of thinking through good reading methodology; (4) "Reading Doctrinally: The Biblical Theology Solution," which, along with (5) "Reading as Meditation: The Exegetical Theology Solution" grows out of the theological and exegetical work of Karl Barth. The approach taken here in this book is closest to Brock's third ap-

proach. Rather than suggesting detailed methods for applying biblical modes of
thought, this book leaves that up to the community of its readers, whether that be
an academic classroom, a church group or some other identifiable set of readers
willing to listen to Scripture and come under its discipline, in sympathy with the
second of the approaches Brock discusses. The approach here is taken with full
awareness of the cultural differences between the worlds of biblical texts and contemporaneous cultures, but with the belief that biblical texts do in fact communicate ideas that transcend those cultures. That would be in contradistinction from
the conclusions of those such as Eckart Otto, *Theologische Ethik des Alten Testaments* (Stuttgart: Verlag W. Kohlhammer, 1994), who thinks that the cultural differences are not spannable. It also differs from the approaches of John Rogerson,
Theory and Practice in Old Testament Ethics, ed. M. Daniel Carroll R. (London:
T & T Clark, 2004), pp. 60-87; and David G. Horrell, *Solidarity and Difference: A
Contemporary Reading of Paul's Ethics* (London: T & T Clark, 2005), who attempt
to bridge such cultural gaps by recognizing in biblical texts universal issues that
resonate with the "discourse ethics" proposed in the work of Jürgen Habermas.
Horrell also sees elements of a more communitarian dimension in Paul that res-
onate with contemporary dialogue.

[3]That is the conclusion of many, though not all, commentators on Genesis. See for
example the explanation of God as "sovereign" Creator in Gordon J. Wenham,
Genesis 1–15 (Waco: Word, 1987), pp. 10, 36-38. For a more accessible association
of God as Creator with kingship, see Walter Brueggemann, *Reverberations of Faith*
(Louisville: Westminster John Knox, 2002), pp. 116-18. For a more detailed development of this idea, see J. Richard Middleton, *The Liberating Image* (Grand Rapids:
Brazos, 2005), pp. 65-70.

[4]This scenario does fit well as evidence of a kind of teleological thinking pervasive
in the world of the Bible. See Matthew Levering, *Biblical Natural Law: A Theocentric
and Teleological Approach* (Oxford: Oxford University Press, 2008), pp. 58-60.

[5]A similar set of thoughts is developed much more extensively in Terence E.
Fretheim: "Israel's God is a relational God who has created a world in which inter-
relatedness is basic to the nature of reality; this God establishes relationships of
varying sorts with all creatures, including a special relationship to the people of
Israel." *God and World in the Old Testament: A Relational Theology of Creation*
(Nashville: Abingdon Press, 2005), p. 16.

[6]This would be a common distinction found in many basic textbooks on ethics. For
the same distinction being made for biblical scholars, consider Wayne Meeks, *The
Origins of Christian Morality* (New Haven, CT: Yale University Press, 1993), pp. 4-5.
For a more nuanced discussion, consider Horrell, *Solidarity and Difference*, pp.
95-97. Horrell tends to blur the distinction between ethics and morality being
maintained in this book.

[7]Easy-to-understand summaries of each of these systems can be found in accessible form in Stephen Wilkens, *Beyond Bumper Sticker Ethics* (Downers Grove, IL: InterVarsity Press, 1995). For virtue ethics, see pp. 115-32; for ethical egoism, see pp. 45-62; for utilitarianism, see pp. 83-98; for duty ethics, see pp. 99-114; for divine command theory, see pp. 169-86.

[8]For the elementary reader, virtue and character can be hard to distinguish. For those interested in the particular nuances, consider the discussion by William P. Brown in the preface to the collection of essays he edited in *Character and Scripture* (Grand Rapids: Eerdmans, 2002), pp. xi-xiii, esp. p. xii.

[9]See Levering, *Biblical Natural Law*, pp. 58-60.

[10]Virtue ethics principles are applied to the analysis of sections of Jesus' teachings, mostly as found in passages in Matthew and Luke, in Daniel J. Harrington and James F. Keenan, *Jesus and Virtue Ethics. Building Bridges Between New Testament Studies and Moral Theology* (Lanham, MD: Rowman & Littlefield, 2002). Their interest is more in seeing how those teachings can conform to the principles of a virtue ethic than to show that the New Testament itself advocates a virtue ethic.

[11]Among the more recent foundational works, consider William P. Brown, ed., *Character and Scripture* (Grand Rapids: Eerdmans, 2002); M. Daniel Carroll R. and Jacqueline E. Lapsley, eds., *Character Ethics and the Old Testament* (Louisville: Westminster John Knox, 2007); and Robert L. Brawley, ed., *Character Ethics and the New Testament* (Louisville: Westminster John Knox, 2007).

[12]For a simple, fuller treatment of philosophical difficulties with "It's right because God says so," and of divine command theory in general, see Wilkens, *Beyond Bumper Sticker Ethics*, pp. 179-86.

[13]Many Christians use the word *Pentateuch* instead. Torah refers to the first five writings in the Bible: Genesis, Exodus, Leviticus, Numbers and Deuteronomy.

[14]Note, for example, the discussions regarding Old Testament ethics in John Barton, *Understanding Old Testament Ethics* (Louisville: Westminster John Knox, 2003), pp. 2-7, 77-127, 163; and Gordon Wenham, *Story as Torah* (Edinburgh: T & T Clark, 2000), pp. 2-4. Note the wide array of biblical passages dealt with in Brown, *Character and Scripture*; and Carroll R. and Lapsley, *Character Ethics and the Old Testament*. Brawley also demonstrates how ethical issues are present throughout Scripture in *Character Ethics and the New Testament*. So also would the more comprehensive paradigmatic treatments of the Old Testament by Waldemar Janzen, *Old Testament Ethics: A Paradigmatic Approach* (Louisville: Westminster John Knox, 1994); and Christopher J. H. Wright, *Old Testament Ethics for the People of God* (Downers Grove, IL: InterVarsity Press, 2004); and the extensive explorations of the New Testament by Hays, *Moral Vision of the New Testament*; Frank Matera, *New Testament Ethics: The Legacies of Jesus and Paul* (Louisville: Westminster John Knox, 1996); and Ben Witherington III, *The Indelible Image: The*

Theological and Ethical Thought World of the New Testament (Downers Grove, IL: InterVarsity Press, 2009).

[15]See Jonathan P. Burnside, *God, Justice and Society: Aspects of Law and Legality in the Bible* (New York: Oxford University Press, 2011), pp. xxxii-xxxv. Burnside's point applies principally to the writings of the Hebrew Bible; in the end, law code, narrative, hymnic, wisdom and prophetic writings all work together to bring more instructive clarity to issues. But that pattern would carry forward then to the New Testament writings, which regard the writings of the Hebrew Bible together as informative Scripture. So, though Paul does not draw on Gospels, both Paul and the Gospels do draw on the same Scriptures.

[16]Those may be questions too heavily oriented to Western cultures. A conversation with an acquaintance working in East Central Africa disclosed an illuminating set of different microethical questions: "Should I beat my wife to show I'm in charge?" "Should I poison my husband?" "Should I take responsibility for myself when it's someone else's job?"

[17]My categories "fatherless" or "unprotected" children are an interpretation of the biblical word for *orphan*. Most people in the world today, especially Westerners, tend to define *orphan* as a child without parents. The cultures reflected in biblical writings envision, instead, children without fathers. Since those cultures are so strongly patriarchal, with men in charge, both husbandless women and fatherless children are totally unprotected, with no immediate familial support systems.

Chapter 2

[1]Gordon Wenham's insights in his *Story as Torah* (Edinburgh: T & T Clark, 2000) are especially helpful here.

[2]Johanna W. H. van Wijk-Bos helpfully explains the difference between Torah, the first five writings of the Bible, all of which instruct, and the individual *tôrâ*, or law, that also instructs. *Making Wise the Simple: The Torah in Christian Faith and Practice* (Grand Rapids: Eerdmans, 2005), p. 3. Her sensitivity to the abuse of Jewish people based on the stereotype of Judaism as a legalistic, law-based religion will also inform this book. However, I will not be as reluctant to talk about legal matters as legal matters when appropriate, since very clearly there are laws in the Torah that bear strong resemblance to legal material also found outside of ancient Israel. Note the comments of James W. Watts: "Rhetorical analysis of the Pentateuch suggests, however, that its description as Torah retains 'law' as its primary, though not exclusive, meaning." *Reading Law: Rhetorical Shaping of the Pentateuch* (Sheffield, UK: Sheffield Academic Press, 1991), p. 154.

[3]Wijk-Bos observes, "The telling of the origins of God's covenant people Israel is thus set into the large framework of God's concern for the whole world." *Making Wise the Simple*, p. 37.

⁴The common recognition of this pattern of the days of creation is simply portrayed in J. Richard Middleton, *The Liberating Image: The* Imago Dei *in Genesis 1* (Grand Rapids: Brazos Press, 2005), pp. 74-77.

⁵The most obvious example here is the Babylonian creation story known as the *Enuma Elish*. Also consider the Utnapishtim story in the *Gilgamesh* epic and the stories of *Atrahasis*, of *Adapa*, of *Aqhat*, of *Kirta*, and of *Baal and Anat*. Excerpts of these stories are found in Victor H. Matthews and Don C. Benjamin, *Old Testament Parallels: Laws and Stories from the Ancient Near East*, 3rd ed. (New York: Paulist, 2006). Consider also the descriptions found in Helmer Ringgren, *Religions of the Ancient Near East*, trans. John Sturdy (London: SPCK, 1973).

⁶The notion of the stories of Genesis 1–11 taking on the pagan gods of Israel's surrounding nations is well established in major commentaries. For a useful summary of those ideas, see Gordon Wenham, *Genesis 1-15* (Waco: Word, 1987), pp. xlviii-l.

⁷For a clear, detailed development of these points, again consult Middleton, *Liberating Image*, pp. 43-90, 108-22.

⁸Wenham, *Story as Torah*, pp. 20-21.

⁹Commentators differ on how this story is to be connected to that of Gen 1:1–2:3. Walter Brueggemann sees the account following Gen 2:4 as one that offers further, intense reflection on humanity in relation to creation. *Genesis* (Atlanta: John Knox Press, 1982), p. 40. Umberto Cassuto sees Gen 2 as a further elaboration of what happened on day six of Gen 1. *A Commentary on the Book of Genesis* (Jerusalem: Magnes Press, 1961), pt. 1, pp. 90- 96. Terence E. Fretheim sees the story dealing with multiple details from Gen 1, even though he postulates separate origins for each account. "The Book of Genesis," in *The New Interpreters Bible* (Nashville: Abingdon Press, 1994), 1:349. Wenham sees Gen 1:1–2:3 as the "overture to the rest of the story" introducing Genesis, but not to be interpreted entirely with the same criteria as the stories that follow. *Genesis 1-15*, p. 40.

¹⁰Phyllis Trible notes that while the man, plants and animals all come from the dust, the woman comes from the same substance as the man, his rib. *God and the Rhetoric of Sexuality* (Philadelphia: Fortress Press, 1978), pp. 94-98. Those observations are taken even further by Christiana De Groot, "Genesis," *The IVP Women's Bible Commentary*, ed. Catherine Clark Kroeger and Mary J. Evans (Downers Grove, IL: InterVarsity Press, 2002), pp. 5-6.

¹¹Walter Brueggemann, "Of the Same Flesh and Bone," *Catholic Biblical Quarterly* 32 (1970): 532-42.

¹²See Fretheim, "Book of Genesis," p. 354.

¹³"Human dominion over the rest of creation is to be an exercise of kingship that reflects God's own kingship. The image of God is not a license for abuse based on arrogant supremacy, but a pattern that commits us to humble reflection of the character of God." Christopher J. H. Wright, *Old Testament Ethics for the People of God* (Downers Grove, IL: InterVarsity Press, 2004), p. 121.

[14]So Wenham, *Genesis 1–15*, p. 71.

[15]Mary Douglas suggests strong connections even between moral aspects of "holiness" as advanced by Leviticus and the creation order of Genesis. *Purity and Danger: An Analysis of Concept of Pollution and Taboo* (London: Routledge, 2002), p. 67.

[16]See Fretheim, "Book of Genesis," pp. 363-64.

[17]More than one commentator has noted the increase in bad human behavior that Genesis chooses to focus on in these early chapters. See Wenham, *Genesis*, p. li; and Fretheim, "Book of Genesis," p. 372.

[18]Cornelius Houtman links this passage with one he regards as more profound, Gen 18:25, a passage to be considered later. "Theodicy in the Pentateuch," in *Theodicy in the World of the Bible*, ed. Antti Laato and Johannes C. de Moor (Leiden: Brill, 2003), pp. 151-53.

[19]Fretheim notes the implications of this that go counter to the mandates of Gen 1:28 and Gen 9:1 to fill the earth. "Book of Genesis," p. 412. Wenham also notes how making a name for themselves reflects basic impiety toward God. *Genesis 1–15*, pp. 239-40.

[20]The observations of Wenham are helpful here. See his *Genesis 1–15*, p. 258.

[21]Technically, the Abraham stories begin with his genealogy in Gen 11:10-32, or more precisely Gen 11:27-32, and end with his death in Gen 25:8 and following genealogy. However, Gen 12:1-3 and Gen 22:16-18 form a purposeful promise bracket around the individual stories appearing between them, as recognized by most commentators. See Paul Williamson, *Abraham, Israel and the Nations: The Patriarchal Promise and Its Covenantal Development in Genesis* (Sheffield, UK: Sheffield Academic Press, 2000), pp. 217-59.

[22]See Wenham, *Genesis 1–15*, pp. 268-69, 274-78, 282.

[23]See Wenham, *Story as Torah*, pp. 20-22, for the prevalence of that terminology for all of Genesis.

[24]Gerhard von Rad comments about the programmatic nature of these promises, which he says "reaches out toward the goal of God's plan for history." *Genesis*, trans. John H. Marks (London: SCM Press, 1972), pp. 160-61. Though some later commentators are reluctant to see such far-reaching import, similar significance is recognized by others, such as Wenham, *Story as Torah*, p. 37; and Fretheim, "Book of Genesis," p. 425. In a more accessible way, the point is extended to the world of narrative theology in Craig G. Bartholomew and Michael W. Goheen, *The Drama of Scripture: Finding Our Place in the Biblical Story* (Grand Rapids: Baker Academic, 2004), first introduced on pp. 53-55.

[25]For a similar sense of emphasis as this survey, see Brueggemann, *Genesis*, pp. 114-15. Wenham shows several alternatives for organizing the development of thought in chapters 12-22, *Genesis 1–15*, pp. 262-63.

[26]See the discussion in Fretheim, "Book of Genesis," p. 446.

[27]Whether this is a covenant renewal (Wenham, *Genesis 1–15*, p. 260, and *Genesis 16–50* [Dallas: Word, 1994], pp. 17, 20, 28), revision (Fretheim, "Book of Genesis," p. 457), or initiation (Williamson, *Abraham, Israel and the Nations*, pp. 217-59) is irrelevant to our discussion here.

[28]Wenham, *Genesis 16–50*, p. 99.

[29]That's a point commonly made in commentaries and word-study books. For a technical presentation, see H. F. Fuhs, "יָרֵא" (*yārē'*) in *Theological Dictionary of the Old Testament*, ed. G. Johannes Botterweck and Helmer Ringgren, trans. David E. Green (Grand Rapids, Eerdmans, 1990), 6:300-313. For examples of people being afraid of God and thus deficient in knowing God, consider Ex 3:6; 20:20. For other examples not covered by this book, see 1 Sam 12:18-20 in the Old Testament and 1 Jn 4:15-18.

[30]Brueggemann touches on the importance both of promise and faith, and on "unfaith" and faith for this section. *Genesis*, pp. 106, 114.

[31]Ibid., pp. 126, 129.

[32]Rogerson notes that Abimelech's question in Gen 20:4 echoes Abraham's of Gen 18:23, placing this in the same ethical discourse framework. *Theory and Practice in Old Testament Ethics*, p. 73.

[33]Wenham considers the entire scene, with its obvious faithlessness, "astonishing." *Genesis 16–50*, p. 75. For an accessible example of an ancient law supporting the practice possibly in view here, see Matthews and Benjamin, *Old Testament Parallels*, pp. 50-51.

[34]For an example of an ancient law supporting the practice, see Matthews and Benjamin, *Old Testament Parallels*, p. 49.

[35]Brueggemann, *Genesis*, p. 151. Wenham offers more details underscoring faithlessness, including links between Gen 16:3 and Gen 3:6. *Genesis 16–50*, pp. 7-8, 12.

[36]Fretheim, "Book of Genesis," p. 454.

[37]I agree here with most recent commentators who note that homosexual behavior is *not* the archetypal sin of the city of Sodom. That city has earlier been described as being wicked (Gen 13:13). The words of Genesis present the attempt of outrageous evil, homosexual rape, against messengers of God in one glaring example of that overall wickedness. Note Fretheim, "Book of Genesis," p. 477; and Wenham, *Genesis 16–50*, p. 55.

[38]This would be an adaptation of Wenham's thesis in *Story as Torah*, pp. 1-4.

[39]See Brueggemann, *Genesis*, pp. 130-31; Wenham, *Genesis 1–15*, p. 299.

[40]Wenham, *Genesis 1–15*, p. 330.

[41]Fretheim, "Book of Genesis," pp. 467-68.

[42]John W. Rogerson finds in this interaction affirmation of Jürgen Habermas's "discourse ethics," with "justice" being the sort of "ethical norm . . . capable of receiving

the acceptance of all involved who could take part in the practical discourse." *Theory and Practice in Old Testament Ethics*, ed. M. Daniel Carroll R. (London: T & T Clark, 2004), p. 72.

[43]Wenham notes not just the implications for thinking about the problem of evil but also similar story details between the two sets of passages in Gen 6–9 and Gen 18–19. *Genesis 16–50*, pp. 40-43. Fretheim comments extensively on the sense of divine justice implied by the scenario unfolding in Gen 18–19. "Book of Genesis," pp. 477-79. Here, we can conclude that God is not violating the Noahic standards, since the judgment is local. God is still dealing with sinful people, but with the righteous as a hedge to his judging activity.

[44]See the discussions of Brueggemann, *Genesis*, pp. 173-76; and Fretheim, "Book of Genesis," pp. 469-70.

Chapter 3

[1]See, with slightly different details, Terence E. Fretheim, *Exodus* (Louisville: John Knox Press, 1991), pp. 14-16.

[2]This would be stronger than the sense implied by the NRSV, that God's knowledge is no more than one of taking notice, or that God "took cognizance of the matter." Umberto Cassuto, *A Commentary on the Book of Exodus*, trans. Israel Abrahams (Jerusalem: Magnes Press, 1967), p. 29.

[3]See Douglas K. Stuart, *Exodus* (Nashville: B & H Publishing, 2006), p. 21.

[4]See Craig G. Bartholomew and Michael W. Goheen, *The Drama of Scripture* (Grand Rapids: Baker Academic, 2004), pp. 64-66.

[5]The deception of the "Hebrew midwives" in Ex 1:15-21 is just the sort of ethically instructive episode referred to by Gordon Wenham, *Story as Torah* (Edinburgh: T & T Clark, 2000), pp. 1-4. See Fretheim, *Exodus*, pp. 31-36 for a discussion of the positive ethics rooted in creation that are portrayed here.

[6]Johanna W. H. van Wijk-Bos, *Making Wise the Simple* (Grand Rapids: Eerdmans, 2005), pp. 15-19, 155-56. Especially relevant is her summary: "God's liberating activity assures ancient Israel of God's loving protective care and of God's desire that the people should be in God's presence. God's covenant, as delineated in Exodus, assures ancient Israel of God's ongoing covenantal relationship" (p. 19).

[7]"As 'priests' they will also make access to God possible for others, for the rest of the world that belongs to God, for people who are not explicitly taken into covenant with this God" (ibid., p. 17).

[8]"Exodus 3:1-12 . . . looks forward . . . to the experience of the sons of Israel at Horeb/ Sinai, an experience parallel to the experience there of Moses." John I. Durham, *Exodus* (Waco: Word, 1987), p. 33.

[9]Walter Brueggemann offers specific details that show the striking covenantal nature of Ex 6:6-8. "The Book of Exodus," in *The New Interpreter's Bible* (Nashville: Abingdon, 1994), 1:734-35.

[10]Durham notes the purposefulness of the interruption, though not by connecting these instructions to the covenant. *Exodus*, p. 153.

[11]Fretheim, *Exodus*, p. 135.

[12]Brueggemann, "Book of Exodus," p. 808; Fretheim, *Exodus*, p. 179.

[13]This is inferred from the general tenor of the writing. Elsewhere, similar rationale is declared explicitly in Deut 6:21-25.

[14]One way historically of viewing biblical law has been to divide it into three categories: civil, ceremonial and moral. Torah's words do not support that distinction. Rather than mistakenly impose that scheme, the approach here seeks to discern a basic sense of morality from laws without saying that some laws are specifically moral while others are not. That resembles the "wisdom" approach found in Andrew Cameron, "Liberation and Desire: The Logic of Law in Exodus and Beyond," in *Exploring Exodus*, ed. Brian S. Rosner and Paul R. Williamson (Nottingham: Apollos, 2008), pp. 142-48.

[15]This contradicts many scholars, such as Cyril S. Rodd's *Glimpses of a Strange Land: Studies in Old Testament Ethics* (Edinburgh: T & T Clark, 2001), whose attitude is cemented in the work of Eckart Otto, *Theologische Ethik des Alten Testaments* (Stuttgart: Verlag W. Kohlhammer, 1994). For a history of attempted solutions to problems created by this cultural gap, see Robert R. Wilson, "Sources and Methods in the Study of Ancient Israelite Ethics," *Semeia* 66 (1995): 55-63.

[16]See Hetty Lalleman, *Celebrating the Law? Rethinking Old Testament Ethics* (Milton Keynes, UK: Paternoster Press, 2004); Gordon J. Wenham, "The Gap Between Law and Ethics in the Bible," *Journal of Jewish Studies* 48 (1997): 17-29; and Christopher J. H. Wright, *Old Testament Ethics for the People of God* (Downers Grove, IL: InterVarsity Press, 2004). Consider also the sophisticated bridging of cultures in the use of "discourse ethics" by John Rogerson, *Theory and Practice in Old Testament Ethics*, ed. M. Daniel Carroll R. (London: T & T Clark, 2004), pp. 68-79.

[17]This "final form" approach is acknowledged by Rodd, *Glimpses of a Strange Land*, p. 79.

[18]Again, the approach of dividing up the laws into civil, ceremonial and moral components is an artificial one that does not hold up under close scrutiny.

[19]Wright, *Old Testament Ethics*, p. 322.

[20]Some traditions, principally Lutheran and Roman Catholic, view Ex 20:17 as two separate commandments, considering the issues raised in Ex 20:1-6 to reflect a single commandment.

[21]Though the unique format of the Ten Commandments leads some to think of them more as policy statements than as laws, their legal import is not questioned. See the brief discussion in Carol Meyers, *Exodus* (Cambridge: Cambridge University Press, 2005), pp. 165-66.

[22]The divine origins of Torah's laws set Israel's laws apart from the laws known from other nations within the ancient Near East. See the summaries in James W. Watts,

Reading Law: Rhetorical Shaping of the Pentateuch (Sheffield, UK: Sheffield Academic Press, 1991), p. 98; and Meyers, *Exodus*, p. 185.

[23]See Meyers, *Exodus*, pp. 190-91. Also consider Wright, *Old Testament Ethics*, pp. 333-37.

[24]That would be counter to what one reads in some translations, such as the NIV's rendering of this verse.

[25]Meyers thinks this commandment presents an unenforceable standard, even though she offers possibilities for how it actually could be enforced. *Exodus*, pp. 165, 178. Brueggemann explains how the commandment proscribes "desire acted upon publicly." "Book of Exodus," p. 849.

[26]Jonathan Burnside asserts that laws such as this and several others in the Torah regulating thoughts offer one major distinctive between how law works in modern contexts and in the Torah. *God, Justice and Society* (New York: Oxford University Press, 2011), p. 11.

[27]David L. Baker, "Last But Not Least: The Tenth Commandment," *Horizons in Biblical Theology* 27 (2005): 7-20.

[28]Rodd, *Glimpses of a Strange Land*, pp. 94-98.

[29]Alexander Rofé cites four examples in Deuteronomy that he considers to be further outworking of the tenth commandment: 19:14; 23:25; 23:26; 24:10-11. Each of those "forbids all trespass into the realm of the other that may cause danger to his property, or to his ownership rights." *Deuteronomy: Issues and Interpretation* (Edinburgh: T & T Clark, 2002), pp. 79-96. For the quote see p. 96.

[30]Burnside distinguishes between the "semantic" approach to law existing in modern societies and what he calls a "narrative" approach that invites questions such as "'What typical situations do the words of this rule evoke?' or more straightforwardly, 'What does it make you think of?' It is a picture-oriented or 'imagistic' approach, rather than a literal one." *God, Justice and Society*, p. 11.

[31]However, consider Wright, *Old Testament Ethics*, p. 296, who makes a case for moral implications in the sabbath.

[32]See the useful overview about marriage customs in ancient Israel in Meyers: "Many texts—such as Gen 2:24 . . . and even legal rulings (e.g., Exod 21:5)—give the impression of a monogamous ideal or norm." *Exodus*, pp. 195-99, esp. p. 199. To that we could also add what we have already observed from the world of Genesis that situations of polygamy almost always reflected disorder. See Gen 4:19-24; 16:1-6; 29:31–30:24. Thinking through all of these texts together would be the sort of practice advocated by Burnside, *God, Justice and Society*, p. xxxiii.

[33]See Wijk-Bos, *Making Wise the Simple*, pp. 181-82.

[34]Wright sees ancient Israelite justice administered between two basic social institutions: the family and locally recognized public authorities, principally the elders at the town or city gate. *Old Testament Ethics*, pp. 301-3.

[35]See Durham for an affirmation of third party adjudication being advanced here. *Exodus*, pp. 323-24.

[36]That appears to be the case in the understanding of this law addressed by Jesus in Mt 5:38-39.

[37]The scholarly discussion is mixed as to whether the statement is requiring literal payments of wounds and body parts or whether it is a metaphoric expression of legal principle. For the former, see Brueggemann, "Book of Exodus," p. 864; and William H. C. Propp, *Exodus 19-40: A New Translation with Introduction and Commentary* (New York: Doubleday, 2006), pp. 227-32. For the second view, preferred here, see the thoughtful legal points in Burnside, *God, Justice and Society*, p. 12; along with Durham, *Exodus*, pp. 323-24; Meyers, *Exodus*, pp. 192-93.

[38]Again, whether the text really means "miscarriage" or "premature birth" is subject to debate. If the latter, then the death penalty could be implied. See Durham, *Exodus*, pp. 324-25.

[39]Brueggemann, "Book of Exodus," p. 865.

[40]See Burnside, *God, Justice and Society*, pp. 27-28.

[41]See the list of patriarchal issues offered by Brueggemann, "Book of Exodus," p. 867.

[42]Meyers, *Exodus*, p. 194.

[43]Rofé discusses this sort of ironic punishment as "symbolic *talio*" or "mirror punishment," whereby the crime becomes the punishment. *Deuteronomy*, pp. 186-87.

[44]Though some commentators connect this law to the preservation of family honor (e.g., Brueggemann, "Book of Exodus," p. 867) the words of the law make no such direct connection to that concern.

[45]Jeffries M. Hamilton identifies four such motivations in the Book of the Covenant: "economic rationale" (Ex 21:21), "moral rationale" (Ex 21:8; 22:27), "theocentric rationale" (Ex 23:6-7) and "historical rationale" (Ex 22:21; 23:9). *Social Justice and Deuteronomy: The Case of Deuteronomy 15* (Atlanta: Scholars Press, 1992), pp. 86-90. Such "motive clauses" do appear in other law codes from the ancient Near East, but not with the frequency or quality that Torah has to offer. See Watts, *Reading Law*, p. 65.

[46]See Wijk-Bos, *Making Wise the Simple*, pp. 180-91, for a helpful focus on the primacy of the regard for the weak. She considers that to be a unifying principle for all of the laws in the Book of the Covenant.

[47]This sort of "imitation of God" concept will be important elsewhere in Torah as well. See Bruce Birch, "Moral Agency, Community, and the Character of God," *Semeia* 66 (1996): 31-33; and Barton, *Understanding Old Testament Ethics* (Louisville: Westminster John Knox, 2003), pp. 50-54. The motif is qualified substantially by Rodd, *Glimpses of a Strange Land*, pp. 65-76, who shows how it is not a dominating, core motif for the Old Testament.

[48]Here is where the points elaborated by those studying "moral formation" are helpful to consider.

[49]A more detailed procedure is suggested by Wright, *Old Testament Ethics*, pp. 321-24. He offers four basic steps: "1. Distinguish the different kinds of law in the text" (p. 321); "2. Analyse the social function and relative status of particular laws and institutions" (p. 322); "3. Define the objective(s) of the law in Israelite society" (p. 322); "4. Preserve the objective but change the context" (p. 323). Within step 3, he lists ten additional questions to help accomplish that: (1) "What kind of situation was this law trying to promote, or prevent?" (2)"Whose interests was this law aiming to protect?" (3) "Who would have benefited from this law and why?" (4) "Whose power was this law trying to restrict and how did it do so?" (5) "What rights and responsibilities were embodied in this law?" (6) "What kind of behavior did this law encourage or discourage?" (7) "What vision of society motivated this law?" (8) "What moral principles, values or priorities did this law embody or instantiate?" (9) "What motivation did this law appeal to?" (10) "What sanction or penalty (if any) was attached to this law, and what does that show regarding its relative seriousness or moral priority?"

Chapter 4

[1]For a detailed demonstration of ethics presented in Leviticus's ritual activity, see Leigh M. Trevaskis, *Holiness, Ethics and Ritual in Leviticus* (Sheffield, UK: Sheffield Phoenix Press, 2011).

[2]Samuel E. Balentine, *Leviticus* (Louisville: John Knox Press, 2002), pp. 153-54.

[3]That exhortation appears six times throughout Leviticus, with four of those in the Holiness Code: Lev 11:44; 11:45; 19:2; 20:7; 20:26; 21:8. It is sometimes viewed as an encouragement to imitate God. See John Barton, *Understanding Old Testament Ethics* (Louisville: Westminster John Knox, 2003), pp. 29-30; 50-53. The perspective advanced here is more similar to Cyril S. Rodd, *Glimpses of a Strange Land: Studies in Old Testament Ethics* (Edinburgh: T & T Clark, 2001), pp. 65-76.

[4]That count is based on an English language search through the NRSV. Three times in Leviticus (Lev 16:32; 21:10; 21:12), the NRSV uses *consecrate* to represent a different Hebrew term from the one being counted here. In one statement, Lev 19:24, the term normally rendered *holy* is translated as "set apart." The count does not reflect the duplication of the word *holy*, translated "most holy" in the NRSV. See also Gordon J. Wenham, *The Book of Leviticus* (Grand Rapids: Eerdmans, 1979), p. 18.

[5]See John G. Gammie, *Holiness in Israel* (Minneapolis: Fortress Press, 1989), pp. 5-9, 26-27, 44.

[6]"If we can abstract pathogenicity and hygiene from our notion of dirt, we are left with the old definition of dirt as matter out of place. This is a very suggestive approach. It implies two conditions: a set of ordered relations and a contravention of that order. Dirt then, is never a unique, isolated event. Where there is dirt there is system. Dirt is the by-product of a systematic ordering and classification of matter,

in so far as ordering involves rejecting inappropriate elements." Mary Douglas, *Purity and Danger* (London: Routledge, 2002), p. 44. Douglas goes on to conclude that "if uncleanness is matter out of place, we must approach it through order" (p. 50). Though she has subsequently modified aspects of her grand theory about what stands behind the sense of purity related to dietary restrictions, those explanations do not significantly alter her basic points here. Those points are being applied only to Leviticus's sense of holiness, not to what makes that entire system cohere. See Mary Douglas, *Jacob's Tears: The Priestly Work of Reconciliation* (Oxford: Oxford University Press, 2004), pp. 159-75.

[7]That is Mary Douglas's ultimate point. See *Purity and Danger*, p. 71.

[8]See the useful distinction between cleanliness and holiness in Wenham, *Book of Leviticus*, pp. 18-24. What is "clean" still must be "sanctified" in order to be considered "holy." Cleanliness is not equivalent to holiness. But what becomes dirty or defiled may need to become clean before it can then be sanctified or set apart. Some items, however, are inherently dirty or unclean and can never be fit for holy use. This becomes clearest in the dietary laws.

[9]Trevaskis interacts critically with Mary Douglas and sees dietary restrictions undergirding a life of obedience, in contrast to the Eden-like death of disobedience. That dietary concern for purity would then be parallel to the morally significant instructions of the Holiness Code. *Holiness, Ethics and Ritual in Leviticus*, pp. 47-107.

[10]For support for that translation of Gen 1:11, 12, 21, 25, see Gordon J. Wenham, *Genesis 1–15* (Waco: Word, 1987), p. 21. The NRSV masks the distinctiveness of created species, saying "various kinds" instead of "after its own kind." Compare the language of Gen 1:11, 12, 21, 25 with Lev 11:16, 22, 29. For a fuller treatment that also links the created order with the morality of Leviticus, see Douglas, *Purity and Danger*, pp. 62-71.

[11]Douglas, *Purity and Danger*, pp. 62-67. See also Philip Peter Jenson, who adds to this more "structuralist" way of classifying the world what he terms a "realist" view that also concentrates "on the inescapable realities of death and life," so that holiness would advance life. *Graded Holiness: A Key to the Priestly Conception of the World* (Sheffield, UK: Sheffield Academic Press, 1992), pp. 56-88.

[12]The concern here is to keep it simple. One could, for example, say that by transmitting bodily uncleanness in the various ways put forward in Leviticus 15 one is inflicting harm on another by making that person unclean and thus unfit for tabernacle activities. But the immediate harm to that person's *well-being* is not the point of such laws.

[13]Based on the NRSV. "The repetition . . . punctuates all these instructions with the constant reminder that they are an integral part of what the God of Sinai requires if Israel is to realize its covenantal commission to become not only a 'priestly kingdom' but also a 'holy nation.'" Balentine, *Leviticus*, pp. 151-52.

[14]Ibid., p. 253.

[15]Kaiser offers a clear and concise list. A man is forbidden to have sexual relations with his: "mother (v. 7), stepmother (v. 8 . . .), sister (v. 9), granddaughter (v. 10), half-sister on the father's side (v. 11), paternal aunt (v. 12), maternal aunt (v. 13), paternal uncle's wife (v. 14), daughter-in-law (v. 15), brother's wife (v. 16), step-daughter or granddaughter (v. 17), or wife's sister while the wife is still living (v. 18)." Walter C. Kaiser, "The Book of Leviticus," in *The New Interpreter's Bible* (Nashville: Abingdon Press, 1994), 1:1125. The simplicity of some of those items is challenged by the very detailed discussion of Jacob Milgrom, *Leviticus 17-22: A New Translation with Introduction and Commentary* (New York: Doubleday, 2000), pp. 1523-49. Specifically, he takes v. 9 to address a "half sister" and v. 17 to address taking both a mother and her daughter as wives simultaneously, when the mother had been previously married. It could also include taking both a mother and her granddaughter when the mother had been previously married (pp. 1546-47).

[16]Though, see Milgrom, *Leviticus 17-22*, pp. 1526-27, who regards v. 6 as a blanket statement covering all immediately near blood relatives in the household, including "the sister and the daughter." Accordingly, the list of vv. 6-18 covers prohibitions "by generation, . . . by blood, . . . and by relationship" (p. 1527).

[17]Ibid., p. 1525. Milgrom observes that people are addressed as singular individuals instead of as a collective "you" or "they." That both personalizes and underscores the violation done to specific family members by the illicit acts.

[18]See Balentine, *Leviticus*, p. 158; Milgrom, *Leviticus 17-22*, pp. 1527, 1530-31; Wenham, *Leviticus*, p. 255.

[19]Milgrom, *Leviticus 17-22*, pp. 1549-50.

[20]See ibid., pp. 1558-65: "Thus both factors combine to create the enormity of the sin of Molek worship: ascribing to Molek the attributes of a deity who can demand child sacrifice and, at the same time, averring that Molek is an agent of YHWH and carries out his will" (p. 1565).

[21]As tempting as it would be to include the instructions in Lev 19:23-25 covering the prohibition of eating of the fruit of newly planted trees in this mix as environmentally sound practice, the words here indicate that it is related to God's ownership and blessing of the land, not to environmentally conscious farming practices.

[22]The extent of the representation of the Ten Commandments is frequently discussed, with some maintaining that all ten are alluded to in one way or another (see Kaiser, "Book of Leviticus," p. 1131; Wenham, *Leviticus*, p. 264), and others, wanting to restrict the references only to the clearly stated concerns against worshiping other gods (v. 4), making images (v. 4), keeping the sabbath (v. 3), and honoring parents (v. 3) (see Balentine, *Leviticus*, p. 161; Milgrom, *Leviticus 17-22*, pp. 1600-1602).

[23]See Milgrom's advocacy for the qualifying term *open. Leviticus 17–22*, p. 1648.

[24]Balentine, *Leviticus*, p. 165; John E. Hartley, *Leviticus*, (Dallas: Word, 1992), pp. 316-17; and Milgrom, *Leviticus 17–22*, pp. 1647-48.

[25]Vengeance taking may be provable in court. The term "implies extralegal retribution, which, although forbidden to men, may be exacted by God." Milgrom, *Leviticus 17–22*, p. 1651.

[26]One could add a third, which precedes these two, namely, proper land management. The laws for giving the land a sabbath rest combine values of hard work with proper land management in a way that reflects the cooperation between people and land advanced in the creation mandate of Genesis 1:28-30; 2:8-9. It also offers relief to hired laborers, slaves and animals. See Johanna W. H. van Wijk-Bos, *Making Wise the Simple* (Grand Rapids: Eerdmans, 2005), pp. 52-54; Christopher J. H. Wright, *Old Testament Ethics for the People of God* (Downers Grove, IL: InterVarsity Press, 2004), pp. 158-62.

[27]See Wright, *Old Testament Ethics*, pp. 200-205, 206-7.

[28]"Love and mercy toward one's neighbor lay at the heart of the jubilee legislation. If all Israel were but 'aliens and [God's] tenant' (v. 23), the transitory nature of all mortals on this earth and the habitations we occupy must be acknowledged." Kaiser, "Book of Leviticus," p. 1174.

[29]Though fully aware of the critical issues connected to the composition of Deuteronomy, I wish to maintain the spirit of the final form reading by dealing with the material on the terms of its own words and as it appears in its literary sequence and setting.

[30]For two examples, consider (1) the *Epic of Gilgamesh*, which, though ancient even for Israel, still was popular enough to be in written form well into the seventh century B.C.E., and (2) the Ugaritic "Stories of Aquat."

[31]At least ninety-six times God is said to be giving something to his people in the book of Deuteronomy.

[32]See Terence Fretheim, *God and World in the Old Testament* (Nashville: Abingdon Press, 2005), pp. 22-27.

[33]"One must not romanticize the Deuteronomic use of the term 'love,' as though it were primarily a 'feeling' or even an aptitude. It concerns, rather, practical acts of obedience in every sphere of daily life." Walter Brueggemann, *Deuteronomy* (Nashville: Abingdon Press, 2001), p. 84.

[34]See the comments in Patrick D. Miller, *Deuteronomy* (Louisville,: John Knox Press, 1990), pp. 101-4.

[35]The language has strong, royal overtones, applying the ancient Near Eastern language of kingship to Israel's God. See Duane L. Christensen, *Deuteronomy 1–21:9* (Nashville: Thomas Nelson, 2001), p. 204; and A. D. H. Mayes, *Deuteronomy* (London: Oliphants, 1979), p. 210.

[36]"God *does* require love; but those, for example, who outwardly obeyed the commandments, but did not love God, were in effect offering God a bribe." Peter C.
Craigie, *The Book of Deuteronomy* (Grand Rapids: Eerdmans, 1976), p. 206.

[37]Rodd cautions against making this a declaration of the imitation of God as a core
ethical principle, noting that doing something in imitation of is quite different
from doing something similar to. *Glimpses of a Strange Land*, p. 68.

[38]See Brueggemann, *Deuteronomy*, pp. 96-97.

[39]"'I have taught you,' is a further reminder of the didactic function of the text of this
book, for Israel will demonstrate her 'wisdom . . . in the eyes of the peoples' by
means of her fidelity to YHWH's commandments." Christensen, *Deuteronomy
1–21:9*, p. 80.

[40]Phraseology similar to Deut 17:13 can be found in Deut 13:11; 19:19-20; 21:21. Sometimes the concern to "purge evil" from their midst appears alone: Deut 22:22, 24,
which deal with adultery; Deut 24:7, which deals with slave-trading fellow Israelites.

[41]Deut 14:29; 15:4, 10, 18; 19:13; 22:7; 24:13, 19; 25:15. Topics here focus on extending
kindness to people (or in one case, birds) in various weak circumstances, except
for Deut 19:13 (murder) and Deut 25:15 (honesty).

[42]Deut 21:14; 22:19, 29, each of which addresses harm to a woman's sexual reputation.

[43]Deut 18:9-12—child sacrifice, along with other religious practices of the Canaanites;
Deut 22:5—crossdressing; Deut 23:18—the fees of a temple prostitute; Deut 25:16—
dishonest weights in business transactions.

[44]Even if, as Mayes suggests (*Deuteronomy*, p. 150), such a comment about the
wisdom of one's law code was common elsewhere in the ancient Near East, the
statement in Deuteronomy at the very least makes a counter offer for the nations
to consider Israel's laws. See Wright, *Old Testament Ethics*, p. 62.

[45]Though the "words" being referred to in Deuteronomy 6:6 may possibly be restricted to the Ten Commandments (see Ronald E. Clements, "The Book of Deuteronomy," in *New Interpreter's Bible*, 2:343; Craigie, *Deuteronomy*, p. 170), it is
more likely that they refer to the entirety of the Deuteronomic instruction from
the "words" of Deut 1:1 on. See Christensen, *Deuteronomy 1–21:9*, p. 143.

[46]Though it is possible that the demand for love reflects its common appearance in
ancient Near Eastern treaties, the family environment makes it a more likely influence for the language depicting the kind of relationship between God and his
people. See Clements, "Book of Deuteronomy," p. 343.

[47]Clements, "Book of Deuteronomy," p. 437; Miller, *Deuteronomy*, p. 145.

[48]See Wright, *Old Testament Ethics*, pp. 85-92.

[49]To see this kind of thinking described in the wider ancient Near Eastern setting,
see Helmer Ringgren, *Religions of the Ancient Near East*, trans. John Sturdy
(London: SPCK, 1973), pp. 42-46, 107-20, 173-75. For evidence that such attitudes
persisted across millennia in Mesopotamia see Karen Rhea Nemet-Nejat, *Daily

Life in Ancient Mesopotamia (Peabody, MA: Hendrickson, 2002), pp. 175-215. Paucity of extant materials hinders forming firm conclusions for Canaanite religious attitudes, but a strong placating streak is discernible. See G. del Olmo Lete, *Canaanite Religion According to the Liturgical Texts of Ugarit* (Winona Lake, IN: Eisenbrauns, 2004), pp. 324-88.

[50]See Miller, *Deuteronomy*, p. 62.

[51]In drawing this analogy, I am fully aware that the biblical senses of covenant are not exact equivalents to the sense of contract as it is applied in Western societies. See the introduction to the concept in Steven L. McKenzie, *Covenant* (St. Louis: Chalice Press, 2000), pp. 1-3.

[52]Miller concludes his final form analysis of the blessings and curses in chapters 27-28 as follows: "The covenantal structure with its encouragement to obedience and sanctions against disobedience is not meant to suggest a one-to-one correspondence between a single act and a single outcome. It is meant to claim a relationship in which choices and acts determine outcomes and consequences. The results are built into the structure of existence by the Lord of the covenant, who points the way the people are to go and directs the way that by their acts they choose to go." *Deuteronomy*, p. 198.

[53]Clements, "Book of Deuteronomy," pp. 512-13.

[54]Miller, *Deuteronomy*, p. 136.

[55]Craigie, *Deuteronomy*, p. 237.

[56]Miller, *Deuteronomy*, pp. 148-49.

[57]Though this may be a hedge against eventual greedy land acquisition by the powerful from the powerless (Brueggemann, *Deuteronomy*, pp. 202-4), the language here does not address the motives for moving boundary markers. That can be done by rich and poor alike. Either case is a disrespect of what sacrally belongs to another.

[58]Clements regards these not as humane concessions but as supporting the morale of the army that must fight with total focus on the battle at hand. "Book of Deuteronomy," p. 439. However, note Miller: "Something here is quite at odds with the enterprise of war. Deuteronomy does not reflect on it; it simply holds to a concern for individual humanity in the midst of its undoing." *Deuteronomy*, p. 160.

[59]Clements, "Book of Deuteronomy," p. 448.

[60]See Craigie, *Deuteronomy*, pp. 287-88; and Brueggemann, *Deuteronomy*, pp. 219-20.

[61]See Alexander Rofé, *Deuteronomy: Issues and Interpretation* (Edinburgh: T & T Clark, 2002), pp. 178-80, who discusses the lack of evidence of a daughter's virginity as comparable to the rebelliousness of the son in Deut 21:18-21. Both show lack of respect to parents, and both bring dishonor to the home.

[62]"The intimacy of sexual relationship is at the heart of the enduring commitment of a man and a woman and the creation of a family. It is not to be taken lightly but is to be jealously guarded." Miller, *Deuteronomy*, p. 163.

[63]Brueggemann, *Deuteronomy*, p. 231. Craigie sees these laws restricted to slaves escaping from foreign countries. *Deuteronomy*, pp. 300-301. See the discussion in Jeffries M. Hamilton, *Social Justice and Deuteronomy* (Atlanta: Scholars Press, 1992), pp. 117-24, in which he points out the tensions of the two sets of laws that do indeed undermine the practice of slavery.

[64]Craigie advocates the broadening of the category "prostitute," based on the Hebrew terminology in v. 18 that employs a different word for "prostitute" from what appears in v. 17. *Deuteronomy*, pp. 301-2.

[65]Ibid., pp. 302-3.

[66]Brueggemann, *Deuteronomy*, p. 233.

[67]Wright, *Old Testament Ethics*, p. 332. Rofé considers the possibility of "palingamy," in which the woman moves between two different sexual partners "in alternation, under the guise of temporary marriages," thus attempting a legal form of adultery. *Deuteronomy*, p. 188.

[68]Though seeing the law's focus as protecting the land from defilement, Brueggemann's comments are instructive: "For the first husband to reengage with her sexually would be to relate to a 'used' woman." *Deuteronomy*, p. 236.

[69]Craigie, *Deuteronomy*, p. 307.

[70]Brueggemann, *Deuteronomy*, p. 237; in contrast to Clements, "Book of Deuteronomy," p. 469.

[71]Clements, "Book of Deuteronomy," p. 475.

[72]Note Gordon J. Wenham, who discusses laws as having lower ethical standards than those alluded to in some biblical stories. "The Gap Between Law and Ethics in the Bible," *Journal of Jewish Studies* 48 (1997): 17-29.

[73]Those wishing a more comprehensive treatment of the worldview ultimately advanced by these writings should consult Wright, *Old Testament Ethics*. He proposes a system that views people interacting with God, one another and their land as a paradigm for how others can learn right from wrong in their social and economic dealings.

[74]This would not only include the sense of purity advocated in dietary issues and defilement issues both of people and land, it would extend to the violent means for Israel acquiring their land in the first place. However objectionable one might find each of these, the words indicate that they are situation specific to the people of Israel, underscoring their unique relationship to God. Those who object to these comments being reserved for only a footnote should remember that this book offers only a basic, introductory explanation for the nonspecialist.

Chapter 5

[1]See Tremper Longman III, *Proverbs* (Grand Rapids: Baker Academic, 2006), pp. 80-81.

[2]See Paul Overland, who also notes other studies that connect Deuteronomy with Proverbs, most notably Deut 6 and Prov 7. "Did the Sage Draw from the Shema?

A Study of Proverbs 3:1-12," *Catholic Biblical Quarterly* 62 (2000): 424-40. For an additional, more detailed survey on the aptness of connections between Proverbs and Deuteronomy, see Katherine J. Dell, *The Book of Proverbs in Social and Theological Context* (Cambridge: Cambridge University Press, 2006), pp. 167-78.

[3]Longman summarizes the problems of correlating wisdom and covenant, and yet points to studies showing how they can work together. *Proverbs*, p. 82. To see integration possibilities, consider Craig G. Bartholomew and Ryan P. O'Dowd, *Old Testament Wisdom Literature: A Theological Introduction* (Downers Grove, IL: InterVarsity Press, 2011), pp. 76, 87-88.

[4]King Solomon is identified as the originator of the Proverbs collection (Prov 1:1), and one could make a claim for Solomonic authorship of much of Proverbs. See Bruce K. Waltke, *The Book of Proverbs: Chapters 1–15* (Grand Rapids: Eerdmans, 2004), pp. 31-36. That does not necessarily make Solomon the "I" speaker of these proverbs, which follow basic literary conventions of seeing instruction in the household environment as coming from the father to the son. See Bartholomew and O'Dowd, *Old Testament Wisdom Literature*, pp. 82-83; and Michael V. Fox, *Proverbs 1–9* (New York: Doubleday, 2000), pp. 80-81.

[5]Fox, *Proverbs 1–9*, p. 145.

[6]Based strictly on Hebrew vocabulary, the comparison does not appear initially apt. Different words for "seek" are used in each passage. The comparison of the similar motif, however, is what highlights a main point of contrast between Proverbs and Torah. For comparisons between the speech in Prov 1:20-33 and the speeches in Jer 7 and Jer 20, which are recognized as Deuteronomic, see Scott L. Harris, *Proverbs 1–9: A Study of Inner-Biblical Interpretation* (Atlanta: Scholars Press, 1995), pp. 67-109.

[7]Richard J. Clifford, "Introduction to Wisdom Literature," in *The New Interpreter's Bible* (Nashville: Abingdon Press, 1997), 5:12; and Bartholomew and O'Dowd, *Old Testament Wisdom Literature*, p. 79.

[8]Leo G. Perdue, *Wisdom and Creation: The Theology of Wisdom Literature* (Nashville: Abingdon Press, 1994), pp. 106-12. In a representative sample, Perdue points out that God creates evil for the day of justice (Prov 16:4); owns just balances (Prov 16:11); is the creator who is mocked when the poor are mistreated (Prov 17:5); creates perception organs (20:12); is maker for both rich and poor people (Prov 22:2).

[9]See Waltke, *Book of Proverbs*, pp. 68-76.

[10]Proverbs is certainly aware that things go wrong in the world, even for those who do right. See the discussions in Bartholomew and O'Dowd, *Old Testament Wisdom Literature*, pp. 96-97; and Raymond C. Van Leeuwen, "The Book of Proverbs," in *New Interpreter's Bible*, 5:25; and Waltke, *Book of Proverbs*, pp. 107-9.

[11]Bartholomew and O'Dowd, *Old Testament Wisdom Literature*, pp. 86-91; Clifford, "Introduction to Wisdom Literature," pp. 8-12; Waltke, *Book of Proverbs*, pp. 68-69.

[12]For an incomplete list of other relevant proverbs, consider Prov 12:16; 14:29; 15:1, 18; 16:32; 19:11; 22:8, 24; 27:4; 29:11; 30:32-33.

[13]That "inclusio" is a commonly recognized structural feature. For further discussion of the centrality of the "fear of the LORD" in relation to Proverbs' overall structure, see Bartholomew and O'Dowd, *Old Testament Wisdom Literature*, pp. 80-82.

[14]See the references under note 49 from chap. 4.

[15]This is more than "theism," which would involve believing in any god. By referring to the fear of the Lord, Proverbs is identifying its words with YHWH, the God of the Israelites, with whom the Israelites are in covenant relationship. Though Proverbs has minimal connections to Torah's covenantal dynamics, it assumes awareness of Torah's covenant God. See Waltke, *Book of Proverbs*, pp. 64-68.

[16]For lists of works consider Fox, *Proverbs 1-9*, pp. 17-23; and Waltke, *Book of Proverbs*, pp. 28-31. Consider also the useful discussion in Bartholomew and O'Dowd, *Old Testament Wisdom Literature*, pp. 38-46, from which the basic summaries of Egyptian and Mesopotamian worldviews are taken in this discussion. They carry further the kinds of corrections found in Roland E. Murphy, *The Tree of Life: An Exploration of Biblical Wisdom Literature* (Grand Rapids: Eerdmans, 2002), pp. 115-26, who noted how Israelite wisdom did much more than accept the standards of Egyptian or Mesopotamian concepts, contrary to what other scholars on wisdom writings had been advocating. He also offers a detailed listing of primary sources of ancient Near Eastern wisdom literature (pp. 151-75). A more complete discussion with conclusions similar to those in Bartholomew and O'Dowd can be found in Longman, *Proverbs*, pp. 42-61.

[17]For a more complete presentation of the kind of postmodern thinking out of which this kind of statement emerges, consider James W. Sire, *The Universe Next Door: A Basic Worldview Catalog*, 5th ed. (Downers Grove, IL: InterVarsity Press, 2009), pp. 214-43.

[18]"Wisdom cannot be attained unless it is desired." Perdue, *Wisdom and Creation*, p. 84.

[19]Longman, *Proverbs*, pp. 74-78.

[20]"If the reader maintains the subject position of the silent adolescent beyond ch. 9, he or she will discover a host of various characters, a virtual cavalcade of heroes and scoundrels in the quest for wisdom, that expand this adolescent's social horizon from what was profiled initially by the parent." William P. Brown, *Character in Crisis: A Fresh Approach to the Wisdom Literature of the Old Testament* (Grand Rapids: Eerdmans, 1996), p. 45.

[21]Consider the discussion in Brown, *Character in Crisis*, pp. 30-43, who analyzes both the initial rebuke and subsequent invitation of wisdom against the straightforward instruction of the father. The net effect is to show how wisdom had much more than static instruction to offer to an ever-changing world.

[22]Brown develops the point that Proverbs addresses situations in a dynamic world,

rather than offering timeless principles evocative of a "moral fascism." Ibid., pp. 22-49.

[23]See Perdue, *Wisdom and Creation*, p. 87.

[24]Though appealing to a popular, nonscholarly audience, the Abrahamic connections, minus the blessing of the nations, is clearly explained in Graeme Goldsworthy, *Gospel and Wisdom: Israel's Wisdom Literature in the Christian Life* (Carlisle, UK: Paternoster, 1987), pp. 63-65.

[25]For a similar point see Murphy, *Tree of Life*, p. 126.

[26]Leeuwen, "Book of Proverbs," p. 24.

[27]On the inadequacies of the simple categories of "synonymous," "antithetic" and "synthetic," see Bartholomew and O'Dowd, *Old Testament Wisdom Literature*, pp. 62-64. For a more detailed discussion, with alternatives, see J. M. LeMon and B. A. Strawn, "Parallelism," in *Dictionary of the Old Testament: Wisdom, Poetry and Writings*, ed. Tremper Longman III and Peter Enns (Downers Grove, IL: IVP Academic, 2008), pp. 502-11. They suggest a balance between the oversimplified categories already mentioned and the more complex analyses offered in recent scholarship, listing eight main tendencies in parallelisms: "of morphological elements," "of number," "staircase," "ballast variant," "positive-negative," "gender-matched," "nominal-pronominal" and "half-line or internal."

[28]"The saying is stated in a general way in order that its truth may remain open for diverse instantiations." Waltke, *Book of Proverbs*, pp. 450-51.

[29]Though it is possible that the proverb implies a deliverance beyond earthly life (Longman, *Proverbs*, p. 230; Waltke, *Book of Proverbs*, pp. 452-53), it is more likely that a more immediate consequence is in view. See Michael V. Fox, *Proverbs 10-31* (New Haven, CT: Yale University Press, 2009), p. 511; and Roland E. Murphy, *Proverbs* (Nashville: Thomas Nelson, 1998), p. 73.

[30]Longman, commenting on this statement, says: "Proverbs are not promises; they are generally true principles, all other things being equal." *Proverbs*, p. 231. See also Murphy: "It is obvious that this is an ideal, not a real, event since the just do go hungry. But the saying expresses the usual Israelite understanding of divine justice. No proverb says it all." *Proverbs*, p. 73.

[31]Some commentators see more structural relationships between proverbs than others. For example, Leeuwen sees Prov 10:1-8 as "a patterned introduction to the fundamental issues of 10:1–15:33," with Prov 10:1 and Prov 10:8 forming the outer bracket opposing wisdom with folly, Prov 10:2-3 and Prov 10:6-7 forming an inner layer, contrasting the righteous with the wicked and Prov 10:4-5 at the core focusing on "human responsibility." "Book of Proverbs," pp. 106-7. Waltke sees Prov 10:1 introducing the collection with the same thematic concern as Prov 1:8, while Prov 10:2-5 form a bracket with Prov 10:15-16 on the same topic of wealth and poverty. *Book of Proverbs*, p. 450. Neither commentator's suggestion is readily transparent.

[32]"We believe, however, that the book's poetic repetitions and many nuanced groupings of proverbs yield countless literary and thus theological patterns and a thematic unity that strengthens and integrates each of the discrete sections of proverbs. Proverbs is not a disconnected group of sayings, but a highly memorable body of teachings with a consistent message about life in God's world—but only when it is read as a whole." Bartholomew and O'Dowd, *Old Testament Wisdom Literature*, p. 82. Coming from a different perspective, a similar point is argued by Brown, *Character in Crisis*, pp. 45-49.

[33]"Sometimes Proverbs condemns the gift or bribe, sometimes it simply observes its power." Leeuwen, "Book of Proverbs," p. 152.

[34]Murphy, commenting on Prov 18:16: "It is rather naïve to think that the 'gift' in this verse is disinterested; access to the great is made possible. While this is not necessarily a bribe that perverts a judgment, neither is it without influence on the formation of opinion. It is open to abuse." *Proverbs*, p. 137. Leeuwen notes: "In pre-industrial societies such as ancient Israel, gifts played a major role in the general exchange of goods and services." "Book of Proverbs," p. 174. He goes on to note that the gift that gains access to people of power "was especially prone to corruption." Longman notes: "It is better to understand the circumstance of a gift to be the issue. If one gives a gift to circumvent justice, then it is wrong. But there are situations where a bribe can open doors to good ends. In other words, the purpose of the bribe is the issue here." *Proverbs*, p. 552.

[35]"Proverbs are, properly speaking, not universal rules; rather, they are situationally oriented, open-ended sayings designed to exercise one's mental and moral faculties and thereby enable the moral agent to size up ethically demanding situations and to act appropriately." Brown, *Character in Crisis*, pp. 13-14. See also Leeuwen, "Book of Proverbs," p. 23.

[36]Waltke, *Book of Proverbs*, pp. 588, 591.

[37]Plato, *The Republic*, bk. 5.20-22, 475E-480A.

[38]Fools "do not have the patience to achieve the goals associated with wisdom . . . nor do they want to listen to people with competence." Longman, *Proverbs*, p. 354. See also Leeuwen, "Book of Proverbs," p. 172.

[39]Longman, *Proverbs*, pp. 61-63.

Chapter 6

[1]Gene M. Tucker summarizes the unique function of the prophet as one who: "(1) presents a communication from God (2) announcing future events." "Prophetic Speech," in *Interpreting the Prophets*, ed. James Luther Mays and Paul J. Achtemeier (Philadelphia: Fortress Press, 1987), p. 39.

[2]Gene M. Tucker, "The Book of Isaiah," in *The New Interpreters Bible* (Nashville: Abingdon, 2001), 6:53.

[3]The courtroom flavor to this is regularly observed. See Joseph Blenkinsopp, *Isaiah*

1–39: A New Translation with Introduction and Commentary (New York: Doubleday, 2000), p. 182; and Tucker, "Book of Isaiah," pp. 52-53. Both commentators note how Isaiah's use of Deuteronomic language here is common in prophetic writings. They also note that Isaiah lacks explicit mention of the covenant here.

⁴See Claus Westermann, *Basic Forms of Prophetic Speech*, trans. Hugh Clayton White (London: Lutterworth, 1967), pp. 129-209, for a basic, detailed description of the judgment speech and its varieties that prevail throughout prophetic literature. Though this has been nuanced by others (see Tucker, "Prophetic Speech," pp. 34-35), the basic sense of accusation and announcement of verdict still is affirmed.

⁵See David L. Petersen, *The Prophetic Literature: An Introduction* (Louisville: Westminster John Knox Press, 2002), pp. 5-8.

⁶For an overview of prophetic roles, see Jack R. Lundbom, *The Hebrew Prophets: An Introduction* (Minneapolis: Fortress Press, 2010), pp. 8-32.

⁷That in part helps to explain the role of prophets as historians in view of Joshua, Judges, Samuel and Kings being known as prophetic books in the Jewish arrangement of Scripture. See Petersen, *Prophetic Literature*, pp. 1-2. The rendering of accounts is regularly recognized as one of the three main roles of the prophet: accounts, speeches and prayers. See Westermann, *Basic Forms of Prophetic Speech*, p. 90; and Tucker, "Prophetic Speech," p. 29. For observations about event interpretation, see Petersen, *Prophetic Literature*, pp. 10-11.

⁸Tucker remarks that the absence of rationale in prophecies of salvation is a "distinctive feature" of Israelite prophecy. "Prophetic Speech," p. 39.

⁹Petersen notes the international scope of many prophetic oracles with an awareness of the accountability of the nations, not merely their ultimate blessing. *Prophetic Literature*, pp. 38-39. He does not connect that last item to the Torah, however.

¹⁰For a sense of the intricacies involved in the process, consider Alexander Rofé, *Introduction to the Prophetic Literature* (Sheffield, UK: Sheffield Academic Press, 1997), pp. 45-53. For a simpler general process, consider Tucker, "Prophetic Speech," pp. 28-29.

¹¹Blenkinsopp notes the "step-by-step description of Israelites: first as a nation like any other . . . then, a large-scale kinship group . . . then a familial unit . . . finally coming back to the 'children' . . . of Yahveh's household castigated in the first stanza." *Isaiah 1–39*, pp. 182-83.

¹²Hans Wildberger, *Isaiah 1–12: A Commentary* (Minneapolis: Fortress Press, 1991), pp. 23-24.

¹³Blenkinsopp, *Isaiah 1–9*, p. 184.

¹⁴Ibid., p. 183. Blenkinsopp settles on that after presenting options. See also Wildberger, *Isaiah 1–12*, pp. 27-28, who also sees covenantal connections between the invading army of v. 7 and the consequences for disobedience spelled out in Ex 23:29, Lev 26:3 and Deut 28:37.

[15]"By contrasting Yahweh's mercy with Israel's iniquity, the prophet wants those survivors to learn their lesson." Tucker, "Book of Isaiah," p. 54.

[16]R. E. Clements comments how the message here "establishes a broad appeal for repentance, rather than pointing to a particular historical epoch of the ministry of the prophet Isaiah." "The Unity of the Book of Isaiah," in *Interpreting the Prophets*, ed. James Luther Mays and Paul J. Achtemeier (Philadelphia: Fortress Press, 1987), p. 51.

[17]This is the general conclusion of those pursuing what is often called "canonical criticism." See the complete essay by Clements, "Unity of the Book of Isaiah," pp. 50-61; and Marvin A. Sweeney, "Formation and Form in Prophetic Literature," in *Old Testament Interpretation: Past, Present and Future*, ed. James Luther Mays, David L. Petersen and Kent Harold Richards (Nashville: Abingdon Press, 1995), pp. 113-26.

[18]Though the messages of prophets are sometimes portrayed as being in conflict with the duties of priests, a careful reading shows that satisfying moral demands is placed on equal footing with cultic demands. See David Noel Freedman, "Between God and Man: Prophets in Ancient Israel," in *Prophecy and Prophets*, ed. Yehoshua Gitay (Atlanta: Scholars Press, 1997), p. 68. Blenkinsopp appropriately remarks that this is not dealing with external versus internal religious expression but rather two forms of external expression that were to come from those internally purified. *Isaiah 1-9*, p. 185. See also Tucker, "Book of Isaiah," p. 58.

[19]Wildberger, *Isaiah 1-12*, pp. 53-58. While not necessarily advocating a strict connection to the covenant of Torah, Blenkinsopp likewise notes the Deuteronomic feel to this segment. *Isaiah 1-9*, p. 185.

[20]Tucker, "Book of Isaiah," p. 65.

[21]John D. Watts, *Isaiah 1-33* (Nashville: Thomas Nelson, 2005), p. 49.

[22]Wildberger, *Isaiah 1-12*, pp. 90-92; and Tucker, "Book of Isaiah," p. 67.

[23]On military protection, see Wildberger, *Isaiah 1-12*, pp. 108-9.

[24]John Barton, *Understanding Old Testament Ethics* (Louisville: Westminster/John Knox, 2003), pp. 134-40. He suggests that Isaiah regards God, the Lord of the universe, as at the top of the chain of importance, with all proceeding from him in the divine order. People who elevate themselves over God would also elevate themselves over that divine order; that self-exaltedness would lead to all sorts of inappropriate behavior. Barton acknowledges that Isaiah never says anything like this explicitly, but it may be an underlying assumption discernible from various statements throughout the writing.

[25]The language of pride appears in Lev 26:19 as something that causes covenantal disloyalty. It also appears in Deut 8:14 as a symptom of people who mistake their own abilities for God's hand of blessing on their lives, and in Deut 17:20 as a potential problem for kings that can be hindered by their persistent awareness of Torah's standards.

[26]Wildberger, *Isaiah 1–12*, pp. 110-11.

[27]In this connection, Wildberger also mentions Prov 20:1; 21:17; 23:20; 31:4. Ibid., p. 201.

[28]See Christopher J. H. Wright, *Old Testament Ethics for the People of God* (Downers Grove, IL: InterVarsity Press, 2004), pp. 17-20. His concept of worldview is quite applicable to the sense of assumption here. He develops the specifics of that concept in relation to Israel in pp. 23-99.

[29]See Cyril S. Rodd, *Glimpses of a Strange Land: Studies in Old Testament Ethics* (Edinburgh: T & T Clark, 2001), pp. 292-95.

[30]An immediate challenge to that point comes both from Barton, *Understanding Old Testament Ethics*, pp. 77-153, and in an even deeper philosophical way from Matthew Levering, *Biblical Natural Law* (Oxford: Oxford University Press, 2008), pp. 23-68. The sophisticated line of reasoning in both writings indicates, however, that the thought patterns they detect as representative of natural law ethics are not a part of the overt encouragement of the words of the Bible themselves, though certainly an allowable derivative from them.

[31]We have already explored some of Isaiah's implied Torah references. While some prophets also offer implied Torah (and even wisdom) references, others are much more direct. Consider, e.g., Hos 8:1: "One like a vulture is over the house of the LORD, / because they have broken my covenant, / and transgressed my law." Jeremiah, Ezekiel and Malachi frequently directly refer to Torah standards. See also Hos 4:6; Amos 2:4; Hab 1:4; Zeph 3:4; Zech 7:12.

[32]See Walter J. Houston, "Exit the Oppressed Peasant? Rethinking the Background of Social Criticism in the Prophets," in *Prophecy and Prophets in Ancient Israel: Proceedings of the Oxford Old Testament Seminar*, ed. John Day (London: T & T Clark, 2010), pp. 101-16.

[33]Rodd, *Glimpses of a Strange Land*, pp. 170-74, 178-82. Rodd addresses the difficulties of assuming a structural problem in society, particularly with a latent desire to see contemporaneous global ills reflected in the prophets' concerns with the poor. "In ancient Israel poverty was a misfortune not a problem" (p. 180). He concludes, "the poor lacked power and honour, and were often subjected to oppression—and attempts were made to prevent them from starving and to secure justice for them. Both were seen to be important and in accord with obedience to God, but it is quite false to suppose that the Israelites thought that God was 'on the side of' the poor and was hostile to the rich" (pp. 181-82).

[34]See, e.g., Is 58:6-7; Jer 2:34; 5:28; 7:6; 22:16; Ezek 16:49; 18:5-18; 22:7; Zech 7:10; Mal 3:5. The references reflect the discussion in Rodd, *Glimpses of a Strange Land*, pp. 171-72.

[35]See Barton, *Understanding Old Testament Ethics*, pp. 97-129. He notes how both the indictments against the nations and Israel appear to reflect standards that most

people would be expected to agree on. The imbalance is that Israel, both northern and southern kingdoms, is held to even tighter standards than the nations. See also Petersen, *Prophetic Literature*, p. 39.

[36]See Rofé, *Introduction to the Prophetic Literature*, pp. 41-43.

Chapter 7

[1]Treating the Gospel separately from Luke's sequel, Acts, is no veiled contradiction of those who have insightfully observed a "narrative unity" between those two works. But I do think that enforcing a tight coordination between them can sometimes stifle the unique voices crying out from each. Stopping to listen to those unique voices is part of the corrective advanced by Mikeal C. Parsons and Richard I. Pervo, *Rethinking the Unity of Luke and Acts* (Minneapolis: Fortress Press, 1993).

[2]Most significant for this is Richard A. Burridge, *What Are the Gospels? A Comparison with Graeco-Roman Biography*, 2nd ed. (Grand Rapids: Eerdmans, 2004).

[3]Ibid., pp. 174-75, 202, 290-91. See also the summary in Richard A. Burridge, *Imitating Jesus: An Inclusive Approach to New Testament Ethics* (Grand Rapids: Eerdmans, 2007), pp. 24, 28-31.

[4]See Joel B. Green, *The Gospel of Luke* (Grand Rapids: Eerdmans, 1997), pp. 21-22; and Luke Timothy Johnson, *The Gospel of Luke* (Collegeville, MN: Liturgical Press, 1991), p. 3.

[5]I am not trying to suggest here that we will observe something we could call "Luke's ethics," but that his presentation will underscore unique emphases about Jesus that are important to a "Life of Jesus ethics." See Frank J. Matera, *New Testament Ethics: The Legacies of Jesus and Paul* (Louisville: Westminster John Knox, 1996), p. 9.

[6]This was observed most famously by Albert Schweitzer, "But it was not only each epoch that found its reflection in Jesus; each individual created Jesus in accordance with his own character. There is no historical task which so reveals a man's true self as the writing of a life of Jesus." *The Quest of the Historical Jesus*, ed. and trans. John Bowden (London: SCM Press, 2000), p. 6. The thesis was carried back into church history by Jaroslav Pelikan, *Jesus Through the Centuries: His Place in the History of Culture* (New Haven, CT: Yale University Press, 1985).

[7]One key popular figure in US history doing that is Thomas Jefferson, *The Jefferson Bible: The Life and Morals of Jesus of Nazareth* (Boston: Beacon Press, 1989). Jefferson excised all miracles from the Gospels, reducing Jesus to a master philosopher. For some summaries of more sophisticated biblical scholarly examples of that perspective, consider Mark Allen Powell, *Jesus as a Figure in History: How Modern Historians View the Man from Galilee* (Louisville: Westminster John Knox, 1998), pp. 25-28, 60-64. Note also the discussion in Burridge, *Imitating Jesus*, pp. 25-28. See the discussion, followed by extensive refutation, in Burridge, *Imitating Jesus*, pp. 33-34.

[8]Though consider Charles H. Talbert, who describes how the Gospel according to

Matthew portrays the relationship between Jesus and his disciples with language evocative of a philosopher and his pupils. *Matthew* (Grand Rapids: Baker Academic, 2010), pp. 20-24. Even then it is the association between them that supports this, not the teaching interaction itself.

[9]Limiting the count just to that expression *kingdom of God* or its counterpart in Matthew, *kingdom of heaven*, there are sixty-seven appearances of it Matthew and Luke. Contrast that with just the use of the word *love*—ten times in reference to a moral exhortation in Matthew and Luke.

[10]Luke combines kingdom language with salvation language, also incorporating other elements of a divine restoration program. For a summary of those, see Joel B. Green, *The Theology of the Gospel of Luke* (Cambridge: Cambridge University Press, 1995), pp. 28-37.

[11]Though the word *love* in various forms, both verbal and nominal, appears fifty-seven times in John, only in five statements does Jesus tells his disciples to love others: Jn 13:34 (twice); 13:35; 15:12; 15:17. Those statements are in his farewell discourse, and fellow disciples are to be the objects of that love.

[12]Burridge, *Imitating Jesus*, pp. 25-28.

[13]These are common observations by Lucan scholars. For a useful introductory discussion of those, consider R. Alan Culpepper, "The Gospel of Luke: Introduction, Commentary, and Reflections," in *The New Interpreter's Bible* (Nashville: Abingdon, 1995), 9:27-30.

[14]For insightful, in-depth analysis of these, see John O. York, *The Last Shall Be First: The Rhetoric of Reversal in Luke* (Sheffield, UK: JSOT Press, 1991).

[15]See Green, *Gospel of Luke*, p. 534.

[16]See also Allen Verhey, *The Great Reversal: Ethics and the New Testament* (Grand Rapids: Eerdmans, 1984), pp. 93-97. For a development of that motif by Luke in parallel to the Pauline presentation of Jesus in Phil 2:5-11, see H. Douglas Buckwalter, *The Character and Purpose of Luke's Christology* (Cambridge: Cambridge University Press, 1996), pp. 231-72.

[17]John Nolland indicates that a betrothed couple entering into sexual relations, as implied by a pregnancy, would be a violation of marriage customs. *Luke 1–9:20* (Dallas: Word, 1989), pp. 49, 104. On the other hand, Lynn Cohick suggests that shame need not necessarily be accorded to an engaged, unwed mother because of the legally binding nature of betrothal. *Women in the World of the Earliest Christians: Illuminating Ancient Ways of Life* (Grand Rapids: Baker Academic, 2009), p. 153. Luke's overt mention of the fact, however, would seem to lead to his implying shame from the reader's perspective.

[18]James Malcolm Arlandson lists "herdsmen" under the category of "the unclean and degraded," among the lowest in society. *Women, Class and Society in Early Christianity: Models from Luke-Acts* (Peabody, MA: Hendrickson, 1997), pp. 102-3.

[19]This is not a list of equally perceived marginalized. John Roth notes that certain "character-types" were expected to receive mercy, whereas "sinners" were not. Thus Luke's merging the two categories signals something new. *The Blind, the Lame, and the Poor: Character Types in Luke-Acts* (Sheffield, UK: Sheffield Academic Press, 1997), pp. 215-20. David A. Neale surveys how Luke takes "sinner" as a character type and uses that as a means of redirecting the extent of rescuing that Jesus performs. *None But the Sinners: Religious Categories in the Gospel of Luke* (Sheffield: Sheffield Academic Press, 1991). Arlandson points out how scholarship has failed to take into consideration the social distinctions of women in the Greco-Roman world, since it would be socially weak women who would be marginalized, not all women. *Women, Class and Society in Early Christianity*, pp. 6-12. Arlandson also provides evidence for other types appearing on this list as also being reckoned among the marginalized (ibid., pp. 22, 113-16). Social perception of tax collectors appears more significant than potential political association. Luke never distinguishes between Judean tax collectors, who collect for Rome, and Galilean tax collectors, who collect for Herod and would therefore not be perceived as selling out politically to Romans. Yet the sense of sleaze associated with the job carries over wherever they exist. According to Ramsay MacMullen, tax collectors were on the list of people to whom cultured Romans were supposed to be snobby. *Roman Social Relations: 50 B.C. to A.D. 284* (New Haven, CT: Yale University Press, 1974), pp. 138-41.

[20]Luke in his storytelling technique is clearly drawing on patterns from Old Testament stories, especially in Genesis 17 and Judges 13. Judith Lieu, *The Gospel of Luke* (Peterborough: Epworth, 1997), pp. 4-6. In those stories, however, people were allowed to question God without consequence. Here, Zechariah is not, unsettling expectations as Luke so often does with his use of the technique known as "defamiliarization." See James L. Resseguie, *Narrative Criticism of the New Testament: An Introduction* (Grand Rapids: Baker Academic, 2005), p. 34.

[21]Suggestions vary as to what is being communicated with that detail: The most likely suggestion is that it sets up the sign being offered to Mary about Elizabeth's condition (Lk 1:36). Culpepper, "Gospel of Luke," pp. 47-48. Lieu thinks it may also point to her desire to avoid her ongoing shame of barrenness until her pregnancy was obvious. *Gospel of Luke*, p. 6. See also Green, *Gospel of Luke*, p. 81.

[22]"In contrast to Zechariah, we notice, Mary holds no official position among the people, she is not described as 'righteous' in terms of observing Torah, and her experience does not take place in a cultic setting. She is among the most powerless people in her society: she is young in a world that values age; female in a world ruled by men; poor in a stratified economy. Furthermore, she has neither husband nor child to validate her existence. That she should have found 'favor with God' and be 'highly gifted' shows Luke's understanding of God's activity as surprising

and often paradoxical, almost always reversing human expectations." Johnson, *Gospel of Luke*, p. 39.

[23]York explains in details how the entire section works as "explicit bi-polar reversal." *Last Shall Be First*, pp. 44-55.

[24]Ibid., pp. 162-63.

[25]For the development of Luke's Christology, wherein Jesus is elevated to a divine level, see Robert F. O'Toole, *Luke's Presentation of Jesus: A Christology* (Rome: Editrice Pontificio Istituto Biblico, 2004), pp. 181-87, 207-16, 221-24. See also Buckwalter, *Character and Purpose of Luke's Christology*, pp. 173-228; C. Kavin Rowe, *Early Narrative Christology: The Lord in the Gospel of Luke* (New York: Walter de Gruyter, 2006).

[26]Nolland, *Luke 1-9:20*, pp. 91-92.

[27]Luke Timothy Johnson, *The Literary Function of Possessions in Luke-Acts* (Missoula, MT: Scholars Press, 1977), p. 91.

[28]For an explanation of the programmatic nature of this citation for Luke's unfolding story of Jesus, see ibid., p. 91.

[29]That would be typical of Luke's appeal to the concept of "sinner," which refers to someone completely alienated from God rather than to specific acts a person has committed. According to Neale this would be typical of the concept as it emerges from Septuaguintal readings of the psalms. *None But the Sinners*, pp. 75-97.

[30]Nolland notes how the leper's actions here are "reminiscent" of Peter's, earlier in the chapter. *Luke 1-9:20*, p. 227.

[31]Halvor Moxnes, "Patron-Client Relations and the New Community," in *The Social World of Luke-Acts: Models for Interpretation*, ed. Jerome H. Neyrey (Peabody, MA: Hendrickson, 1991), pp. 252-53.

[32]Johnson describes how these stories also underscore Jesus' prophetic credentials. *Literary Function of Possessions*, pp. 96-103.

[33]Resseguie cites this as a classic example of "defamiliarization." *Narrative Criticism of the New Testament*, pp. 34-36. My summary here damages Luke's version, since Luke does not inform the reader of Simon's name or inhospitality until later in the story. "The narrative invites stock responses from the reader only to overturn and dismantle those familiar expectations at the end" (p. 36).

[34]To assume that she is a prostitute, as many commentators do, is to change the story. *Sinner* is a shame label, not a label meant to identify a specific activity or infraction of norms. The story draws on competing "courts of reputation." See David A. deSilva, *The Hope of Glory: Honor Discourse and New Testament Interpretation* (Collegeville, MN: Liturgical Press, 1991), pp. 3-8. One court is from Jesus' perspective and the other from Simon's. The readers are urged to pick Jesus'.

[35]Luke surprises the readers with Jesus' sudden indication that the woman knew she had been forgiven by Jesus sometime prior to this incident. See Green, *Gospel of*

Luke, pp. 313-14; also Neale, *None But the Sinners*, p. 146. This would be another element of reordering in Luke's defamiliarizing technique.

[36]Lieu cautions against making too much of the mere phenomenon of women supporting men. It's the comparative status of having been delivered from demonic possession, as opposed to having been chosen, like the male apostles, that adds extra bite to this. *Gospel of Luke*, pp. 60-61. See also Arlandson, *Women, Class and Society in Early Christianity*, pp. 131-34.

[37]See Sverre Bøe, *Cross-Bearing in Luke* (Tübingen: Mohr Siebeck, 2010), esp. pp. 126-27.

[38]Green, *Gospel of Luke*, pp. 381-82; and Johnson, *Gospel of Luke*, pp. 153, 155-56.

[39]Culpepper, "Gospel of Luke," p. 227.

[40]Samaritans would be regarded by Jews as inferior to them, due to centuries of animosity between the two groups. "Their affiliation to the congregation of Israel was never denied, only considered doubtful." John Nolland, *Luke 9:21–18:34* (Dallas: Word, 1993), p. 536.

[41]Lieu, *Gospel of Luke*, p. 87.

[42]Green, *Gospel of Luke*, p. 434.

[43]"Martha's anxiety and concern are understandable enough. But her self-preoccupation and resentment led her to break the rules of hospitality far more radically than did her sister, for she asked a stranger to intervene in a family rivalry." Johnson, *Gospel of Luke*, pp. 175-76.

[44]Green, *Gospel of Luke*, pp. 465-66.

[45]In correcting his host, "Jesus is hardly the model guest." Culpepper, "Gospel of Luke," p. 286.

[46]Nolland, *Luke 9:21–18:34*, p. 749.

[47]Green, *Gospel of Luke*, pp. 578-86.

[48]"The word choice by Luke . . . corresponds to the portrayal of Mammon in 16:13 as an idol competing for human allegiance against God, which portrayal the Pharisees mock. In light of the sayings which follow, it is instructive to note that the term *bdelygma* is also used to designate sham outward worship (Isa. 1:13 and 66:3), immoral financial dealings (Deut 25:16), and the remarrying of a divorced wife (Deut 24:4)!" Johnson, *Gospel of Luke*, p. 250.

[49]Nolland, *Luke 9:21–18:34*, p. 828.

[50]Johnson, *Gospel of Luke*, p. 261.

[51]Neale, *None But the Sinners*, p. 177.

[52]Culpepper, "Gospel of Luke," p. 357.

[53]"Zacchaeus is not just another story of one who repents but the living proof of the realization of the promise of forgiveness of sin and the dawning of the day of God's mercy." Neale, *None But the Sinners*, p. 189.

[54]The words of Lk 2:34-35 in context probably do not refer to the death of Jesus di-

rectly, but more likely to the conflict the life of Jesus will engender in the rest of the story, conflict that reaches its zenith at the cross. See Green, *Gospel of Luke*, pp. 149-50. Culpepper elaborates on the "paradigmatic character" of Lk 4:16-30, pointing to his death. "Gospel of Luke," p. 108.

[55]Moxnes, "Patron-Client Relations and the New Community," p. 259.

[56]Johnson, *Gospel of Luke*, p. 347.

[57]Green, *Gospel of Luke*, pp. 822-23.

[58]Neale regards this mandate as the epitome of what has been going on all along in the Gospel with stories of sinners repenting before Jesus. *None But the Sinners*, p. 189.

[59]See O'Toole, *Luke's Presentation of Jesus*, pp. 113-40.

[60]O'Toole restricts the role of the prophet to having "knowledge not possessed by others" (such as knowing others' thoughts); performing miracles, suffering and being rejected; and predicting the future, the last of which he features at length. He also mentions the performance of miracle and symbolic actions. He makes no mention at all of the prophet as one who speaks God's words and indicts God's people. Ibid., pp. 42-51.

[61]Johnson, *Literary Function of Possessions*, pp. 91-94; and O'Toole, *Luke's Presentation of Jesus*, pp. 29-31.

[62]Johnson points out how the section running from Lk 7:1-8:3 fuels the prophetic image of Jesus by reflecting the responses of the crowds to Jesus as though he were a prophet. *Literary Function of Possessions*, pp. 96-103.

[63]Lieu remarks how John's harsh images have echoes with words in Amos and Isaiah. *Gospel of Luke*, p. 24.

[64]Green notes how that response reemerges in Lk 3:12, 3:14, 10:25, 18:18, as well as in Acts 2:37, 16:30, 22:10. *Gospel of Luke*, p. 177.

[65]O'Toole shows convincingly how that activity is associated both with God, sometimes as "the Father," and with Jesus. Luke's narrative often uses Jesus' pronouncements of forgiveness to point to him being more than just a human prophet. *Luke's Presentation of Jesus*, pp. 213-15.

[66]See Rowe, *Early Narrative Christology*, pp. 199-201.

[67]In noting the intensifying prophetic message in the travel section, Johnson states that Jesus "is at once a) calling to the crowds for conversion and warning them of being lost if they do not convert; calling to individuals from among the crowd to become his disciples; b) experiencing rejection at the hands of the Pharisees/ Lawyers and in turn threatening them with rejection; c) instructing his disciples. In a word, the core of the faithful people is being prepared on the road to Jerusalem. Those who are going to reject are rejecting, those who are going to convert are being called; those who are following are being instructed." *Literary Function of Possessions*, p. 112.

[68]"If a man's heart is centered on his earthly possessions, he will be incapable of responding to God's visitation; if his heart is centered on the kingdom, he will give away his possessions and find his treasure with God. In both responses, the disposition of possessions is a sign of the response of the heart to God." Johnson, *Literary Function of Possessions*, p. 155.

[69]That is not a point discussed in chapter six. Typical examples of that activity would include acts such as Isaiah walking naked and barefoot as a sign of what was about to happen to the Egyptians when carried away as captives by the Assyrians (Is 20:1-5), or Ezekiel building ramps in the ground against a brick, as though a city, to show how Jerusalem would undergo a lengthy siege (Ezek 4:1-7). For an in-depth study of the phenomenon, consider W. D. Stacey, *Prophetic Drama in the Old Testament* (London: Epworth Press, 1990).

[70]O'Toole also regards Jesus' activity of teaching in the temple immediately afterward as symbolic of the temple having been cleansed. *Luke's Presentation of Jesus*, pp. 50-51.

[71]"The most important reversal portrayed in the Gospel is that which takes place in the life of Jesus. He is the son conceived by the Holy Spirit, empowered by the Spirit to reverse the plight of all those without honor, the one transfigured in the presence of disciples, the one who proclaims the good news of the kingdom. Yet he is destined (δει) to suffer death on the cross. By humbling himself, however, he prepares for God's great exaltation—the resurrection and his ascension into heaven. Jesus thus becomes the model to be followed (9.22ff.; 14.26ff.; 17.25ff.) for those wishing to experience the exaltation side of God's bi-polar reversal." York, *Last Shall Be First*, pp. 171-72.

[72]This is an adaptation of the concept as explained by Stephen E. Fowl, *The Story of Christ in the Ethics of Paul: An Analysis of the Function of the Hymnic Material in the Pauline Corpus* (Sheffield, UK: JSOT Press, 1990), pp. 92-95. Fowl applies the concept initially as a means for deriving ethics from a story of Christ in Phil 2:5-11, a story reflecting a similar humility-to-exaltation pattern.

[73]See Bøe, *Cross-Bearing in Luke*, pp. 116-26.

[74]Burridge, *Imitating Jesus*, p. 31.

[75]Bøe, *Cross-Bearing in Luke*, pp. 89, 93; and Green, *Gospel of Luke*, p. 372.

[76]Bøe helpfully connects this to the statement in Lk 9:46 of disciples asserting their own greatness. He proceeds to disavow tendencies to impose modern notions of the "self," ascetic notions of denial of substances or early Christian notions of the embracing of martyrdom. Instead, he sees "that denying oneself in order to follow Jesus indicates a relational character of self-denial; the loyalties of a disciple should not be to 'oneself,' but to Jesus. Self-denial indicates surrender, a handing over. This again indicates that self-denial is an individual project, a most personal affair—but not private in the sense of a secret or sentimental issue. The need to

confess Christ publicly and to carry the cost is evident in Luke 9.23-27." *Cross-Bearing in Luke*, p. 100.

[77]Ibid., pp. 126-27.

[78]"The disciples are thus called to imitate the one whose leadership style reversed the ways of worldly rulers in accordance with God's divine principle—the humble servant will be exalted (1.47-55)." York, *Last Shall Be First*, p. 171.

[79]"Luke's intentional development of a sympathetic view of the 'sinner' is unique among the Gospels. No other canonical Gospel shows such an interest in developing the role of the 'sinner' into one with whom the reader can not only sympathize, but ultimately identify. It is but a short step from understanding the plight of the lost son to recognizing elements of our own experience in his struggles. Luke's 'sinner' has evolved from a despised element of society (Lk. 3.12; 5.28; 6.32ff.) to a sympathetic figure with whom the reader is encouraged to identify (Lk. 7.36-50; 13.1-5; 15.1-32)." Neale, *None But the Sinners*, p. 164.

[80]Green, *Gospel of Luke*, p. 272.

[81]Ibid., pp. 273-75.

[82]Johnson, *Literary Function of Possessions*, pp. 142-43.

Chapter 8

[1]See Richard Burridge, *Imitating Jesus* (Grand Rapids: Eerdmans, 2007), pp. 33-34; Dale C. Allison Jr., *Studies in Matthew: Interpretation Past and Present* (Grand Rapids: Baker Academic, 2005), pp. 142-47; and Graham N. Stanton, *A Gospel for a New People: Studies in Matthew* (Edinburgh: T & T Clark, 1992), pp. 64-71, 323.

[2]See Ulrich Luz, *The Theology of the Gospel of Matthew*, trans. J. Bradford Robinson (Cambridge: Cambridge University Press, 1995), pp. 1-6.

[3]Richard A. Burridge, *What Are the Gospels?* (Grand Rapids: Eerdmans, 1994.), pp. 135-36, 166.

[4]Ibid., pp. 135-36, 156-66.

[5]For an exhaustive list of repetitions, grouped by additional features, see Dale C. Allison Jr. and W. D. Davies, *A Critical and Exegetical Commentary on the Gospel According to Saint Matthew* (Edinburgh: T & T Clark, 1988), 1:88-92.

[6]The official term for Greek-based literature is σύγκρισις or *syncrisis*. See Stanton, *A Gospel for a New People*, pp. 77-84. It is close to a Hebrew-based literary technique, *qal vahomer*, an argument that moves from the lesser to the greater. See Phillip Sigal, *The Halakhah of Jesus of Nazareth According to the Gospel of Matthew* (Leiden: Brill, 2008), p. 83. For ancient examples of and instruction in the technique see Libanius's Progymnasmata: *Model Exercises in Greek Prose Composition and Rhetoric*, trans. Craig A. Gibson (Atlanta: Society of Biblical Literature, 2008), pp. 321-53, also pp. 51-53, 99; and *Progymnasmata: Greek Textbooks of Prose Composition and Rhetoric*, trans. George A. Kennedy (Leiden: Brill, 2003), pp. 52-55.

Also Dale C. Allison Jr., *The New Moses: A Matthean Typology* (Minneapolis: Fortress Press, 1993), p. 12. The basic vocabulary often associated with simple comparisons includes words such as the following: ὡς, ὅμοιος, ὁμοιόω, ὥσπερ, ὡσεί, οὕτως, μείζων, παραβολή. These terms abound in Matthew, though Luke does use ὡς and ὡσεί slightly more. See Luz, *Matthew 1–7*, trans. James E. Crouch (Minneapolis: Fortress Press, 2007), pp. 25-38.

[7]For syncrisis with Israel, see William L. Kynes, *A Christology of Solidarity: Jesus as the Representative of His People in Matthew* (Lanham, MD: University Press of America, 1991), pp. 15-20. For syncrisis with Moses, see Allison, *New Moses*. For warrant for syncrisis with a messianic Son of David, see Lidija Novakovic, *Messiah, the Healer of the Sick* (Tübingen: Mohr Siebeck, 2003).

[8]The official term is *mimesis*. See Burridge, *Imitating Jesus*, p. 31, who notes its prevalence in Greco-Roman *bioi* as denoting "imitation of a good example to follow, or a bad one to avoid." For an excellent summary of the imitation motif in Matthew, see Allison, *Studies in Matthew*, pp. 147-53.

[9]Of Matthew's thirty-seven references to the kingdom, only five use "kingdom of God": Mt 6:33; 12:28; 19:24; 21:31, 43.

[10]For an encapsulation of this practice and its origins, see Everett Ferguson, *Backgrounds of Early Christianity*, 3rd ed. (Grand Rapids: Eerdmans, 2003), p. 538.

[11]This scholarly commonplace might confuse those who have been told that the Messiah is predicted all over the Old Testament. Consider one definitive scholarly voice among many: "When one looks up the term *māšîaḥ* (Hebrew) or *christos* (Greek), both referring to an anointed person, one is surprised to learn that the term is never used in the Old Testament of a future Jewish ruler—never." Ben Witherington III, *The Indelible Image: The Theological and Ethical Thought World of the New Testament*, vol. 1, *The Individual Witnesses* (Downers Grove, IL: IVP Academic, 2009), p. 70. The term is based on Old Testament images, but is not itself a specific Old Testament hope.

[12]For an in-depth, historical treatment of the concept that is rooted in actual Jewish writings from the period, consider John J. Collins, *The Scepter and the Star: The Messiahs of the Dead Sea Scrolls and Other Ancient Literature* (New York: Doubleday, 1995), pp. 31-41.

[13]One famous expression is found in the collection of Jewish synagogue hymns called the *Psalms of Solomon*. Hymn 17 reflects these sentiments clearly: "See, Lord, and raise up for them their king, / the son of David, to rule over your servant Israel / . . . to purge Jerusalem from Gentiles / . . . He will judge peoples and nations in the wisdom of his righteousness / . . . and their king shall be the Lord Messiah." Quoted from *The Old Testament Pseudepigrapha*, ed. James H. Charlesworth (London: Darton, Longman & Todd, 1985), 2:667.

[14]One famous expression of this is found among the Dead Sea Scrolls in a fragment

known as 4Q521: "and the earth will listen to his anointed one [i.e. Messiah]. . . . For the Lord . . . will honour the pious upon the throne of an eternal kingdom, freeing prisoners, giving sight to the blind . . . he will heal the badly wounded and will make the dead live, he will proclaim good news to the poor." Quoted from *The Dead Sea Scroll: Study Edition*, ed. Florentino García Martínez and Eibert J. C. Tigchelaar (Leiden: Brill, 1998), 2:1045.

[15]Collins, *Scepter and the Star*, pp. 102-35.

[16]See Luz, *Matthew 1–7*, pp. 15-18.

[17]See N. T. Wright, *The New Testament and the People of God* (London: SPCK, 1992), pp. 385-86; Michael A. Knibb, "The Exile in the Literature of the Intertestamental Period," *Heythrop Journal* 18, no. 3 (1976): 253-72.

[18]See Mt 1:22-23; 2:14-15, 17-18, 23; 4:13-16; 8:16-17; 12:15-21; 13:13-15, 34-35; 21:4-5; 27:9-10. A high proportion of these fulfillment statements appear in this opening segment. Jesus' arrival is part of a divine plan. See Bauer, "Literary and Theological Function of the Genealogy in Matthew's Gospel," pp. 129-59.

[19]Ibid., p. 155.

[20]For a full development of recompense, consider Blaine Charette, *The Theme of Recompense in Matthew's Gospel* (Sheffield, UK: Sheffield Academic Press, 1992), pp. 119-61.

[21]Allison, *New Moses*, pp. 172-80; Stanton, *Gospel for a New People*, p. 80.

[22]Klyne Snodgrass points out that advocating going beyond what a law says is certainly not against the law. "Matthew and the Law," in *Treasures Old and New: Contributions to Matthean Studies*, ed. David R. Bauer and Mark Alan Powell (Atlanta: Scholars Press, 1996), pp. 120-22.

[23]That observation is a commonplace observed by many commentators. For one example, see R. T. France, *The Gospel of Matthew* (Grand Rapids: Eerdmans, 2007), p. 325. Jesus is called teacher by a scribe (Mt 8:19), by Pharisees (Mt 9:11), by "some of the scribes and Pharisees" (Mt 12:38), by "collectors of the temple tax" (Mt 17:24), by a young man who had many possessions he was unwilling to give up to follow Jesus (Mt 19:16, 22), by disciples of Pharisees, along with Herodians (Mt 22:16), by some Sadducees (Mt 22:24), by a lawyer from among the Pharisees (Mt 22:36).

[24]Again, that observation is a commonplace for many commentators. For one example, see ibid., p. 293.

[25]France likewise notes the possibility of an "echo" of the mercy of Mt 9:13, also noting how each of these stories in this segment are meaningfully linked to each other. *Gospel of Matthew*, p. 366.

[26]That is probably an adaptation of Leviticus's "You shall be holy, for I the LORD your God am holy" (Lev 19:2). Burridge, *Imitating Jesus*, pp. 216-17.

[27]Ibid., pp. 77-78.

[28]See Richard A. Edwards, *Matthew's Narrative Portrait of Disciples: How the Text-*

Connoted Reader Is Informed (Harrisburg, PA: Trinity Press International, 1997), pp. 28-39. For little-faith disciples in Mt 16–20, see Jeannine K. Brown, *The Disciples in Narrative Perspective: The Portrayal and Function of the Matthean Disciples* (Atlanta: Society of Biblical Literature, 2002). Note also Michael J. Wilkins, *Discipleship in the Ancient World and Matthew's Gospel*, 2nd ed. (Grand Rapids: Baker Books, 1995), p. 172.

[29]Novakovic, *Messiah, the Healer of the Sick*, pp. 159-63.

[30]The words here resemble the words of messianic hope mentioned in footnote 14 of this chapter, from 4Q521 among the Dead Sea Scrolls.

[31]To see that developed in detail, consider Young S. Chae, *Jesus as the Eschatological Davidic Shepherd: Studies in the Old Testament, Second Temple Judaism, and in the Gospel of Matthew* (Tübingen: Mohr Siebeck, 2006), pp. 205-12; also Novakovic, *Messiah, the Healer of the Sick*, pp. 131-32.

[32]The case for Jesus as a gentle king here is developed independently by Deirdre J. Good, *The Meek King* (Harrisburg, PA: Trinity Press International, 1999), pp. 82-93; and Jon Laansma, *"I Will Give You Rest": The Rest Motif in the New Testament with Special Reference to Mt 11 and Heb 3–4* (Tübingen: Mohr Siebeck, 1997), pp. 209-22.

[33]For a detailed description of the Jewish halakhic nuances of this interaction, see Sigal, *Halakhah of Jesus of Nazareth*, pp. 156-71.

[34]See France, *Gospel of Matthew*, p. 490: the sign makes sense only to those who know of Jesus' resurrection.

[35]So Richard B. Hays, *The Moral Vision of the New Testament* (San Francisco: HarperCollins, 1996), pp. 105-6; and Stanton, *Gospel for a New People*, p. 189.

[36]So France, *Gospel of Matthew*, p. 591.

[37]The word she uses for the "dogs" among which she considers herself in v. 27 is κυνάρια—"bitches."

[38]Charles H. Talbert provides examples of teachers challenging the commitment of those wanting to be disciples. *Matthew* (Grand Rapids: Eerdmans, 2010), p. 190.

[39]Allison and Davies, *Matthew*, p. 270.

[40]Stanton, *Gospel for a New People*, pp. 185-89.

[41]France, *Gospel of Matthew*, p. 641; Talbert, *Matthew*, pp. 204-5.

[42]France, *Gospel of Matthew*, p. 694; Hays, *Moral Vision of the New Testament*, pp. 101-2; and Talbert, *Matthew*, p. 221.

[43]Stanton, *Gospel for a New People*, pp. 214-21.

[44]Ps 22:1 (Ps 21:2 LXX) is evoked with the words of Mt 27:46: "My God, my God, why have you forsaken me?" Prior to that Matthew uses the vocabulary of the LXX psalm in narrative descriptions and asides: foes casting lots for his garments (Ps 22:18/21:19—Mt 27:35); head-shaking derision (Ps 22:6/21:7—Mt 27:39); mockery (Ps 22:7/21:8—Mt 27:41); taunts to trust God (Ps 22:9/21:10—Mt 27:43-44).

[45]This is developed nicely in France, *Gospel of Matthew*, pp. 1112-13.

[46]Hays, *Moral Vision of the New Testament*, p. 109.

[47]Charette, *Theme of Recompense*, pp. 121-40.

[48]Talbert demonstrates how association with a teacher was thought of as a transformative experience within the Greco-Roman world. *Matthew*, pp. 20-24. Though Matthew fits within that environment, Matthew also purposefully declares that Jesus is more than just another teacher. Being "with Jesus" is, in Matthew's world, being with the presence of God (Mt 1:23; 28:20).

[49]See Stanton, *Gospel for a New People*, pp. 371-77.

[50]See Dale B. Martin, who surveys conflicting views about the body in the Greco-Roman world, noting that for some, disease was perceived as a form of invasion needing to be repulsed. That would lead many to assume a demonic invasion and a disease invasion to be inseparable. Matthew is not communicating that, even if he does put the two different forms of invasion into the same category of cure. *The Corinthian Body* (New Haven, CT: Yale University Press, 1995), pp. 139-62.

[51]Again, note *Psalms of Solomon* 17. See the discussion in Collins, *Scepter and the Star*, pp. 53-56.

[52]The warning of Mt 7:21-23 makes that clear: "Not everyone who says to me, 'Lord, Lord,' will enter the kingdom of heaven, but only the one who does the will of my Father in heaven. On that day many will say to me, 'Lord, Lord, did we not prophesy in your name, and cast out demons in your name, and do many deeds of power in your name?' Then I will declare to them, 'I never knew you; go away from me, you evildoers.'"

[53]See France, *Gospel of Matthew*, pp. 826-27; and Talbert, *Matthew*, p. 253.

[54]Often the "little ones" are considered to be anyone in need. See the discussion in Stanton, *Gospel for a New People*, pp. 207-31, for why the expression should probably be restricted to disciples.

[55]Charette offers a compelling case for the importance of those two motivations as adaptations of the Abrahamic promises and Mosaic covenantal blessings and curses. See his *Theme of Recompense in Matthew's Gospel*.

[56]That is the standard grouping found in most commentaries. See the discussion in Charles H. Talbert, *Reading the Sermon on the Mount: Character Formation and Ethical Decision Making in Matthew 5-7* (Grand Rapids: Baker Academic, 2004), pp. 21-26. Though there is much diversity in how subunits of these chapters should be perceived, recognition of the basic threefold division is quite widespread.

[57]Eugene Boring, "The Gospel of Matthew," in *The New Interpreter's Bible* (Nashville: Abingdon Press, 1995), 8:177.

[58]See Donald A. Hagner, *Matthew 1-13* (Dallas: Word, 1993), pp. 91-92; and Talbert, *Reading the Sermon on the Mount*, p. 50.

[59]"The nine pronouncements are thus not statements about general human virtues—

most appear exactly the opposite to common wisdom." Boring, "Gospel of Matthew," p. 178.

[60]France notes that the overall sense is the same, whether salt would be used for flavoring or for preservation. *Gospel of Matthew*, p. 174.

[61]See the useful discussion in Snodgrass, "Matthew and the Law," pp. 114-18. Though the sense of something coming to pass as formerly predicted may be in view with the use of the word *fulfill*, it more likely refers to the sense of completing requirements. The importance of law is then underscored with hyperbole in Mt 5:18-19 "to persuade the reader that scripture is of permanent validity and is to be practiced as the will of God" (ibid., p. 118).

[62]Donald A. Hagner, "Ethics and the Sermon on the Mount," *Studia Theologica* 51 (1997): 47; and Snodgrass, "Matthew and the Law," pp. 120-22.

[63]So Talbert, *Reading the Sermon on the Mount*, pp. 70-71, as opposed to Allison and Davies, *Matthew*, p. 509, who see anger as the same as hatred, and therefore a source for murder. For more explanation see Allison, *Sermon on the Mount*, pp. 61-62.

[64]Allison and Davies, *Matthew*, p. 526; and Talbert, *Reading the Sermon on the Mount*, pp. 74-76.

[65]Sigal, *Halakhah of Jesus of Nazareth*, p. 114.

[66]Allison develops this possibility in detail, noting especially Jesus being slapped (Mt 26:67), his garments being taken from him (Mt 27:35) and someone being forced to carry Jesus' cross (Mt 27:32), along with connections between Mt 5:38-42 and Is 50:4-11. *Studies in Matthew*, pp. 219-22. See also France, *Gospel of Matthew*, pp. 220-21.

[67]Lev 19:34 directly connects Israelites loving aliens as themselves with doing to them what they would have wanted done when they were aliens in Egypt. Connections between love and mercy are not uncommon in Second Temple literature. See *Testament of Naphthali* 8.1-8 and *Testament of Gad* 6.1-7 among the *Testaments of the Twelve Patriarchs*; see also Cairo *Damascus Document* 6.20-7.1 and Philo, *De Virtutibus* 102-8, 20-21, where he elaborates on Leviticus 19:34.

[68]For a similar point, see Hagner, "Ethics and the Sermon on the Mount," pp. 52-53. See John Howard Yoder, *What Would You Do? A Serious Answer to a Standard Question* (Scottdale, PA: Herald Press, 1992), pp. 11-24, whose popular-level refutation of the logic of self-defense does not overrule the microethical boundaries of this scenario. It is difficult to move from a microsetting to a macro-one, whether one is advocating "just war" or pacifism.

[69]Allison, *Sermon on the Mount*, pp. 7-8; and Talbert, *Reading the Sermon on the Mount*, p. 78.

[70]So most commentators. Note France, *Gospel of Matthew*, pp. 250-51.

[71]Allison and Davies, *Matthew*, p. 661.

[72]Talbert considers Mt 7:1-12 as a continuous unit on judgment, with vv. 1-5 elaborating how not to do it, and vv. 6-12 how: discerningly (v. 6), with wisdom asked persistently from God (vv. 7-11), in the way one would want it done to oneself (v. 12). *Reading the Sermon on the Mount*, pp. 131-32. In support of the line pursued here, see France, *Gospel of Matthew*, pp. 273-73.

[73]"Certain commands must be *radicalized*: this applies to the great ethical commands, especially those enjoining concern for one's fellow human beings. Other commands must be *downplayed*: this applies to commands concerned with ritual and rite." Birger Gerhardsson, *The Ethos of the Bible*, trans. Stephen Westerholm (Philadelphia: Fortress Press, 1979), pp. 44-45. See also Hays, *Moral Vision of the New Testament*, pp. 99-101.

[74]Faithfulness is probably a better translation than "faith." Donald A. Hagner also notes Old Testament antecedents to these concerns in Is 1:17, Jer 22:3, Hos 6:6, Zech 7:9-10, Mic 6:8 and Hab 2:4. *Matthew 14-28* (Dallas: Word, 1995), p. 670.

[75]"Matthew . . . was presumably of the opinion that the love commandment was supreme, that if a conflict should arise among the commandments all the rest should be subordinated to that of love." Ulrich Luz, *The Theology of the Gospel of Matthew*, trans. J. Bradford Robinson (Cambridge: Cambridge University Press, 1995), p. 53.

[76]That example is elaborated by Talbert, *Reading the Sermon on the Mount*, pp. 87-88.

[77]As I am writing this, a homosexual rights group has succeeded in shutting down a Christian adoption agency because that agency refused to facilitate adoptions by same-sex partners, effectively harming thousands of lives over the refusal to grant a privilege that could be satisfied elsewhere. Shutting down an agency of mercy over nonconformity to a fringe practice would certainly exemplify straining out a gnat while swallowing a camel (Mt 23:24).

Chapter 9

[1]For a detailed demonstration of this with regard to Romans, consider N. T. Wright, "Romans and the Theology of Paul," in *Society of Biblical Literature Seminar Papers* (Atlanta: Scholars Press, 1992), pp. 184-92. See also Francis Watson, *Paul and the Hermeneutics of Faith* (London: T & T Clark, 2004), pp. 276-77. Though Watson does not see Paul developing an Old Testament theological narrative, he does see that Paul derives his theology about what Jesus does from his reading the Torah and the Prophets.

[2]On the conversion of Paul, see Alan Segal, *Paul the Convert: The Apostolate and Apostasy of Saul the Pharisee* (New Haven, CT: Yale University Press, 1990). For the importance of Paul's Jewishness, consider relevant articles in *The Dictionary of Paul and His Letters*, ed. Gerald F. Hawthorne and Ralph P. Martin (Downers Grove, IL: InterVarsity Press, 1993), esp. W. R. Stegner, "Jew, Paul the," pp. 503-11. For Paul's Jewish view of holiness, see Calvin Roetzel, *Paul: The Man and the Myth*

(Edinburgh: T & T Clark, 1999), pp. 30-38. For a succinct overview of Paul's theology and its Jewish connectedness, see Michael J. Gorman, *Apostle of the Crucified
Lord* (Grand Rapids: Eerdmans, 2004), pp. 131-45. For a useful presentation of the
range of scholarship on this topic, see David G. Horrell, *An Introduction to the
Study of Paul*, 2nd ed. (London: T & T Clark, 2006), pp. 57-105.

[3]See Victor Paul Furnish, *Theology and Ethics in Paul* (Nashville: Abingdon, 1968),
whose descriptions of this relationship are still the starting point for this topic.

[4]For a brief description of some of these specifics, see Gorman, *Apostle of the Crucified Lord*, pp. 65-71.

[5]This will receive further discussion in the introductory section of chap. 10.

[6]For particulars on Paul as letter writer and the relative dating of letters, consider
Gorman, *Apostle of the Crucified Lord*, pp. 74-96; and Horrell, *An Introduction to
the Study of Paul*, pp. 44-49.

[7]For scholarly conclusions on dating reflecting contrasting theological perspectives,
consider D. A. Carson and Douglas J. Moo, *An Introduction to the New Testament*,
2nd ed. (Grand Rapids: Zondervan, 2005); and Carl R. Holladay, *A Critical Introduction to the New Testament* (Nashville: Abingdon Press, 2009).

[8]The more noteworthy examples include Rom 12:14, 19-21 (see Mt 5:39-47; Lk 6:27-
35); 1 Cor 7:10-11 (see Mt 5:32; 19:3-9; Mk 10:2-9; Lk 16:18); 1 Cor 11:23-26 (see Mt
26:26-29; Mk 14:18-21; Lk 22:21-23); Rom 13:9-10 and Gal 5:14 (see Mt 7:12; 22:35-40;
Mk 12:28-31). 1 Cor 9:14 alludes to a command of Jesus without exactly quoting it.

[9]For Jesus as exemplar, see chap. 7. Paul appeals to Jesus as exemplar in 1 Cor 11:1,
Rom 15:1-3 and Phil 2:5-8.

[10]Ephesians, which follows Galatians, is actually a bit longer. For specifics on mea-
surements, see Bruce M. Metzger, *The Canon of the New Testament* (Oxford: Clarendon Press, 1987), pp. 297-99.

[11]See the discussion in Robert Banks, *Paul's Idea of Community*, rev. ed. (Peabody,
MA: Hendrickson, 1994), pp. 31-36; also Jerome Murphy-O'Connor, *St. Paul's
Corinth: Texts and Archaeology*, 3rd ed. (Collegeville, MN: Liturgical Press, 2002),
pp. 178-84.

[12]Roy E. Ciampa and Brian S. Rosner suggest that she may have been an Ephesian
businesswoman with agents traveling between Corinth and Ephesus, where Paul
is as he writes the letter (1 Cor 16:8). *The First Letter to the Corinthians* (Grand
Rapids: Eerdmans, 2010), p. 77. Craig S. Keener notes that possibility, but suggests
that the reverse also be possible, that Chloe lived in Corinth and was a member of
the church there. *1-2 Corinthians* (Cambridge: Cambridge University Press, 2005),
p. 24. Banks allows for the possibility that Chloe may even have sponsored a
church group in her house. *Paul's Idea of Community*, pp. 33-34.

[13]For variations in the complexity of the situation, compare Thiselton with Winter:
Anthony C. Thiselton, *The First Epistle to the Corinthians* (Grand Rapids: Eerdmans,

2000), pp. 32-36; Bruce W. Winter, *After Paul Left Corinth: The Influence of Secular Ethics and Social Change* (Grand Rapids: Eerdmans, 2001), pp. 1-3.

[14]Some may disagree with grouping 1 Cor 5–6 and 1 Cor 8–10 as individual issues. For at least one treatment of Paul's ethics that combines both chapters 5–6 and 8–10, see David G. Horrell, *Solidarity and Difference* (London: T & T Clark, 2005), pp. 140-52, 168-82.

[15]For a detailed overview of important issues for reading New Testament letters, see David E. Aune, *The New Testament in Its Literary Environment* (Philadelphia: Westminster Press, 1987), pp. 158-225. For a simpler overview of Paul as a letter writer, consider Gorman, *Apostle of the Crucified Lord*, pp. 74-97; and Horrell, *An Introduction to the Study of Paul*, pp. 44-55.

[16]Either one is possible. For representative contrasting views, see discussions in Joseph A. Fitzmyer, *First Corinthians* (New Haven, CT: Yale University Press, 2008), pp. 141-42, who favors Corinth, and Ciampa and Rosner, *First Letter to the Corinthians*, p. 77, who argue for Chloe as a resident of Ephesus, with business associates traveling to Corinth.

[17]This is an adaptation of the thoughts of J. Christiaan Beker, *Paul the Apostle: The Triumph of God in Life and Thought* (Philadelphia: Fortress Press, 1984), pp. 23-25.

[18]The expression τὸ αὐτὸ λέγητε is an adaptation of the common τὸ αὐτὸ φρονεῖν. See G. Adolph Deissmann, *Bible Studies: Contributions Chiefly from Papyri and Inscriptions to the History of the Language, the Literature, and the Religion of Hellenistic Judaism and Primitive Christianity*, trans. Alexander Grieve (Edinburgh: T & T Clark, 1901), p. 256. For the commonness of the concept of harmony in Greco-Roman rhetoric and its reflection in 1 Corinthians 1–4, see Martin, *The Corinthian Body* (New Haven, CT: Yale University Press, 1995), pp. 38-47, 56-58.

[19]Paul's self-description as rhetorically ungifted is itself a common rhetorical device, perhaps indicating that Paul is indeed sufficiently trained. See Martin, *Corinthian Body*, pp. 48-55.

[20]Stiff competition between secular teachers, whose students were expected to be fiercely loyal to them, was part of the normal Corinthian scene. See Winter, *After Paul Left Corinth*, pp. 36-39.

[21]Ibid., pp. 40-43. Winter suggests that the cultural climate of the philosophical Sophists had infiltrated the Corinthian culture, influencing believers to apply the standards of the unconverted world to their converted teachers. See also Keener, *1–2 Corinthians*, pp. 29-30.

[22]Gordon D. Fee, *The First Epistle to the Corinthians* (Grand Rapids: Eerdmans, 1987), p. 67.

[23]See Martin Hengel, *Crucifixion in the Ancient World and the Folly of the Message of the Cross* (Philadelphia: Fortress Press, 1977), pp. 1-9. Ciampa and Rosner say, "The cross was a shocking image in the ancient world—of evil, shame, rejection

and punishment." *First Epistle to the Corinthians*, p. 92. For a development of the issues associated with competing views of honor and shame between Paul and the Corinthian elites, consider Raymond Pickett, *The Cross in Corinth: The Social Significance of the Death of Jesus* (Sheffield, UK: Sheffield Academic Press, 1997), pp. 39-58.

[24]See Pickett, *Cross in Corinth*, p. 74.

[25]"The cross, then, constitutes the point at which, and/or the means through which, God's presence and promise becomes operative as that which actualizes and transforms." Thiselton, *First Epistle to the Corinthians*, p. 156.

[26]Paul does not elaborate on the new covenant here, but his awareness of the Spirit as the agent of that covenant is clear from his writings. See Gordon Fee, *God's Empowering Presence: The Holy Spirit in the Letters of Paul* (Peabody, MA: Hendrickson, 1994), pp. 812-13. For the origin of the concept, see Jer 31:31-34 and Ezek 36:24-27, two passages that Paul merges in 2 Cor 3:2-6.

[27]Ibid., p. 110.

[28]Fee, *First Epistle to the Corinthians*, p. 136. Since Fee's commentary was published, scholarship on 1 Corinthians has increasingly attributed most of the problems in the Corinthian church to social tensions stemming from the value system of a social elite that is at odds with those from a more common way of life. See the survey of the development of this prevailing view in Thiselton, *First Epistle to the Corinthians*, pp. 25-28.

[29]Fee, *First Epistle to the Corinthians*, pp. 194-95.

[30]The segment from 1 Cor 5:1–6:20 actually contains three different issues: how to deal with a sexually immoral man living in incest (1 Cor 5:1-13), lawsuits between church members (1 Cor 6:1-11), the sexual immorality of a man visiting a prostitute (1 Cor 6:12-20). For explanations as to how they are linked, see both Fee, *First Epistle to the Corinthians*, pp. 194-96; and Ciampa and Rosner, *First Letter to the Corinthians*, pp. 237-51.

[31]Richard B. Hays, *First Corinthians* (Louisville: John Knox Press, 1997), p. 82.

[32]See Winter, *After Paul Left Corinth*, pp. 45-47. Winter points to specific legal sanctions against a man marrying his father's widow.

[33]Keener offers concrete, historical evidence for the easy possibility of such a scenario. *1–2 Corinthian*, p. 48. Winter suggests instead that the father is still living, with the son in an adulterous-incestuous relationship with an older woman. *After Paul Left Corinth*, pp. 47-49. The latter would have elicited severe legal sanctions that resemble the kind of action Paul is urging the Corinthians to take.

[34]See Andrew D. Clarke, *Secular and Christian Leadership in Corinth: A Socio-Historical and Exegetical Study of 1 Corinthians 1–6* (Leiden: E. J. Brill, 1993), pp. 73-88. Note also Winter, *After Paul Left Corinth*, pp. 53-57; and Martin, *Corinthian Body*, pp. 69-70.

[35]Perhaps they were claiming the same rights and privileges of the elite in their immoral, gluttonous behavior often associated with coming of age. See Winter, *After Paul Left Corinth*, pp. 76-93.

[36]See Jerome Murphy-O'Connor, *Keys to First Corinthians: Revisiting the Major Issues* (Oxford: Oxford University Press, 2008), pp. 17-18.

[37]Brian S. Rosner suggests that Paul desires them to be "confessing the sin of the erring brother as if it were their own." *Paul Scripture and Ethics: A Study of 1 Corinthians 5–7* (Leiden: E. J. Brill, 1994), p. 72.

[38]If Winter is correct, the penalty that Paul advocates the church enact mirrors what would happen under Roman law if an elite Roman were to enter into an adulterous, incestuous relationship: banishment and stripping of citizenship and property. Winter, *After Paul Left Corinth*, pp. 44-57. That would make Paul's comments even more situational specific, rather than generic for all churches.

[39]See Victor Paul Furnish, *Theology and Ethics in Paul* (Nashville: Abingdon, 1968), pp. 224-27. For more focused theological treatment, see Hermann Ridderbos, *Paul: An Outline of His Theology*, trans. John Richard De Witt (Grand Rapids: Eerdmans, 1975), pp. 253-58.

[40]For possible connections between Deuteronomy and the catalog of 1 Cor 5:9-11, see Rosner, *Paul, Scripture and Ethics*, pp. 68-70. For possible connections with the Decalogue, see Thiselton, *First Epistle to the Corinthians*, pp. 411-12. On the Corinthian culture, see Winter, *After Paul Left Corinth*, pp. 45-47.

[41]Paul's Torah awareness informs his sense of holiness. See Fee, *First Epistle to the Corinthians*, p. 215. Martin analyzes this as reflecting attitudes about disease. *Corinthian Body*, pp. 168-174. He is directly refuted by Karl Olav Sandnes, *Belly and Body in the Pauline Epistles* (Cambridge: Cambridge University Press, 2002), pp. 214-15. For a discussion of holiness issues connecting the Torah and 1 Cor 5, see Rosner, *Paul, Scripture and Ethics*, pp. 67-68, 73-80.

[42]Paul's actual injunction is that they "not even eat with such a one" (1 Cor 5:11). That would reflect the social significance of meals for the Corinthian culture, a major form of social bonding, as noted by Thiselton, *First Epistle to the Corinthians*, p. 415.

[43]Winter notes how 1 Cor 6:1-8 connects not only with 1 Cor 5:1-13 but with chapters 1–4. *After Paul Left Corinth*, p. 73.

[44]So Fee, *First Epistle to the Corinthians*, pp. 231-32; and Fitzmyer, *First Corinthians*, p. 251.

[45]See Winter, *After Paul Left Corinth*, pp. 58-71. Also useful is the detailed discussion of various options in Thiselton, *First Epistle to the Corinthians*, pp. 419-21, 424-25.

[46]This will receive further elaboration in 1 Cor 8:1–11:1. See Thiselton, *First Epistle to the Corinthians*, p. 437.

[47]The word in Greek translated "believer" is ἀδελφός, "brother." The Roman culture dominating Paul's Corinth frowned on family members taking one another to

court, finding it disgraceful. See Winter, *After Paul Left Corinth*, pp. 70-71.

[48]So also Keener, *1–2 Corinthians*, p. 54.

[49]See Ciampa and Rosner, *First Letter to the Corinthians*, pp. 240-41, who show both the commonalities and distinctives of the three lists in 1 Cor 5:9-11; 6:9-10.

[50]Most commentators regard these as Corinthian slogans about claims to personal rights. Winter regards them as typical of the cavalier attitude of young men who have come of age and have assumed the "toga virilis." *After Paul Left Corinth*, pp. 86-93. Others see in them permissive standards of the unconverted being inappropriately asserted by some in the believing community in Corinth. See Ciampa and Rosner, *First Letter to the Corinthians*, p. 252; Fitzmyer, *First Corinthians*, p. 263. For a detailed discussion of the hedonistic worldview that may stand behind all these slogans, consider Sandnes, *Belly and Body in the Pauline Epistles*, pp. 191-99.

[51]Are the comments about God's destruction of food and body part of the slogan that Paul refutes, or the first part of Paul's response to the food slogan? See the discussions in Ciampa and Rosner, *First Letter to the Corinthians*, p. 254; Murphy-O'Conner, *Keys to First Corinthians*, pp. 22-26; and Thiselton, *First Epistle to the Corinthians*, pp. 462-63. All three conclude that "God will destroy both one and the other" is part of the slogan, not Paul's response.

[52]See Sandnes, who also suggests that freedom from food laws in the Torah may have led the Corinthian believers to think that they were free from any physical restrictions, including sexual activity. *Belly and Body in the Pauline Epistles*, pp. 191-97.

[53]In raising the topic of men visiting prostitutes Paul may be addressing people who think that their connection to Christ puts them on a different spiritual plane. Fee, *First Epistle to the Corinthians*, pp. 250-51. Or the men may be visiting prostitutes because their wives were denying them sexually (see 1 Cor 7:5). Ibid., p. 271. More likely, he is addressing the twisted attitudes in the unbelieving culture that on the one hand celebrated sexual license, and on the other relegated husband and wife sex to procreation, not pleasure, with husbands expecting to find such pleasure elsewhere. For a discussion of youthful promiscuity, see Winter, *After Paul Left Corinth*, pp. 86-93. For the connection between promiscuity outside the home and abstinence within, see Ciampa and Rosner, *First Letter to the Corinthians*, pp. 250-51. They also survey, and reject, other options for understanding this passage: (1) that it is generalizing about sexual immorality, after denouncing the specifics of incest in 1 Cor 5:1; (2) that it is still dealing with incest, but in a different way; (3) that it may be dealing with either sacred or temple prostitution.

[54]Though some recent scholarship, following Martin, *Corinthian Body*, pp. 174-79, has approached this passage as a boundary solidifying text with the community's purity the foremost concern, purity language is absent from 1 Cor 6:12-20. Instead, one finds the language of ownership, control and domination.

[55] Though 1 Cor 5:13 may appear to be an exception, even there the quotation of Deut 17:7 is a final comment to cement what he has been saying, not his starting point, nor his core ethic.

[56] Suggestions include a false split between the spiritual and physical existence of humanity, so that physical expressions such as sexual intimacy would be beneath "spiritual" people who know that the current age is to be dissolved at the coming of Jesus (Fee, *First Epistle to the Corinthians*, pp. 269-70); response to a crisis, possibly a famine, perhaps alluded to in 1 Cor 7:26 (Winter, *After Paul Left Corinth*, pp. 216-32); a response to the influence of values from Cynic philosophy (Will Deming, *Paul on Marriage and Celibacy: The Hellenistic Background of 1 Corinthians 7*, 2nd ed. [Grand Rapids: Eerdmans, 2004], pp. 107-13). None of these have widespread acceptance.

[57] So Fee, *First Epistle to the Corinthians*, p. 275, who is followed by most commentators.

[58] Each of those passages does so differently, with vv. 17-24 emphasizing how social realities are transcended by the gospel and vv. 29-31 how future awareness related to the gospel should lead them to transcend present concerns. See discussions in Fee, *First Epistle to the Corinthians*, pp. 307-21, 335-42; and Thiselton, *First Epistle to the Corinthians*, pp. 544-45, 580-83, whose work upgrades Fee's on this point.

[59] Deming denies a connection between this chapter and thoughts derived from Gen 2:24. *Paul on Marriage and Celibacy*, pp. 115. However, the sense of authority over the body is introduced in 1 Cor 6:12, not with the concept of "it is permitted" (ἔξεστιν), as Deming argues against (p. 116), but with the sense of "I will not be dominated by anything" (οὐκ ἐγὼ ἐξουσιασθήσομαι ὑπό τινος). It is the sense of ruling over the body (οὐκ ἐξουσιάζει) that 1 Cor 7:4 revisits in a different way. That sense is what is connectable to Gen 2:24.

[60] Those effects would seem to be more related to moral and religious influences of the believing spouse on the unbelieving spouse and children than to undefined, perhaps even immaterial, special effects. See Murphy-O'Connor, *Keys to First Corinthians*, pp. 45-53, 56-57; and Thiselton, *First Epistle to the Corinthians*, pp. 528-30.

[61] "'Peace' for Paul refers to reconciliation, both vertical with God and horizontal between human beings. . . . Paul is saying in v. 15 that if your unbelieving spouse leaves, you are free to remarry, but don't forget that at the core of your Christian identity is the recognition that you are those who restore relationships as peacemakers." Ciampa and Rosner, *First Letter to the Corinthians*, p. 304. Fee sees in Paul's thinking Jewish influence that encourages good behavior before Gentiles to win their favor, in this case so that the unbelieving spouse might be saved as the believing spouse stays in the marriage. *First Epistle to the Corinthians*, pp. 303-5.

[62] For the possibility, see Ciampa and Rosner, *First Letter to the Corinthians*, p. 357.

[63]For more detail on these possibilities, see Thiselton, *First Epistle to the Corinthians*, pp. 594-98.

[64]So Winter, *After Paul Left Corinth*, pp. 241-52.

[65]Again, that translation is not universal. It could refer either to the man or the woman of the couple. If to the man, as the term was often used, it would deal with his passions. If to the woman, it could refer to her being at or just past the marriageable age for women. See the discussion in ibid., pp. 246-49. It is highly improbable that the scenario refers to a man keeping his virgin daughter from marrying, a view refuted in most modern commentaries.

[66]This may involve participating in temple sacrifices themselves, or merely in temple banquets in the aftermath of the sacrifice. See Murphy-O'Connor, *Keys to First Corinthians*, pp. 114-19. Winter restricts this to banquets in the Temple of Poseidon at Isthmia, in connection with the revived Isthmian games, and under the aegis of the imperial cult. *After Paul Left Corinth*, pp. 269-81. John Fotopoulos, after surveying archaeological evidence for dining facilities associated with twenty different temples in and around first-century Corinth, including the Temple of Poseidon at Isthmia, only finds definitive evidence for such facilities in use in the temple to Aesklepius. *Food Offered to Idols in Roman Corinth* (Tübingen: Mohr Siebeck, 2003), pp. 49-157. See also the detailed archaeological and primary textual data in Murphy-O'Connor, *St. Paul's Corinth*, pp. 5-191. Trying to define any specific sites of banqueting for Corinthian Christians is probably too difficult in view of Paul's own lack of specificity.

[67]The NRSV uses the term *liberty* (1 Cor 8:9). Winter argues convincingly that "right" is a better term. *After Paul Left Corinth*, pp. 280-81. Based on that, he sees that the banquets for the Isthmian games are in view, since associations with other temples would not have been thought of in terms of "rights." Thiselton generalizes this as a "right to choose," which Paul goes on to subsume beneath the necessity of caring for others, regardless of rights. *The First Epistle to the Corinthians*, pp. 649-50.

[68]The situation here is often framed as one of the "strong" versus the "weak," especially as regarding relative faith. Note the brief survey in Fotopoulos, *Food Offered to Idols in Corinth*, pp. 188-91. Paul's actual language frames it not as "strong" versus "weak" but as those claiming knowledge versus those with weak consciences, which might also involve social stratification. See the useful discussion in Fitzmyer, *First Corinthians*, pp. 333-34.

[69]The term *conscience* means something different from the common notion of the little voice inside telling a person what to do. Thiselton, after surveying the history of the study of the term, eventually explains the concept as being akin to self-awareness, such that it reflects on the level of confidence that what one is doing is correct. *First Epistle to the Corinthians*, pp. 640-44. Those with weak consciences are susceptible to being carried along by the crowd into activities they have no business engaging in.

[70] Ibid., p. 640. Fotopoulos offers evidence that dining at temple facilities could lead people to think that they were dining in the actual presence of deity. *Food Offered to Idols in Roman Corinth*, pp. 175-76. Murphy-O'Connor admits the validity of such evidence, but cites further evidence that questions how seriously people regarded that presence. *Keys to First Corinthians*, pp. 118-19.

[71] See Fitzmyer, *First Corinthians*, p. 332.

[72] Thiselton, *First Epistle to the Corinthians*, p. 663.

[73] As part of the mixed agenda, Paul also implies his unwillingness to be beholden to anyone in Corinth as a client, which would undermine his desire to see a faction-free community. See Keener, *1–2 Corinthians*, p. 79. He supports that with a fascinating use of a regulation from the Torah that at face value has nothing to do with paying people (1 Cor 9:9; see Deut 25:4). Ciampa and Rosner offer an explanation of the usage of this verse as an example of *qal vahomer*, an argument from lesser to greater: if God is concerned about animals, how much more humans. They cite Philo and Josephus, who also employ the same technique with the same verse. *First Letter to the Corinthians*, pp. 404-7. Paul offers further support (1 Cor 9:14) by alluding to a command from Jesus that those who proclaim the Gospel should earn their living from that, and from nothing else. Paul appears to override the command from Jesus with the exemplar of Jesus. See Horrell, *Solidarity and Difference*, pp. 214-22.

[74] See Fitzmyer, *First Corinthians*, p. 373, and Fee, *First Epistle to the Corinthians*, pp. 433-35. Note the insightful discussion in Sandnes, *Belly and Body in the Pauline Epistles*, pp. 199-211. He shows how Paul's appeal to Torah's wilderness texts on eating and drinking resembles a common Second Temple thought that connects improper attitudes about food, drink and sex to idolatry.

[75] Fee points out useful connections between 1 Cor 10 and the "Song of Moses" in Deut 32, from which the line about sacrificing to demons and not to God is drawn (see Deut 32:17). *First Epistle to the Corinthians*, pp. 448-49, 472. See also Ciampa and Rosner, *First Letter to the Corinthians*, pp. 479-83.

[76] See Thiselton, *First Epistle to the Corinthians*, pp. 796; and Horrell, *Solidarity and Difference*, pp. 214-31.

[77] As a reminder, we are not covering issues 4-6 and 9 because they do not have the same extensive treatment of ethical implications. See the introduction to this chapter.

[78] For the link between this section and 1 Cor 8:1–11:1, see Thiselton, *First Epistle to the Corinthians*, p. 799.

[79] See implications of this in Fee, *First Epistle to the Corinthians*, p. 586. Thiselton elaborates further on the difficulties of distinguishing certain gifts from others. *First Epistle to the Corinthians*, pp. 936-88.

[80] Most commentators agree that particular gift is tongues, which he mentions last and which is the only gift appearing in all the lists of gifts in this section. See Fee,

First Epistle to the Corinthians, pp. 571-72. Martin discusses "tongues" as "high status activity" for the Corinthian church. *Corinthian Body*, pp. 87-88.

[81]The dichotomy between whether this passage emphasizes diversity or unity is certainly false, since both are strong elements of the passage. For the former see Fee, *First Epistle to the Corinthians*, pp. 582-83. For the latter see Thiselton, *First Epistle to the Corinthians*, pp. 928-30.

[82]For examples of the commonness of the analogy, see Martin, *Corinthian Body*, pp. 92-94.

[83]While Greco-Roman philosophers often used body imagery to cement hierarchical relationships within the state, Paul reverses the pattern to show how what is regularly dishonored by others is honored by God. Ibid., pp. 94-96.

[84]Contra Fitzmyer, *First Corinthians*, pp. 487-89, as one representative. "Love is not set over against the gifts . . . rather love is the *way* in which the gifts are to function." Fee, *First Epistle to the Corinthians*, p. 628.

[85]See Frank J. Matera, who notes Paul's shift to a first person praise of love in 1 Cor 13:4-7 as typical of his appeal to his own example, as he has done throughout the letter (1 Cor 4:1-16; 9:1-27; 10:33–11:1), and which he considers modeled on Christ's own activity (1 Cor 11:1). *New Testament Ethics* (Louisville: Westminster John Knox, 1996), p. 151.

[86]Commentators regularly note Paul's pattern of a supporting core to his specific points of exhortation in this letter. Thus, chap. 9 supports what he says in chap. 8, and leads to his further application and resolution in chap. 10, just as chap. 13 supports what he says in chap. 12, leading to further application and resolution in chap. 14. For a useful, concise description of that, see Ciampa and Rosner, *First Letter to the Corinthians*, pp. 560-61.

[87]Thiselton surveys the scholarly suggestions offered: (1) some were denying any possibility of any life after death, thought to have been a common notion for many; (2) some were thinking that a form of spiritual resurrection had already occurred; (3) some were struggling with the notion of a bodily resurrection, since a bodily existence after death would be thought of as an inferior existence; (4) there may be a mixture of perspectives indicated, with "some" believing one and "some" believing another. *First Epistle to the Corinthians*, pp. 1172-76.

[88]For a description not only of that perspective but a survey of attitudes of death and the afterlife in the Greco-Roman world, see Martin, *Corinthian Body*, pp. 108-20. For an accessible summary of relevant primary texts reflecting these attitudes, consider Keener, *1–2 Corinthians*, pp. 122-23. For a discussion of these attitudes as an elitist view, see Winter, *After Paul Left Corinth*, pp. 105-9.

[89]See the supporting grammatical presentation in Fee, *First Epistle to the Corinthians*, pp. 722-28, whose explanation also reflects the position of the majority of commentators.

⁹⁰See Thiselton, *First Epistle to the Corinthians*, pp. 1169-72.

⁹¹See Sandnes, *Belly and Body in the Pauline Epistles*, pp. 182-87.

⁹²Though some see this as a quotation from an anti-Epicurean slogan instead of a quotation from Isaiah, the words here in 1 Cor 15:32 match identically the words from Is 22:13 in the Greek LXX. See the brief discussion in Thiselton, *First Epistle to the Corinthians*, pp. 1252-53.

⁹³It appears as a line in the play *Thais*. See the discussion in Winter, *After Paul Left Corinth*, pp. 98-100, whose computer search strongly links the words to that play by Menander.

⁹⁴For the second time in this letter, Paul uses the expression "I say this to your shame" to show the Corinthian believers that they are not as honorable before God as they think (see 1 Cor 6:5). In both places he is concerned that their lack of awareness of the effects of the cross and the resurrection has blunted their sense of right and wrong. For the importance of honor and shame, and Paul's correction of Corinthian believers to consider honor before God over honor before others, see Thiselton, *First Epistle to the Corinthians*, p. 1257.

⁹⁵For a development of the centrality of that thought for Paul's ethics throughout his epistles, consider J. Paul Sampley, *Walking Between the Times: Paul's Moral Reasoning* (Minneapolis: Fortress Press, 1991), pp. 7-24.

Chapter 10

¹Krister Stendahl observes that Paul explains "justification rather than forgiveness." *Paul Among Jews and Gentiles* (London: SCM, 1976), pp. 23-40.

²Craig S. Keener, *Romans* (Eugene, OR: Cascade Books, 2009), p. 30.

³*Salvation*—Rom 1:16; 11:11; 13:11. *Save*—Rom 5:9-10; 8:24; 9:27; 10:1, 9-10, 13; 11:14, 26. Seven of those verbs are in the future tense.

⁴"Paul's overall descriptive term for the final victory of God in the coming age, when the last enemy shall have been destroyed and God shall reign as the unchallenged Sovereign above all, is *salvation*." Victor Paul Furnish, *Theology and Ethics in Paul* (Nashville: Abingdon, 1968), p. 122.

⁵David Noy, *Foreigners at Rome: Citizens and Strangers* (London: Duckworth, 2000), pp. 15-16. That figure is most likely the higher limit and would have been reasonably constant throughout the first century. It is based on records for the "corn dole," food imports and numbers of residential buildings, among other factors.

⁶Robert Jewett estimates enough to make a trajectory of "several thousands" by the year 64, when Nero persecuted Christians in the city, perhaps dozens of house-based congregations spread across the city with twenty to forty participants. That would allow a range of 600-1,200. *Romans* (Minneapolis: Fortress, 2007), pp. 61-62.

⁷For a description of that see Michael J. Gorman, *Apostle of the Crucified Lord* (Grand Rapids: Eerdmans, 2004), pp. 67-69.

[8]Though the "reasons for Romans" are a subject of wide scholarly debate, this basic position finds support from the following discussions: Robert Jewett, *Romans* (Minneapolis: Fortress, 2007), pp. 1, 44, 74, 80-91; James C. Miller, *The Obedience of Faith, the Eschatological People of God, and the Purpose of Romans* (Atlanta: SBL, 2000), pp. 5-19; A. J. M. Wedderburn, *The Reasons for Romans* (Minneapolis: Fortress, 1988); F. F. Bruce, "The Romans Debate—Continued," in *The Romans Debate,* ed. K. P. Donfried, rev. ed. (Peabody, MA: Hendrickson, 1991), pp. 175-94.

[9]James D. Hester, "The Rhetoric of *Persona* in Romans," in *Celebrating Romans,* ed. S. E. McGinn (Grand Rapids: Eerdmans, 2004), pp. 95-103.

[10]For a simple description of Paul's Pharisaical background, including the importance of separating from Gentiles, consider Gorman, *Apostle of the Crucified Lord,* p. 53. For greater scholarly detail, consider Calvin Roetzel, *Paul: The Man and the Myth* (Edinburgh: T & T Clark, 1999), pp. 24-38.

[11]*Letter of Aristeas,* line 142, cited in James H. Charlesworth, *The Old Testament Pseudepigrapha* (London: Darton, Longman & Todd, 1983, 1985), 2:22.

[12]This appears most clearly in Paul's letter to the Galatians.

[13]Such possibilities are reflected in Gal 2:11-14 and Acts 21:27-30.

[14]For the social dynamics involved here, see Stephan Joubert, *Paul as Benefactor* (Tübingen: Mohr Siebeck, 2000), pp. 206-9.

[15]See Peter Lampe, "The Roman Christians of Romans 16," in Donfried, *Romans Debate,* p. 218.

[16]This modifies Jewett, *Romans,* pp. 87-88, also drawing on observations of Peter Stuhlmacher, "The letter is an exposition and clarification of that gospel vis-à-vis the criticism Paul knows to be rampant in Rome." "The Purpose of Romans," in Donfried, *Romans Debate,* p. 237.

[17]For a concise display of this, see Keener, *Romans,* pp. 14, 160-62. For a detailed refutation of Romans 14–15 as hypothetical, based on the specifics of 1 Corinthians 8–10, see Mark Reasoner, *The Strong and the Weak: Romans 14.1–15.13 in Context* (Cambridge: Cambridge University Press, 1990), pp. 24-44, though Reasoner sees more than a regard for Jewish *kashruth* in the quarrel. Consider as an alternative to Reasoner, N. T. Wright, "The Letter to the Romans," in *The New Interpreter's Bible* (Nashville: Abingdon Press, 2002), 10:730-33.

[18]Keener, *Romans,* pp. 162-63; and James D. G. Dunn, *Romans 9–16* (Dallas: Word, 1988), pp. 800-802.

[19]Points made here in developing Romans' argument grow out of my earlier published work. See Peter Gosnell, "Law in Romans: Regulation and Instruction," *Novum Testamentum* 51 (2009): 252-71.

[20]The summary that follows within this paragraph is neither intended to describe the theme of Romans nor its purpose, but instead to summarize core aspects of major theological points dealt with in the growing argument of the letter, espe-

cially in its regard for "the gospel." The description matches the basic set of expectations associated with God's restorative plan, expectations that are certainly addressed in main sections of the letter. See the general descriptions of the "Divine Plan of Salvation" and "God's Gospel" in Joseph A. Fitzmyer, *Romans* (New York: Doubleday, 1992), pp. 108-10.

²¹See Hermann Ridderbos, *Paul: An Outline of His Theology*, trans. John Richard De Witt (Grand Rapids: Eerdmans, 1975), pp. 253-58, esp. pp. 257-58.

²²So most commentators, even if there is disagreement about other aspects of what this opening conveys. See Jewett, *Romans*, pp. 97-98; and Wright, "Letter to the Romans," pp. 416-19.

²³For one Second Temple Jewish instance of that sort of obedience, note *Testament of Judah* 13:1, in Greek: ὑπακούειν ἐντολῆς κυρίου θεοῦ.

²⁴"Whereas there are many forms of obedience, including obedience under the law, Paul speaks here of the special sort of obedience produced by the gospel." Jewett, *Romans*, p. 110. See also Hester, "Rhetoric of *Persona* in Romans," pp. 89-91.

²⁵The meaning of the term *righteousness* in Romans is a deeply discussed issue. For a broad overview see David G. Horrell, *An Introduction to the Study of Paul*, 2nd ed. (London: T & T Clark, 2006), pp. 75-77. Horrell summarizes four main positions: (1) righteousness "imputed"—one is declared right before God; (2) righteousness "imparted"—one is made right before God; (3) one is transferred from the realm of "sin" to God's righteous realm, and incorporated into God's people; (4) denoting who belongs to God's people now, who will experience final vindication from God on judgment day. The approach taken here reflects elements from all four, noting that Paul deals with the obedience of believers now, in view of what they are not yet. Warrant for such a combination emerges from the detailed discussion in J. A. Ziesler, *The Meaning of Righteousness in Paul: A Linguistic and Theological Enquiry* (Cambridge: Cambridge University Press, 1972). Ziesler observes, "The gospel is power exactly in that God's righteousness is revealed in it, and that means his activity, his powerful activity. This righteousness then is both demand and gift, as in Mt. 5; it is the new life, the moral renewal of the believer, which yet remains always God's righteousness. It is gospel, partly because this new life is now a gracious possibility, but perhaps primarily because it is also justification, restoration to right relationship, acquittal, purely by God's grace, and quite apart from anything man has done, will do, intends to do, or even is now beginning to do" (p. 187). See also Keener, *Romans*, p. 29.

²⁶Consider the following terms abounding in English translations of Romans: *just, justice, justify, right, righteous, unrighteous, unrighteousness, injustice, obey, obedience, disobedience, good, bad, evil, lawless, sin, transgression, trespass.*

²⁷Elsewhere in Romans, Paul equates strong faith in God with being "fully convinced" about God doing what he says he will do (Rom 4:21), or God having done what

the good news claims he has done such that one can be "fully convinced" about participating in certain covenantally forbidden activities, such as eating unclean food or working on the sabbath (Rom 14:2-5).

[28]Commentators frequently note the similarity of the language and concerns of Rom 1:18-25 and the Second Temple writing *Wisdom of Solomon*, especially *Wisdom 13:1-10; 14:21-31.*

[29]Paul probably begins with same-sex activity as the height of out-of-touchness because it exhibits the contrary-to-nature argument of idolatry from the previous verses. As God is exchanged for idols (Rom 1:23, 25), so natural intercourse for unnatural (Rom 1:26). See Fitzmyer, *Romans*, p. 285; and Keener, *Romans*, pp. 37-40.

[30]Though Paul's interlocutor could be a general, perhaps even pagan, moralist, commentators tend to agree that the primary candidate is "a Jew who judges himself superior to the pagan because of his people's privileges." Fitzmyer, *Romans*, p. 297.

[31]Thomas Schreiner shows how sin as a power leads to sinful activity and a universal charge of sinfulness. *Romans* (Grand Rapids: Baker Books, 1998), p. 164. Francis Watson sees Paul's use of Scripture in Rom 3:10-20 as his way of presenting the "law as a failed project." *Paul and the Hermeneutics of Faith* (London: T & T Clark, 2004), pp. 67-71.

[32]Regardless of where one lands on the "faith in Christ" versus "faithfulness of Christ" discussion, the verb *believe* indicates that faith is always required as a response to what God has done in Christ. However, I remain unpersuaded by the recent trend to talk about the "faithfulness of Christ" rather than the more traditional "faith in Christ." See Stanley E. Porter, "The Rhetorical Scribe: Textual Variants in Romans and Their Possible Rhetorical Purpose," in *Rhetorical Criticism and the Bible*, ed. Stanley E. Porter and Dennis L. Stamps (Sheffield, UK: Sheffield Academic Press, 2002), pp. 416-18; Jewett, *Romans*, p. 268; and Keener, *Romans*, pp. 57-58.

[33]The language here strongly resembles the language of Rom 1:17, where "the righteousness of God is *revealed* through faith for faith." Here, "the righteousness of God has been *disclosed* . . . through faith in Christ Jesus, for all who believe." The words in Rom 3:21-22 certainly echo the words of Rom 1:17, along with their regard for "the righteousness of God."

[34]On liberation see Fitzmyer, *Romans*, pp. 122-23. On the power of sin see Douglas J. Moo, *The Epistle to the Romans* (Grand Rapids: Eerdmans, 1996), p. 230.

[35]Whether the expression "sacrifice of atonement" refers to *expiation*, a washing away of sins, or *propitiation*, the satisfaction of God's wrath, does not change the overall direction of Paul's ethics. Liberation from a sin-dominated world takes place regardless of either definition. For arguments in favor of the latter, which is preferred here, consider Moo, *Epistle to the Romans*, pp. 231-36. Paul has already been discussing God's wrath in a significant way in the context.

[36]"[God's] failure to punish Israel's sins, that is, by completely rejecting Israel as his people, did not mean that he was unfairly generous (one of the questions raised by the aborted discussion in 3:1-8)." James D. G. Dunn, *Romans 1–8* (Dallas: Word, 1988), p. 181.

[37]The discussion here is an extension of what has already been surveyed in note 25 of this chapter. A legal declaration certainly fits Paul's use of the terminology in his treatment of Abraham in Rom 4. But the effects of the cross and the resurrection are so strong that God is not merely overlooking people's wrongdoing (as in Rom 3:25) when others really know better. Paul describes the rightness before God as real, a resurrection empowered justification (Rom 4:25). God has no charge against those who belong to him through Christ (Rom 8:33). See Keener, *Romans*, pp. 27-29.

[38]Simon J. Gathercole, among others, offers necessary revisions to the historical revision of the "New Perspective on Paul." *Where Is Boasting: Early Jewish Soteriology and Paul's Response in Romans 1–5* (Grand Rapids: Eerdmans, 2002). He has shown how a sense of personal merit derived from Torah-keeping did exist in various major Second Temple Jewish expressions. Note in addition the useful analysis in Jewett, *Romans*, pp. 295-96, which incorporates the social categories of honor and shame, under which "boasting" naturally falls. That allows the conclusion that boasting in one's merit and boasting based on nationalistic alignment need not be mutually exclusive.

[39]Consider Andrew T. Lincoln, "Abraham Goes to Rome," in *Worship, Theology and Ministry in the Early Church: Essays in Honor of Ralph P. Martin*, ed. M. J. Wilkins and T. E. Paige (Sheffield, UK: Sheffield Academic Press, 1992), esp. pp. 172-76. Note also Keener, *Romans*, pp. 67-68.

[40]Rom 5:1-11 are more normally included as the introduction to the material that spans the rest of chaps. 5-8, especially because they address God's love (Rom 5:5, 8; 8:35, 39), the hope for future glorification (Rom 5:2-5; 8:20-25) and the Spirit at work in believers' lives (Rom 5:5; 7:6; 8:1-27). See Fitzmyer, *Romans*, pp. 96-97. Here, they are being treated as more transitional, concluding aspects of the argument from chaps. 1-4 before launching into more ethically relevant material. See Jewett, *Romans*, pp. 346-47; and Keener, *Romans*, p. 73.

[41]Though it would be premature at this point to declare that Paul received his view of sin as a power from his reading of Gen 4:7 in Hebrew (the LXX offers a different reading that omits the word *sin*), later Jewish tradition does connect the sense of sin as some sort of lurking power with the human inclination toward evil, the *yetser hara*. See the Palestinian Targum manuscript B of Genesis 4 from the Cairo *Damascus Document*: "Indeed sin crouches at the gate of your heart; but I have placed in your hand control over the evil inclination, and you shall rule over it, whether for better or for worse." Cited from Michael L. Klein, trans. and ed.

Genizah Manuscripts of Palestinian Targum to the Pentateuch (Cincinnati: Hebrew Union College Press, 1986), 1:6.

[42]E. P. Sanders helpfully explains how in Romans 6:7 the term *justify* expresses a transference from the control of sin's dominion. The NRSV masks that by translating δεδικαίωται as "freed from." *Paul and Palestinian Judaism: A Comparison of Patterns of Religion* (London: SCM Press, 1977), pp. 470-72. The ensuing description of the material in this part of Romans is not substantially different from what can be found in pre-Sanders writings. Consider, for example, the basic summary in F. F. Bruce, *Paul: Apostle of the Heart Set Free* (Grand Rapids: Eerdmans, 1977), pp. 330-32.

[43]See Jewett, *Romans*, p. 408. We saw such statements in 1 Corinthians. For example, you are unleavened, therefore be unleavened (1 Cor 5:7); you are washed, sanctified, justified, therefore be washed, sanctified, justified (1 Cor 6:9-11).

[44]Paul's word ἐπιθυμίαις, "passions," is common to the Greco-Roman philosophical dialogue. It appears in Rom 1:26; 6:12; 7:7, 8; 13:14. See Stanley K. Stowers, *A Rereading of Romans: Justice, Jews, and Gentiles* (New Haven, CT: Yale, 1994), pp. 278-80, for the resemblance between Paul and the philosophical tradition of refuting Stoic views that knowledge triumphs over inner struggles. Consider further the possibilities for Rom 6 offered by Emma Wasserman, *The Death of the Soul in Romans 7* (Tübingen: Mohr Siebeck, 2008), pp. 81-83, 130-36.

[45]"Since wages are paid in increments as well as at the end of a task, the death that Paul has in mind is a present reality that will extend into the future." Jewett, *Romans*, p. 426.

[46]"The alternative offered by the gospel is holiness which ends in eternal life, where 'holiness' is probably more clearly conceived as a process . . . 'sanctification,' that is, the progressive transformation from inside out (cf. 2:28-29), so that the final rising with Christ is but a continuation and completion of the whole process." Dunn, *Romans 1–8*, p. 356.

[47]For the new covenant orientation of Rom 2:14-15 and its possible reference to Gentiles doing what has been placed on their hearts by virtue of being Christian converts, see N. T. Wright, "The Law in Romans 2," in *Paul and the Mosaic Law*, ed. J. D. G. Dunn (Grand Rapids: Eerdmans, 2001), pp. 143-48; Akio Ito, "ΝΟΜΟΣ (ΤΩΝ) ΈΡΓΩΝ and ΝΟΜΟΣ ΠΙΣΤΕΩΣ: The Pauline Rhetoric and Theology of ΝΟΜΟΣ," *Novum Testamentum* 45, no. 3 (2003): 250-51; Jewett, *Romans*, pp. 212-24; and Klyne Snodgrass, "Gospel in Romans: A Theology of Revelation," in *Gospel in Paul: Studies on Corinthians, Galatians and Romans for Richard Longenecker*, ed. L. A. Jervis and P. Richardson (Sheffield, UK: Sheffield Academic Press, 1994), pp. 304-6. Snodgrass shows how the statements in Rom 2 are connectable to those in Rom 6.

[48]For connections between Rom 7:6 and the new covenant passages of Jeremiah and Ezekiel, see James D. G. Dunn, "'The Law of Faith,' 'the Law of the Spirit,' and 'the

Law of Christ," in *Theology and Ethics in Paul and His Interpreters: Essays in Honor of Victor Paul Furnish*, ed. Eugene H. Lovering Jr. and Jerry L. Sumney (Nashville: Abingdon Press, 1996), pp. 69-70. For an explanation of the role of the Spirit in the "replacement" of the old with the new covenant in Rom 7:6, see Gordon Fee, *God's Empowering Presence* (Peabody, MA: Hendrickson, 1994), pp. 506-8. Fee notes, "The consequence of such 'release' is that we 'serve' God no longer under Torah but by the Spirit, through whom, he will go on to explain in 8:4-13, the purpose of Torah is carried out in our lives" (p. 507).

[49]For pertinent Greco-Roman moral concepts reflected in this passage consider Troels Engberg-Pedersen, *Paul and the Stoics* (Louisville: Westminster John Knox, 2000), pp. 239-46; Stowers, *A Rereading of Romans*, pp. 258-84; and Wasserman, *Death of the Soul in Romans 7*.

[50]Stowers, *Rereading of Romans*, pp. 278-79. Though Stowers is convinced that Paul is addressing Gentiles only and not a mixed Jew-Gentile audience as is preferred here, he offers a thoroughly illuminating discussion of Rom 7:7-25 as an example of προσωποποιία, "speech in kind," wherein Paul assumes the persona of the ἀκρατής, the person who fails to control personal passions (pp. 269-72). He portrays the discussion of "the mastery of the will" as a moral commonplace. Significant terms and phrases from that commonplace are reflected in Rom 7:7-25. Paul's point is that the law is an enemy to any person, Jew or Gentile, struggling with the mastery of passions, courtesy of the effects of the reign of sin on the "flesh."

[51]Ibid., p. 280.

[52]"The use of the singular is significant. It brings out the fact that the law's requirements are essentially a unity, the plurality of commandments being not a confused and confusing conglomeration but a recognizable and intelligible whole." C. E. B. Cranfield, *The Epistle to the Romans* (Edinburgh: T & T Clark, 1975), 1:384.

[53]"Paul here puts it beyond dispute that the antitheses of vv 5-9 do not denote the before and after of conversion.... [E]ven those whom he has described confidently as 'in the spirit' (v 9) may yet live in and for the flesh. And if they do so, if they let that become the dominant force in their living, they are back on the way to death, the mindset of the flesh." Dunn, *Romans 1–8*, p. 457.

[54]See Fitzmyer, *Romans*, p. 492.

[55]"The end of God's creative purposes is resurrection, not incarnation." Dunn, *Romans 1–8*, p. 483.

[56]The thoughts reflected in the summary overview of these chapters is generally expressed by most commentators, even if the specifics on their supporting details and import can differ. See Cranfield, *Epistle to the Romans*, 2:445-50; James D. G. Dunn, *Romans 9–16*, Word Biblical Commentary 38B (Dallas: Word, 1988), pp. 518-21; Fitzmyer, *Romans*, pp. 99-100; Jewett, *Romans*, pp. viii-ix; and Wright, "Epistle to the Romans," pp. 620-26.

[57]Sanders, *Paul and Palestinian Judaism*, pp. 482, 491, 550-52, and *Paul, the Law and the Jewish People* (Philadelphia: Fortress Press, 1983), pp. 154-60. For a discussion of Christ as both the goal and termination of the Law's covenantal obligations, see Watson, *Paul and the Hermeneutics of Faith*, pp. 329-41, esp. pp. 332-33; for τέλος as "goal" instead of "end," see Jewett, *Romans*, pp. 619, 622. For τέλος as the termination of one program giving way to another, see Dunn, *Romans 9–16*, pp. 589-90, as well as relevant Greek lexica.

[58]Furnish, *Theology and Ethics in Paul*, pp. 102-6.

[59]Ibid., pp. 104, 188-89. Furnish comes to that conclusion based on his comparison of the language of Rom 2:18 with Rom 12:2. See also Moo, *Epistle to the Romans*, pp. 757-58.

[60]"The 'mind' is a key category in Paul's vision of renewal (cf. 7:25 and 8:5-8). Instead of the 'unfit mind' of 1:28, Paul holds out a vision of a mind renewed, able now at last to think for itself what will please God, instead of being darkened by the deceitfulness of sin (see also the suggestive 'we have the mind of the Messiah' in 1 Cor 2:16)." Wright, "Epistle to the Romans," p. 705. See also Frank J. Matera, *New Testament Ethics* (Louisville: Westminster John Knox, 1996), pp. 193-95.

[61]Jewett offers a useful study of the term for "sober judgment" and its significance for what Paul portrays here. *Romans*, pp. 732-42. He observes, "By making these unique faith relationships the 'measure of all things,' so to speak, Paul defines 'sober-mindedness' as the refusal to impose the standard of one's own relationship with God onto others. The same thought is reiterated in 14:4, 22-23 in the admonition not to interfere with the faith relationships that other believers have with the Lord. This verse therefore stands as a bulwark against elitist conceptions of 'divine-men,' superleaders and geniuses who claim precedence over others because of their gifts and benefactions" (p. 742).

[62]*Sententiae* (Latin) or *gnōmai* (Greek) are short, pithy statements of advice, often appearing in moral instruction within the Greco-Roman world. See Abraham J. Malherbe, *Moral Exhortation: A Greco-Roman Sourcebook* (Philadelphia: Westminster Press, 1986), pp. 109-11.

[63]So also Jewett, *Romans*, p. 756.

[64]For a detailed discussion of how these sayings might stem from traditions about Jesus, consider Michael Thompson, *Clothed with Christ: The Example and Teaching of Jesus in Romans 12.1-15* (Sheffield, UK: JSOT Press, 1991), pp. 96-110. He regards it an open question as to whether Paul was consciously depending on those traditions.

[65]For that distinction worked out in more careful detail, see my article, "Law in Romans," pp. 252-71.

[66]For a useful expansion of this line of reasoning consider Wright, "Epistle to the Romans," pp. 716-20. Wright regards the words of Rom 13:1-7 as general advice in

keeping with what has been said in Rom 12:14-21 about believers not pursuing vengeance. Government is the divinely ordained way for order to be established in societies. These words do not express a deep theory of government. Until Jesus returns to establish his ultimate lordship over the earth, believers generally should submit to such authorities as they uphold basic societal order.

[67]Paul may be moving from ἐντολή to λόγος for stylistic reasons. Dunn appeals to the "word of divine revelation" from Rom 9:6, 9, 28, and then notes that the Ten Commandments are the ten "words" in Ex 34:38 and Deut 10:4. *Romans 9–16*, p. 778. By contrast Fitzmyer limits ἐντολή in Rom 13:9 to the Decalogue. *Romans*, p. 679.

[68]It would be methodologically wrong to assume that the definition for coveting discussed in chap. 3 of this book in relation to Exodus is the exact same sense that Paul deals with here. But we have already seen in this chapter how coveting in its Greco-Roman environment coincides with the moral-philosophical discussion of the mastery of the will. See note 49 of this chap.

[69]Dunn, *Romans 9–16*, pp. 775, 777; Fitzmyer, *Romans*, pp. 677, 679. Dunn also connects the concern for "love" here with Rom 5:5, 8:28, 12:9, and the concern for "fulfillment" with Rom 8:4, as well as with Rom 1:5, 3:31, 9:31-32, 10:6-8. *Romans 9–16*, p. 775. Richard Hays connects the uses of δικαίωμα in Rom 2:26 and Rom 8:4. That explanation provides a foundation for Paul's point in Rom 13:10. "The Role of Scripture in Paul's Ethics," in *Theology and Ethics in Paul and His Interpreters*, ed. E. H. Lovering Jr. and J. L. Sumney (Nashville: Abingdon, 1996), pp. 36-37.

[70]Paul makes no explicit connection between his thoughts here and any words he may know from Jesus such as those found in Mt 22:39 (with Mt 7:12) and Mk 12:30-31. Jewett notes that "the frequent citations of Lev 19:18 by early Christian writers makes it likely that Paul is following a tradition established by Jesus." *Romans*, pp. 812-13. He notes further that "Paul takes an independent line with this tradition . . . treating it as no other NT writer did as a summary of the law" (p. 813). Though Lev 19:18 may not be frequently *cited* in Jewish literature, it is commonly *referred* to. See *Jubilees* 7.20 and 20.2; *Testament of Reuben* 6.9; *Testament of Levi* 17.5; *Testament of Judah* 18.3; *Testament of Issachar* 3.3 and 5.2; *Testament of Zebulon* 5.1; *Testament of Gad* 4.2; *Testament of Benjamin* 3.3-5 and 10.3. Jewett likewise cites the Cairo *Damascus Document* 6:20-21. *Romans*, p. 806. And he refers to the teachings of Hillel and Akiba (p. 813). On the use of Lev 19:18 in Rom 13:9, consider Hays, "The hermeneutical reconfiguration of the law is achieved not through appeal to the teaching of Jesus or to some other normative consideration but through a rereading of Scripture itself." "Role of Scripture in Paul's Ethics," pp. 35-36. For a view more in favor with Rom 13:9 reflecting words from Jesus, see Thompson, *Clothed with Christ*, pp. 132-40.

[71]The NRSV's use of the term *desires* masks the fact that this is the nominal form of

the verb "to covet." Paul is talking about passions, with regard to the "flesh," recalling the dialogue of Rom 7:7-24. See Dunn, *Romans 9–16*, p. 791; and Jewett,
Romans, p. 828.

[72]So also Wright, "Epistle to the Romans," p. 729.

[73]Commentators regularly observe the commonness of the idiom of making "provision." Jewett cites texts that reflect on "legal, administrative and business contexts" of the expression. It implies that people give purposeful attention to some
activity. *Romans*, p. 828.

[74]This is a slightly different take from most commentators, who automatically
assume that the "some" actually means the "strong." Reasoner may be correct to
conclude that "strong" and "weak" are social labels already circulating within
Roman Christian communities. *Strong and the Weak*, pp. 45-63. But Paul may be
using that point to get his readers to rethink what those labels actually mean in
view of the cross and the resurrection. Some of the "some" may not be as "strong"
as they think. See Rom 14:22-23.

[75]See the third "important issue" in this chapter's introduction.

[76]See Lincoln, "Abraham Goes to Rome," pp. 174-76; and Keener, *Romans*, pp. 67-68.

[77]Jewett discusses how this refers to serious harm that leads to a form of destruction,
as declared in the next sentence. *Romans*, p. 860.

[78]Keener, *Romans*, pp. 43, 163.

[79]Most commentators correctly note how *faith* in this context applies to engaging in
disputed practices. However, the importance of faith as a recurrent motif also
points to something more. "In other words, you are either with Abraham or with
Adam. You are either living, like Abraham, in unwavering trust in God and God's
promises; or you are turning away from God and living by some other means."
Wright, "Epistle to the Romans," p. 742.

[80]See the discussion earlier in this chapter under "The Unfolding Argument."

[81]"What is required is that the strong should actually help the weak by taking something of the weight of the burden which they have to carry off their shoulders on
to their own." Cranfield, *Romans*, p. 30.

[82]Jewett, *Romans*, pp. 878-80.

[83]For connections between Psalm 69:9 and potential divided loyalties within believing communities in Rome, see Dunn, *Romans 9–16*, p. 839. Thompson also
notes the potential for abuse from those outside the Christian community, who
would not understand why a convert, as a fellow Gentile, might appear to be
acceding to Jewish customs deemed to be strange or inferior. *Clothed with Christ*,
p. 223.

[84]His citation of the psalm "is the only instance in the Pauline letters where a biblical
precedent is cited for Jesus' passion." Jewett, *Romans*, p. 879.

[85]See Hays, "Role of Scripture in Paul's Ethics," p. 30, for παράκλησις, "encour-

agement" (Rom 15:4), as moral exhortation. Contrast with Dunn, *Romans 9–16*, pp. 839-40, for general "encouragement" leading to hope.

[86]Gosnell, "Law in Romans," pp. 268-71.

[87]For a similar observation about the role of the mind, and its transformation under Christ, see Thompson, *Clothed with Christ*, pp. 81-83.

[88]Ibid., p. 81.

[89]See Fee, *God's Empowering Presence*, pp. 540-41.

[90]Ibid., p. 569.

[91]Gosnell, "Law in Romans," pp. 256-58.

[92]Though the list is not presented as an exhaustive one for Paul, it does show many of the core basics that one can find in discussions on Paul's ethics. See principally Furnish, *Theology and Ethics in Paul*; and Sampley, *Walking Between the Times* (Minneapolis: Fortress Press, 1991). Also see Richard A. Burridge, *Imitating Jesus* (Grand Rapids: Eerdmans, 2007), pp. 98-115; and Richard B. Hays, *The Moral Vision of the New Testament* (San Francisco: HarperCollins, 1996), pp. 16-46.

Bibliography

Allison, Dale C., Jr. *The New Moses: A Matthean Typology.* Edinburgh: T & T Clark, 1993.

———. *The Sermon on the Mount: Inspiring the Moral Imagination.* New York: Crossroad, 1999.

———. *Studies in Matthew: Interpretation Past and Present.* Grand Rapids: Baker Academic, 2005.

Allison, Dale C., Jr., and W. D. Davies. *A Critical and Exegetical Commentary on the Gospel According to Saint Matthew.* 3 vols. International Critical Commentary. Edinburgh: T & T Clark, 1988, 1991, 1997.

Arlandson, James Malcolm. *Women, Class, and Society in Early Christianity: Models from Luke-Acts.* Peabody, MA: Hendrickson, 1997.

Aune, David E. *The New Testament in Its Literary Environment.* Philadelphia: Westminster Press, 1987.

Baker, David L. "Last But Not Least: The Tenth Commandment." *Horizons in Biblical Theology* 27 (2005): 7-20.

———. *Tight Fists or Open Hands? Wealth and Poverty in Old Testament Law.* Grand Rapids: Eerdmans, 2009.

Ballentine, Samuel E. *Leviticus.* Louisville: John Knox Press, 2002.

Banks, Robert. *Paul's Idea of Community.* Rev. ed. Peabody, MA: Hendrickson, 1994.

Bartholomew, Craig G., and Michael W. Goheen. *The Drama of Scripture: Finding Our Place in the Biblical Story.* Grand Rapids: Baker Academic, 2004.

Bartholomew, Craig G., and Ryan P. O'Dowd. *Old Testament Wisdom Literature: A Theological Introduction.* Downers Grove, IL: InterVarsity Press, 2011.

Barton, John. *Understanding Old Testament Ethics.* Louisville: Westminster John Knox, 2003.

Bauer, David R. "The Literary and Theological Function of the Genealogy in Matthew's Gospel." In *Treasures New and Old: Contributions to Matthean Studies.* Edited by David R. Bauer and Mark Allan Powell, pp. 129-59. Atlanta: Scholars Press, 1996.

Beker, J. Christian. *Paul the Apostle: The Triumph of God in Life and Thought*. Philadelphia: Fortress Press, 1984.

Betz, Hans Dieter. *The Sermon on the Mount: A Commentary on the Sermon on the Mount, Including the Sermon on the Plain (Matthew 5:3–7:27 and Luke 6:20-49)*. Minneapolis: Fortress Press, 1995.

Birch, Bruce. "Moral Agency, Community, and the Character of God." *Semeia* 66 (1996): 23-41.

Birch, Bruce, and Larry L. Rasmussen. *Bible and Ethics in the Christian Life*. Minneapolis: Augsburg, 1976.

Blenkinsopp, Joseph. *Isaiah 1–39: A New Translation with Introduction and Commentary*. Anchor Bible Commentary 19. New York: Doubleday, 2000.

Bøe, Sverre. *Cross-Bearing in Luke*. Wissenschaftliche Untersuchungen zum Neuen Testament 278. Tübingen: Mohr Siebeck, 2010.

Boring, Eugene M. "The Gospel of Matthew." In *The New Interpreter's Bible*, 8:87-505. Nashville: Abingdon Press, 1995.

Brawley, Robert L., ed. *Character Ethics and the New Testament: Moral Dimensions of Scripture*. Louisville: Westminster John Knox Press, 2007.

Brock, Brian. *Singing the Ethos of God: On the Place of Christian Ethics in Scripture*. Grand Rapids: Eerdmans, 2007.

Brown, Jeannine K. *The Disciples in Narrative Perspective: The Portrayal and Function of the Matthean Disciples*. Atlanta: Society of Biblical Literature, 2002.

Brown, William P., ed. *Character and Scripture: Moral Formation, Community, and Biblical Interpretation*. Grand Rapids: Eerdmans, 2002.

———. *Character in Crisis: A Fresh Approach to the Wisdom Literature of the Old Testament*. Grand Rapids: Eerdmans, 1996.

Bruce, F. F. *Paul: Apostle of the Heart Set Free*. Grand Rapids: Eerdmans, 1977.

———. "The Romans Debate—Continued," in *The Romans Debate*, edited by Karl P. Donfried, pp. 175-94. Rev. and expanded ed. Peabody, MA: Hendrickson, 1991.

Brueggemann, Walter. "The Book of Exodus." In *The New Interpreter's Bible*, 1:675-981. Nashville: Abingdon Press, 1994.

———. *Deuteronomy*. Nashville: Abingdon Press, 2001.

———. *Genesis*. Atlanta: John Knox Press, 1982.

———. "Of the Same Flesh and Bone." *Catholic Biblical Quarterly* 32 (1970): 532-542.

———. *Reverberations of Faith*. Louisville: Westminster John Knox, 2002.

Buckwalter, H. Douglas. *The Character and Purpose of Luke's Christology*. Society for New Testament Studies Monograph Series 89. Cambridge: Cambridge University Press, 1996.

Burnside, Jonathan P. *God, Justice and Society: Aspects of Law and Legality in the Bible*. New York: Oxford University Press, 2011.

Burridge, Richard A. *Four Gospels, One Jesus? A Symbolic Reading.* Grand Rapids: Eerdmans, 1994.

————. *Imitating Jesus: An Inclusive Approach to New Testament Ethics.* Grand Rapids: Eerdmans, 2007.

————. *What Are the Gospels? A Comparison with Graeco-Roman Biography.* 2nd edition. Grand Rapids: Eerdmans, 2004.

Cameron, Andrew. "Liberation and Desire: The Logic of Law in Exodus and Beyond." In *Exploring Exodus,* edited by Brian S. Rosner and Paul R. Williamson, pp. 123-53. Nottingham: Apollos, 2008.

Carroll R., M. Daniel, and Jacqueline E. Lapsley, eds. *Character Ethics and the Old Testament.* Louisville: Westminster John Knox, 2007.

Carson, D. A., and Douglas J. Moo. *An Introduction to the New Testament.* 2nd edition. Grand Rapids: Zondervan, 2005.

Carter, Philippa. *The Servant-Ethic in the New Testament.* New York: Peter Lang, 1999.

Cassuto, Umberto. *A Commentary on the Book of Genesis.* Translated by Israel Abrahams. Jerusalem: Magnes Press, 1961.

————. *A Commentary on the Book of Exodus.* Translated by Israel Abrahams. Jerusalem: Magnes Press, 1967.

Chae, Young S. *Jesus as the Eschatological Davidic Shepherd: Studies in the Old Testament, Second Temple Judaism, and in the Gospel of Matthew.* Wissenschaftliche Untersuchungen zum Neuen Testament 216. Tübingen: Mohr Siebeck, 2006.

Charette, Blaine. *The Theme of Recompense in Matthew's Gospel.* Journal for the Study of the New Testament Supplement Series 79. Sheffield: Sheffield Academic Press, 1992.

Charlesworth, James H., ed. *The Old Testament Pseudepigrapha.* 2 vols. London: Darton, Longman & Todd, 1983, 1985.

Christensen, Duane L. *Deuteronomy 1–21:9.* Word Biblical Commentary 6A. Nashville: Thomas Nelson, 2001.

Ciampa, Roy E., and Brian S. Rosner. *The First Letter to the Corinthians.* Grand Rapids: Eerdmans, 2010.

Clarke, Andrew D. *Secular and Christian Leadership in Corinth: A Socio-Historical and Exegetical Study of 1 Corinthians 1–6.* Arbeiten zur Geschichte des antiken Judentums und des Urchristentums 18. Leiden: E. J. Brill, 1993.

Clements, Ronald E. "The Book of Deuteronomy." In *The New Interpreter's Bible,* 2:269-538. Nashville: Abingdon Press, 1998.

————. "The Unity of the Book of Isaiah." In *Interpreting the Prophets.* Edited by James Luther Mays and Paul J. Achtemeier, pp. 50-74. Philadelphia: Fortress Press, 1987.

Clifford, Richard J. "Introduction to Wisdom Literature." In *The New Interpreter's Bible*, 5:1-16. Nashville: Abingdon Press, 1997.

Cohick, Lynn H. *Women in the World of the Earliest Christians: Illuminating Ancient Ways of Life*. Grand Rapids: Baker Academic, 2009.

Collins, John J. *The Scepter and the Star: The Messiahs of the Dead Sea Scrolls and Other Ancient Literature*. New York: Doubleday, 1995.

Cosgrove, Charles H. *Appealing to Scripture in Moral Debate: Five Hermeneutical Rules*. Grand Rapids: Eerdmans, 2002.

Craigie, Peter C. *The Book of Deuteronomy*. New International Commentary on the Old Testament 5. Grand Rapids: Eerdmans, 1976.

Cranfield, C. E. B. *The Epistle to the Romans*. 2 vols. International Critical Commentary. Edinburgh: T & T Clark, 1975, 1979.

Culpepper, R. Alan. "The Gospel of Luke. Introduction, Commentary, and Reflections." In *The New Interpreter's Bible*, 10:1-490. Nashville: Abingdon Press, 1995.

Danker, Frederick W. *Jesus and the New Age: A Commentary on St. Luke's Gospel*, Philadelphia: Fortress Press, 1988.

De Groot, Christiana. "Genesis." In *The IVP Women's Bible Commentary*. Edited by Catherine Clark Kroeger and Mary J. Evans, pp. 1-27. Downers Grove, IL: InterVarsity Press, 2002.

Deissmann, G. Adolf. *Bible Studies: Contributions Chiefly from Papyri and Inscriptions to the History of the Language, the Literature, and the Religion of Hellenistic Judaism and Primitive Christianity*. Translated by Alexander Grieve. Edinburgh: T & T Clark, 1901.

Dell, Katherine J. *The Book of Proverbs in Social and Theological Context*. Cambridge: Cambridge University Press, 2006.

Deming, Will. *Paul on Marriage and Celibacy: The Hellenistic Background of 1 Corinthians 7*. 2nd ed. Grand Rapids: Eerdmans, 2004.

DeSilva, David A. *The Hope of Glory: Honor Discourse and New Testament Interpretation*. Collegeville, MN: Liturgical Press, 1991.

Douglas, Mary. *Jacob's Tears: The Priestly Work of Reconciliation*. Oxford: Oxford University Press, 2004.

———. *Purity and Danger: An Analysis of Concept of Pollution and Taboo*. London: Routledge, 2002.

Dunn, James D. G. "'The Law of Faith,' 'the Law of the Spirit,' and 'the Law of Christ.'" In *Theology and Ethics in Paul and His Interpreters: Essays in Honor of Victor Paul Furnish* , pp. 62-82. Edited by Eugene H. Lovering Jr. and Jerry L. Sumney. Nashville: Abingdon Press, 1996.

———. *Romans 1-8*. Word Biblical Commentary 38A. Dallas: Word, 1988.

———. *Romans 9-16*. Word Biblical Commentary 38B. Dallas: Word, 1988.

Durham, John I. *Exodus*. Word Biblical Commentary 3. Waco: Word, 1987.

Edwards, Richard A. *Matthew's Narrative Portrait of Disciples: How the Text-Connoted Reader is Informed*. Harrisburg, PA: Trinity Press International, 1997.

Engberg-Pedersen, Troels. *Paul and the Stoics*. Louisville: Westminster John Knox, 2000.

Fee, Gordon D. *The First Epistle to the Corinthians*. New International Commentary on the New Testament. Grand Rapids: Eerdmans, 1987.

———. *God's Empowering Presence: The Holy Spirit in the Letters of Paul*. Peabody, MA: Hendrickson, 1994.

Ferguson, Everett. *Backgrounds of Early Christianity*. 3rd ed. Grand Rapids: Eerdmans, 2003.

Fitzmyer, Joseph A. *First Corinthians*. Anchor Bible Commentary 32. New Haven, CT: Yale University Press, 2008.

———. *Romans*. Anchor Bible Commentary 31. New York: Doubleday, 1992.

Fotopoulos, John. *Food Offered to Idols in Roman Corinth*. Wissenschaftliche Untersuchungen zum Neuen Testament 151. Tübingen: Mohr Siebeck, 2003.

Fowl, Stephen E. *The Story of Christ in the Ethics of Paul: An Analysis of the Function of the Hymnic Material in the Pauline Corpus*. Journal for the Study of the New Testament Supplement Series 36. Sheffield, UK: JSOT Press, 1990.

Fowl, Stephen E., and L. Gregory Jones. *Reading in Communion: Scripture and Ethics in Christian Life*. Grand Rapids: Eerdmans, 1991.

Fox, Michael V. *Proverbs 1–9*. Anchor Bible Commentary 18a. New York: Doubleday, 2000.

———. *Proverbs 10–31*. Anchor Bible Commentary 18b. New Haven, CT: Yale University Press, 2009.

France, R. T. *The Gospel of Matthew*. New International Commentary on the New Testament. Grand Rapids: Eerdmans, 2007.

Freedman, David Noel. "Between God and Man: Prophets in Ancient Israel." In *Prophecy and Prophets*, pp. 57-87. Edited by Yehoshua Gitay Atlanta: Scholars Press, 1997.

Fretheim, Terence E. "The Book of Genesis." In *The New Interpreter's Bible*, 1:319-674. Nashville: Abingdon Press, 1994.

———. *Exodus*. Louisville: John Knox Press, 1991.

———. *God and World in the Old Testament: A Relational Theology of Creation*. Nashville: Abingdon Press, 2005.

Fuhs, H. F. "יָרֵא." In *Theological Dictionary of the Old Testament*, 6:300-13. Edited by G. Johannes Botterweck and Helmer Ringgren. Translated by David E. Green. Grand Rapids, Eerdmans, 1990.

Furnish, Victor Paul. *Theology and Ethics in Paul*. Nashville: Abingdon, 1968.

Gammie, John G. *Holiness in Israel*. Minneapolis: Fortress Press, 1989.

García Martínez, Florentino, and Eibert J. C. Tigchelaar, eds. *The Dead Sea Scrolls: Study Edition.* 2 vols. Leiden: Brill, 1997, 1998.

Gathercole, Simon J. *Where Is Boasting: Early Jewish Soteriology and Paul's Response in Romans 1-5.* Grand Rapids: Eerdmans, 2002.

Gerhardsson, Birger. *The Ethos of the Bible.* Translated by Stephen Westerholm. Philadelphia: Fortress Press, 1979.

Goldsworthy, Graeme. *Gospel and Wisdom: Israel's Wisdom Literature in the Christian Life.* Carlisle, UK: Paternoster Press, 1987.

Good, Deirdre J. *Jesus the Meek King.* Harrisburg, PA: Trinity Press International, 1999.

Gorman, Michael J. *Apostle of the Crucified Lord: A Theological Introduction to Paul and His Letters.* Grand Rapids: Eerdmans, 2004.

Gosnell, Peter W. "Law in Romans: Regulation and Instruction." *Novum Testamentum* 51 (2009): 252-71.

Green, Joel B. *The Gospel of Luke.* Grand Rapids: Eerdmans, 1997.

———. *The Theology of the Gospel of Luke.* Cambridge: Cambridge University Press, 1995.

Gustafson, James. "The Place of Scripture in Christian Ethics." *Interpretation* 24 (1970): 430-55.

Hagner, Donald A. "Ethics and the Sermon on the Mount." *Studia Theologica* 51 (1997): 4-59.

———. *Matthew 1-13.* Word Biblical Commentary 33A. Dallas: Word, 1993.

———. *Matthew 14-28.* Word Biblical Commentary 33B. Dallas: Word, 1995.

Hamilton, Jeffries M. *Social Justice and Deuteronomy: The Case of Deuteronomy 15.* Atlanta: Scholars Press, 1992.

Harrington, Daniel J., and James F. Keenan. *Jesus and Virtue Ethics: Building Bridges Between New Testament Studies and Moral Theology.* Lanham: Rowan & Littlefield, 2002.

Harris, Scott L. *Proverbs 1-9: A Study of Inner-Biblical Interpretation.* Atlanta: Scholars Press, 1995.

Hartley, John E. *Leviticus.* Word Biblical Commentary 4. Dallas: Word, 1992.

Hays, Richard B. *First Corinthians.* Louisville: John Knox Press, 1997.

———. *The Moral Vision of the New Testament: A Contemporary Introduction to New Testament Ethics.* San Francisco: HarperCollins, 1996.

———. "The Role of Scripture in Paul's Ethics." In *Theology and Ethics in Paul and His Interpreters,* pp. 30-47. Edited by E. H. Lovering Jr. and J. L. Sumney. Nashville: Abingdon, 1996.

Hengel, Martin. *Crucifixion in the Ancient World and the Folly of the Message of the Cross.* Philadelphia: Fortress Press, 1977.

Hester, James D. "The Rhetoric of *Persona* in Romans." In *Celebrating Romans: Template for Pauline Theology,* pp. 83-103. Edited by S. E. McGinn. Grand Rapids: Eerdmans, 2004.

Holladay, Carl R. *A Critical Introduction to the New Testament.* Nashville: Abingdon Press, 2009.

Horrell, David G. *An Introduction to the Study of Paul.* 2nd ed. London: T & T Clark, 2006.

———. *Solidarity and Difference: A Contemporary Reading of Paul's Ethics.* London: T & T Clark, 2005.

Houston, Walter J. "Exit the Oppressed Peasant? Rethinking the Background of Social Criticism in the Prophets." In *Prophecy and Prophets in Ancient Israel: Proceedings of the Oxford Old Testament Seminar,* pp. 101-16. Edited by John Day. London: T & T Clark, 2010.

Houtman, Cornelius. "Theodicy in the Pentateuch." In *Theodicy in the World of the Bible,* pp. 151-82. Edited by Antti Laato and Johannes C. de Moor. Leiden: Brill, 2003.

Ito, Akio. "ΝΟΜΟΣ (ΤΩΝ) ἜΡΓΩΝ and ΝΟΜΟΣ ΠΙΣΤΕΩΣ: The Pauline Rhetoric and Theology of ΝΟΜΟΣ." *Novum Testamentum* 45 (2003): 237-59.

Janzen, Waldemar. *Old Testament Ethics: A Paradigmatic Approach.* Louisville: Westminster John Knox, 1994.

Jefferson, Thomas. *The Jefferson Bible: The Life and Morals of Jesus of Nazareth.* Boston: Beacon Press, 1989.

Jenson, Philip Peter. *Graded Holiness: A Key to the Priestly Conception of the World.* Journal for the Study of the Old Testament Supplement Series 106. Sheffield, UK: Sheffield Academic Press, 1992.

Jewett, Robert. *Romans.* Minneapolis: Fortress, 2007.

Johnson, Luke Timothy. *The Gospel of Luke.* Collegeville, MN: Liturgical Press, 1991.

———. *The Literary Function of Possession in Luke-Acts.* Missoula, MT: Scholars Press, 1977.

Joubert, Stephan. *Paul as Benefactor.* Wissenschaftliche Untersuchungen zum Neuen Testament 124. Tübingen: Mohr Siebeck, 2000.

Kaiser, Walter C. "The Book of Leviticus." In *The New Interpreter's Bible,* 1:983-1191. Nashville: Abingdon Press, 1994.

Keener, Craig S. *1-2 Corinthians.* Cambridge: Cambridge University Press, 2005.

———. *Romans.* Eugene, Oregon: Cascade Books, 2009.

Kennedy, George A., trans. *Progymnasmata: Greek Textbooks of Prose Composition and Rhetoric.* Leiden: Brill, 2003.

Kingsbury, Jack Dean. *Matthew: Structure, Christology, Kingdom.* Philadelphia: Fortress Press, 1975.

Klein, Michael L., ed. and trans. *Genizah Manuscripts of Palestinian Targum to the Pentateuch.* 2 vols. Cincinnati: Hebrew Union College Press, 1986.

Knibb, Michael A. "The Exile in the Literature of the Intertestamental Period." *The Heythrop Journal* 17, no. 3 (1976): 253-72.

Knight, Douglas A., ed. *Ethics and Politics in the Hebrew Bible: Semeia 66.* Atlanta: Scholars Press, 1995.

Kynes, William L. *A Christology of Solidarity: Jesus as the Representative of His People in Matthew.* Lanham, MD: University Press of America, 1991.

Laansma, Jon. *"I Will Give You Rest."* Wissenschaftliche Untersuchungen zum Neuen Testament 98. Tübingen: Mohr Siebeck, 1997.

Lalleman, Hetty. *Celebrating the Law? Rethinking Old Testament Ethics.* Milton Keynes, UK: Paternoster Press, 2004.

Lampe, Peter. "The Roman Christians of Romans 16." In *The Romans Debate,* pp. 216-30. Edited by Karl P. Donfried. Rev. ed. Peabody, MA: Hendrickson, 1991.

Leeuwen, Raymond C. Van. "The Book of Proverbs." In *The New Interpreter's Bible,* 5:17-264. Nashville: Abingdon Press, 1997.

LeMon, J. M., and B. A. Strawn. "Parallelism." In *Dictionary of the Old Testament: Wisdom, Poetry and Writings,* pp. 502-15. Edited by Tremper Longman III and Peter Enns. Downers Grove, IL: IVP Academic, 2008.

Lete, G. del Olmo. *Canaanite Religion According to the Liturgical Texts of Ugarit.* Winona Lake, IN: Eisenbrauns, 2004.

Levering, Matthew. *Biblical Natural Law: A Theocentric and Teleological Approach.* Oxford: Oxford University Press, 2008.

Libanius. *Libanius's* Progymnasmata: *Model Exercises in Greek Prose Composition and Rhetoric.* Translated by Craig A. Gibson. Atlanta: Society of Biblical Literature, 2008.

Lieu, Judith. *The Gospel of Luke.* Peterborough, UK: Epworth Press, 1997.

Lincoln, Andrew T. "Abraham Goes to Rome." In *Worship, Theology and Ministry in the Early Church: Essays in Honor of Ralph P. Martin,* pp. 163-79. Edited by Michael J. Wilkins and Terrence E. Paige. Journal for the Study of the New Testament Supplement Series 87. Sheffield, UK: Sheffield Academic Press, 1992.

Longman, Tremper, III. *Proverbs.* Grand Rapids: Baker Academic, 2006.

Longman, Tremper, III, and Raymond B. Dillard. *An Introduction to the Old Testament.* 2nd edition. Nottingham: Inter-Varsity Press, 2007.

Lundbom, Jack R. *The Hebrew Prophets: An Introduction.* Minneapolis: Fortress Press, 2010.

Luz, Ulrich. "The Disciples in the Gospel According to Matthew." In *The Interpretation of Matthew,* pp. 115-48. Edited by Graham N. Stanton. Edinburgh: T & T Clark, 1995.

———. *Matthew 1-7.* Translated by James E. Crouch. Minneapolis: Fortress Press, 2007.

———. *The Theology of the Gospel of Matthew.* Translated by J. Bradford Robinson. Cambridge: Cambridge University Press, 1995.

MacMullen, Ramsay. *Roman Social Relations: 50 B.C. to A.D. 284.* New Haven, CT: Yale University Press, 1974.

Malchow, Bruce V. *Social Justice in the Hebrew Bible: What Is New and What Is Old.* Collegeville, MN: Liturgical Press, 1996.

Malherbe, Abraham J. *Moral Exhortation: A Greco-Roman Sourcebook.* Philadelphia: Westminster Press, 1986.

Martin, Dale B. *The Corinthian Body.* New Haven, CT: Yale University Press, 1995.

Marxsen, Willi. *New Testament Foundations for Christian Ethics.* Edinburgh: T & T Clark, 1993.

Matera, Frank J. *New Testament Ethics: The Legacies of Jesus and Paul.* Louisville: Westminster John Knox, 1996.

Matthews, Victor H., and Don C. Benjamin. *Old Testament Parallels: Laws and Stories from the Ancient Near East.* 3rd ed. New York: Paulist, 2006.

Mayes, A. D. H. *Deuteronomy.* London: Oliphants, 1979.

McKenzie, Steven L. *Covenant.* St. Louis: Chalice Press, 2000.

Meeks, Wayne A. *The Origins of Christian Morality: The First Two Centuries.* New Haven, CT: Yale University Press, 1993.

Metzger, Bruce M. *The Canon of the New Testament.* Oxford: Clarendon Press, 1987.

Meyers, Carol. *Exodus.* Cambridge: Cambridge University Press, 2005.

Middleton, J. Richard. *The Liberating Image: The* Imago Dei *in Genesis 1.* Grand Rapids: Brazos Press, 2005.

Milgrom, Jacob. *Leviticus 17–22: A New Translation with Introduction and Commentary.* Anchor Bible Commentary 3a. New York: Doubleday, 2000.

Miller, James C. *The Obedience of Faith, the Eschatological People of God, and the Purpose of Romans.* Atlanta: SBL, 2000.

Miller, Patrick D., Jr. *Deuteronomy.* Louisville: John Knox Press, 1990.

———. "The World and Message of the Prophets." In *Old Testament Interpretation Past, Present and Future: Essays in Honor of Gene M. Tucker,* pp. 97-112. Edited by James Luther Mays, David L. Petersen and Kent Harold Richards. Nashville: Abingdon Press, 1995.

Moo, Douglas. *The Epistle to the Romans.* Grand Rapids; Eerdmans, 1996.

Moxnes, Halvor. "Patron-Client Relations and the New Community." In *The Social World of Luke-Acts: Models for Interpretation,* pp. 241-68. Edited by Jerome H. Neyrey. Peabody, MA: Hendrickson, 1991.

Murphy-O'Connor, Jerome. *Keys to First Corinthians: Revisiting Major Issues.* Oxford: Oxford University Press, 2009.

———. *St. Paul's Corinth: Texts and Archeology.* 3rd ed. Collegeville, MN: Liturgical

Press, 2002.

Murphy, Roland E. *Proverbs*. Word Biblical Commentary 22. Nashville: Thomas Nelson, 1998.

———. *The Tree of Life: An Exploration of Biblical Wisdom Literature*. Grand Rapids: Eerdmans, 2002.

Neale, David A. *None But the Sinners: Religious Categories in the Gospel of Luke*. Journal for the Study of the New Testament Supplement Series 58. Sheffield, UK: Sheffield Academic Press, 1991.

Nemet-Nejat, Karen Rhea. *Daily Life in Ancient Mesopotamia*. Peabody, MA: Hendrickson, 2002.

Nolland, John. *Luke 1–9:20*. Word Biblical Commentary 35A. Dallas: Word, 1989.

———. *Luke 9:21–18:34*. Word Biblical Commentary 35B. Dallas: Word, 1993.

———. *Luke 18:35–24:53*. Word Biblical Commentary 35C. Dallas: Word, 1993.

Novakovic, Lidija. *Messiah, the Healer of the Sick*. Wissenschaftliche Untersuchungen zum Neuen Testament 2/170. Tübingen: Mohr Siebeck, 2003.

Noy, David. *Foreigners at Rome: Citizens and Strangers*. London: Duckworth, 2000.

O'Toole, Robert F. *Luke's Presentation of Jesus: A Christology*. Studia Biblica 25. Rome: Editrice Pontificio Istituto Biblico, 2004.

Otto, Eckart. *Theologische Ethik des Alten Testaments*. Stuttgart: Verlag W. Kohlhammer, 1994.

Overland, Paul. "Did the Sage Draw from the Shema? A Study of Proverbs 3:1-12." *Catholic Biblical Quarterly* 62 (2000): 424-40.

Parsons, Mikeal C., and Richard I. Pervo. *Rethinking the Unity of Luke and Acts*. Minneapolis: Fortress Press, 1993.

Pelikan, Jaroslav. *Jesus Through the Centuries: His Place in the History of Culture*. New Haven, CT: Yale University Press, 1985.

Perdue, Leo G. *Wisdom and Creation: The Theology of Wisdom Literature*. Nashville: Abingdon Press, 1994.

Petersen, David L. *The Prophetic Literature: An Introduction*. Louisville: Westminster John Knox Press, 2002.

———. "Rethinking the Nature of Prophetic Literature." In *Prophecy and Prophets*, pp. 23-40. Edited by Yehoshua Gitay. Atlanta: Scholars Press, 1997.

Phillips, Anthony. "Prophecy and Law." In *Israel's Prophetic Tradition: Essays in Honour of Peter R. Ackroyd*, pp. 217-30. Edited by Richard Coggins, Anthony Phillips and Michael Knibb. Cambridge: Cambridge University Press, 1982.

Pickett, Raymond. *The Cross in Corinth: The Social Significance of the Death of Jesus*. Journal for the Study of the New Testament Supplement Series 143. Sheffield, UK: Sheffield Academic Press, 1997.

Porter, Stanley E. "The Rhetorical Scribe: Textual Variants in Romans and Their

Possible Rhetorical Purpose." In *Rhetorical Criticism and the Bible,* pp. 403-19. Edited by Stanley E. Porter and Dennis L. Stamps. Journal for the Study of the New Testament Supplement Series 195. Sheffield, UK: Sheffield Academic Press, 2002.

Powell, Mark Allen. *Jesus as a Figure in History: How Modern Historians View the Man from Galilee.* Louisville: Westminster John Knox, 1998.

Pregeant, Russell. *Knowing Truth, Doing Good: Engaging New Testament Ethics.* Minneapolis: Fortress Press, 2008.

Propp, William H. C. *Exodus 19–40: A New Translation with Introduction and Commentary.* Anchor Bible Commentary 2a. New York: Doubleday, 2006.

Rad, Gerhard von. *Genesis: A Commentary.* Translated by John H. Marks. London: SCM Press, 1972.

Reasoner, Mark. *The Strong and the Weak: Romans 14.1–15.13 in Context.* Society for New Testament Studies Monograph Series 103. Cambridge: Cambridge University Press, 1990.

Resseguie, James L. *Narrative Criticism of the New Testament: An Introduction.* Grand Rapids: Baker Academic, 2005.

Ridderbos, Herman. *Paul: An Outline of His Theology.* Translated by John Richard De Witt. Grand Rapids: Eerdmans, 1975.

Ringgren, Helmer. "Prophecy in the Ancient New East." In *Israel's Prophetic Tradition: Essays in Honour of Peter R. Ackroyd,* pp. 1-11. Edited by Richard Coggins, Anthony Phillips and Michael Knibb. Cambridge: Cambridge University Press, 1982.

———. *Religions of the Ancient Near East.* Translated by John Sturdy. London: SPCK, 1973.

Rodd, Cyril S. *Glimpses of a Strange Land: Studies in Old Testament Ethics.* Edinburgh: T & T Clark, 2001.

Roetzel, Calvin. *Paul: The Man and the Myth.* Edinburgh: T & T Clark, 1999.

Rofé, Alexander. *Deuteronomy: Issues and Interpretation.* Edinburgh: T & T Clark, 2002.

———. *Introduction to the Prophetic Literature.* Biblical Seminar 21. Sheffield, UK: Sheffield Academic Press, 1997.

Rogerson, John W. *Theory and Practice in Old Testament Ethics.* Edited by M. Daniel Carroll R. Journal for the Study of the Old Testament Supplement Series 405. London: T & T Clark, 2004.

Rogerson, John W., Margaret Davies and M. Daniel Caroll R. eds. *The Bible in Ethics: The Second Sheffield Colloquium.* Journal for the Study of the Old Testament Supplement Series 207. Sheffield, UK: Sheffield Academic Press, 1995.

Rosner, Brian S. *Paul, Scripture and Ethics: A Study of 1 Corinthians 5–7.* Arbeiten zur Geschichte des antiken Judentums und des Urchristentums 22. Leiden: E. J. Brill, 1994.

Roth, S. John. *The Blind, the Lame, and the Poor: Character Types in Luke-Acts.* Journal for the Study of the New Testament Supplement Series 144. Sheffield, UK: Sheffield Academic Press, 1997.

Rowe, C. Kavin. *Early Narrative Christology: The Lord in the Gospel of Luke.* Beihefte zur Zeitschrift für die neutestamentliche Wissenschaft 139. Berlin: Walter de Gruyter, 2006.

Rowland, Christopher. "Prophecy and the New Testament." In *Prophecy and Prophets in Ancient Israel: Proceedings of the Oxford Old Testament Seminar,* pp. 410-30. Edited by John Day. London: T & T Clark, 2010.

Sampley, J. Paul. *Walking Between the Times: Paul's Moral Reasoning.* Minneapolis: Fortress Press, 1991.

Sanders, E. P. *Paul and Palestinian Judaism: A Comparison of Patterns of Religion.* London: SCM Press, 1977.

Sandnes, Karl Olav. *Belly and Body in the Pauline Epistles.* Society for New Testament Studies Monograph Series 120. Cambridge: Cambridge University Press, 2002.

Schrage, Wolfgang. *The Ethics of the New Testament.* Translated by David E. Green. Edinburgh: T & T Clark, 1988.

Schreiner, Thomas R. *Romans.* Baker Exegetical Commentary on the New Testament. Grand Rapids: Baker, 1998.

Schweitzer, Albert. *The Quest of the Historical Jesus.* Translated and edited by John Bowden. London: SCM Press, 2000.

Segal, Alan. *Paul the Convert: The Apostolate and Apostasy of Saul the Pharisee.* New Haven, CT: Yale University Press, 1990.

Seitz, Christopher R. *Prophecy and Hermeneutics: Toward a New Introduction to the Prophets.* Grand Rapids: Baker Academic, 2007.

Sigal, Phillip. *The Halakhah of Jesus of Nazareth According to the Gospel of Matthew.* Leiden: Brill, 2008.

Sire, James W. *The Universe Next Door: A Basic Worldview Catalog.* 5th ed. Downers Grove, IL: InterVarsity Press, 2009.

Snodgrass, Klyne. "Gospel in Romans: A Theology of Revelation." In *Gospel in Paul: Studies on Corinthians, Galatians and Romans for Richard Longenecker,* pp. 304-6. Edited by L. A. Jervis and P. Richardson. Journal for the Study of the New Testament Supplement Series 108. Sheffield, UK: Sheffield Academic Press, 1994.

———. "Matthew and the Law." In *Treasures New and Old: Contributions to Matthean Studies,* pp. 99-127. Edited by David R. Bauer and Mark Allan Powell. Atlanta: Scholars Press, 1996.

Stacey, W. D. *Prophetic Drama in the Old Testament.* London: Epworth, 1990.

Stanton, Graham N. *A Gospel for a New People: Studies in Matthew.* Edinburgh: T & T Clark, 1992.

Stegner, W. R. "Jew, Paul the." In *The Dictionary of Paul and His Letters,* pp. 503-11. Edited by Gerald F. Hawthorne and Ralph P. Martin. Downers Grove: Inter-Varsity Press, 1993.

Stendahl, Krister. *Paul Among Jews and Gentiles.* London: SCM Press, 1976.

Stowers, Stanley K. *A Rereading of Romans: Justice, Jews, and Gentiles.* New Haven, CT: Yale University Press, 1994.

Stuart, Douglas K. *Exodus.* Nashville: B & H Publishing, 2006.

Stuhlmacher, Peter. "The Purpose of Romans." In *The Romans Debate,* pp. 231-42. Edited by Karl P. Donfried. Rev. ed. Peabody, MA: Hendrickson, 1991.

Sweeney, Marvin A. "Formation and Form in Prophetic Literature." In *Old Testament Interpretation: Past, Present and Future: Essays in Honor of Gene M. Tucker,* pp. 113-26. Edited by James Luther Mays, David L. Petersen and Kent Harold Richards. Nashville: Abingdon Press, 1995.

Talbert, Charles H. *Matthew.* Grand Rapids: Baker Academic, 2010.

———. *Reading the Sermon on the Mount: Character Formation and Ethical Decision Making in Matthew 5–7.* Grand Rapids: Baker Academic, 2004.

Tannehill, Robert C. *The Narrative Unity of Luke-Acts: A Literary Interpretation.* Vol. 1. Philadelphia: Fortress, 1986.

Thiselton, Anthony C. *The First Epistle to the Corinthians.* Grand Rapids: Eerdmans, 2000.

Thompson, Michael. *Clothed with Christ: The Example and Teaching of Jesus in Romans 12:1-15.* Journal for the Study of the New Testament Supplement Series 59. Sheffield, UK: JSOT Press, 1991.

Trevaskis, Leigh M. *Holiness, Ethics and Ritual in Leviticus.* Hebrew Bible Monographs 29. Sheffield, UK: Sheffield Phoenix Press, 2011.

Trible, Phyllis. *God and the Rhetoric of Sexuality.* Philadelphia: Fortress Press, 1978.

Tucker, Gene M. "The Book of Isaiah." In *The New Interpreter's Bible,* 6:25-552. Nashville: Abingdon Press, 2001.

———. "Prophetic Speech." In *Interpreting the Prophets,* pp. 27-40. Edited by James Luther Mays and Paul J. Achtemeier. Philadelphia: Fortress Press, 1987.

Verhey, Allen. *The Great Reversal: Ethics and the New Testament.* Grand Rapids: Eerdmans, 1984.

———. *Remembering Jesus: Christian Community, Scripture and the Moral Life.* Grand Rapids: Eerdmans, 2002.

Waltke, Bruce K. *The Book of Proverbs: Chapters 1-15.* New International Commentary on the Old Testament. Grand Rapids: Eerdmans, 2004.

Wasserman, Emma. *The Death of the Soul in Romans 7.* Wissenschaftliche Untersuchungen zum Neuen Testament 256. Tübingen: Mohr Siebeck, 2008.

Watson, Francis. *Paul and the Hermeneutics of Faith.* London: T & T Clark, 2004.

Watts, James W. *Reading Law: Rhetorical Shaping of the Pentateuch.* Biblical Seminar

59. Sheffield, UK: Sheffield Academic Press, 1991.

Watts, John D. *Isaiah 1–33*. Word Biblical Commentary 24. Nashville: Thomas Nelson, 2005.

Wedderburn, A. J. M. *The Reasons for Romans*. Minneapolis: Fortress, 1988.

Wenham, Gordon J. *The Book of Leviticus*. New International Commentary on the Old Testament 3. Grand Rapids: Eerdmans, 1979.

———. "The Gap Between Law and Ethics in the Bible." *Journal of Jewish Studies* 48 (1997): 17-29.

———. *Genesis 1–15*. Word Biblical Commentary 1. Waco, TX: Word, 1987.

———. *Genesis 16–50*. Word Biblical Commentary 2. Dallas: Word, 1994.

———. *Story as Torah*. Edinburgh: T & T Clark, 2000.

Westermann, Claus. *Basic Forms of Prophetic Speech*. Translated by Hugh Clayton White. London: Lutterworth, 1967.

Wijk-Bos, Johanna W. H. van. *Making Wise the Simple: The Torah in Christian Faith and Practice*. Grand Rapids: Eerdmans, 2005.

Wildberger, Hans. *Isaiah 1–12: A Commentary*. Minneapolis: Fortress Press, 1991.

Wilkens, Stephen. *Beyond Bumper Sticker Ethics*. Downers Grove, IL: InterVarsity Press, 1995.

Wilkins, Michael J. *Discipleship in the Ancient World and Matthew's Gospel*. 2nd edition. Grand Rapids: Baker, 1995.

Williamson, Paul R. *Abraham, Israel and the Nations: The Patriarchal Promise and Its Covenantal Development in Genesis*. Journal for the Study of the Old Testament Supplement Series 315. Sheffield, UK: Sheffield Academic Press, 2000.

Wilson, Robert R. "Sources and Methods in the Study of Ancient Israelite Ethics." *Semeia* 66 (1995): 55-63.

Winter, Bruce W. *After Paul Left Corinth: The Influence of Secular Ethics and Social Change*. Grand Rapids: Eerdmans, 2001.

Witherington, Ben, III. *The Indelible Image: The Theological and Ethical Thought World of the New Testament*. Vol. 1, *The Individual Witnesses*. Downers Grove, IL: IVP Academic, 2009.

Wright, Christopher J. H. *Old Testament Ethics for the People of God*. Downers Grove, IL: InterVarsity Press, 2004.

Wright, N. T. "The Law in Romans 2." In *Paul and the Mosaic Law*, pp. 288-314. Edited by J. D. G. Dunn. Grand Rapids: Eerdmans, 2001.

———. "The Letter to the Romans." In *The New Interpreter's Bible*, 10:395-770. Nashville: Abingdon Press, 2002.

———. *The New Testament and the People of God*. London: SPCK, 1992.

———. "Romans and the Theology of Paul." In *Society of Biblical Literature Seminar Papers*, pp. 184-213. Atlanta: Scholars Press, 1992.

Yoder, John Howard. *What Would You Do? A Serious Answer to a Standard Question.* Scottdale, PA: Herald Press, 1992.

York, John O. *The Last Shall Be First: The Rhetoric of Reversal in Luke.* Journal for the Study of the New Testament Supplement Series 46. Sheffield, UK: Sheffield Academic Press, 1991.

Ziesler, J. A. *The Meaning of Righteousness in Paul: A Linguistic and Theological Enquiry.* Society for New Testament Studies Monograph Series 20. Cambridge: Cambridge University Press, 1972.

SCRIPTURE INDEX

Finding the Textbook You Need

The IVP Academic Textbook Selector
is an online tool for instantly finding the IVP books
suitable for over 250 courses across 24 disciplines.

www.ivpress.com/academic/textbookselector